EXPLORER

FLORIDA

Emma Stanford

Page 2: number plates
Page 3: lifeguard's hut, Fort Lauderdale
Page 4: oak tree, Panhandle
Page 5(a): American alligator
Page 5(b): Bahia Mar yacht marina
Page 6: Gumbo Limbo Nature Trail
Pages 6/7: Fort Lauderdale beach
Page 7: boat at John Pennekamp Coral Reef State Park
Page 8: on the Anhinga Trail, Everglades National Park
Page 9: launch of the Space Shuttle Columbia
Page 51: South Beach
Page 109: detail of a shiny 'hog'
Page 137: 'The Spirit of Ecstasy'
Page 173: colourful shells, Captiva Island
Page 199: palm tree
Page 237: water-bike on St Pete Beach

Written by Emma Stanford
Original photography by Clive Sawyer

Reprinted 2002
Reprinted 2001. Information verified and updated.
Revised third edition 1998
First published 1993

Edited, designed, produced and distributed by AA Publishing,
Maps © Automobile Association Developments Ltd 1993, 1996, 1998, 2001
Distributed in the United Kingdom by AA Publishing

A CIP catalogue record for this book is available from the British Library.

ISBN 0 7495 1610 0

Published by AA Publishing (a trading name of Automobile Association Developments Limited, whose registered office is Millstream, Maidenhead Road, Windsor, SL4 5GD. Registered number 1878835).

Colour separation by Fotographics Ltd
Printed and bound in Italy by Printer Trento srl

How to use this book

ORGANISATION

Florida Is, Florida Was

Discusses aspects of life and culture in contemporary Florida and explores significant periods in its history.

A–Z

Breaks the state down into regional chapters, and covers places to visit, including walks and drives. Within this section fall the Focus On articles, which consider a variety of subjects in greater detail.

Travel Facts

Contains the strictly practical information that is vital for a successful trip.

Hotels and Restaurants

Lists places to stay and places to eat alphabetically by region. Entries are graded budget, moderate or expensive.

ABOUT THE RATINGS

Most of the places described in this book have been given a separate rating. These are as follows:

▶▶▶	**Do not miss**
▶▶	**Highly recommended**
▶	**Worth seeing**

Contents

TURTLE
CROSSING

TONS O' FUN
GLASS BOTTOM & SNORKEL TOURS

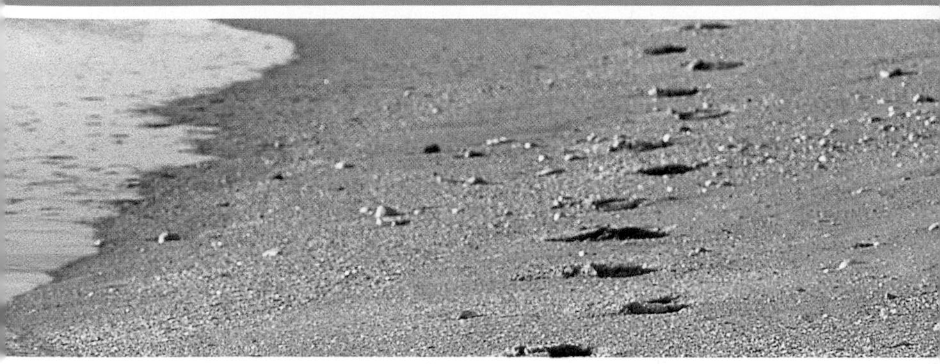

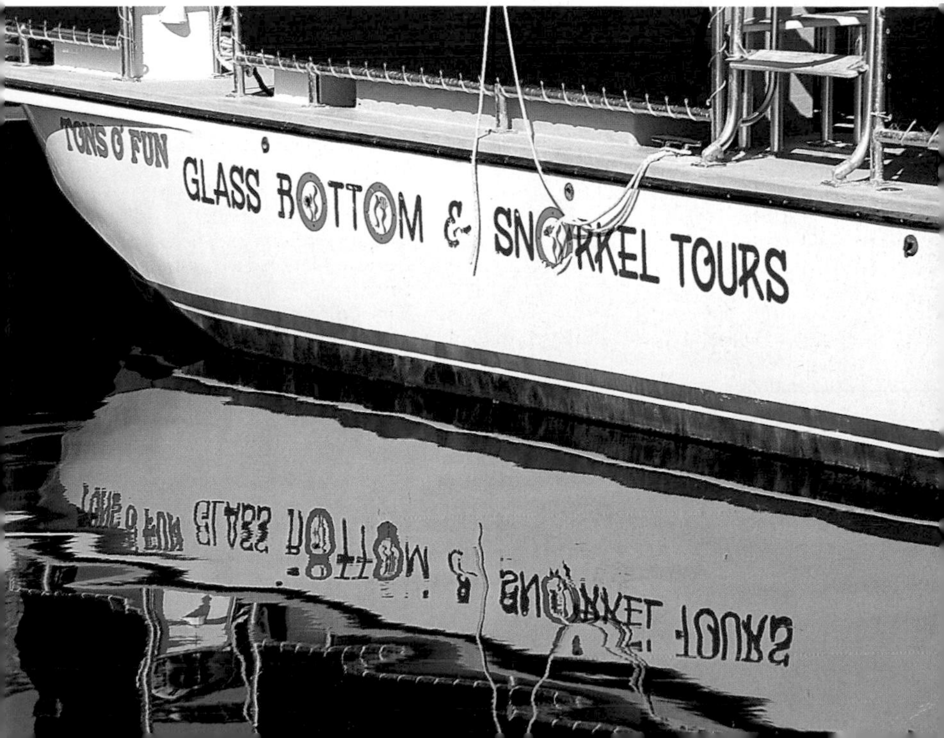

Emma Stanford has written, edited and contributed to a variety of books on California, Hawaii, the Caribbean, France and Spain, as well as Mediterranean port guides for the US Navy. She has written *Explorer Florida*, *Explorer Hawaii*, *Essential Orlando*, *Essential Florida*, *Travellers Caribbean Cruising including Miami* and *CityPack Los Angeles* for the AA.

My Florida

The green heron sat with his back to me studiously ignoring my poised camera, and continued to survey the brackish water for signs of life – and lunch. A moorhen stepped gingerly from lilypad to lilypad; above, a pair of snowy egrets preened in an elaborate courtship ritual. I'd decided to give the alligator-wrestling a miss and ended up transfixed by one of Florida's most appealing sideshows, the spectacular birdlife that had 19th-century naturalist John James Audubon falling off his perch with excitement as he toured the Florida Keys with a sketch-book in the 1830s.

Florida's main events – art deco in Miami Beach, Orlando's amazing theme parks, the subtropical Florida Keys, fabulous golfing, the dazzling white-sand beaches – are every bit as alluring as the brochures claim. But, for me, part of the fun is to venture beyond the hype and discover some of Florida's less well-publicised attractions.

The Great Outdoors, showcased by Florida's admirable network of well-maintained state parks, is one surprise. The peninsula may be flat for the most part, but it is far from featureless. Woodland trails and wildlife spotting, canoe runs and snorkelling or diving in freshwater springs make a grand change from foot-slogging around the theme parks. There is superb fishing from piers, jetties and bridges, or Hemingway-esque types can head for deeper waters on the trail of wahoo, tarpon and marlin.

On the cultural front, Florida offers several world-class art galleries, while in recent years there has been a growing interest in the state's colourful past with restored historic houses, ancient Native American sites and local history museums offering a fascinating insight into early Florida lifestyles from the Native Americans encountered by 16th-century Spanish explorers to pirates, planters and pioneer farmers.

Florida is an ideal two-centre holiday destination, so venture out beyond Miami and the theme park experience and explore another side of the Sunshine State.

Emma Stanford

Florida Is & Was

GEORGIA
ALABAMA
L Seminole
Crestview
Milton
Ponce de León
Marianna
Chattahoochee
Monticello
Quincy
Maclay State Gardens
Fort Walton Beach
Pensacola
National Museum of Naval Aviation
Point Washington
Tallahassee
Apalachicola
Wakulla Springs
Panama City
St Marks
Perry
Apalachee Bay
Port St Joe
Apalachicola
Cape San Blas
St George Island
0 50 100 150 200 km
0 50 100 miles

Movie set in Miami

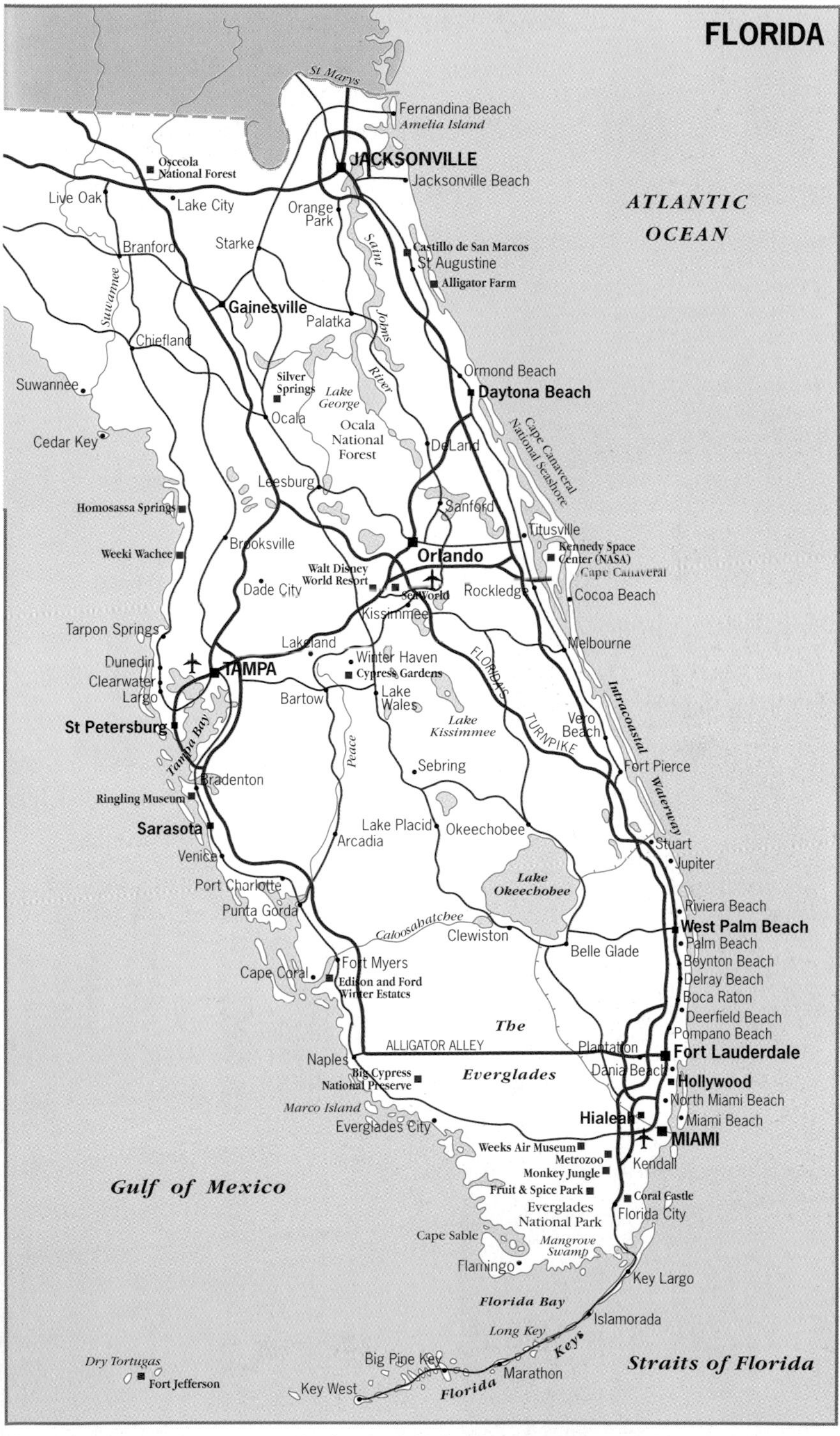
FLORIDA
ATLANTIC OCEAN
Gulf of Mexico
Straits of Florida
St Marys
Fernandina Beach
Amelia Island
JACKSONVILLE
Jacksonville Beach
Osceola National Forest
Live Oak
Lake City
Orange Park
Branford
Starke
Castillo de San Marcos
St Augustine
Alligator Farm
Suwannee
Gainesville
Palatka
Saint Johns River
Chiefland
Ormond Beach
Daytona Beach
Silver Springs
Lake George
Ocala
Ocala National Forest
Cedar Key
DeLand
Cape Canaveral National Seashore
Leesburg
Homosassa Springs
Sanford
Titusville
Weeki Wachee
Brooksville
Orlando
Kennedy Space Center (NASA)
Cape Canaveral
Walt Disney World Resort
SeaWorld
Dade City
Rockledge
Cocoa Beach
Kissimmee
Tarpon Springs
Lakeland
Melbourne
Dunedin
Winter Haven
Cypress Gardens
TAMPA
Clearwater
Largo
Bartow
Lake Wales
FLORIDA'S TURNPIKE
Intracoastal Waterway
Vero Beach
St Petersburg
Tampa Bay
Peace
Lake Kissimmee
Sebring
Fort Pierce
Bradenton
Ringling Museum
Sarasota
Lake Placid
Okeechobee
Arcadia
Stuart
Venice
Jupiter
Port Charlotte
Lake Okeechobee
Punta Gorda
Riviera Beach
Caloosahatchee
West Palm Beach
Clewiston
Palm Beach
Belle Glade
Fort Myers
Boynton Beach
Cape Coral
Edison and Ford Winter Estates
Delray Beach
Boca Raton
Deerfield Beach
The Everglades
Pompano Beach
ALLIGATOR ALLEY
Plantation
Fort Lauderdale
Naples
Big Cypress National Preserve
Dania Beach
Hollywood
Marco Island
North Miami Beach
Hialeah
Miami Beach
Everglades City
MIAMI
Weeks Air Museum
Metrozoo
Kendall
Monkey Jungle
Fruit & Spice Park
Coral Castle
Everglades National Park
Florida City
Cape Sable
Mangrove Swamp
Flamingo
Key Largo
Florida Bay
Islamorada
Long Key
Florida Keys
Dry Tortugas
Fort Jefferson
Big Pine Key
Marathon
Key West

11

If you were to pick a tree to represent northern Florida it would be the stately live oak, while the symbol of the south would be the palm. In central Florida, the citrus family rules and groves of glossy orange, lemon, grapefruit and lime trees bask in the famous Florida sunshine.

Florida and orange juice are synonymous. As far as statistics go, the state is one of the world's largest citrus-growing regions, and its groves produce around 25 per cent of the orange juice and 50 per cent of the grapefruit juice on the world market. Spanish explorers introduced oranges to Florida in the 16th century, and by the time the first grapefruit was planted in 1825, wild orange trees could be found all over the state. With the introduction of water and rail transport in the 1880s, citrus growers multiplied in the central Florida region. Their glossy-leaved groves spread southeast to Indian River, around Fort Pierce, then down to Miami after the frosts of 1894–5. The marvellously fragrant white orange blossom was adopted as Florida's official state flower in 1909; orange juice became the state beverage in 1967.

AN INFINITE VARIETY Florida's citrus fruits come in all shapes and sizes – hefty Duncan white and rosy-pink grapefruits, oranges, tangerines, tangelos (tangerine-grapefruits), Temple oranges (tangerine-oranges), lemons, limes and the nut-sized kumquat. Marmalade, preserves, sweets, orange-blossom honey and even citrus wine are a tribute to the ingenuity of local residents.

Most citrus fruit requires at least 300 days of sunshine and take 12 months to mature. The citrus harvest begins in October with grapefruits and ends in July with oranges. Ripe fruit can be left on the tree for several months, so it is not unusual to see last year's crop surrounded by the new season's blossom. A mature grapefruit tree can produce around 1,000 fruits each season.

A Florida citrus grove

KEY LIME PIE The Key lime is a small, round, yellowish-coloured fruit which is a Florida speciality, and the essential ingredient of Key lime pie. This delicious tangy dessert is said to have been invented by a cook named Sarah at the Curry Mansion in Key West. However, the authentic preparation of Key lime pie – the consistency of the pie crust, and the choice between meringue (for purists) or whipped cream topping – remains a contentious issue in kitchens across the state (see suggested recipe).

Key lime pie filling
4 eggs
14 oz can condensed milk
½ cup Key lime juice
1 tsp lemon essence
8 tbs sugar
Separate eggs. Beat together yolks, condensed milk and juice. Add one pinch salt. Beat whites to soft peaks; add lemon essence and beat in sugar. Fold one-third of egg-white mixture into lime filling and place in pie shell. Top with remaining egg white. Bake at 180°C/350°F for 20–25 minutes. Chill before serving.

Transporting the oranges

TASTE THEM FRESH! Roadside stalls piled high with fresh fruit and vegetables are a familiar sight throughout Florida. Beyond the Greater Miami city limits, Miami-Dade County is one of the top 100 citrus-producing counties in the United States. The winter harvest of Homestead is laden with avocados (once known as alligator pears), cucumbers, canteloupes and water-melons, limes, strawberries and tomatoes. Buy them fresh from the farmers' markets or roadside stalls or stop by a U-pick for a real taste experience.

In the central region, look for glossy purple aubergines, squashes and okra. There are apples, pears and pecan nuts in the north.

BLACK GOLD The fertile drained Everglades region around Lake Okeechobee is another source of fruit and vegetables. It is also the land of black gold – not oil, in this case, but sugar-cane. Its huge crop makes Clewiston the sugar capital of the state. Half the nation's raw sugar consumption (around 1½ million pounds) is hand-harvested here by machete-wielding labourers. Clewiston's other claim to fame is its cabbage palm business, which supplies the fresh hearts of palm dished up in chic Florida restaurants.

The southern corner of the state yields an abundance of exotic tropical fruits. Home-grown bananas, carambolas (star fruit), figs, guavas and papayas can be found in local supermarkets. The origins of the mango crop can be traced back to a shipment of 35 mango trees delivered from Calcutta in 1888.

❑ Florida will use any excuse for a festival. For two fruit-inspired extravaganzas, check out the annual Plant City Strawberry Festival in February and June's Monticello Watermelon Festival, whose hotly contested melon seed-spittin' competition requires unusual skills. ❑

Anchored to the North American continent by Georgia and Alabama, the Florida peninsula is bordered on each side by salt water. The state can claim a tidal shoreline extending over 8,000 miles (12,870km) via hundreds of sandy beaches, wide bays, estuaries, lagoons and a host of offshore islands.

AROUND THE COAST Florida's east coast is protected from the Atlantic by a string of barrier islands. These islands taper off like stepping stones into the gentle curve of the Florida Keys, to Key West, just 90 miles (145km) from Cuba. The rounded southern tip of the peninsula contains the Everglades, a vast swampland region that stretches over 10 million acres (4 million ha) and crumbles into the waterways of the Ten Thousand Islands region off Florida's lower west coast. Sandbars and islands line the west coast and the Gulf of Mexico, while the northern Gulf shore of the Panhandle offers some of the finest barrier-island beaches, created by blinding white quartz sand washed down from the Appalachian Mountains over thousands of years. Areas of these magnificent coastal dunes are protected as part of the **Gulf Islands National Seashore** (see page 245).

FLOWING WATER Inland northern Florida is a land of rolling hills and pine forests, freshwater springs and swift tannin-stained rivers like the Apalachicola, Blackwater and Suwannee. Below Florida's thin covering of soil, deep fissures in the limestone foundations release freshwater springs fed by subterranean watercourses. **Wakulla Springs**, south of Tallahassee, claims to be one of the world's deepest springs.

At **Florida Caverns State Park**, near Marianna, there is an opportunity to look below the earth's surface. This is the only place in the state where the water table drops sufficiently to reveal spectacular stalagmites and stalactites in limestone caverns.

STILL WATERS A low ridge extends from the north into the lakeland region of central Florida. Forests give way to prairie land and an estimated 30,000-plus lakes and ponds varying in depth from a few inches to around 30 feet (9m). **Lake Okeechobee** is the second largest body of fresh water wholly within the United States, some 750 square miles (1,940sq km) in total area, but only 14 feet (4m) deep at its lowest point. This freshwater reservoir is the starting point of the Everglades, the primary source of a 50-mile-wide (80km) river of grass that extends across the state to the Gulf of Mexico. The **Everglades National Park** covers only one-seventh of the true Everglades region, but acts as a showcase for its diverse flora and fauna.

THE EVERGLADES Patches of brilliant green signal the presence of hardwood 'hammocks', the local name for stands of trees which have found a slightly elevated limestone outcrop on which to take root above the swamp. Ranging in size from just a few feet to several acres, they are a refuge for bobcats, deer, hawks, owls and other wildlife. Pine groves and areas of cypress swamp (one of the finest for sightseeing purposes is **Corkscrew Swamp**) also provide useful animal habitats. Coastal mangrove forests flourish where the Everglades meet the Gulf. The nutrient-rich, brackish water trapped in the mangroves' complex root system creates an ideal habitat for numerous native animals and birds.

BAYS AND ISLANDS The mangrove-lined back bays of the west coast are a fascinating unofficial wildlife refuge teeming with fish and wading

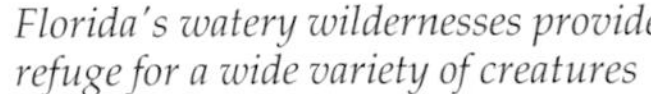

Florida's watery wildernesses provide refuge for a wide variety of creatures

birds. This is a favourite haunt of manatees, too. These gentle, endangered 3,000-pound (1,360kg) sea cows enjoy a plentiful supply of river weed and water hyacinths in the warmer waters. On the Gulf, the islands of **Sanibel** and **Captiva** are renowned for their seashell beaches, as is **Cayo Costa State Park**, where sea turtles lay their eggs. **Pine Island Sound** is a favourite playground of the friendly bottlenose dolphin.

❑ Midway up the east coast, nature lovers should not miss two exceptional protected areas: the **Canaveral National Seashore** and **Merritt Island National Wildlife Refuge**. The latter harbours 21 endangered species in its freshwater lagoons, saltwater marshes and hammocks – all close to the Kennedy Space Center. In winter, the population is swelled by a magnificent roll call of migrating birds. ❑

THE FLORIDA KEYS are a 150-mile (240km) chain of fossilised coral-rock islands, short on beaches but fringed by reefs. Vegetation is sparse, with pockets of tropical hardwoods, slash pine, mangroves and prickly pears. The Gulf Stream flows in a north direction around the Florida Keys and the southern tip of the peninsula, warming the reef-strewn seas. This is a diver's paradise, well served with aquatic parks such as the **John Pennekamp Coral Reef State Park** off Key Largo and the vast **Biscayne National Park**, south of Miami. The Atlantic waters are still warm enough for diving as far north as the Gold Coast.

Dolphins haunt west coast bays

Florida's subtropical climate, with its distinct growing seasons, is augmented by extraordinarily diverse natural habitats that support a wealth of native and imported plant life. Brilliant hibiscus, oleander, colourful azaleas, scented gardenias and clouds of bougainvillaea gladden the eye; palms, sea grapes and magnificent live oaks cast welcoming shadows in the heat.

EVERGLADES FLORA Botanists from around the world have marvelled at the sheer variety of plant life that flourishes in Florida. No fewer than 2,000 plant species, both temperate and tropical, grow side by side in the Everglades. **Sawgrass**, a marsh plant edged with small sharp teeth and a menace to explorers, predominates in the region, covering nearly 8 million acres (3.2 million ha) of Everglades.

Willows, **pines** and tropical hardwoods, such as **mahogany** and **live oak**, grow on outcrops of limestone creating shady hammocks. The **gumbo limbo**, affectionately known as the 'tourist tree' for its peeling red bark, reminiscent of sunburned skin, is also found here. An unwelcome addition is the parasitic **strangler fig**. Its seed, carried on the wind or by birds, lodges in the host tree; as the strangler fig grows, it drops a tangled mass of aerial roots to the ground while wrapping itself around the host trunk depriving it of light, water and nutrients.

Hammock woods are also festooned with air plants (epiphytes) such as **orchids** and **bromeliads**. Although attached to a host tree, these plants are non-parasitic, gathering water and nutrients that run down the bark. **Spanish moss**, which tumbles from live oaks such as cypresses, is another epiphyte.

In addition to lovely orchids such as the creamy vanilla orchid, mule-ears and fragant night-blooming epidendrum, there is a wealth of beautiful Everglades flowers. They include colourful pink gerardia, morning glory, spider lilies, purple pickerel weed and Glades lobelia, yellow carpets of splatterdock and water lilies.

An exotic hibiscus bloom

❑ For a gentle introduction to what plants to look out for, visitors to Miami should head for the peaceful surroundings of Fairchild Tropical Gardens in South Miami. Other glorious gardens around the state include A B Maclay State Gardens in Tallahassee; Cypress Gardens in Winter Haven; Harry P Leu Gardens in Orlando; Marie Selby Botanical Gardens in Sarasota; and Washington Oaks State Park, on Anastasia Island. The prize for the biggest banyan tree goes to the Edison Winter Estate in Fort Myers. ❑

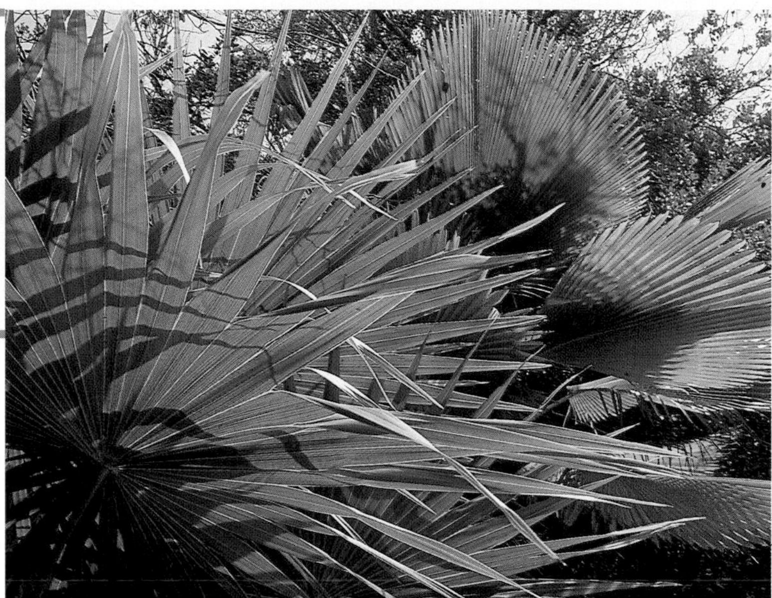

Native Keys palms

TREES OF THE SWAMPLANDS Cypress trees can grow at depths of water in which most trees would drown. It is thought that their curious cone-like 'knees' help them to breathe. Dwarf **pond cypress** is the most common variety. Though few lofty **bald cypresses** survived the 1930s lumber era, you can still see these formidable 600- to 700-year-old giants in Big Cypress Swamp and Corkscrew Swamp, north of the Everglades National Park.

PINES AND PALMS On higher ground, **saw palmetto** and **slash pine** forests survive on next to no soil, finding purchase in hollows and potholes filled with a rich residue of peat and marl. The feathery, non-native **Australian pine**, found throughout Florida, is considered a pest. This tree is fast encroaching on native species, and determined attempts are being made to eradicate it.

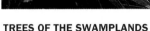

Palms are an essential ingredient of the Florida skyline. Of the hundreds of palms to be seen, 11 species are native to the state. **Cabbage palms**, **coconut palms**, **queen palms** and the elegant **royal palm** appear in hammocks and along the roadside, as do the tall, thin **Washingtonia palm** and the fan-tailed **traveller's palm**, while the squat **jelly palm** is common in northern parts of the state. In the Panhandle, glossy **magnolia** forests interrupt the endless march of pine, and the live oaks in this area are awe-inspiring.

PLANTS OF THE COAST Mangroves probably form the single most important plant system in Florida. They stabilise the shoreline, reduce storm damage, filter run-offs and feed and harbour a multitude of land, sea and air creatures. Their ability to obtain fresh water from salt water is unique. There are several types of mangroves, such as **red mangroves**, supported on arched prop roots, which grow closest to the water's edge; **black mangroves** which push up hundreds of pencil-thin root tips (pneumatophores) to help them breathe; and **white** and **buttonwood mangroves** which are found higher up the shore.

Coastal hammocks are **sea grape** territory, with their round, leathery leaves and bunches of fruit used to make jellies. Clumps of **sea oats** anchor the coastal dunes and are protected by law.

Florida's abundant bird life guarantees good birdwatching. On an early morning stroll along the beach you'll almost certainly spot brown pelicans, gulls galore, terns, scurrying sanderlings and maybe a cormorant or two.

EARLY RECORDS Florida's birds have fascinated and enchanted visitors from the early days. One of the first records of native bird life, Catesby's *Natural History of Carolina, Florida and the Bahama Islands*, was published in London in 1731. A century later, renowned American ornithologist John James Audubon ventured down through Florida to Key West gathering material for his epic *Birds of America*. Audubon's detailed descriptions of the rare roseate spoonbill, flocks of flamingos and pristine white snowy egret 'arrayed in more brilliant apparel than I have seen before' were translated into beautiful etchings. Yet less than a century ago these same birds were on the verge of extinction, slaughtered for their gorgeous plumage, a popular period-fashion accessory.

BIRDS OF THE WETLANDS
Everglades National Park is one of the most remarkable natural preserves in the world. Together with its northern neighbors, Big Cypress and Corkscrew swamps, it supports an extraordinary treasury of bird life. As well as providing sanctuary, they are a prime breeding and feeding ground for myriad species of wading birds. The **roseate spoonbill** has survived here, though it is still on the endangered list. A Florida native with rose-colored plumage, red eyes and a bald head, it has a distinctive spatulate beak which it sweeps from side to side to trap food.

The endangered **wood stork** nests in swampland cypress hammocks. Largely white, it has black-tipped wings with a span of more than 5 feet (1.5m); it feeds on fish using its sensitive beak to feel beneath the water's surface. White clusters of apple snail eggs cling to Everglades trees and plants from May through September. The adult snails are the sole diet of the few hundred remaining **Everglades kites**, with their curved bills designed to extract the snails' bodies. The eggs are also an important food source for the jerky-legged **limpkin**, an ibis-like wading bird.

❑ One of the strangest birds is the anhinga, or snakebird, which swims through the water with only its thin, flexible neck above the surface. Anhingas dive to skewer fish on their pointed beaks, surface, flip their catch into the air, and retrieve and swallow it with practiced aplomb. Despite its aquatic lifestyle, the anhinga's feathers are not waterproof, so it is common to see it drying its wings by the water's edge. ❑

HERONS, EGRETS AND PELICANS
The **great blue heron** and dainty **little blue heron** can be seen throughout the state. The Keys are the best place to spot the **great white heron**, which stands almost 5 feet (1.5m) tall. Its yellow-green legs distinguish it from the **great egret**, which stalks on spindly black legs.

The smaller **snowy egret** barely survived the plume hunters. Its beak and legs are black, but its large feet are gold-coloured. **Cattle egrets** arrived from Africa in the 1950s. They feed off insects disturbed by cattle and can often be spotted perched on a cow's back.

The ubiquitous **brown pelican** is a familiar sight on the coast, perched on pilings, bobbing on the swell, or skimming low over the waves in search of food.

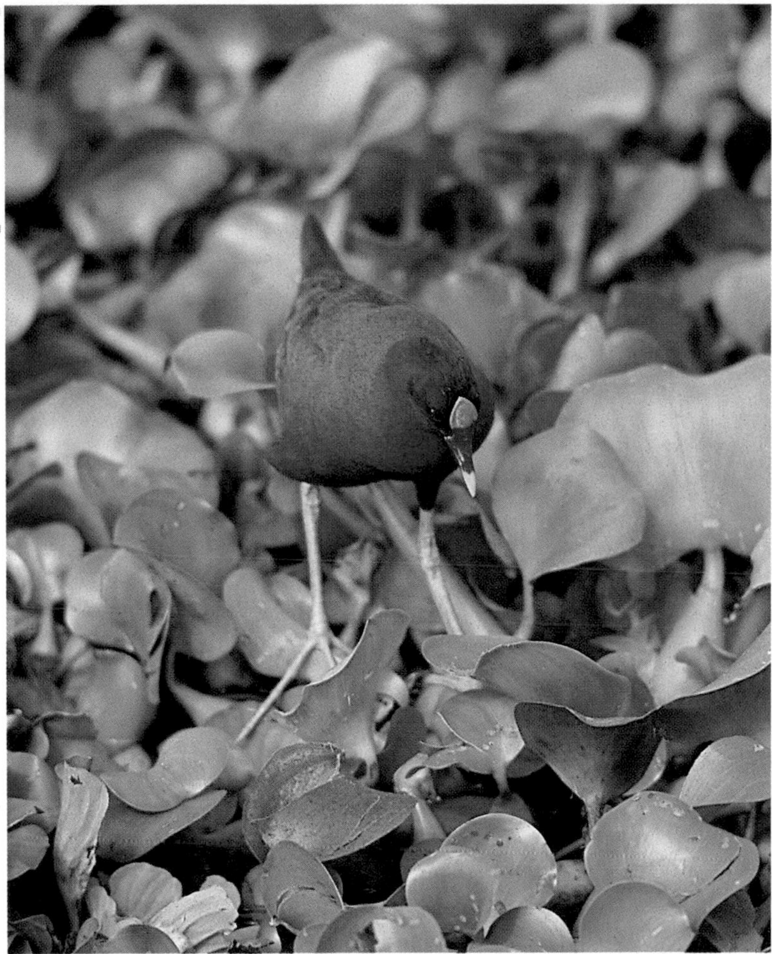

Purple gallinule

RAPTORS Birds of prey are a dramatic addition to Florida's wide blue skies. The handsome **red-shouldered hawk**, with its black-and-white back feathers and reddish breast, lives off frogs, lizards and snakes. It can often be seen perched on telegraph poles or fence posts near roadsides. **Ospreys** are also seen throughout the state, building nests close to water where they catch fish using their powerful talons.

Among other birds of prey are graceful **swallow-tailed kites**, **black** and **turkey vultures** and the endangered **Southern bald eagle**. Rangers in the Everglades and at Merritt Island, on the Atlantic coast, will point out the eagles' enormous nests, which can measure more than 6 feet (2m) across.

BIRDS OF THE WOODLANDS In woods throughout the state, woodpeckers can be heard if not seen, drilling into dead wood for beetles and ants. The **pileated woodpecker** has a distinctive red crest that contrasts with the black plumage on its back. Another woodland resident, the **barred owl** is named for the distinctive brown stripes on its breast. Also look for minute **gnatcatchers** zipping around the bushes, or the crimson flash of a jaunty **red cardinal**.

The alligator is to Florida what the kangaroo is to Australia – part of the scenery and a favourite tourist attraction. The world's first alligator attraction, the St Augustine Alligator Farm on Anastasia Island, was founded in 1893, leading the way for a host of imitators.

THE AMERICAN ALLIGATOR An adult male alligator can grow up to 16 feet (5m) or more, though most are around 12 feet (3.5m), and females are usually 8 to 9 feet (2.5–2.7m) in length. These cold-blooded reptiles need to bask in the sun to warm up enough to function. During the winter dry season, they earn the sobriquet 'Keeper of the Everglades', because they fulfill an important role by digging sizeable 'gator holes' in the ground. Water seeps in to fill these holes, providing life-sustaining oases for plants, birds, fish and other animals. Alligators mate in the spring, and the female lays 20–60 leathery eggs around June. If the temperature rises above 90°F (31°C), the hatchlings will be male; if it falls below 87°F (30°C) they will be female. Baby alligators feed themselves from the start, hunting crayfish, frogs, insects and snakes. Alligators will eat anything. They may appear slow and awkward, but they can move at frightening speeds, and their powerful jaws can snap shut with a force of 1,200 pounds per square inch. Do not attempt to feed them as you could end up on their menu.

THE AMERICAN CROCODILE This shy reptile is a much rarer sight, found only in the saltwater Florida Bay area. A lighter greenish-gray colour, crocodiles have narrow tapering snouts, and the teeth of their upper and lower jaws are visible in profile (an alligator's lower set of teeth fits inside its upper jaw).

ON THE ENDANGERED LIST Florida's most visible endangered mammal is the **manatee** (see panel page 204), a huge and gentle sea cow inhabiting rivers and coastal areas. Here the slow-moving creature is particularly at risk from boat traffic (41 per cent of manatee deaths are caused by watercraft collisions). The best time to see them is during the cool winter months (Nov–Mar) when they venture upstream to find warm spring waters. Another endangered Everglades inhabitant is the beautiful tawny **Florida panther**. The 30–50 remaining big cats, 6 feet (1.8m) long and weighing 60–130 pounds (27–60kg), are seriously threatened

Young alligators are on their own as soon as they leave the egg

Gently smiling jaws

by the destruction of their natural habitat through (among other things) mercury poisoning in the food chain. Female panthers can give birth to two to four kittens every other year, while an adult male will range more than 500 square miles (1,300sq km) hunting for deer, raccoons, wild pigs and other prey.

The dainty **Key deer** is also living on borrowed time as development eats away its limited habitat on Big Pine Key and the surrounding islands. The smallest sub-species of the white-tailed deer, Key deer grow to only around 24–28 inches (60–70cm) in height. Around 70 out of a population numbering 250–300 deer are killed by motorists every year.

OTHER MAMMALS Racoons and opossums share an often fatal attraction for highways. **Racoons** that make it across can be seen along the water's edge searching for food, while **opossums**, along with **squirrels** and **wild turkeys**, root about in the woodlands, keeping a wary eye out for hungry short-tailed **bobcats**.

Cotton rats, **marsh rabbits**, **otters**, and **spotted skunks** inhabit marshland regions throughout the state.

Armadillos arrived from Central America in the 19th century. They dig and burrow into timber for insects and fungi, scour the ground for fruit and rely on their speed for protection. The armadillo's shell is made of tough plates covered and joined by leathery skin. In spring, females give birth to four offspring, all of the same sex.

LIZARDS, SNAKES AND AMPHIBIANS Native **green lizards** and **skinks** are regulars to the woodland scene, while **Cuban lizards** (the male has a puff sack on his throat) can be spotted in urban areas. The largest and most poisonous Florida snake is the **water moccasin**, a relative of the rattlesnake; **pygmy rattlesnakes**, **black rat snakes** and **indigo** and **king snakes** are other reptiles to watch out for. **Walking catfish** are one of Florida's strangest sights.

❑ Turtle-watching is a fascinating Florida pastime. Leatherback turtles, which can grow up to 6 feet (1.8m) long and weigh a ton (literally), and loggerhead, green, rare hawksbill and Kemp's Ridley turtles all swim in Florida waters and must leave the relative security of the ocean to lay their eggs on the beach during the nesting season (1 May–31 Oct). Federal laws have been introduced to protect the remaining nesting areas, and state laws prohibit bright lights on the beach at certain times as these may confuse hatchlings heading for the ocean. ❑

Writer and artist Frederic Remington, known chiefly for his portrayals of the Old West, complained that Florida's cow-hunters sadly lacked 'the bilious fierceness and rearing plunge which I had associated with my friends out West', though his artistic nature allowed that 'they are picturesque in their unkempt, almost unearthly wildness'. One of his subjects was folk hero Bone Mizell, who listed branding cattle with his teeth among his accomplishments.

LIFE ON THE PRAIRIE The Spanish introduced cattle and horses to Florida in the 16th century. Livestock thrived in the rolling green central prairie region south of Gainesville, now known as Paynes Prairie, a state preserve near Micanopy. When prospective settlers rejected the cattle and land that the Spanish offered them, the missions taught local Native Americans to herd the livestock instead, and they proved very adept in their new rôle.

White settlers arrived from the north in the 19th century, and brought their own methods of herding cattle. For instance, Remington noted their use of cur dogs to round up the herd, sparing their horses, and remarked on the newcomers' practice of building strong log corrals approximately a day's march apart all through the woods of the vast ranch lands.

Cowboy boots – an essential item of Western gear, sold off the shelf

During the 1930s, Brahman cattle were introduced and cross-bred with native species. Herds of these hump-backed beasts are a familiar sight in fields along the roadside, often providing a comfortable perch for white cattle egrets. Among the inhabitants at the **Babcock Crescent B Ranch**, outside Fort Myers, are Senepol cattle, quarter horses, named for the quarter-mile races they run, and a herd of bison. An adventurous swamp-buggy ride will take you to the 70-year-old commissary, once the company stores, where saddles still hang over the verandas and cowboys go swaggering by (see page 205).

CATTLE TOWNS Arcadia is a sleepy cattle town 20 miles (32km) north of the Babcock ranch. High noon in the restored main street looks like a scene from a Western movie. Though present-day cowboys are more likely to roll into town in a battered pick-up than on horseback, the twice-yearly rodeo is as traditional as they come, and the local Western outfitters are equipped with the classic clothes – pearl-buttoned shirts, string ties and cowboy boots.

Kissimmee, just outside Orlando, is a curious combination of cattle town and theme park dormitory. The Kissimmee Sports Arena has a

popular Friday night rodeo, with authentic bronco-riding, calf-roping and barrel-racing, and the town hosts the twice-yearly Silver Spurs Rodeo.

Another realistic cattle town is **Davie**, just outside Fort Lauderdale. Davie has hitching posts galore, cacti, swinging saloon doors on the town hall and even a 'ride-through' service at the local McDonald's.

WHERE CHAMPIONS ARE BORN At the heart of the state, **Marion County** is the cornerstone of Florida's thoroughbred horse country. More than 27,000 Floridians are employed in the state's billion-dollar equine industry; 400 of its 600 farms and training centres are in Marion County, ranged around the county seat of Ocala.

Florida competes heavily with California and Kentucky, the other major equine centres. The Sunshine State enjoys advantages similar to Kentucky, with its famous bluegrass. Florida has its own limestone-enriched pastureland, which accounts for the strong, light bones of dynamic Kentucky Derby winners, such as the great Needles and, more recently, Unbridled.

Drive US 301, or better still, minor roads such as SR 200, for a beguiling

Excitement at Davie's rodeo

vista of rolling green meadows and pristine white fencing, interspersed with galloping thoroughbred horses. Many of the farms you will find along these roads are open to the public.

For details, call the **Florida Thoroughbred Breeders' and Owners Association** (tel: 352/629-2160).

❑ For a close look at Florida's ranch culture, nothing beats a good rodeo. Fans from all over the state and beyond head to Arcadia's **All Florida Championship Rodeo**, 124 Herd Street (March and October, tel: 863/494-2014); and Kissimmee's **Silver Spurs Rodeo**, Silver Spurs Arena, US 192 East (February and September/October, tel: 407/677-6336). Friday night **rodeos** take place at the Kissimmee Sports Arena at 8pm (tel: 407/933-0020); and Davie's Wednesday-night **Jackpot Rodeos** take place at the Davie Rodeo Arena, 6591 SW 45th Street (tel: 954/475-9787). ❑

It may sound like a cliché, but Florida really is a giant cultural melting pot. The state 'where everyone is from somewhere else' welcomes around 1,000 new residents every day, and the diversity of Florida's demographic profile is probably only rivalled by that of another great magnet for immigrants, California.

Home-grown migrants from the northern states (and a healthy proportion of Canadians) account for the majority of the population growth. However, where once newcomers were largely retiree 'snowbirds' flocking south to enjoy an ice-free winter and tax advantages, Florida's present-day migrants are much more likely to include large numbers of young professionals and families equally intent on the good life in the sun and the work opportunities offered by a burgeoning business sector. North Americans are not alone in recognizing Florida's possibilities. A relatively short hop to the south, Latin America and the Caribbean have provided another source of enthusiastic migration and, as the word spread about Florida's boom economy and increasingly attractive leisure profile in the 1990s, significant numbers of European migrants also jumped aboard the bandwagon bound for the Sunshine State.

Multicultural faces in the crowd

MULTICULTURAL MAKE-UP There is nothing new in Florida's multicultural make-up. From the initial influx of curious pioneers in the 18th century, the state has never attracted one stereotypical settler or any one nationality in particular. The original European occupants of the peninsula, the Spanish, were replaced by French noblemen, English adventurers, American planters and Creek Native Americans whose descendants, the Seminoles, are considered Florida natives even though they have inhabited the state for only 200 years. Over the following century or so, Caribbean islanders introduced Bahamanian architecture to the Keys, the Scots built golf courses in Dunedin, Cubans brought cigars to Tampa and Greek sponge-divers introduced bouzouki music and spinach pastries to Tarpon Springs.

Florida's multicultural diversity is one of the state's most appealing characteristics and locals like to celebrate with a calendar of festivals, attractions and special events. For example, you could experience a Greek-style Epiphany Day (6 January) with Greek Orthodox religious processions, music, dancing and feasting in Tarpon Springs; or take part in the colourful Caribbean-style Goombay Festival (first weekend of June) in Miami's funky Coconut Grove district.

CULTURAL ATTRACTIONS In the southern part of the state, you will find several Seminole-owned and

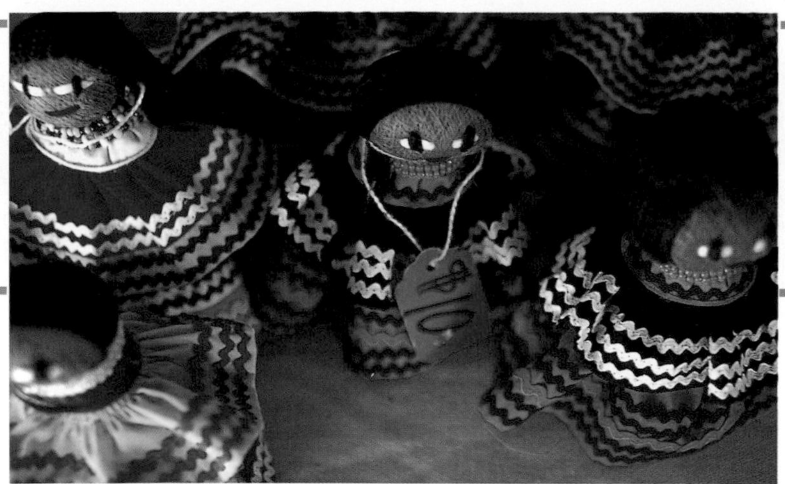

Artefacts of Floridian culture and history: traditional Seminole Indian dolls

operated attractions that offer a chance to learn a little more about Florida's Native Americans. Tourist villages on the Tamiami Trail (US 41) west of Miami and the Ah-Tha-Thi-Ki Museum outside Fort Lauderdale, demonstrate traditional Seminole crafts and culture. Rather less traditional but popular Everglades air-boat rides and alligator-wrestling are also available. Gambling presents a different type of entertainment, with a major new casino resort on reservation lands close to Miami.

The significant role of Miami's Cuban community in shaping the modern city will be reflected in a new museum dedicated to the Cuban experience in Florida, under construction in the city's landmark Freedom Tower, where many Cuban refugees of the 1950s and 1960s were processed on their arrival in the US.

For a dash of vintage Cuba in the heart of Miami, check out nightclubs devoted to the pre-Revolutionary Havana sound, watch dominoes players click-clacking away at tables beneath the trees on the pavements of Calle Ocho (SW 8th Street) in Little Havana and make a reservation for pop diva Gloria Estefan's traditional Cuban restaurant on Miami Beach.

Miami Beach itself celebrates more than 200 years of Jewish history in the state with the Sanford L Ziff Jewish Museum of Florida, housed in a former South Beach synagogue. There is also an emotionally moving Holocaust Memorial.

Heading north up to the Gold Coast, the Morikami Museum and Japanese Gardens in Delray Beach commemorate a colony of Japanese pineapple farmers with beautifully landscaped grounds, crafts displays and demonstrations of the traditional Japanese tea ceremony.

❑ Cracker culture has a better press in Florida than in most other southern states, where the word has been used disparagingly to describe the poor and disadvantaged. In Florida, Cracker refers to anything that's native to Florida.

Cracker architecture can be seen in the wooden pioneer homes throughout the state. A good example would be the Cracker homestead on the Marjorie Kinnan Rawlings State Historic Site, south of Gainesville. Meanwhile, Cracker cooking is a byword for southern-style barbecue, grits (cracked corn porridge), catfish and hearty portions. ❑

Florida is a magnet for sports lovers. Everything from golf and canoeing to greyhound racing and jai alai finds loyal supporters in this sports-crazy state, and millions of holiday-makers every year can also enjoy the excellent facilities.

In Palm Beach County alone there are more than 145 golf courses, 1,100 tennis courts and 47 miles (75km) of oceanfront beaches offering scuba diving, surfing, sailing and other watersports, plus sportfishing. Baseball, croquet, greyhound racing, jai alai and two polo clubs just about complete the sporting picture in this one small area.

COURSES AND COURTS Florida's **golf** courses are glorious. The Sunshine State has developed into a top golfing destination well supplied with challenging courses designed by the likes of Pete Dye and Tom Fazio, plus a tremendous choice of excellent public courses. This is the birthplace of Jack Nicklaus, after all. Naples, on the west coast, claims to be the 'Golfing Capital of the World'. Although golf is played all year round, winter is by far the busiest season.

Tennis aces can have a ball

Tennis resorts and training schools are another intrinsic feature of the Florida sporting scene, and the state is home to Nick Bolletieri's tennis camp, training ground for many tennis greats. Sports-oriented resorts are a popular alternative to traditional hotels.

HEAD FOR THE WATER As the first rays of sun streak the Atlantic Ocean, **surfers** can be seen crouching over their boards waiting to catch the first wave of the day. **Waterskiers** and **jet-skiers** carve trails through the water and **catamarans** zip to and fro. There is also **parasailing** for the adventurous or **pedalboats** for those less inclined to get wet.

Marinas are packed with charter boats offering **sportfishing** excursions for marlin, pompano, sailfish and shark. Islamorada in the Florida Keys claims to be the 'Sportfishing Capital of the World' – Pompano on the Gold Coast and Destin in the Panhandle might beg to differ.

Meanwhile, **scuba divers** and **snorkellers** flock to the Gold Coast and Keys to explore the dazzling coral reefs and artificial dive sites warmed by the Gulf Stream.

One way of exploring Florida's inland water courses is by **canoe**. The Blackwater and Suwannee rivers in the Panhandle, the Myakka and Peace rivers near Arcadia, the southern tip of the Everglades and the Keys are just a few of the prime locations. Saltwater and freshwater **fishermen** on the rivers and back bays should obtain a fishing licence, available from tackle shops.

A SPORTS LOVERS' PARADISE Spectator sports such as basketball and football attract enthusiastic crowds. Baseball, in its season, does

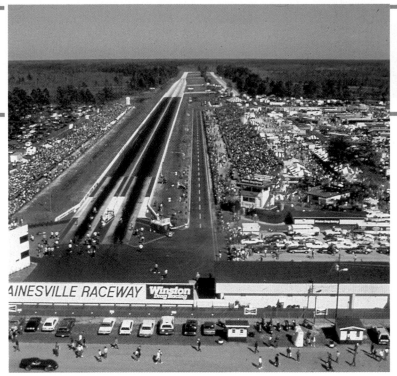

Sport is big in Gainesville

the same. February signals the arrival of major league teams from around the country for the start of the six-week spring training programme.

Central Florida welcomes the Houston Astros to Kissimmee, and the Atlanta Braves to Orlando's Walt Disney World Resort.

On the west coast, the New York Yankees practice in Tampa, the Philadelphia Phillies in Clearwater, the Boston Red Sox and Minnesota Twins train in Fort Myers, and the Toronto Blue Jays warm up in Dunedin.

Over on the east coast, the St Louis Cardinals take up residence in Jupiter, while the Los Angeles Dodgers claim Vero Beach. Fans can turn up to watch the practice sessions, and the Grapefruit League games, which attract a million-plus fans each year. Attending these smaller games can be just as exciting as regular league play-offs.

No motor racing fan should leave Florida without a visit to Daytona,

❑ Pari-mutuel betting was legalized in Florida in 1931. It opened the doors to a flood of sporting activities, including the now widely popular grey-hound racing, horse-racing, which takes place on four courses in Miami alone, and the fast and furious ball game of jai alai, which is something of a Florida speciality. ❑

the 'Birthplace of Speed' and home of 'the other 24-hour race'. US stock-car racing was virtually born here at the Daytona Speedway, and February's Race Weeks culminate in the world-famous Daytona 500. There are stock-car race tracks around the state from West Palm Beach to Tampa and Pensacola. Sebring's 12-hour endurance race is another classic, and downtown Miami hosts an annual springtime Grand Prix.

Mickey Mouse hit Florida in 1971, when Walt Disney's Magic Kingdom opened its doors outside Orlando. However, the state's love affair with theme parks was already well established.

Cypress Gardens, near Winter Haven, Florida's first and longest continuously operated theme park, has been packing them in since the mid-1930s. Further encouraged by the success of Disney, themed attractions have sprung up around the state, and exotic animals and birds have come to roost in a wide variety of specially created 'natural habitats' from the African plains of Tampa's Busch Gardens to Orlando's SeaWorld. There is fun on tap at water parks, zoos, adventure zones, miniature golf courses and arcades.

WALT DISNEY WORLD® RESORT Disney continues to draw the crowds as one of the world's number-one tourist destinations. The **Magic Kingdom**, with its cast of Disney characters from Cinderella to Dumbo; **Epcot**'s 'science-with-a-smile' and cultural exhibits; and **Disney-MGM Studios** were joined in 1998 by **Disney's Animal Kingdom**, which has exotic landscapes and close encounters with animals, as well as with dinosaurs, Disney characters and great rides. The Disney complex also includes three unique water parks, **Blizzard Beach**, **Typhoon Lagoon** and **River Country**, plus the sprawling **Downtown Disney** entertainment district, which is excellent for shopping and dining. The nightclubs of Downtown Disney's **Pleasure Island** offer plenty of after-dark entertainment.

UNIVERSAL CHALLENGE Near by there is hot competition in the form of **Universal Studios Orlando**. At **Universal Studios**, *E.T.*, *Back to the Future*'s Doc Brown and *Terminator 2* are among others, the theme for rides which are cute, stomach-churning and hair-raising, in turn. Universal's **Islands of Adventure** park, opened in 1999, breathes life into favourite cartoon characters, from Spider-Man and Popeye to Dr Seuss, in dramatically themed zones with shows and rides to match. Between the entrances to both parks is **Universal Studios CityWalk**, full of shopping, dining and entertainment options. Also under Universal's wing, not far from the parks, is a major water park, **Wet 'n' Wild** – the water playground of choice if you want to get wet in the International Drive area.

MORE AROUND ORLANDO Still in Orlando, **SeaWorld Orlando**, Florida's most popular marine park, features an all-star cast of whales, dolphins, sea lions and otters. You can also see Penguin Encounter; an eerie collection of eels, venomous fish and sharks in Terrors of the Deep; plus a nightly Polynesian dinner show. Don't miss **Discovery Cove,** SeaWorld's new sister park, where interactive marine adventures are a speciality, along with bottlenose dolphin and stingray encounters.

In Kissimmee, the local splash zone is **Water Mania**. Both parks offer children's versions of the big slides, as well as drier options such as sunbathing.

A half-hour drive away, **Cypress Gardens** combine spectacular botanical gardens with waterskiing extravaganzas, variety shows, the new Wings of Wonder butterfly conservatory and Nature's Way animal habitat exhibit, an elaborate model railroad, and – the park's kitsch trademark –the crinolined Southern Belles, who pose on the beautiful manicured lawns.

TAMPA ADVENTURES Some 90 minutes by car from Orlando is **Busch Gardens** in Tampa. Spreading out from a re-created Serengeti Plain, with its array of African wildlife, themed districts re-create places on

the African continent, from a Moroccan souk to a southern African village. A dolphin theatre, an ice show, rides and children's play areas acompany the wildlife – of which there is a lot. **Adventure Island**, a mile away, makes a splash with its Tampa Typhoon water slide, a leisurely ride through a simulated rain forest and many other adventures.

PANHANDLE DUO The Panhandle's Panama City Beach has **Shipwreck Island Water Park** with six landscaped acres (2.5ha) of pools and slides, sundecks and snack bars, and **Miracle Strip Amusement Park**, a gigantic fairground packed with good, old-fashioned rides such as the giant Ferris wheel, a 2,000-foot (610m) roller coaster, swinging gondolas and a host of contests and sideshows.

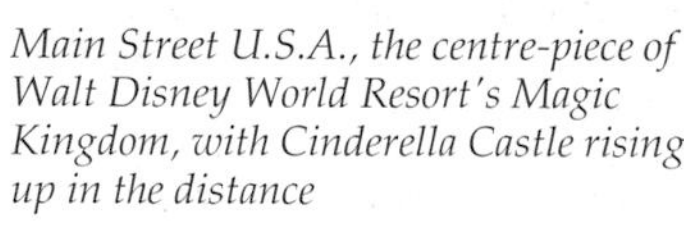

Main Street U.S.A., the centre-piece of Walt Disney World Resort's Magic Kingdom, with Cinderella Castle rising up in the distance

❑ Best of the rest:
Miami: Miami Seaquarium.
Keys and Everglades: Theater of the Sea, Islamorada.
Central Florida: Wild Waters and Silver Springs, Ocala.
Gold Coast: Lion Country Safari, West Palm Beach.
East Coast: Adventure Landing, Jacksonville Beach.
West Coast: Weeki Wachee Spring, north of Tampa.
Panhandle: Gulfarium, Fort Walton Beach. ❑

French science fiction writer Jules Verne predicted Florida's space age future in his novel, From Earth to the Moon, *published in 1863. Verne described 'Florida ... shaken to its very depths' by the lift-off of a rocket named* Columbiad. *Was it coincidence or intent which named the 1980s Columbia Space Shuttle programme? Was there a well-read scientist with a sense of humour at work?*

INTO THE SPACE RACE The first scientific studies exploring the use of rockets for space flight were published in the early 20th century. During the 1930s, German scientists made dramatic leaps forward in the development of rocket technology, culminating in the World War II V-2 guided missile. Later many of these scientists continued their work in peacetime for the United States and the Soviet Union. By the late 1950s, the space race was on. In October 1957, the Soviets launched *Sputnik 1* into Earth's orbit, followed in January 1958 by the Americans' *Explorer 1*. When the National Aeronautics and Space Administration (NASA) was set up later that year, it selected the missile-testing range at Florida's Cape Canaveral Air Force Station as its test base and inaugurated the *Mercury* manned space programme. Once again the Soviets got there first with Yuri Gagarin's manned space flight in *Vostok 1* on 12 April, 1961. Less than a month later, on 5 May, Alan Shepard became the first American in space, with a 15-minute sub-orbital flight in a *Mercury* capsule.

❑ The centre-piece of NASA's space programme for the future is a truly international affair. Space Station Freedom will be an orbiting scientific research facility and launch point for further trips to the moon. The component parts are being transported into orbit by a series of Space Shuttle flights, where they can be assembled by astronauts. Designs for the main structure, a 508-foot (155m) horizontal boom, incorporate docking facilities for the Space Shuttle and four special-purpose modules – two US, one Japanese and one European – which will provide accommodation and work space for up to eight people. Canada is contributing a maintenance depot and a mobile service unit. ❑

GEMINI* AND *APOLLO Work on the giant Launch Complex 39 began in 1962 across the Banana River from Cape Canaveral. NASA's operations moved across the water to Merritt Island in 1964, the first year of the two-man *Gemini* missions. An estimated 400,000 visitors took the opportunity to tour the newly named Kennedy Space Center Complex.

After several unmanned launches, the first manned *Apollo* flight was accomplished in December 1968, with a three-man crew. On 20 July, 1969, Neil Armstrong and Edwin 'Buzz' Aldrin Jr's moonwalk from *Apollo 11* made them the first men on the moon.

THE SPACE SHUTTLE NASA's next target was to develop a reusable manned spacecraft, the Space Transportation System (STS), better known as the Space Shuttle. Three basic elements make up the Space Shuttle system: a 212-foot (64.5m) Orbiter, shaped like an airplane; two solid-fuel booster rockets; and an external tank containing liquid

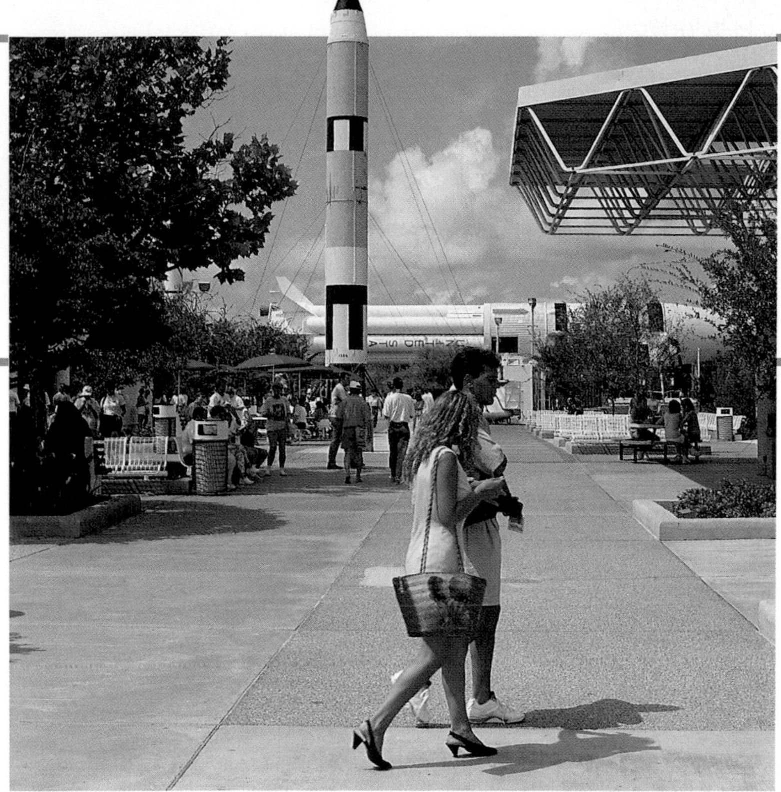

Kennedy Space Center, Rocket Garden

hydrogen (fuel) and liquid oxygen (an oxidiser). These elements produce a degree of flexibility that permits the Orbiter to take off like a rocket, orbit like a spacecraft and return to Earth, landing on a runway like a glider or an airplane. At lift-off, the combined Space Shuttle system stands 184 feet (56m) high and weighs 4½ million pounds (2 million kg). The boosters, used up at lift-off, are jettisoned after about two minutes and parachute to Earth where they are retrieved and reused. The 15- by 60-foot (4.5 by 18m) cargo bay can transport bulky cargoes such as communications and scientific research satellites into the Earth's orbit. Disabled spacecraft and hardware can be recovered and repaired in the bay, and loads weighing as much as 32,000 pounds (14,500kg) can be brought back to Earth.

The Space Shuttle's maiden voyage in 1981 marked the real beginning of space travel. These reusable craft are designed for years of service, allowing for routine space flights that will service the space station programmes of the 21st century.

WINDOW INTO SPACE Florida is the heart of America's pioneering space programme, and there is no better place to see the story unfold than at Kennedy Space Center (see pages 192–3 and 196). The centre's 70-acre (28ha) Visitor Complex is the gateway to an in-depth look at space travel, with dozens of displays, collections of memorabilia and space hardware, re-creations and film footage of great moments in the exploration of space. There are bus tours to Launch Complex 39 and the historic Cape Canaveral Air Force Station launch sites, as well as IMAX movies, and the Astronaut Memorial, a huge granite 'space mirror' which tracks the sun throughout the day and commemorates US astronauts who have died in the line of duty.

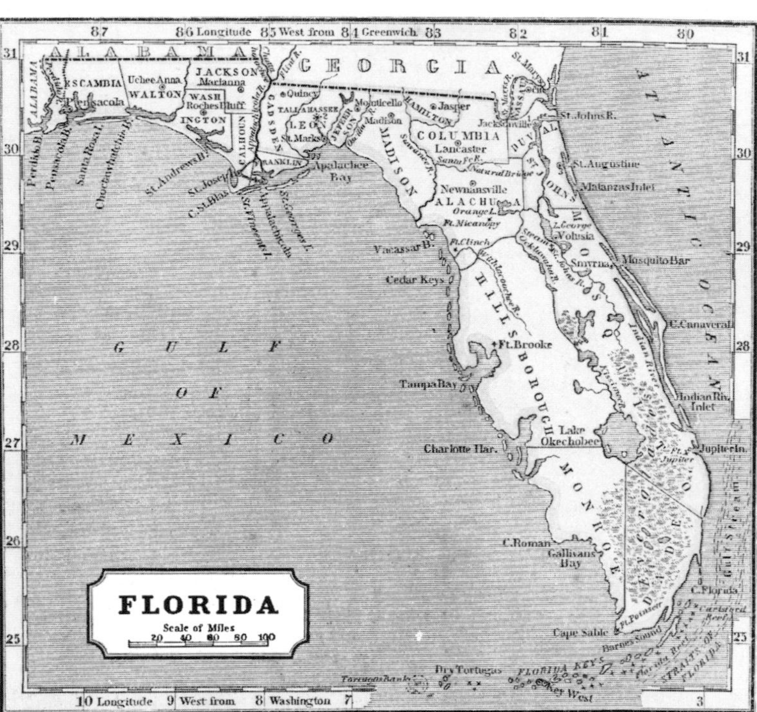

Cypress swamp, primeval-looking Florida landscape

Most of the Florida peninsula tacked on to the bottom right-hand corner of North America is just about as flat as a pancake. Its highest point, near the border with Georgia, is a mere 345 feet (105m) above sea level. Thus, the story of its origins is something of a surprise.

FIRE AND WATER About 200 million years ago, when the ancient continent of Pangaea began to break apart, a chain of island volcanoes rose from the sea, curving south from the mainland toward Cuba and the Bahamas. As the sea level rose and fell during the period of the Pleistocene era, these volcanoes were gradually eroded. Deep sea-filled trenches formed and gathered sediment to create massive limestone deposits reaching depths of 18,000 feet. Fossilised remains found in the north indicate that Florida was still under water while dinosaurs roamed the rest of the continent. Its warm waters were home to the prehistoric forerunners of turtles, sharks, whales and manatees (sea cows).

EMERGENCE OF DRY LAND Around 20 to 30 million years ago, Florida finally appeared as a flat, swampy plateau cemented to the mainland by millions of years worth of collected sediment, coated with a rich phosphorous residue from the waves. As the last Great Ice Age advanced from the north, gigantic glaciers devoured the sea and Florida doubled in size as the waters receded. No glaciers reached very far south, so Florida became a safe haven for all manner of creatures, from mammoths and sabre-toothed tigers to tiny deer, wolves, bears and swamp-dwelling alligators. Their fossilised remains are frequently uncovered by phosphate mining operations.

FROM ISLAND TO PENINSULA After the Ice Ages came the rains. The rains flooded the porous limestone, creating underground freshwater reservoirs, transformed sinkholes into springs and filled numerous rivers and thousands of lakes. The outline of the peninsula was still being shaped by the changing sea level, as can be seen from the graduated terraces sloping away from the center of the state into the Gulf of Mexico, but around 6,000 years ago the Florida of today was recognisable. Florida's 1,350-mile (2,170km) seashore, fringed with islands and coral reefs, enclosed a land rich in plant life, animal life and fresh water – a land ripe for human habitation.

Fairchild Tropical Gardens, Miami

Columbus discovered the Americas when his progress westward was impeded in 1492. Convinced that India was just around the corner, he christened the offshore islands the 'West Indies' and the native inhabitants 'Indians'.

THE FIRST-COMERS Some historians believe that the first Americans migrated from Asia across the Bering Strait after the last Ice Age, some 20,000 years ago. This extraordinary journey may have continued for up to 10,000 years, as different groups of migrants gradually spread out over the North and South American continents. There is no trace of any large native primate from which humans could have evolved here, so it is possible that all 'Americans', from the Inuit (Eskimos) of Alaska and Canada to the Araucanian people of Chile, are descended from the first Mongoloid migrants. However, there is a growing argument which supports the theory that certain South American groups developed separately and are unrelated.

Archaeologists believe the first Floridians arrived in the northern Panhandle region about 10,000 to 12,000 years ago. The traditional view maintains that these first settlers arrived as part of the general migration south, but similarities between early Florida culture and the cultures of some of the tribes of Central and South America indicate a remigration north.

Native American totem pole

The first migrants were hunter/gatherers who arrived in a promised land of sunny skies and rich hunting, surrounded by a bountiful ocean. Armed with simple flint-tipped spears, they roamed the peninsula and subsisted on mammoth, bison, boar, deer, fish and shellfish, quail, duck and goose.

EARLY SETTLEMENT By 5000 BC, groups of Native Americans had settled in villages along the St Johns River. These semi-permanent communities practiced the orderly disposal of refuse, and their dumps, known as middens, have provided archaeologists with precise clues to the habits and culture of the original settlers. Mounds of discarded shells indicate a healthy seafood diet; broken arrowheads and weapons chart the development from crude spears to more sophisticated hunting methods; and, from around 2000 BC, a startling cultural advance is demonstrated by the presence of shards of pottery. This is a clear guide to the highly developed culture of these southern tribes, as the art of fashioning clay vessels and baking them was not discovered for another eight centuries in most of North America.

Cultivation of maize began around 1000 BC, giving rise to the emergence of crude irrigation schemes particularly in the Lake Okeechobee area of central south Florida. Advances in the tribes' ability to feed themselves led to something of a population explosion, and settlements gradually

Remnants of a proud culture

appeared across the entire peninsula. Estimates of the aboriginal population around the time of the arrival of the Spanish vary enormously, with a median of about 100,000 spread throughout the state and divided into tribes. The peoples included the Timucuans in the central and northern areas and the Apalachee in the north and east Panhandle region. Tampa Bay was settled by the Tocobega, while Calusas hunted on the southwest coast, and Tequestas controlled the Everglades and southeastern shores.

A RICH CULTURE The apparent lack of a written language among Florida's original Native Americans has proved a major stumbling block in furthering our understanding of the everyday life of the peninsula's early inhabitants. Archaeological investigations at important historical sites, such as Crystal River (see page 204), are still uncovering more questions than answers, though several significant cultural periods have been identified, such as the Deptford culture (500 BC–AD 300), the Weedon Island culture (AD 300–900) and the Safety Harbor culture (900–onwards until contact with Europeans).

Jean Ribaut, a French mariner who helped colonise Florida, described the Native Americans in the mid-16th century as 'of tawny colour, hawk nosed and of a pleasant countenance'. They wore light deerskin coverings and coloured earrings made from inflated fish bladders, and intricate tattoos. Ribaut was impressed by the Native Americans' hunting methods – disguised in deerskins and horns, they could sneak up close to their prey for the kill.

Tribal government was administered by chieftains, who were advised by elders and priests. Animal sacrifices were made to appease the sun god, and first-born children were sacrificed in demonstration of fealty to the tribal chief. Human bones, up to 6,000 years old, were discovered in burial sites. Reserved for important figures, these burial mounds increased in size and ingenuity until they became massive earthworks visible for miles around on complex road and canal systems which developed along similar lines to those of the ancient Aztec and Mayan civilisations of South and Central America.

THE BEGINNING OF THE END The arrival of the first explorers from Europe signalled trouble ahead for Florida's early inhabitants. The greatest threats were neither weapons nor land disputes, but European ailments such as measles and chicken pox, against which the Native American population had no defence.

When Spanish explorer Juan Ponce de León sailed from his base in Puerto Rico on 3 March, 1513, he was going in search of the lost island of Bimini and its legendary fountain of eternal youth. A month later, on Easter Sunday, he landed near present-day St Augustine and named the new territory La Florida, *after the Spanish Eastertide Feast of Flowers,* Pascua Florida.

Ponce de León's explorations led him around the Keys (the Spanish for island is *cayo*) – which he named *Los Martires* because they reminded him of a chain of martyred men – and up the west coast of the peninsula to Charlotte Harbor, now known as Fort Myers. He was met by Native Americans shouting in Spanish. Whether the Spanish words had been learned from contacts with South American natives or from forays by slave hunters is not known.

The first attempt to colonise Florida was a disaster. Ponce de León returned in 1521 with 200 settlers and missionaries, but their settlement was attacked before the foundations were complete, and the Spanish retired to Cuba, where Ponce de León died from an arrow wound.

Exploring the past

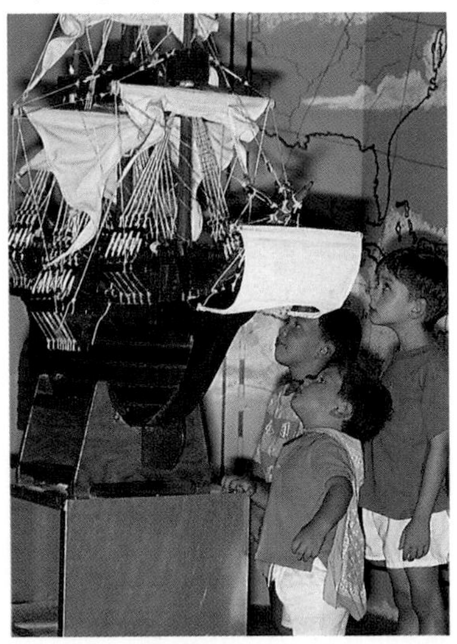

❑ Italian navigator and explorer John Cabot may have been the first European to see Florida when he sailed down the North American coast on a charting mission for King Henry VII of England. Although he never set foot ashore, 16th-century maps of Cabot's voyages appear to confirm that he sighted the Florida peninsula. ❑

DREAMS OF GOLD In 1528, Pánfilo de Narváez landed in Tampa Bay with a force of 400 men. They trailed north into the Panhandle in search of gold, leaving instructions for their ships to join them. Disease and tribal raids took their toll, the ships never turned up and the few remaining men of the expedition set sail in makeshift boats from which there were only four survivors (who reappeared in Mexico some eight years later).

There were still dreams of undiscovered pots of gold when Hernando de Soto fielded a further expedition in 1539. Setting out from Tampa Bay in March of that year, de Soto led his 1,000 battle-hardened *conquistadores* and fortune-seekers deep into North America's interior. They ventured as far as North Carolina and Alabama, where de Soto died of a fever on the Mississippi River after three years of fruitless searching. By this time the promise of gold was beginning to wear a little thin. It is now believed that any gold the Native Americans possessed had probably been recovered from Spanish shipwrecks along the coast.

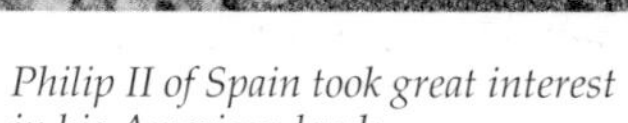
Philip II of Spain took great interest in his American lands

EUROPEAN INROADS Tristán de Luna y Arellano made the next attempt to establish a permanent Spanish settlement on the peninsula. This nobleman and veteran of several campaigns sailed into Pensacola Bay with a total of 1,500 soldiers, priests and craftsmen in 1559. Their luck was no better, and the combination of Luna's shortsighted management, crippling food shortages and a violent hurricane forced them to retreat in 1561.

By this time, although the Spanish had continually failed to establish a foothold on their vast new territory, their presence was being felt in a far more long-reaching and insidious fashion. European diseases were savagely decimating the Native American population, and raids by slave traders from strongholds in the West Indies were driving the Native Americans from their traditional homelands. Within 200 years, the original inhabitants of Florida would no longer exist.

For a record of these lost Floridians, we are indebted to the French. Spurred by Spain's failure to colonise, French explorer Jean Ribaut made several forays along the Florida coast. In 1564, a colony of Huguenots founded a settlement on the St Johns River at Fort Caroline. Here, Ribaut and his cartographer Jacques le Moyne, compiled a fascinating account of the local tribes complete with detailed descriptions of Native American dress, customs and practices.

This French Protestant enterprise proved too much for Spanish Catholic pride, and Philip II dispatched Pedro Menéndez de Avilés to dislodge the French. Menéndez landed south of the St Johns River on 28 August, 1565, on the feast of St Augustine. Not long after this, the Huguenots were defeated.

❑ Menéndez was also commanded by Philip II to spread the Catholic faith throughout the New World; he set about his task with unprecedented patience and humanity. Jesuit priests were established at Tampa Bay and Charlotte Harbor, and by the 17th century the Native American Catholic reserves were formed. ❑

St Augustine grew to become the oldest continuously inhabited European settlement in the United States – despite numerous attempts by hostile raiders, England's Sir Francis Drake included, to remove it from the face of the earth.

On learning of Menéndez's victory over the French colonists, Philip II of Spain declared it was a wholly justifiable 'retribution ... upon the Lutheran pirates', which would act as a lesson to all. However, Spain's problems with foreign fortune-hunters, particularly those on the high seas, were only just beginning.

THE PLUNDERERS PLUNDERED Throughout the 16th and 17th centuries, Spanish treasure fleets, laden with gold, silver, copper and precious stones plundered from Spain's West Indian and South American colonies, ploughed slowly homeward around the southern tip of Florida. They attracted buccaneers like bees to honey. Attacking the lumbering galleons from smaller, swifter craft, pirates could easily escape with their booty and hide out in the impenetrable maze of coastal mangrove swamps and play hide-and-seek around the Florida Keys.

❑ Potential profits far outweighed the danger, as Francis Drake soon discovered. Drake returned from a successful foray to the New World with Spanish booty worth some £1½ million, was knighted by Queen Elizabeth I on the docks at Deptford, and sent straight back to colonise North America – all the time continuing to deny that he harboured any hostility towards Spain. ❑

Booty from a treasure ship

DISASTER AT SEA The treasure ships had numerous natural hazards to face as well, including treacherous tides, knife-edged coral reefs concealed in the shallows and violent storms which descended with little warning. On 4 September, 1622, a fleet of Spanish galleons, guarded by men-o'-war, upped anchor in Havana harbour and set sail for home. Among the vessels were the *Nuestra Señora de Atocha* and the *Santa Margarita*, both lying low in the water, weighed down by their priceless cargoes. The following evening, they and six other vessels lay at the bottom of the Florida Straits, victims of a violent hurricane which had also killed no fewer than 550 men.

It was some 350 years before a marine salvager and Florida legend named Mel Fisher located the site and its fabulous golden bounty, part of which is now on show at the **Mel Fisher Maritime Museum** in Key West (see pages 100 and 106).

BLACK CAESAR'S DOMAIN The Keys had long been a haven for smugglers and pirates ('wrecking' constituting a significant part of the economy), and there are more wrecks cluttering up the reefs here than anywhere else around the coast. Some ships, no doubt, fell prey to natural disasters, but many others are said to have been lured to their fate by false signals, the victims of legendary pirates such as the notorious Black Caesar. Reputed to be an escaped slave, Black Caesar distinguished himself by single-handedly capturing small vessels from his base just north of Key Largo. He then graduated to the post of trusted henchman to the infamous Edward Teach, alias Blackbeard.

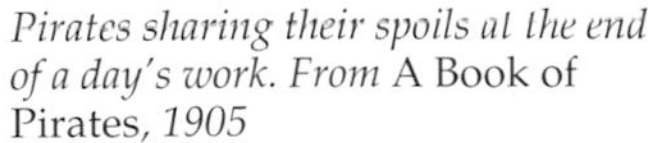

Pirates sharing their spoils at the end of a day's work. From A Book of Pirates, *1905*

Caesar's lust for wealth and power, and his wanton cruelty forced the authorities to act. In 1718, flying the *Jolly Roger* flag, Lieutenant Robert Maynard captured Teach's ship, the *Queen Anne's Revenge*. Teach was killed in the course of the battle, and Black Caesar was brought back in chains to Virginia, where he was hanged.

GASPARILLA The Treasure Coast area around Fort Pierce and Vero Beach is another fruitful spot for salvagers – 11 vessels of the Spanish Plate Fleet sank here in 1715. On the Gulf Coast, gold coins have been washed ashore at Naples after heavy storms, and there was certainly plenty of shipping and pirate action around Tampa Bay and the Charlotte Harbor area. This is where legendary mutineer-turned-buccaneer, José Gaspar – also known as Gasparilla – carved his violent niche into the folklore of Florida.

Captiva Island is said to have been named after one of his more famous exploits – the abduction of the Spanish infanta and her escort of 11 Mexican maidens in 1801. Once he landed on the island, Gaspar handed the captive maidens over to his crew and claimed the Spanish princess for himself. When she refused to co-operate with him, he had her executed.

❑ According to local storytellers, José Gaspar was a high-ranking gentleman who staged a bloody mutiny on the Spanish galleon *Florida Blanca* in 1785. As Gasparilla, he terrorised passing sea traffic for 37 years, capturing or sinking some 36 ships between 1784 and 1795. ❑

Gaspar's sea-faring days came to an end in 1822 when an American warship, masquerading as a British trader, attacked his pirate ship with a blast from a concealed gun battery. Realising that the game was up, Gasparilla committed suicide by leaping overboard. The day of the big-time Florida pirates was almost over, though the Laffite brothers, French pirates, and the mysterious Tavernier, their associate, were still harrying American ships from south of the border well into the 19th century.

During the 17th century, British slave traders made frequent raids into Spanish territory to capture native Florida tribes-people. The cattle-herding skills of the Native Americans, acquired while living in segregated reserves under the Spanish, were highly prized and sought-after.

BRITISH OPPORTUNISTS Raids were becoming more daring by the beginning of the 18th century, and the British slave traders had formed an alliance with the Creek tribes, members of the Muskogeah Native American tribe from Alabama, Georgia and the Carolinas. After the raids, many of the Creeks stayed on, occupying former Spanish farmlands and other Native American territory. Because they had deserted their own tribes in the north, they became known as *Seminoles*, from a Creek word meaning 'runaways' or 'wanderers'.

When Spain and Britain ended the Seven Year War with the Treaty of Paris in 1763, Britain received Florida in exchange for Cuba. As the Spanish sailed away with the remnants of the aboriginal population, the British moved in with their Creek allies, and the two communities co-existed amicably enough.

Vast tracts of land were swiftly annexed and granted to settlers, together with financial inducements. Rice, sugar-cane and indigo plantations were carved out of the fertile soil by African slaves, many of whom were assimilated into Native American communities through servitude and marriage.

SPANISH REOCCUPATION Britain occupied Florida for only 20 years. With British reserves severely depleted by the American Revolution, Spain saw a golden opportunity to reclaim lost American territory. They landed a force at Pensacola, and captured west Florida in 1781. Four years later, the Second Treaty of Paris saw Florida back in Spanish hands – but it was to bring its old conqueror little joy.

The Seminoles largely ignored the Spanish jurisdiction and soon found their land claims being disputed by a steady flow of white settlers from the north. Native American migrants continued to move south, and escaped African slaves from the Southern states sought refuge in Spanish territory, incurring the wrath of Georgia's powerful planters.

THE FIRST SEMINOLE WAR Tension built up along the border between Florida and Georgia, and relations between the Seminoles and the white settlers were worsening. General (later President) Andrew Jackson leaped upon the flimsiest pretext to thunder into Florida and attack the Seminoles by the Suwannee River. This was the First Seminole War of 1817–18.

DESPERATE MEASURES In 1819, Spain canceled its $5 million debt to the United States and left Florida for good, opening the door to a further influx of white settlers. In 1823, an attempt was made to restrict the Seminoles to a single reservation in central west Florida. It failed. The Removal Act of 1830 sought an even more drastic solution – Seminoles were exiled to reservations in Arkansas, west of the Mississippi. Senior chieftains journeyed west to view the land in 1832, but after just one chief had agreed to sign away his tribal lands, the process was halted by the arrival of a man named Osceola.

THE SECOND SEMINOLE WAR Young, handsome and confident, Osceola was widely respected, and he succeeded in uniting the various tribes to fight the Second Seminole

A Seminole family

War, which lasted seven long and bloody years (see also page 43). His capture, by trickery, while he was negotiating under a flag of truce in 1837, prompted a considerable public outcry. He died a year later, incarcerated in Fort Moultrie, South Carolina.

Osceola was succeeded by Chief Coacoochee (Wild Cat), but the spirit of the Seminoles had been broken, and they were no match for the United States' forces with their superior weaponry.

❑ Osceola, who was part European, had no shortage of grievances against the United States. One of his main ones was against the kidnappers of his wife Che-cho-ter (Morning Dew). This was an insult to his tribe and family he could never forgive. ❑

SURRENDER AND SURVIVAL Some 3,000 Seminoles travelled the so-called 'Trail of Tears' across the Mississippi in 1842. A handful of renegades, led by Chief Billy Bowlegs, slipped into the Everglades and continued to harry settlers and the army into the Third Seminole War of 1855. But the Seminoles were finally forced to surrender in 1858, and the chief was escorted west. An additional 300 Seminoles retreated deep into the Everglades, emerging only to trade alligator skins, deer-hides and small amounts of produce. It is their descendants who make up the present-day Seminole population and the smaller Miccosukee group. In 1911, the US government allocated reservation lands to Florida's Native Americans.

When Spain cancelled her debt to the United States by relinquishing control of the Florida peninsula in 1819, General Andrew Jackson was appointed the territory's first governor. 'Old Hickory', as he was known for his reputation to be as tough as this wood, arrived to take up his post in 1821, but only remained three months before heading for Washington, where he eventually became president in 1828.

A CENTRAL GOVERNMENT One of the most important questions facing Floridians was where to establish their state government. The two major settlements, Pensacola and St Augustine, were a three weeks' journey apart at opposite sides of the peninsula. In 1832, two scouts were sent out on horseback, one from each of the principal towns, and they met midway between the two, in the rolling hills of northern Florida. It was here that the town of Tallahassee was built.

By 1824, Florida's early legislative councils were convening in three log cabins near the site of the present-day Capitol building in Tallahassee. These cabins were replaced by a two-storey masonry structure in 1826, but as Florida moved towards state-hood, a larger and more impressive building was thought to be appropriate. Congress found $20,000 and commissioned a Capitol, which was completed just in time to welcome the new state government on 3 March, 1845.

Union guns at Fort Brady during the Civil War

SETTLEMENT AND SLAVERY During the 1820s, land grants and financial inducements encouraged a steady stream of white settlers to northern Florida, where they planted cotton, rice, tobacco and sugar-cane, stole Native American lands, and forced African Americans into slavery. The port of Jacksonville, founded in 1821, helped open up the interior. Pioneers ventured down the St Johns River to set up their trading posts and grew indigo and citrus fruits along the river banks and into the interior.

Down in the Keys, Caribbean immigrants were introducing their own distinctive architecture and establishing plantations growing fruits such as pineapples, bananas and mangoes.

One of Florida's early senators, David Levy Yulee, was Caribbean born. His sugar plantation and mill near Homosassa, on the Gulf Coast, was operated by 1,000 slaves. As in other Southern states, the slavery system was the backbone of the plantation economy, and it is estimated that some 25,000 slaves laboured under the yoke of King Cotton in Florida.

❑ The cotton industry turned little Apalachicola (now famous for its oysters) into the third largest port on the Gulf coast during the 1830s. Another claim to fame is Dr John Gorrie's ice-making machine, invented here in 1848. It led eventually to the development of air-conditioning and refrigeration. ❑

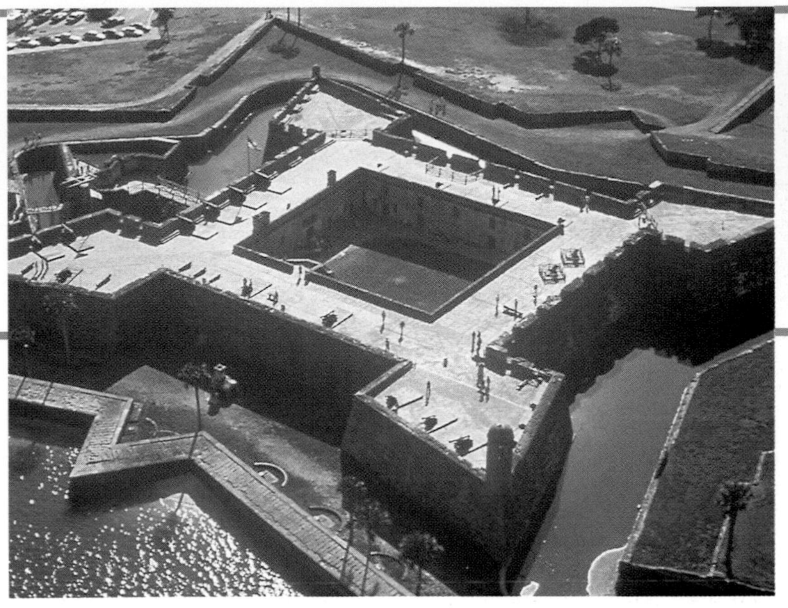

The Castillo de San Marcos, in St Augustine, Florida's most historic fortress

Florida's population almost doubled, from 34,370 to 66,500, between 1830 and 1845. Skirmishes between the Native Americans and white settlers became more frequent and bloody, and the government's efforts to deport the Native Americans by the Removal Act of 1830 resulted in the Second Seminole War (1835–1842). Fort Lauderdale, Fort Myers and Fort Pierce were all founded in response to the war. The total bill ran to more than $40 million (see also pages 40–1).

THE CIVIL WAR During a brief respite, the first cross-state railroad was built between Fernandina and Cedar Key. It opened in 1861. But Florida had barely recovered from its internal conflicts when pressure from wealthy plantation owners ensured that the 16-year-old state seceded from the Union on 10 January, 1861. Allied to the Confederate states, Florida went to war against the Union – and, as history tells us, lost.

Florida's main task in the Civil War was to provide food for the Confederate army, though Key West, among other places, remained loyal to the North and became a vital staging post for Union troops. The Confederates won a battle at Olustree, near Lake City, and Tallahassee became the only Confederate capital east of the Mississippi not to fall to Union forces, when a 'cradle and grave' troop of old men and boys successfully repelled the Northerners at the Battle of Natural Bridge in March 1865.

Two months later, after General Robert E Lee surrendered the Confederate cause at Appomattox, the Union flag was run up above the state capitol.

❑ Florida still takes pride in its Confederate history. After the war ended, many senior Confederate figures were forced to flee, among them Secretary of State Judah P Benjamin. Benjamin took refuge with Major Robert Gamble on his plantation at Ellenton, near Tampa. Today, the house is immaculately restored as the J P Benjamin Memorial (see page 204). ❑

At the end of the Civil War, President Andrew Jackson appointed a provisional government to oversee the reconstruction of Florida. It was not for some 20 years, however, until the coming of the railroad, that the state finally flourished.

AFRICAN AMERICAN RIGHTS A constitutional convention met in October 1865, the secession order was annulled, and laws were introduced to safeguard African Americans' civil rights. But the changes were largely superficial, and although the state government eventually bowed to pressure to include the African American population in its political processes, the requirements for those seeking high office automatically disqualified most African American candidates.

There were some exceptions, however. When the vote was granted to all male citizens of Florida aged 21 and over (including African Americans) in 1868, Jonathan C Gibbs, Florida's first African American cabinet member, was elected. Born of free parents in Philadelphia, Gibbs came to Florida after the Civil War to serve as a Presbyterian missionary. He was appointed secretary of state in 1869.

Meanwhile, nine-tenths of Florida's African Americans were working in the fields. In the 1870s, the Florida chapter of the Ku Klux Klan began to terrorise local African Americans. Despite these injustices, Harriet Beecher Stowe – whose anti-slavery epic *Uncle Tom's Cabin* had done so much to rally the abolitionists when it was published in 1852 – did note that Florida's African Americans were better off than those in neighbouring states.

❑ By the 1870s, even tourists were venturing into the interior of Florida – albeit from the comfortable confines of the luxury steamboats that plied the St Johns River. ❑

OPENING UP THE STATE In spite of the threat of yellow fever and malaria, there were plenty of settlers eager to make a go of it in Florida's wide open spaces. Citrus plantations boomed, and in 1881 the state sold 4 million acres (1.6 million ha) of central Florida to Hamilton Disston, who drained land in the Kissimmee and Caloosahatchee valleys to build settlements and for farming.

THE RAILROAD BARONS In the 1880s, two businessmen were to transform the state by building railroads. Henry B Plant pioneered a cross-state railroad to Tampa on the Gulf Coast; Henry M Flagler decked the Atlantic Coast with a necklace of luxurious resort hotels stretching from Jacksonville to Key West, linked by his East Coast Railroad.

State land grants in exchange for development were a powerful incentive for the railroad builders. For every mile of track between Kissimmee and Tampa, Plant received 5,000 acres (2,020ha) of virgin territory. In 1884, with just 63 hours to spare on the contract, he made it into Tampa and began work on the \$3½ million, 500-room Tampa Bay Hotel.

WIDER CONNECTIONS Plant also added to his growing transportation system a steamship service to Key West and Cuba. In 1885, Vincente Martinez Ybor moved his Cuban cigar-making industry from Key West to Tampa Bay. That same year inventor Thomas Alva Edison found a good spot beside the Caloosahatchee River at Fort Myers, down the coast from Tampa, to build himself a winter home.

Tampa's Cuban connection generated anti-Spanish propaganda and in 1898 Teddy Roosevelt and his Rough

Locomotives old and new

Riders, the first Regiment of US Cavalry Volunteers, rode into town en route to the Spanish–American War in Cuba. A young British journalist named Winston Churchill covered the news story from the comfort of Plant's hotel.

EAST COAST SPLENDOUR Though Plant was a prime mover in the development of Florida, the state's transition to a fashionable winter holiday area was largely due to the efforts of Henry Flagler. Honeymooning in St Augustine in the early 1880s, Flagler was disappointed by the lack of facilities and determined to bring the resort up to standard. The magnificent Spanish-Moorish-Revival-style Ponce de León Hotel opened in 1888. The Hotel Ormond at Ormond Beach followed in 1890. The Royal Poinciana opened in Palm Beach in 1894.

During the winter of 1894–5, a terrible frost destroyed citrus plantations as far south as Fort Lauderdale. In 1896, Miami pioneer Julia Tuttle persuaded Flagler to extend his East Coast Railroad line to Miami, where citrus trees still flourished, by sending him a bouquet of orange blossoms untouched by the big freeze further north. Flagler's railroad eventually reached Key West in 1912, a year before his death.

❑ Though the Ponce de León Hotel is now a college and the Hotel Ormond and Royal Poinciana have disappeared, there is one exceptional reminder of the days when Florida's Atlantic Coast was the premier winter playground of the Vanderbilts and Rockefellers. **The Breakers** at Palm Beach, originally a Flagler creation, was rebuilt in the 1920s after a fire, and its seven-storey Italian Renaissance-style façade, lofty ceilings and magnificent furnishings are still a sight to behold. ❑

In 1912, when Henry Flagler steamed into Key West aboard his famous 'Railroad That Went to Sea', it was the culmination of a dream. This had been a romantic project from its inception, but it cost Flagler dearly.

The last section of the East Coast Railroad system, extending from Homestead south of Miami down through the Keys, took seven years and several million dollars to complete. But somehow anything seemed possible in Florida at the beginning of the new century.

NEW FRONTIERS Entrepreneur Carl Fisher arrived in Miami as Flagler was celebrating. There he met New Jersey horticulturist John Collins who was struggling to transform a failed avocado plantation into a residential development on a strip of sand 3 miles (5km) out in Biscayne Bay. Fisher advanced Collins $50,000 to develop the land in exchange for a 200-acre (80-ha) plot. They built a wooden bridge across to the mainland, the longest in the country at the time, and in 1915 Fisher started a dredging operation which would almost double the size of the island, now known as Miami Beach.

As the mangrove wilderness was tamed, elegant hotels, shopping malls, golf courses and tennis courts sprang up along the beach. Across the bay, industrialist millionaire James Deering built himself a magnificent mansion, Vizcaya; further up the coast, self-taught architect Addison Mizner was enchanting the well-to-do with his Spanish-Mediterranean-inspired creations in Palm Beach. By the 1920s, Florida was definitely on the map, and everybody wanted a little piece of it.

REAL ESTATE MADNESS It was with a sense of adventure that the first 'tin-can tourists' drove the length and breadth of the country in their shiny new Fords, Oldsmobiles and Packards. The shortage of hotels could not deter them. They set up tented cities on the beach and dined out of tin cans. And they were easy targets for the squadrons of smooth-talking salesmen who hurried south as rumours spread of the real estate mania. The Marx Brothers even made a film about it called *Coconuts*. These shark-like salesmen, the 'binder boys', made fortunes overnight reselling options on undeveloped land to the uninitiated. Elaborate advertising campaigns, involving huge sums of money, further fuelled the dreams of those who raced south to invest in a little Florida sunshine.

THE ENTREPRENEURS George Merrick, founder of America's first planned community, spent $3 million in a single year advertising his Coral Gables development in Miami. This was one of the finest results of the land-boom era, and one of the most enduring. Its French, Dutch South African and Chinese neighbourhoods are still regarded as some of the most desirable residential areas in Miami (see page 54).

Inspired by Carl Fisher's success in Miami Beach, Charlie Rodes tackled the swamps of Fort Lauderdale. By dredging a series of parallel channels, he raised a neat clutch of 'finger islands' which gave the city a Venetian look – and earned Rodes a fortune.

Meanwhile, Addison Mizner was doing so well in Palm Beach that he and his brother, Winston, snapped up 16,000 acres (6,500 ha) of land around the fishing hamlet of Boca Raton. In 1925, they launched an advertising campaign which incorporated the slogan 'I'm the Greatest Resort in the World!', and sold $26 million worth of contracts before they had built a single Venetian-style bridge.

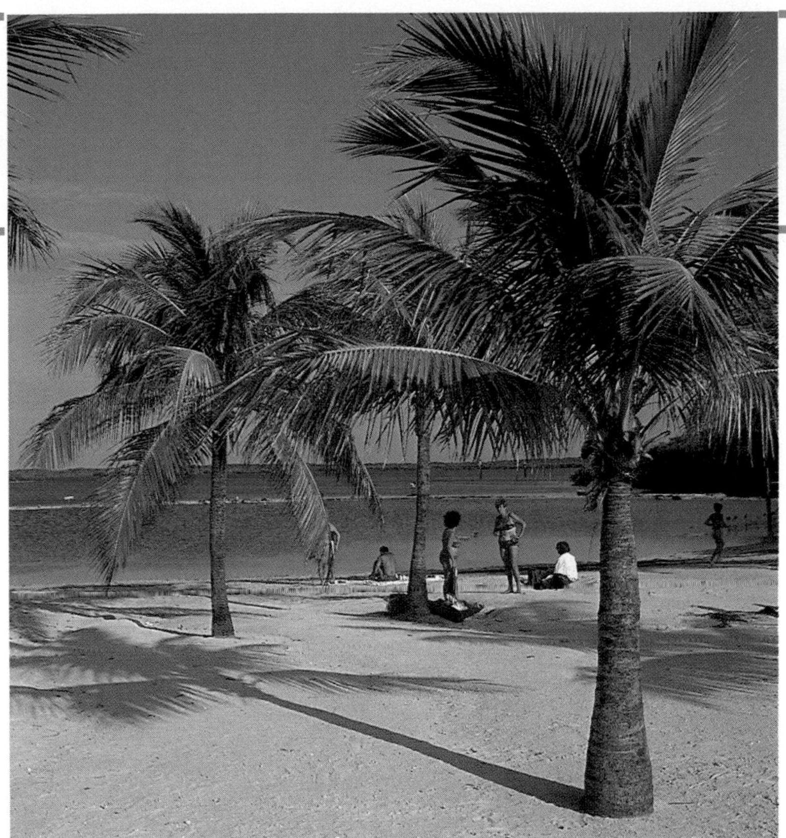

END OF A DREAM The land boom reached its height in 1925, and within a year Mizner's Boca Raton was already being decried as 'Beaucoup Rotten'. Disaster hit the resort when Miami was struck by a hurricane, and a couple of banks collapsed the following spring. Property investors realised they'd been duped when they took stock of their precious plots. Some plots were under water in swamps, while others were buried beneath mosquito-infested mangrove thickets. Things went from bad to worse. A drastic hurricane swept across the lower edge of the state in 1928, leaving more than 2,000 people dead and millions of dollars' worth of property destroyed. In the wake of this catastrophe came the stock market crash of 1929, which marked the beginning of the 1930s Depression years.

Florida's sunshine has drawn visitors to the state for more than 100 years

❏ The land boom also hit the Gulf Coast. Property guru Wilson Fuller wrote a book describing his experiences in St Petersburg, where his creative practices allowed him to transform a single investment of $50,000 into $270,000 in a few simple moves. Just down the coast, in Sarasota, circus king John Ringling threw causeways across the bay to the barrier-island Longboat Key, where he built an attractive shopping district to spare his wife and guests the trouble of journeying to Palm Beach. ❏

The collapse of the land boom and the ensuing Great Depression left a string of paper millionaires turned paupers – and an unpleasant taste in the mouths of many investors.

Florida suffered less than the rest of the United States. Here, while the rest of the country was locked into gloom, was one of the few bright spots on the horizon: the promise of sunny skies and palm-fringed beaches still worked its magic.

THE 1930s After a quiet start, the rest of the decade was actually a time of expansion for the state. Hardest hit by the crash, Miami was also the first to recover, and confident new building programmes signalled that the city was on the road to recovery. Miami Beach blossomed with the construction of art deco hotels and embraced the Moderne style a few years later.

The Hialeah Park Race Track opened in 1931 to celebrate the legalisation of pari-mutuel betting. This drew a large and enthusiastic crowd to the greyhound tracks, as well as to the jai alai *frontons* (as the venues for this pelota-like game are known). Legalised betting also attracted the attention of organised crime, and the gangster Al Capone retired to a heavily guarded estate on Palm Island where he died in 1947. With no state income tax or inheritance tax, and its inviting climate, Florida also welcomed less infamous retirees.

During the mid-1930s, the state benefited from a number of wide-ranging federal-aid programmes. Land reclamation, public buildings and transport were covered by the brief, as were cultural, educational and welfare projects.

When Flagler's former Overseas Railroad was destroyed by the Labor Day hurricane of 1935, federal relief workers picked over the ruins and built the Overseas Highway. Meanwhile, the Florida Emergency Relief Agency (FERA) worked together with local residents to gentrify Key West, which rapidly attracted literary types.

TOURISTS AND ASTRONAUTS By the early 1940s, Florida's population of 2 million was outnumbered by tourists in winter. Between 1945 and 1954, to cope with the demand, more hotel rooms were built in Greater Miami alone than in all the rest of the United States. In 1959, the nation's first scheduled domestic jet air service commenced between New York and Miami, and brought a new generation of tourists.

Jet airliners were not the only hardware streaking across Florida's wide blue yonder. In 1958, the Cape Canaveral Air Force Station, halfway

Mural in downtown Tampa

up Florida's Atlantic Coast, was chosen by the newly established National Aeronautics and Space Administration (NASA) as a testing ground for its early satellite and rocket programmes. Later, NASA built its own facility nearby. World attention was focused on the Kennedy Space Center's monitors for the historic *Apollo 11* moonwalk, when Neil Armstrong carried mankind one step further into the future.

THE DISNEY PHENOMENON Mickey Mouse arrived in 1971. Preparations for the theme park began quietly in the early 1960s, when Walt Disney targeted the state – and specifically the area near Kissimmee and Orlando – as the ideal site for his new venture. Good communications and transportation, plus year-round sunshine were all factors in his choice, along with the availability of huge tracts of undeveloped land – possibly the greatest attraction of all.

Appalled by the commercial sprawl that had sprung up around his California Disneyland, Disney was determined to control the surroundings on this project. Executives were sworn to secrecy as agents began to buy land. By the time an announcement was made in 1965, Disney had amassed 28,000 acres (11,330 ha), a site twice the size of Manhattan. The Magic Kingdom opened its doors in 1971, Epcot in 1983, Disney-MGM Studios in 1989, and Disney's Animal Kingdom in 1998. Together they make up the world's number-one tourist destination and have attracted more than 500 million visitors since 1971.

INTO THE FUTURE Florida continues to grow from strength to strength. Tourism, born in the 1880s, is now the backbone of the state's wealth as it moves into the 21st century. Florida's financial sector and high-tech industries are also booming, and attract an increasingly youthful quota of new residents. During the 1990s, attempts to address major ecological concerns such as pollution and damage to reefs and wetlands made some progress, but there is still much to do if Florida's precious wilderness areas and wildlife are to be preserved for the next generation.

STRETCHING ALONG THE GLITTERING blue waterfront of Biscayne Bay, Miami is a palm-fringed beach resort, a financial powerhouse and a gateway to Latin America, all rolled into one. Dynamic, exotic and forward-looking, the city's profile has never been higher. Not bad for a far-flung pioneer settlement that rose from the swamps little more than a century ago.

Today, Miami-Dade County covers an area of 1,955 square miles (5,060sq km) and has two million residents, but when pioneer settler Julia Tuttle arrived by mailboat in 1875, all she found were the remains of Fort Dallas, a Seminole trading post and a few scattered plantations around the bay.

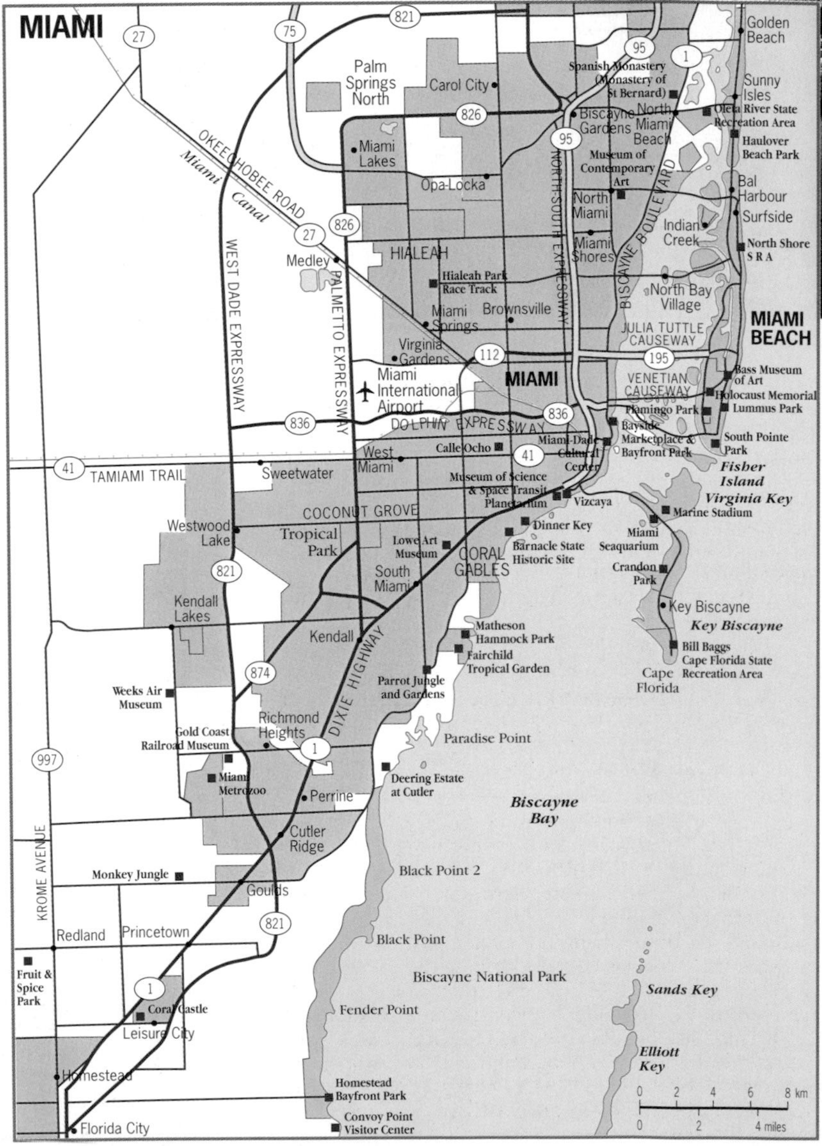

A-Z Miami

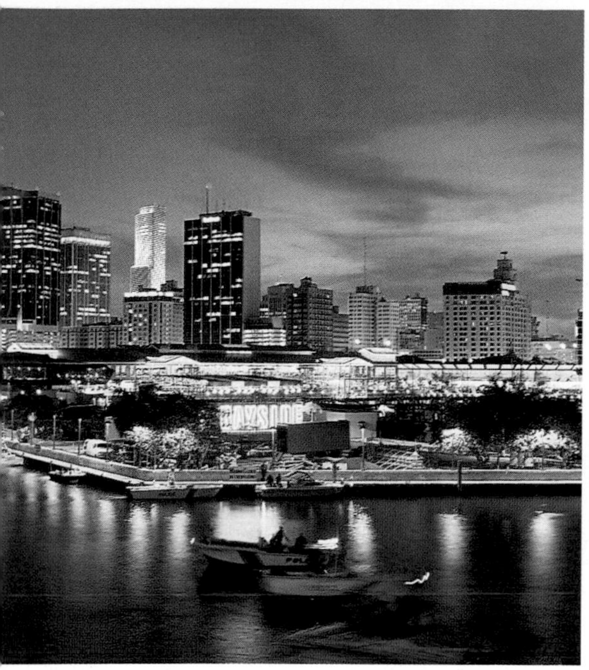

Left: the Downtown skyline rises dramatically behind the blazing lights of Bayside Marketplace

During the terrible winter frost of 1894–5, which decimated citrus groves as far south as Palm Beach, the enterprising Mrs Tuttle sent a bouquet of fresh orange blossoms to railroad baron Henry Flagler, persuading him to extend his railway tracks south to Miami. They duly arrived, followed by a stream of wealthy Northerners who built palatial winter retreats on the foreshore, while developers such as George Merrick created elegant **Coral Gables**, and Carl Fisher and John Collins landscaped an offshore avocado plantation into **Miami Beach**.

For all its vast size, Miami is very much a conglomeration of neighbourhood villages, each with a distinctive flavour – from the elegant **Art Deco** and **SoBe** areas of Miami Beach to neo-Bohemian **Coconut Grove**. Downtown rejuvenation has transformed the formerly bleak financial district with landmark concrete-and-glass architecture and a state-of-the-art sports arena; and an impressive $250-million Performing Arts Center is due to open in 2002. The latest up-and-coming area is the Design District just north of downtown.

Bordering the financial district to the west, **Little Havana** is the spiritual home of the city's one million Cubans (although many of them no longer live there). The Hispanic influence has added a definite twist to Miami's character and culture, and the community is well-represented in both local government and financial institutions. The city also attracts growing communities of Caribbean islanders, Latin Americans and an increasing number of Europeans to its multicultural mix, and the result is one of the most cosmopolitan and intriguing cities in the country.

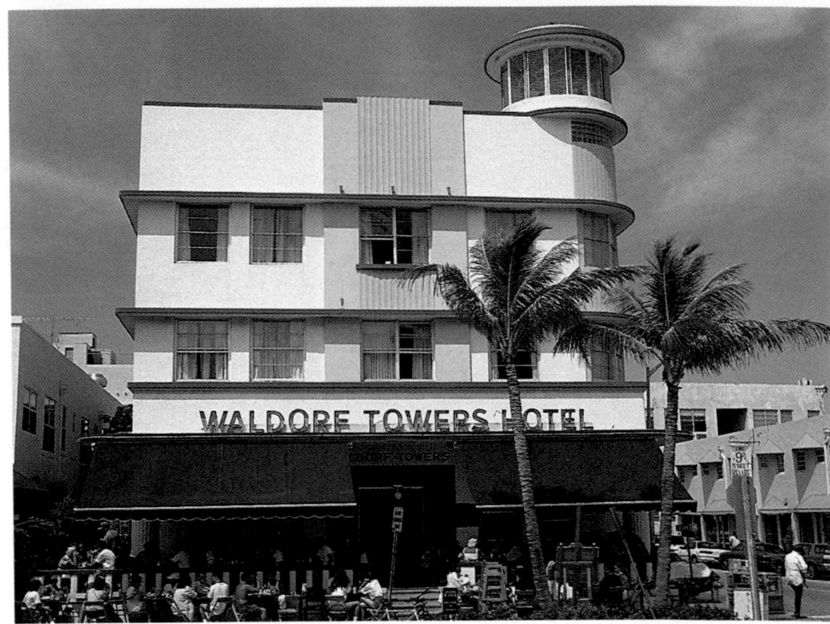

The 1930s have been brought back to life on Miami Beach's Ocean Drive

Miami's neighbourhoods

ART DECO DISTRICT AND MIAMI BEACH Rocketing to worldwide fame as one of the most recognisable jet-set haunts of the 1990s, the stylish Art Deco District covers a mere 12-block portion of Miami Beach, which is actually a 7-square-mile (18sq km) barrier island linked to the mainland by causeways across Biscayne Bay. But this historic district contains more than 800 art deco buildings listed on the National Register of Historic Places, and is the centre-piece of the ultra-chic area known as **SoBe** (South Beach), which occupies the southern tip of Miami Beach and stretches out to around 28th Street.

Miami Beach's building boom began in earnest after World War I with a flourish of Mediterranean Revival architecture relying heavily on romantic styles from the Old World. The earliest art deco buildings date from the mid-1920s and are richly decorated with local images such as palm trees and flamingos, earning the soubriquet 'tropical deco'. The less whimsical Moderne style of the 1930s heralded the new age of mass production, with streamlined aerodynamic designs and vibrant materials, including chrome, glass block and neon.

Today, SoBe's main drag is **Ocean Drive**, where strikingly restored art deco hotels overlook the green swathe of Lummus Park and the Atlantic a few steps away. Restaurants, cafés and other watering-holes packed together on the pavement, invite you to sit back and watch the fascinating parade of pedestrians, dog walkers, in-line skaters and limos which regularly brings traffic to a complete standstill (particularly at night, when SoBe is transformed into the nightlife centre of the city).

There is excellent shopping in designer stores on Collins Avenue and the attractive open-air Lincoln Road Mall,

▶▶▶ CITY HIGHLIGHTS

Art Deco District *pages 52–3*

Bayside Marketplace *page 59*

Coconut Grove *pages 53–4*

Fairchild Tropical Garden *page 60*

Key Biscayne *page 63*

Lowe Art Museum *page 62*

Miami Metrozoo *page 64*

Museum of Science & Space Transit Planetarium *pages 66–7*

Parrot Jungle *page 67*

Vizcaya Museum and Gardens *page 68*

plus numerous good restaurants and dozens of hotels to suit all tastes and budgets, from surprisingly affordable hostels to elegant little boutique hotels housed in art deco gems. Several of the biggest and grandest beach resort hotels are found just to the north of SoBe. Further north are the quieter districts of Surfside, Bal Harbour (with a sophisticated shopping centre) and Sunny Isles – a popular option for family holidays, with affordable accommodation, great beaches, fishing and watersports facilities.

COCONUT GROVE When Doctor Horace P Porter opened his Cocoanut (*sic*) Grove Post Office in 1873, there were only two coconut palms growing in the grove. However, the name caught on when the town of Coconut Grove was incorporated in 1919, and a plentiful supply of palm fronds now cast their shadows on the shopfronts and outdoor cafés of this pleasant Mediterranean-style neighbourhood. Bordering Biscayne Bay, Coconut Grove is a ten-minute drive south of downtown Miami. Its intimate village-like atmosphere has long attracted visiting artists and writers; veteran Everglades conservationist Marjorie Stoneman Douglas lived here for more than 70 years.

Coconut Grove was the product of a friendship between early settlers Charles and Isabella Peacock and Yankee visitor Ralph Middleton Munroe. Munroe encouraged the Peacocks to establish a small hotel in 1884, which prospered with the arrival of Henry Flagler's railroad 12 years later. Rustic camps began to spring up along the bayfront, and eventually Munroe built his own home, **The Barnacle**, now a state historic site (see page 57).

The Peacock Inn expanded and soon employed a number of Bahamian immigrants, who constructed their distinctive wood-frame 'conch houses' along Charles Avenue. The city's Bahamian heritage is celebrated in style every June when the lively **Goombay Festival** takes

FESTIVAL TIMES
Festivals are big in the Grove. In January, there is the annual Taste of the Grove food festival; while the annual three-day Arts Festival in February includes demonstrations, lectures and live jazz. Autumn brings the Columbus Day Regatta, during which more than 65 vessels compete in 21 classes over a weekend. In December, there is the crazy King Mango Strut Parade, a good-natured spoof on the Orange Bowl Parade.

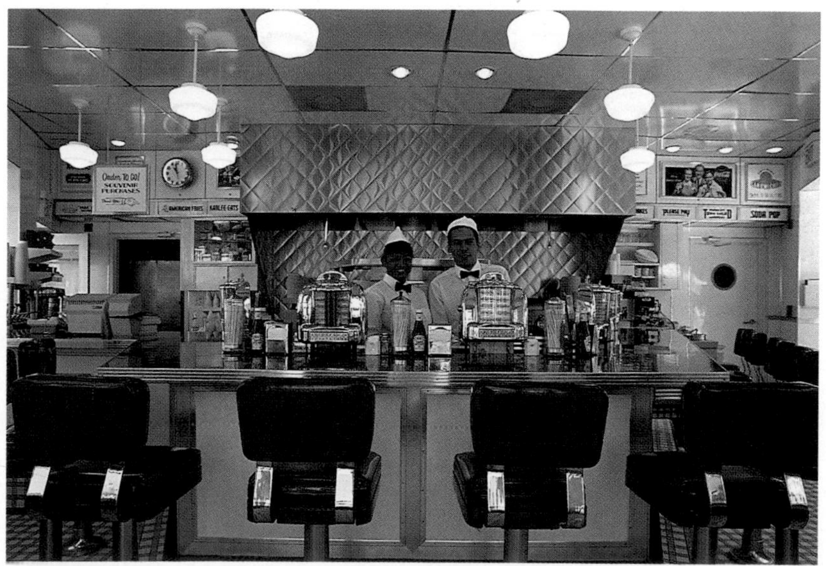

Milkshakes and bar-top jukeboxes at a 1950s-style retro haunt in Coconut Grove

MIAMI DESIGN DISTRICT Brainchild of leading South Beach developer Craig Robins, the Design District is Miami's latest happening neighbourhood. Since 1995, almost $25 million have been ploughed into the 18-block 'village' north of downtown, and refurbished old buildings are taken up by exciting interior design and furniture showrooms, galleries and restaurants. Notable occupants of this 'SoHo of the South' already include Holly Hunt, Highlights and Waterworks, and Robins has plundered his own extensive contemporary art collection to adorn public spaces.

place, complete with processions, 'junkanoo' bands and street stalls. On the corner of Charles Avenue, the decorative 1920s **Coconut Grove Playhouse**, opened as a cinema in 1926, is now home to one of south Florida's leading theatre companies (see page 79).

At the heart of the Grove, boutiques, galleries and restaurants line Main Highway and Commodore Plaza; the up-market Streets of Mayfair and neon-lit CocoWalk on Grand Avenue offer more of the same. Down on the waterfront, you'll find Dinner Key, named after a favourite picnic spot of the area's early residents. There is also David Kennedy Park with a bayshore fitness course, walking trails and children's playground. To the north, the **Vizcaya Museum and Gardens** and the **Museum of Science and Space Transit Planetarium** are major attractions.

CORAL GABLES At the height of the 1920s land boom, developer George Merrick laid the foundations for America's first planned community, Coral Gables. Almost 70 years later, Merrick's exclusive estate remains one of the most prestigious neighbourhoods in town. Between the broad main boulevards, quiet tree-lined streets wind past villas and walled compounds, fountains, plazas and green open spaces. Coral Gables House, on Coral Way, was Merrick's boyhood home.

The development of **The Villages** was Merrick's pet project. Although he never travelled, he gave these enclaves architectural styles ranging from French town houses to colonial Dutch South African. The community was entered through gateways such as the imposing **Puerto del Sol** at the intersection of Douglas Road and the Tamiami Trail. Among this neighbourhood's highlights are the Spanish Mediterranean-style **City Hall** on Miracle Mile and Merrick's stunning **Biltmore Hotel**, on Anastasia Avenue, easily identified by its 16-storey tower, a replica of Seville's Giralda Tower.

Coral Gables' main thoroughfare, **Miracle Mile**, is known for its good restaurants and shopping. To the

Colonnade Building, Coral Gables

south is the University of Miami, founded on land donated by Merrick. Here, the **Lowe Art Museum** exhibits the Kress Collection of Renaissance and baroque art. Further south, on the bayshore, is the **Fairchild Tropical Garden**, one of the largest tropical botanical gardens in the Continental United States.

DOWNTOWN A mixture of gleaming skyscrapers, older office blocks, cultural centres and building sites, Miami's downtown district is now on the way up after several decades of neglect. Downtown Miami spans both sides of the Miami River, with its main thoroughfare, Flagler Street, running east–west from the bayfront.

Two important arts centres on Flagler Street are the 1920s **Gusman Center for the Performing Arts** (174 E Flagler), which plays host to the highly regarded Florida Philharmonic Orchestra, as well as an annual film festival, and the **Miami-Dade Cultural Center** (see page 62). Flagler Street has a variety of major stores and small shops, but **Bayside Marketplace** attracts more shoppers. Just next door is the new **American Airlines Arena** multipurpose sports and entertainment venue. Parking is a problem downtown, so use the cheap and efficient Metromover transport system.

LITTLE HAVANA Since the 1960s, Cuban refugees and immigrants have been resettling in Miami. They have brought their language, customs and heroes to this 3½-acre (1.5-ha) district just west of downtown, and infused it with a distinctive Latin American flavour.

SW 8th Street, better known as **Calle Ocho**, is the commercial heart of the district and the place to find a good Cuban sandwich or a window full of votive statues; buy a handrolled cigar or an embroidered *guayabera* shirt, or check out the action in **Domino Park**, on the corner of 15th Street. A night out in a Cuban restaurant is an experience, and the annual March fiesta is one of Miami's biggest and best street parties.

LUNCH IN LITTLE HAVANA

A meal in itself, a Cuban sandwich is constructed on a heroic scale. Locals gather on the pavements outside the sandwich shop windows sipping tiny cups of Cuban coffee while they wait for their sandwiches to be built. Long, crusty loaves of Cuban bread are split and piled high with ham, pork, Swiss cheese and pickles, then baked in a pizza oven and finished off with mild-to-hot peppery sauce.

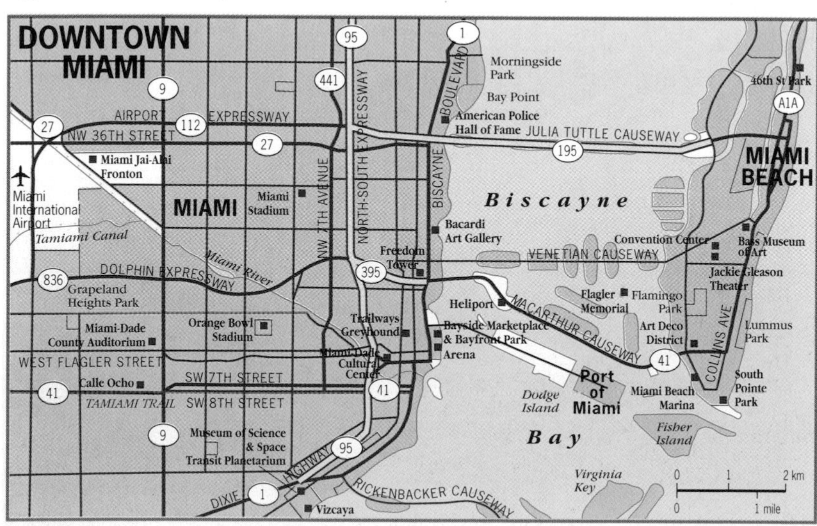

Walk

Through the Art Deco District

Start on Ocean Drive at 5th Street, and walk north.

Take the Lummus Park sidewalk for the best view of the outstanding art deco hotels en route to the **Art Deco Welcome Center**, 1001 Ocean Drive (*Open* Mon–Fri 11–6, Sat 10–10, Sun 11–10).

Turn left on 10th Street for two blocks.

Pass **Essex House** (1001 Collins Avenue) with its beautifully restored foyer adorned by a mural and an etched-glass flamingo window. Then check out the friezes on the former **Washington Storage Building** (1001 Washington Avenue), where snow-birds once stored their furnishings after the winter season. Today it houses the fascinating **Wolfsonian-FIU Museum of Art and Design 1885–1945** (*Open* Mon–Tue, Fri–Sat 11–6, Thu 11–9, Sun noon–5. *Admission: inexpensive*).

Turn right on Washington.

Along Washington, look for two art deco-era public buildings: the old **Miami Beach City Hall** (1130 Washington); and the **US Post Office** (1300 Washington).

At **Espanola Way**, turn left.

This quaint Mediterranean-inspired side street is a great place to window shop or stop for a cold drink.

Turn right on to Pennsylvannia.

A couple of blocks north, the pedestrianised **Lincoln Road Mall** is a terrific shopping, dining and entertainment district.

To complete the circuit, head east on Lincoln Road, turn right on Collins, and left on 15th Street to rejoin Ocean Drive.

Pastel colours characterise the restored façades of Miami's Art Deco District

Walk

Coconut Grove

Start at the corner of Grand Avenue and Main Highway, at the heart of the Coconut Grove shopping district. Walk down Main Highway.

The first stop is the **Coconut Grove Playhouse** (3500 Main Highway), rebuilt in 1927 after a hurricane. Its Spanish rococo façade has elaborate stuccowork, parapets and twisted barley-sugar columns.

On the right, **Charles Avenue** was the home of the Grove's first black community, founded in the 1880s. Note the traditional Miami-Bahamian 'conch' architecture.

Continue on Main Highway for five minutes to the corner of Devon Road on the right.

The ivy-clad **Plymouth Congregational Church** was erected in 1916, and resembles a Spanish mission building, constructed of hand-cut local coral rock. Palms flank the 400-year-old walnut and oak door (from a monastery in the Pyrenees), and there is a pretty garden cloister.

Return from Devon Road along Main Highway.

Hiding behind a tangled wall of trees, the secluded **Barnacle State Historic Site** (3845 Main Highway) is the oldest Miami home still on its original foundations. The cleverly restored 1891 pioneer residence includes many original furnishings, and Coconut Grove resident and naval architect Ralph Midleton Munroe's wooden ketch, *Micco*, is on display in the boathouse (see page 58).

Continue to retrace your steps back along Main Highway to CocoWalk where you will find boutiques, outdoor cafés and restaurants galore.

The Barnacle State Historic Site is a gracious reminder of Coconut Grove's early days

One for crime buffs: the United States' largest police museum

▶ American Police Hall of Fame

3801 Biscayne Boulevard; tel: 305/573-0070
Open: daily 10–5:30. Admission: moderate

More than 11,000 law enforcement-related exhibits, the most extensive collection in the United States, are located in these former Miami FBI headquarters. Police vehicles, weaponry, jail cells, stocks and a pillory (for a hands-on experience of old-fashioned justice), and other sobering sights, such as an authentic electric chair, are on display.

Exotic foliage adorns the high-rise façade of the Bacardi Imports building

▶ Bacardi Art Gallery

2100 Biscayne Boulevard; tel: 305/573-8511 ext 366
Open: Mon–Fri 9–5

North of downtown, the eye-catching 1930s blue-and-white mosaic-tiled Bacardi Imports building makes an unusual local landmark. A small museum (*Admission free*) documents the Bacardi family history. Visitors by appointment only.

▶▶ Bal Harbour

9700 Collins Avenue, Miami Beach; tel: 305/866-0311
Open: Mon–Fri 10–9, Sat 10–7, Sun noon–6

This is an exclusive, beautifully laid-out shopping mall, with a handful of notable European designer boutiques joining the ranks of top American stores, including Saks Fifth Avenue and Neiman Marcus.

▶▶ Barnacle State Historic Site

3485 Main Highway, Coconut Grove; tel: 305/448-9445
Open: Fri–Sun for tours at 10, 11:30, 1 and 2:30
Admission: inexpensive

One of the oldest homes in Miami, the Barnacle was built by Coconut Grove pioneer and naval engineer Ralph Midleton Munroe in 1891. The historic two-storey building has period furnishings, a steep hipped roof shaped like a barnacle and views across the bay (see Walk, page 57).

►► Bass Museum of Art

2121 Park Avenue, Miami Beach; tel: 305/673-7530
Open: Tue–Sat, 10–5, Sun 1–5. Admission: moderate
Housed in an elegant 1930s Streamline former library, the Bass displays a notable permanent collection of Renaissance, baroque and rococo art; American, Asian and contemporary works, textiles and tapestries, as well as a section containing architectural plans and photographs detailing the development of Miami Beach. To house all these various elements, the museum has almost doubled in size with the opening of improved galleries, a café-terrace and shops in an $8-million expansion programme designed by celebrated architect Arata Isozaki, and inaugurated in mid-2000. The Bass also hosts frequent historic and contemporary exhibitions of American and international art.

► Bayfront Park

100 Biscayne Boulevard
The 32-acre (13-ha) Bayfront Park skirts the shoreline from Bayside Marketplace to the cruise ships in the port of Miami. Joggers pound past the palm trees incessantly, and there is an amphitheatre which hosts popular open-air concerts. Plaques around the **John F Kennedy Memorial Torch of Friendship** represent Miami's friendly ties with Latin America: the gap in the row of plaques is being reserved for Cuba, which will be added when relations with the communist Castro regime change.

►►► Bayside Marketplace

401 N Biscayne Boulevard; tel: 305/577-3344
Open: Mon–Thu 10–10, Fri and Sat 10am–11pm, Sun 11–9
Right on the bay, fronting the downtown district, this is one of Miami's busiest attractions. There are more than 150 shops – ranging from wacky gift stores to popular clothing outlets and a Warner Bro Studio and Disney store. South American crafts stalls, sellers of cheap sunglasses and sports outfitters vie for attention, while entertainment is provided by street performers, and there are plenty of restaurants, bars and coffee shops.

The dockside bustles with charter boats heading off on sightseeing trips around the bay. Bayside is also the terminal for the **Water Taxi** service, which operates a daily downtown Miami Shuttle between a variety of hotel, restaurant and shopping locations, as well as several popular destinations along Miami Beach (see **Excursions**, page 69). Live music enlivens the atmosphere at night, and the restaurants, which include the tastes of Mexico, China, Thailand and Italy, are sure to satisfy any craving.

► Biscayne Nature Center

4000 Crandon Boulevard, Key Biscayne
This is the place to brush up on southeast Florida's fascinating natural history. Among the activities offered are marine life expeditions, walks through coastal hammocks, fossil rock reefs and on the beach, plus bike and canoe trips. All trips are led by a naturalist guide and are by reservation only. For details of local history lectures, tours and reservations, tel: 305/642-9600.

Entertainment on the Bayside

ROCK SOLID
In the course of constructing his coral testimonial to lost love, the diminutive Leedskalnin shifted some 1,100 tons of rock single-handedly. He furnished the castle with stone tables and chairs, and a telescope pointed at the North Star. There's also a 9-ton swinging gate that can be opened with a gentle push.

▶ Coral Castle

28655 S Dixie Highway, Homestead; tel: 305/248-6344
Open: daily 9–6. Admission: moderate
When Edward Leedskalnin, a 26-year-old Latvian immigrant, was left at the altar by his fiancée, he found solace in building this unique castle out of solid coral rock. Constructed between 1920 and 1940, the 3-acre (1.2-ha) castle is one of south Florida's original tourist attractions (see panel).

▶ Coral Gables Merrick House and Gardens

907 Coral Way; tel: 305/460-5361
Open: Wed and Sun only, 1–4 (guided tours); gardens daily until dusk. Admission: inexpensive
The boyhood home of Coral Gables developer George Merrick, this modest house surrounded by attractive gardens was founded in 1903. After his father's death in 1911, George continued to buy land, and his estate was the basis for his dream of a brand-new city. The house has been carefully restored in the style of the 1920s, and many of the furnishings are genuine family pieces, including portraits and Mrs Merrick's grand piano.

▶ Deering Estate at Cutler

16701 SW 72nd Avenue; tel: 305/235-1668
Open: daily 10–5. Admission: moderate
Charles Deering's waterfront preserve on Biscayne Bay could not be more different from his brother James's elegantly manicured Vizcaya estate. Purchased by Miami-Dade County in 1985, it's now a park, with acres of mangroves, pinelands, palms and tropical hardwood hammocks. You can tour the grounds on foot or by bus, and a 3-hour guided canoe trip is offered twice daily. Deering's stone mansion and a timber-framed hotel, which was the original property on the estate, are both being restored and are open to visitors.

Masts bristle in Dinner Key Marina

▶ Dinner Key Marina

3400 Pan American Drive, Coconut Grove
Start/finish point of the annual Columbus Day Regatta (October), this was where early Grove residents used to set out on boat and picnic expeditions, hence the name. Today you can admire the art deco Miami City Hall, originally built as the Pan Am seaplane terminal, wet your whistle at one of the marina's many waterfront bars, rent charter boats and go windsurfing.

▶▶▶ Fairchild Tropical Gardens

10901 Old Cutler Road; tel: 305/667-1651
Open: daily 9:30–4:30. Admission: moderate
More than 80 acres (32 ha) of spreading lawns, lakes and exotic species from around the globe comprise these wonderful botanical gardens. Take the 2-mile (3km) bus ride to get a feel for what's offered, from the coastal keys habitat to a lush miniature rain-forest section. The 'must-see' area is the McLamore Arboretum, with its flowering trees and shrubs, a 560-foot-long (170m) pergola draped in exotic vines and a collection of desert plants. The Palmetum Walk offers an extraordinary variety of palm trees. Don't miss the Windows to the Tropics hothouse for displays of tender orchids, aroids and bromeliads.

A cool vista in Fairchild Tropical Garden

▶ Freedom Tower

600 Biscayne Boulevard

A famous downtown landmark, impossible to miss, the 1925 Spanish-Mediterranean-style Freedom Tower was built to house the *Miami News*, and was modelled on the Giralda Tower in Seville, Spain. Across from Bayfront Park, it earned its present name when it served as a refugee-processing centre for more than 600,000 Cubans during the 1962 crisis. It is being restored to house a museum of the Cuban experience in Miami.

▶ Fruit and Spice Park

24801 SW 187th Avenue, Redland; tel: 305/247-5727
Open: daily 10–5. Admission: inexpensive

More than 500 varieties of fruits, vegetables, herbs, nuts and spices, gathered from every corner of the earth, flourish in the grounds of this unusual botanic park near Homestead. There are guided tours around the park at weekends, as well as tours of the local historical districts and a well-socked gift shop.

▶ GameWorks

The Shops at Sunset Place, 5701 Sunset Drive, South Miami; tel: 305/667-4263
Open: Mon–Fri 11am–2am, Sat 10am–2am, Sun 10am–midnight

Steven Spielberg helped design this chain of activity centres that will delight bored kids (and their parents), with a wide selection of state-of-the-art games played in themed zones. If battling dinosaurs or aliens, or testing your co-ordination skills with simulated jet-ski, motor-cycle or baseball action appeals, this should be fun.

▶ Gold Coast Railroad Museum

12450 SW 152nd Street; tel: 305/253-0063
Open: Mon–Fri 11–3, Sat–Sun 11–4. Admission: inexpensive

This collection of historic locomotives includes the *Ferdinand Magellan*, the only Pullman car designed specifically for US presidents. Definitely a must for train buffs, with weekend train rides around the 68-acre (27.5-ha) site.

HOLOCAUST MEMORIAL

Poignantly located at 1933–1945 Meridian Avenue in Miami Beach, the centre-piece of this moving memorial is a 42-foot-high (12.9m) bronze arm rising out of the ground, with sculptured figures climbing the arm symbolising the search for escape. A memorial wall listing victims' names and a meditation garden complement the sculpture.

A sample of the more than 8,000 works of art at the Lowe Art Museum on the University of Miami campus

HIALEAH PARK
Miami's most appealing thoroughbred race course is the handsome 1925 French-Mediterranean complex at Hialeah. The racing season runs from March to May. On race days, Hialeah Park opens early for the horses to work out, and breakfast is served at the track. For more information, tel: 305/885-8000.

►► Haulover Beach Park

10800 Collins Avenue, Sunny Isles Beach; tel: 305/947-3525

This large recreational park offers the best of Florida's natural attractions, including a 2-mile (3km) stretch of hotel-free seashore, complete with golden sands, Atlantic surf, a nine-hole golf course, deep-sea fishing, picnic areas with barbecue facilities, boat hire and walking trails.

►►► Key Biscayne see page 63.

►►► Lowe Art Museum

1301 Stanford Drive, Coral Gables; tel: 305/284-3535
Open: Tue, Wed, Fri and Sat 10–5, Thu noon–7, Sun noon–5
Admission: inexpensive

This excellent small museum on the University of Miami campus houses the fine, and beautifully displayed, Kress Collection of Renaissance and Baroque Art, and a broad spectrum of American works of art, Native American, Western, Oriental and Pre-Columbian arts and crafts.

► Miami Children's Museum

8603 S Dixie Highway (Vizcaya Metrorail Station); tel: 305/663-8800

The former Miami Youth Museum is breaking ground with a new $11-million complex due to open in the autumn of 2001. It will be one of the ten largest children's museums in the US, with plenty of interactive exhibits, outdoor areas and early childhood development activities.

►► Miami-Dade Cultural Center

101 W Flagler Street
Art Museum: Tue–Fri 10–5, Sat–Sun 12–5; tel: 305/375-3000. Admission: inexpensive
Historical Museum: Mon–Sat 10–5 (Thu until 9), Sun 12–5; tel: 305/375-1492. Admission: inexpensive

One of downtown's most celebrated architectural showpieces, Philip Johnson's Mediterranean-style complex houses the **Miami Art Museum**, which concentrates on art from the 1940s to the present, and hosts major touring exhibitions; the **Historical Museum of Southern Florida**; and the **Miami-Dade Public Library**. The Historical Museum offers an interesting glimpse into Florida's history, from prehistory to the present.

This former coconut plantation in Biscayne Bay, once a haunt of wreckers and hunters, is a favourite weekend retreat for Miami's city dwellers. It is linked to the mainland by the Rickenbacker Causeway, which forms an impressive curve across the bay.

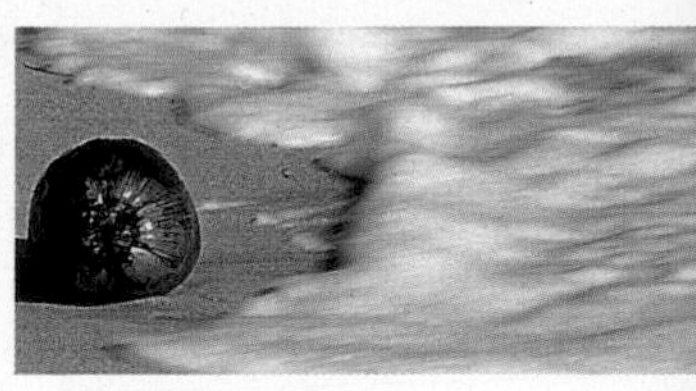

Virginia Key Key Biscayne's sister island is fringed by **Hobie Beach**, with plenty of parking for those who want to fish, swim and windsurf. Further on, the golden domed **Miami Seaquarium** gives visitors a chance to get face to face with dolphins, sharks and whales (see page 64). Another major attraction is Virginia Key's **Miami Marine Stadium**, which stages 'Pops by the Bay' summer concerts, international rowing regattas and powerboat racing.

Key Biscayne Bear Cut Bridge makes the short hop from Virginia Key to Key Biscayne. At the north end of the island, Bear Cut becomes Crandon Boulevard. The boulevard bisects the lush 500-acre (200-ha) **Crandon Park**, where jogging paths and 2½ miles (4km) of public beaches welcome outdoor enthusiasts and offer facilities for picnics. The park's ocean side is lined with luxury hotels and condominiums, and the first-class resort facilities include one of the finest 18-hole golf courses in the country, plus a tennis complex that plays host to international tournaments. At the north end of the beach, the **Marjorie Stoneman Douglas Biscayne Nature Center** offers hands-on marine encounters and a varied programme of walks and talks on Florida's natural world.

BRIDGE WITH A VIEW
The William M Powell Bridge rises 75 feet (23m) above the water to eliminate the need for a drawbridge. The Old Rickenbacker Causeway Bridge, which was replaced by the Powell Bridge, is now a fishing pier with good views of downtown Miami.

Away from it all The southern tip of the island is given over to the **Bill Baggs Cape Florida State Recreation Area**, originally named Cape Florida by early explorer Ponce de León in 1513. This 406-acre (165-ha) preserve is the site of Florida's oldest lighthouse and the oldest surviving structure in South Florida. The **Cape Florida Lighthouse** was erected in 1825 to warn ships off the treacherous reefs along the coastline. A 122-step spiral staircase climbs up the brick structure to an observation post with panoramic views of the bay. Below, there is a reconstructed New England-style keeper's cottage with period furnishings.

Near the beach area, edged by pines and sea grapes, a concession stand sells snacks and bait and hires out tackle, snorkels, bicycles and gear for windsurfers. At the bayside sea wall, you can hook snook, bonefish or grouper. There are walking trails, good birdwatching and turtles nesting in season.

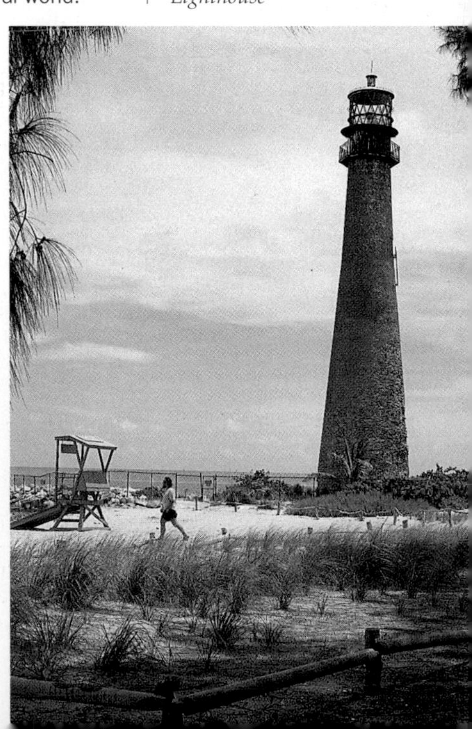

Cape Florida Lighthouse

Siesta-time for one of Miami Metrozoo's inhabitants

HURRICANE ALERT
Hurricanes occur in Florida between June and November, with August to October being the peak season for storms. In 1992, Hurricane Andrew slammed into Florida's east coast just south of Miami, doing an estimated $20 billion in damage, killing at least 22 people and leaving thousands homeless.

►►► Miami Metrozoo

12400 SW 152nd Street, Kendall; tel: 305/251-0400
Open: daily 9:30–5:30 (last tickets sold at 4)
Admission: moderate

Miami has a zoo to be proud of with this well-planned and thoughtfully executed, largely cageless zoo. Metrozoo's 290-acre (117-ha) site features areas of simulated African jungle and veldt, and Asian and European forest, which are home to more than 800 animals representing 191 species. Unimpeded by old-fashioned bars, animals roam on islands surrounded by moats in convincingly re-created habitats. Among the major attractions are the Tiger Temple and the African Plains exhibit, where giraffes, ostriches and zebras graze on a simulated plain. A 2-mile (3km) monorail circuit takes visitors around the zoo and its aviary, with stops along the way for the displays at the Wildlife Shows, the Children's Petting Zoo and the Ecology Theater, where alligator petting offers a real Florida experience. The permanent koala exhibit is another popular highlight.

►► Miami Seaquarium

4400 Rickenbacker Causeway; tel: 305/361-5705
Open: daily 9:30–6. Admission: expensive

Founded in 1955, the Seaquarium cannot help but show its age. As a family attraction it is a reliable favourite and houses a huge variety of marine life, from dolphins and sea lions to rescued manatees and turtles. A wide choice of attractions includes live shows, touch tanks and a nesting area for giant turtles and several species of sea birds. But the Seaquarium's star crowd-pullers are undoubtedly Salty the sea lion, Lolita the killer whale (who has recently attracted the attention of campaigners who wish to see her released from her cramped quarters), and the most famous dolphin of them all, Flipper (the *Flipper* movies and TV show were filmed here). The Seaquarium also operates the Water And Dolphin Exploration programme (WADE), a two-hour, hands-on dolphin experience (information and reservations, tel: 305/365-2501).

High jinks at the Miami Seaquarium

► Miccosukee Indian Village/Airboat Tours

30 miles (48km) west of Miami on Tamiami Trail (US 41); tel: 305/223-8380
Open: daily 9–5. Admission: inexpensive

This is a classic tourist attraction, but an enjoyable one none the less. There is alligator-wrestling, and airboat tours into the Everglades (the latter are an unforgettable experience). Traditional Miccosukee food and crafts are sold at the cultural centre.

Although most families make a beeline for the theme parks, Miami also has plenty to offer the young and the young-at-heart. Beaches beckon, resort hotels run special programmes for junior guests, restaurants welcome children, and there are many attractions designed specifically for families.

Fun is the name of the game at the **Museum of Science & Space Transit Planetarium**, which also arranges family kayaking excursions in Florida Bay. There are games galore at the Spielberg-inspired **GameWorks** complex in South Miami, and the new **Miami Children's Museum** is ideal for small children.

Animal magic Southern Florida's sunny climate has given local zoological parks the edge over many of their cold-weather cousins. Top favourites are **Miami Metrozoo** and **Parrot Jungle**, where carefully re-created habitats provide a home away from home for hundreds of exotic species. In addition to the on-site playgrounds and children's petting areas, frequent animal shows aim to educate as well as entertain.

Miami Seaquarium, across the Rickenbacker Causeway, is another must. Exhibits include rescued manatees and there are great shows that combine snippets of fascinating information with amazing feats. Visiting toddlers can be pushed around in the comfort of special dolphin-shaped push-chairs which are available at the park entrance.

Water, water everywhere Water babies are in luck on Miami's beaches. Gently sloping sandbars extend for several hundred yards before reaching deep water, so there is plenty of shallow swimming and paddling. Public beaches have concession stands, shaded picnic areas and umbrella and deck-chair hire. The **Bill Baggs Cape Florida State Recreation Area**, on Key Biscayne, is an excellent spot for families, with a beach, picnic shelters, a café, playground, fishing piers, bait for sale and tackle for hire, plus bikes and trikes to ride on the woodland trails. A marina complex is planned; meanwhile visitors can hire kayaks and windsurfing gear for a spree on the ocean waves.

The **Biscayne National Park** (see page 89) offers great family snorkelling and scuba-diving excursions. Or take a dip in the historic **Venetian Pool** in Coral Gables, which is more sedate, but its calm waters, snack bar and changing facilities are ideal for young children.

Sport The Florida Marlins play baseball in town, and there is hot National Basketball Association action from the home team, the Miami Heat. American football notables, the Miami Dolphins, pack the Pro-Player Stadium during football season, from September to December.

The Miami Jai Alai Fronton features this fast and furious Basque sport and lots of local colour.

WEEKEND ITINERARY

Day one: Head for Coconut Grove's Vizcaya Museum and Gardens, and the Museum of Science & Space Transit Planetarium. Lunch in Coconut Grove. Explore Coral Gables and seek out the Villages; or make for the Miami Seaquarium. Then it's Bayside Marketplace for shopping and sunset drinks. Dinner in Little Havana.

Day two: Water taxi to Miami Beach from Bayside Marketplace. Stop for brunch in the Art Deco District. Return to Bayside for a Biscayne Bay cruise.

Older children may enjoy a few hours under sail on the bay

ORCHIDS IN BLOOM
Most subtropical orchids grow on trees, so you need to look up to see their beautiful flowers. Their trailing aerial roots gather water and food released by tree bark after rain. Many orchids are scented, and they come in an amazing variety of colours.

▶ Monkey Jungle

14805 SW 216th Street; tel: 305/235-1611
Open: daily 9:30–5. Admission: expensive
Set among the flower nurseries south of the city, Monkey Jungle is renowned for its free-ranging macaque colony, where the monkeys cavort high above the visitors in the enclosed covered walkways below. However, other inhabitants such as gibbons, black spider monkeys, colobus and tamarins are secured behind the bars of conventional cages set in the shade of a hardwood hammock. A collection of parrots provides a splash of colour. There are three semi-educational shows rotating throughout the day, and a gift shop piled high with kitsch monkey memorabilia.

▶ Museum of Contemporary Art (MoCA)

770 NE 125th Street, North Miami; tel: 305/893-6211
Open: Tue–Sat 11–5, Sun noon–5. Admission: inexpensive
Though this slick 23,000-square-foot (2,135sq m) gallery space is somewhat off the beaten track, Miami's latest arts museum takes an innovative and at times provocative approach to the contemporary arts scene, with eight to ten exhibitions annually for a variety of media. The permanent collection includes works by Roy Lichtenstein, Laury Rivers and Claes Oldenberg.

▶▶▶ Museum of Science & Space Transit Planetarium

3280 S Miami Avenue, Coconut Grove; tel: 305/854-4247
Open: daily 10–6. Admission: moderate
This museum, with more than 140 touchable exhibits and live demonstrations, sets out to win over children from the word go. Kids can have fun learning about science, from the principles of physics to human health issues. Travelling exhibitions in conjunction with the Smithsonian Institute are a regular feature and are beautifully presented. There are plans to develop a new

Sign language: an inmate of Monkey Jungle

$200 million Science Center of the Americas together with the Smithsonian. There is also a Wildlife Center displaying reptiles such as a large albino Burmese python, iguanas and tortoises, and injured birds of prey being rehabilitated before their release back into the wild. The separate Planetarium (combination ticket), a tribute to the wonders of space travel, puts on fantastic multimedia laser and astronomy shows (for information, tel: 305/854-2222).

▶▶▶ Parrot Jungle

11000 SW 57th Avenue, South Miami; tel: 305/666-7834
Open: daily 9–6 (weather permitting). Admission: expensive
Set in magnificent jungle gardens filled with gorgeous flowering plants and palms, Parrot Jungle has been in operation since 1936. The 30-acre (12-ha) wildlife habitat supports around 1,100 rare and exotic birds, as well as alligators, monkeys, giant tortoises and koi fish. Many of the birds are free-flying and will come to you for seeds. There's an entertaining trained bird show which displays the talents of assorted parrot prodigies, a gift shop laden with 'parrot-phernalia' and a snack bar. The planned relocation of Parrot Jungle to a new, more central site on Watson Island, across from Miami Beach, is scheduled for mid-2002, and the old site will become an animal preserve.

▶ South Pointe Park

Washington Avenue at Biscayne Boulevard
On the southern tip of Miami Beach, this 17-acre (7-ha) park is a popular recreational spot with a beach and fitness course. Fishermen are welcome, and there is a children's playground, picnic areas and barbecue grills. Concerts are staged at an amphitheatre.

▶ Spanish Monastery

16711 W Dixie Highway, North Miami Beach; tel: 305/945-1462
Open: Mon–Sat 10–4, Sun noon–4. Admission: inexpensive
Founded in Segovia, Spain, in 1141, the former Monastery of St Bernard was spotted by newspaper magnate William Randolph Hearst while he was on an art-buying trip to Europe in the 1920s. Hearst had the cloisters dismantled and shipped across the Atlantic to be added to his vast San Simeon estate in California, but when Florida customs officials replaced the blocks in the wrong cases, the project was abandoned. The painstaking five-year task of piecing it all together was finally undertaken 25 years later, and the eminently satisfactory result is now an Episcopal church and favourite wedding venue.

▶▶ Venetian Pool

2701 DeSoto Boulevard, Coral Gables; tel: 305/460-5356
Closed: Mon in winter; call for schedules. Admission: inexpensive
In a moment of inspiration, George Merrick transformed an obsolete quarry into this delightful, Venetian-inspired swimming hole landscaped with beaches and bridges, striped poles and quaint grottoes. The astonishingly blue lagoon must rate as one of the first themed waterparks. The Miami Opera performed here (in the drained pool) in 1926, and swimming stars Johnny Weissmuller and Esther Williams also made appearances.

WEEK'S ITINERARY

Day one and day two: As for the weekend itinerary (see page 65).

Day three: Biscayne Nature Center walk; or just relax on Key Biscayne.

Day four: Parrot Jungle; picnic in Matheson Hammock Park; Fairchild Tropical Garden.

Day five: Hialeah; Spanish Monastery; cool off on the Sunny Isles Beaches.

Day six: Everglades National Park, Main Visitor Center, near Homestead; return via Coral Castle.

Day seven: Metrozoo and Weeks Air Museum.

Companionship in Parrot Jungle

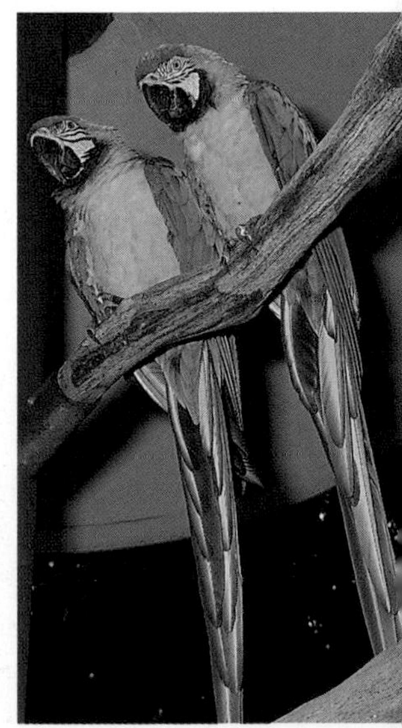

Villa Vizcaya, a bit of Italy in America

SPANISH CONNECTIONS
James Deering named his Biscayne bayside estate for its Spanish connections. Vizcaya means 'elevated place' in the Basque language of the northern Spanish region which lies on the Bay of Biscay (Biscayne is a corruption of Biscay). His chosen motif was a caravel sailing ship similar to the Spanish vessels which once put into Biscayne Bay to replenish their supplies of fresh water. A small bronze caravel decorates the entrance gate to Vizcaya on S Miami Avenue.

▶▶▶ Vizcaya Museum and Gardens

3251 S Miami Avenue, Coconut Grove; tel: 305/250-9133
Open: daily 9:30–5; gardens until 5:30. Admission: moderate

On the northern boundary of Coconut Grove, this fabulous neo-Renaissance villa was built between 1914 and 1916 as a winter residence for industrialist James Deering. A great admirer of European architecture and style, Deering was an avid collector. When he began work on Vizcaya, Deering sent young designer Paul Calfin to Europe, and between them they furnished the house with carpets from Portugal, ceilings from Italy, chandeliers from France, Roman statuary and antique treasures from the finest periods of European design. The building itself is the work of F Burrell Hoffman, who was a mere 29 years old at the time, and who created an elegant northern Italian-style villa built around a courtyard.

The house is now a museum. Each of the 34 rooms on display represents a particular style, such as the gracious 18th-century English Adams library featuring a concealed door in the bookcase, the magnificent Rococo Salon and the Renaissance Hall. The extensive grounds were landscaped with a combination of Italian- and French-pattern formal gardens which lead down to Biscayne Bay and a Venetian waterlanding, while the entire estate is surrounded by a native hammock of mature tropical hardwoods.

Refreshments are available in a pleasant café-restaurant, and there is a gift shop.

▶ Weeks Air Museum

14710 SW 128th Street, Kendall; tel: 305/233-5197
Open: daily 10–5. Admission: moderate

This museum in Tamiami Airport is just the place to check out the history of flight. Dedicated to the preservation and restoration of historic planes, it focuses on World War II models. Among the painstakingly restored exhibits are a P–51 Mustang and a Grumann J2F–6 'Duck'. There are intricate scale models, video booths and a gift shop.

Excursions

Boat tours, rental and charter

Club Nautico of Miami Beach, *Pier E, International Yacht Harbor, 300 Alton Road* (tel: 305/673-2502). Full-, half-day, and hourly powerboat rental. Also Club Nautico of Key Biscayne, *5420 Crandon Boulevard, Key Biscayne* (tel: 305/361-9217); and *Coconut Grove, 2560 S Bayshore Drive* (tel: 305/858-6258).

Heritage of Miami II, *Bayside Marketplace Marina, 401 Biscayne Boulevard* (tel: 305/442-9697). One- and two-hour sightseeing cruises aboard a twin-masted, 85-foot (26m) schooner. Admire Vizcaya, Key Biscayne and the downtown skyline from the water.

Island Queen Cruises, *Bayside Marketplace* (tel: 305/379-5119). Narrated 90-minute cruises feature Millionaires' Row and cruise ships in the Port of Miami. Daily departures on the hour from 11–5, and at 7pm: also at 6pm Fri–Sun. Luxury yachts for charter.

Kelley Fishing Fleet, *Haulover Resort Marina, 10800 Collins Avenue, North Miami Beach* (tel: 305/945-3801). Half- and full-day deep-sea fishing trips (9–12:30, 1:45–5:30, 8pm–midnight) for individuals and groups. Also two- to three-day fishing and diving trips to the Bahamas.

Sailboats of Key Biscayne Rentals and Sailing School, *Crandon Marina, 4000 Crandon Boulevard, Key Biscayne* (tel: 305/361-0328). A variety of small sailing boats (Cat-25s, J24s) for rental by the hour or half-day. Tuition is available.

Water taxis

The Miami water taxi service is a fun way to get around (tel: 954/467-6677, toll-free from Miami); services operate daily from around 11am (check times). Destinations on Miami Beach include the Lincoln Mall and the Miami Beach Marina in South Beach. The water taxis also serve key hotel, shopping, and dining locations in the downtown district, the Port of Miami, and Key Biscayne. All-day passes are good value.

KAYAKS AND CANOES
For a chance to paddle your own canoe up the unspoiled Oleta River or explore the islands of Biscayne Bay, contact Urban Trails Kayak, Haulover Park, 10800 Collins Avenue, Miami Beach (tel: 305/947-1302). Canoes can also be hired directly from the Oleta River State Recreation Area, 3400 NE 163 Street, North Miami (tel: 305/919-1846). The park has a sandy beach, fishing and picnic facilities, and is often visited by Atlantic bottlenose dolphins and, in winter, manatees.

The Bayside Marketplace is excellent for boat tours and water taxis

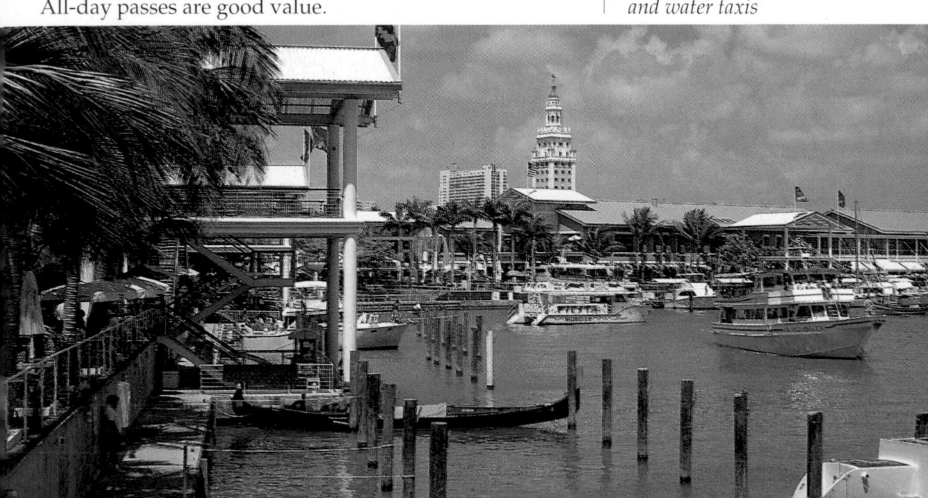

DAY CRUISES
Take a mini-cruise to the Bahamas for the ultimate day out. Discovery Cruise Line (tel: 305/534-7787) offers mini-cruises ranging from one-day excursions to the Bahamas to a couple of hours 'to nowhere', from Miami and Fort Lauderdale. For short day cruises, dinner cruises and party excursions, try Celebration-Floribbean Hospitality (tel: 305/445-8456). They offer buffet meals, entertainment and casino facilities at a bargain price.

Bus tours

Free Way Miami, *Suite 307, 25 SE 2nd Avenue* (tel: 305/579-9820). Daily departures for the three-hour The Great Miami tour with stops at Miami Beach and the Art Deco District, Coral Gables and Coconut Grove. Advance reservations required.

Miami Nice Excursions, *18090 Collins Avenue, Sunny Isles Beach* (tel: 305/949-9180). Daily city attractions, art deco and shopping tours, plus trips to the Everglades and Florida Keys. Advance reservations required.

Cycling and in-line skating

Several neighbourhood districts of Miami can be explored by bike. Make sure you take plenty of water.

The **Miami Beach Bike Center**, *601 5th Street, Miami Beach* (tel: 305/674-0150), offers a wide range of beach cruisers and mountain bikes for hourly, daily or weekly rental. Guided cycle tours of the Art Deco District are also available on the first and third Sunday of each month, departing at 10:30.

Another popular option is to explore the parks and paths of Key Biscayne on cycles hired from **Key Cycling**, *61 Harbor Drive, Key Biscayne* (tel: 305/361-0061), or from the concession within the **Bill Baggs Cape Florida State Recreation Area** (which also hires out in-line skates).

In-line skating is the 'coolest' (and an increasingly popular) way to travel on Ocean Drive; even the Miami Police Department do it! Rental is available from the kiosk on Lummus Park opposite 14th Street, or from **Fritz's Skate & Bike Shop**, *726 Lincoln Road* (tel: 305/532-1954). Make sure you include hand- and knee-guards for safety.

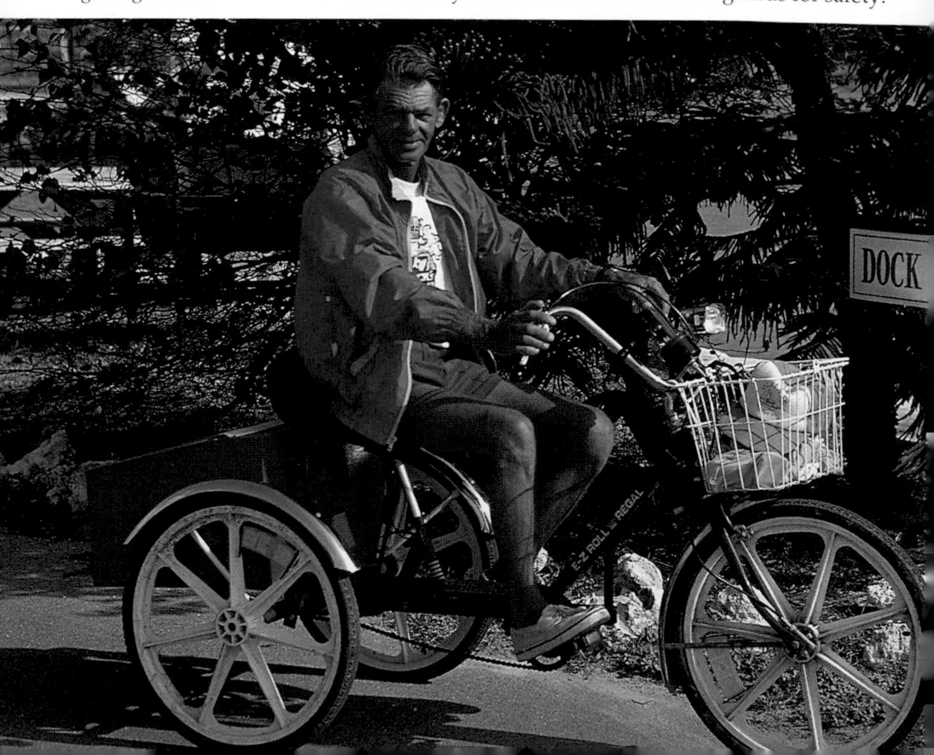

Another fun way of getting around

Driving tours

Miami is so spread out that visiting just a handful of sights can take a whole day. For a scenic drive, take the S Bayshore Drive–Main Highway–Old Cutler Road route around **Biscayne Bay** to the popular South Miami attractions near Homestead. **Miami Beach** is easily explored by car, from the art deco delights along Ocean Drive (see panel) to Bal Harbour, the pricey hotels and beaches of upper Collins Avenue. The only way to get a real feel for **Coral Gables** is by car; maps are available from the Coral Gables City Hall on Miracle Mile. Or have a look at **Little Havana** with a drive down Calle Ocho (SW 8th Street).

Two superb national park sites are an easy day trip away, beyond the Greater Miami city limits. **Biscayne National Park** (9 miles/14.5km east of Homestead) is a 181,550-acre (73,475-ha) aquatic preserve with glass-bottom boats and diving tours. Several gateways provide access to the famous **Everglades National Park** (see pages 90–1). The eastern entrance and park headquarters are 10 miles (16km) southwest of Homestead; the northern entrance at Shark Valley lies 25 miles (40km) west of downtown Miami via the Tamiami Trail (US 41).

The **Gold Coast** begins just north of Miami with Route A1A providing a slow route along the coast or the fast I–95 thundering north–south a few miles inland. The yachts and shops of **Fort Lauderdale** can be reached in under an hour and the exclusive millionaires' enclave of **Palm Beach** is well worth a day's outing.

(For car hire information, see page 84.)

Rickshaw tours

Majestic Rickshaw, *Coconut Grove*. A Coconut Grove night-time speciality (particularly at weekends). Hail a bicycle rickshaw on Grand Avenue or Main Highway between 8pm–2am for a spin around the block, or take a moonlit ride along the bayshore.

Walking tours

Art Deco Welcome Center, *Ocean Front Auditorium, 1001 Ocean Drive, Miami Beach* (tel: 305/531-3484). The Miami Design Preservation League's information centre welcomes visitors to the famous Art Deco District with a tiny shop full of postcards, posters and art deco memorabilia. This is the place to find a self-guided audio tour which takes you on a walking tour of 14 significant art deco sites (allow around one hour).

For an extended version, try to catch one of the excellent 90-minute guided tours which depart at 6:30pm on Thursdays and 10:30am on Saturdays; or by request for groups.

Historical Museum of Southern Florida, *101 W Flagler Street* (tel: 305/375-1492). Tours galore – from walking and bicycling excursions to moonlit gourmet canoe trips – balance fun with insight. Call ahead for prices and schedules.

DECO ROVERS
The latest transport fad in terminally trendy SoBe and the Art Deco District is a cartoon-like little electric buggy known as a Deco Rover. They can be hired from 215 6th Street (between Washington and Collins); tel: 305/538-0202. Scooters are also available for hire.

Snorkelling at Shark Reef, Biscayne National Park

By the mid-1970s, Miami Beach was almost beachless. Development on the island and erosion by the ocean had brought hotels and other buildings literally to the water's edge.

ENTER THE CAVALRY
The city called for the cavalry, and between 1977 and 1981, the US Army Corps of Engineers mounted a vast $51 million beach reconstruction operation dumping millions of tons of sand along the ocean-shore to form a 300-foot-wide (90m) stretch of beach. From Sunny Isles in the north to South Pointe Park, the 10-mile (16km) strip is divided into a series of beaches, each with its own character. Key Biscayne and its island neighbour, Virginia Key, offer an additional 4 miles (6.5km) of beach space; there is Oleta River State Recreation Area north of the city, and the oceanfront Matheson Hammock Park in the south.

Miami Beach and North Miami
South Pointe Park Washington Avenue. Not the best beach, but there is good fishing and snorkelling from the pier (beware of currents), as well as picnic areas with barbecues, footpaths, children's playground, fitness course and a scenic view of the Port of Miami across the bay.

First Street Beach The epicentre of Miami's surfing culture. A beach bar-restaurant pumps up the volume. Volleyball.

Lummus Park Sixth to 14th streets. On the beach side of Ocean Drive, there are windsurfing and deck-chair rentals, refreshments and a playground.

21st Street Beach Start of the two-mile **Miami Beach Boardwalk**, this is a favourite with many members of the gay community. Unofficially, topless bathing is more or less tolerated between First Street Beach and Surfside. Refreshments are available.

35th Street Beach Hemmed in by high-rise buildings, but relatively peaceful. Refreshments and good swimming.

46th Street Beach Near the Fontainebleau Hilton. A happy-go-lucky crowd of watersport fans from Miami University makes its presence felt; refreshments available plus excellent swimming.

North Shore State Recreation Area 79th to 87th streets. A 40-acre (16-ha) oasis of subtropical vegetation and sandy shores. Picnic areas with barbecues, playground, cycle trail, fitness course, fishing and boat hire.

Surfside Beach 93rd Street. A quieter neighbour of the Bal Harbour area beaches which fill up with wealthy northerners in the winter. Fine swimming can be had; popular with French-Canadians.

Haulover Beach 10800 Collins Avenue. Combines beach, dunes and parkland with facilities including picnic areas, playground, boat hire, tennis and golf.

Sunny Isles 163rd to 192nd streets. Two miles (3km) of blustery beach, with windsurfing, jet-ski and sailboat hire. Fishing from the pier; refreshments are available.

Oleta River State Recreation Area 3400 NE 163rd Street. On the mainland, with good swimming from a man-made beach. Cycle trail, canoeing, boating and picnic facilities; dolphins, manatees and land mammals can also be seen.

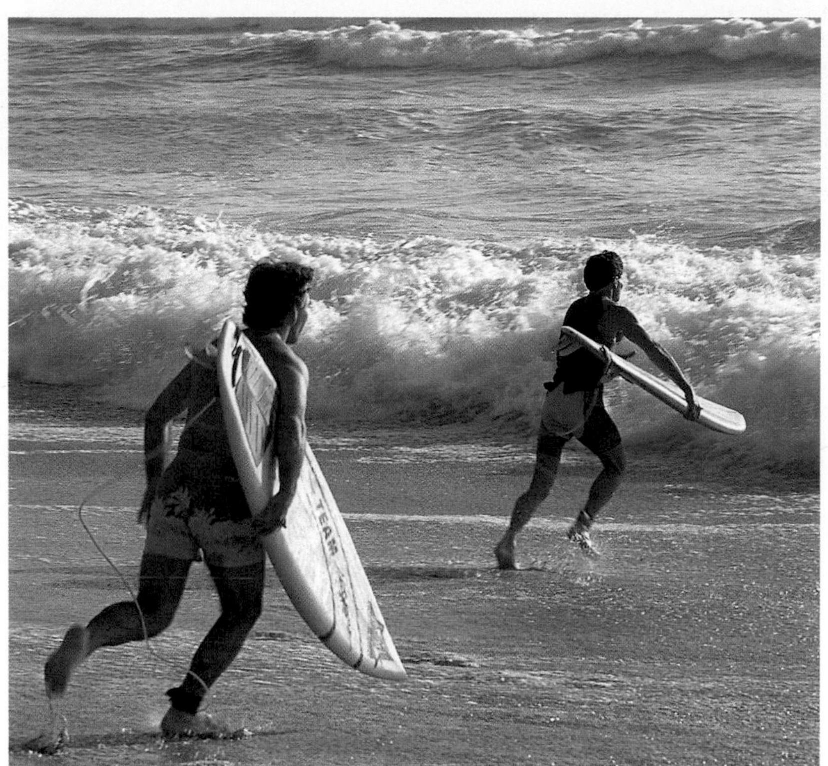

Running for the big one: surfing is the archetypal Florida sport

Key Biscayne, Virginia Key and South Miami

Bill Baggs Cape Florida State Recreation Area Key Biscayne. On the southern tip of thc island, this preserve has ocean beaches, a historic lighthouse, walking trails, windsurfing and cycle hire, fishing on the bayside, picnic areas, and refreshments (see also page 63).

Crandon Park 4000 Crandon Boulevard. Parkland and beach at the northern end of Key Biscayne, which has picnicking and refreshment facilities, playground, cycling trails, fitness course and boat hire.

Hobie Beach Rickenbacker Causeway. Windsurfers and surfboaters skim across the bay around the causeway and picnic on narrow, pine-fringed strips of sand along the roadside. You will find picnic tables, refreshments and watersport equipment for hire (see also page 63).

Virginia Key Beach At the island's south end, running northeast from the causeway, this area has picnic facilities with barbecues and walking trails, plus a number of secluded coves edged by woodlands.

Matheson Hammock Park 9610 Old Cutler Road.
A beautiful bayside beach in a country park south of Coral Gables. Picnic tables, refreshments, playground, walking trails, fitness course, fishing, boat hire, golf and tennis.

FLEA MARKETS AND FACTORY OUTLETS

One of the largest flea markets in South Florida, the Opa-Locka/Hialeah Flea Market, 12705 NW 42nd Avenue, gathers 1,200 wholesale and retail vendors on its sprawling site seven days a week. For factory outlet bargains, head 30 minutes south of Miami to Prime Outlets at Florida City, 250 E Palm Drive (SW 344th Street), where you will find 60 brand-name outlets including a Nike Factory Store, Levi's Outlet by Design and OshKosh B'Gosh (*Open* Mon–Sat 10–9, Sun 11–6).

Shopping

Shopping is big news in Miami, and there are numerous huge shopping malls. Neighbourhood shopping is fun, too, with a wide array of fashion boutiques, small galleries and speciality stores.

On the souvenir front, South Florida's subtropical surroundings have spawned a flourishing business in Florida kitsch, with flamingo and palm-tree motifs appearing on just about everything from T-shirts and china to flashing flamingo Christmas tree lights.

Downtown going north Downtown's pride and joy is **Bayside Marketplace**, *401 N Biscayne Boulevard* (see also page 59). This 16-acre (6.5-ha) waterfront site combines shopping with live entertainment and international restaurants. The latest fashions and sportswear rub price tags with great crafts and gift items. Look for brightly coloured South American appliqué cotton knits, jewellery and leather items.

Part of the Omni hotel complex, **Omni International Mall**, *1601 Biscayne Boulevard*, has been somewhat overshadowed by Bayside. However, it still has 75 shops and 12 restaurants, plus a wonderful gilt carousel which is a hit with junior shoppers.

Out near the airport, Miami's latest mega-mall is taking shape: the **Dolphin Mall** features more than 200 outlet, dining and entertainment venues and comes complete with theme park-style rides.

On the bargain trail, take a detour to the **Fashion District**, *NW Fifth Avenue between 24th and 29th streets*, where designer clothes, accessories and locally made fashions are offered at factory outlet shops and discount stores. More than 250 department stores and boutiques are gathered in the popular **Aventura Mall**, *19501 Biscayne Boulevard* in North Miami. Bloomingdales, Guess?, Gap, a 24-screen cinema and a host of restaurants draw the crowds.

Shopping in CocoWalk is a real experience

Miami Beach On Miami Beach, the Art Deco District is a shopper's delight. A two-block strip of Collins Avenue between 6th and 8th streets has attracted fashion leaders such as Nicole Miller and Kenneth Cole. A historic gem in its own right, **Española Way** features a clutch of tempting antiques shops and small galleries crammed with 1930s and 1940s furniture, furnishings and bric-à-brac.

Big spenders should head straight for the shops at **Bal Harbour**, *9700 Collins Avenue* (see also page 58). A limo's length from Millionaires' Row, the darlings of European design, along with America's top stores – including Florida's largest Neiman Marcus – cater for well-heeled residents and visitors in a very up-market setting.

North Miami Beach is home to the three-level **Mall at 163rd Street**, *1421 NE 163rd Street*, the world's first Teflon-coated indoor mall, with 100 speciality shops and stores including Burdines.

Coconut Grove Coconut Grove's metamorphosis from hippie to hip has made it a front-runner for the title of sunglass capital of the world. These Florida essentials have been raised to an art form and a whole fleet of chic optical boutiques can be found anchored amid the fun atmosphere of the Grove.

Cascades of greenery, Mexican-tiled fountains, elegant boutiques, restaurants and several sophisticated night clubs inhabit the exclusive **Streets of Mayfair**, *2911 Grand Avenue*.

A further galaxy of trendy nightspots, bars and café-restaurants is perched above two levels of boutiques at the Grove's other hotspot, **CocoWalk**, *3015 Grand Avenue*. The clothes-conscious will find everything from Western wear to lingerie on the shelves, and there is a good book and map shop as well. **Main Highway** is crammed with both everyday and outlandish fashions, as well as poster and card shops, great T-shirts and amazing children's toys.

Another favourite shoppers' haunt is **Commodore Plaza**, whose tempting galleries sell colourful South American and Haitian art, Native American jewellery, furnishings and toys.

Coral Gables going south On Coral Way, between LeJeune and Douglas, the four-block **Miracle Mile** shopping district is lined with antiques shops, galleries, boutiques and interior design emporiums. For something a little more affordable, head for the modernistic **Miracle Center**, *3301 Coral Way*. To the south, you'll find **The Shops at Sunset Plaza**, 5701 Sunset Drive, South Miami – fun and family oriented, with an FAO Schwarz toystore, Virgin Megastore and IMAX cinema among its attractions.

West of US 1, the **Dadeland Mall**, *7535 N Kendall Drive*, is a popular shopping centre with five department stores, 165 shops and a well-stocked food court. Also in the Kendall area, **The Falls**, *US Highway 1 at S.W. 36th Street*, is home to a million-gallon waterscape and around 100 prestigious stores and restaurants set among tropical surroundings.

Miami's top shopping malls are generally open from Monday to Saturday 10–9, and from Sunday 11am or noon–5 or 6.

Mobile stalls sell cheap and cheerful souvenirs

LINCOLN ROAD

Once hailed as the Fifth Avenue of the South, Miami Beach's Lincoln Road shopping district fell on hard times until its stunningly successful multimillion dollar face-lift. Along this pedestrian concourse, which runs west from Washington Avenue between 16th and 17th streets, are 12 landscaped blocks decorated with fountains, trees, sculpture and eye-catching pavement designs. There are dozens of boutiques and more than 20 galleries, plus restaurants and outdoor cafés that offer a mile of alfresco dining at night.

Food and drink

In recent years, Miami has emerged as one of the trendiest culinary crucibles in the United States, if not the world – and this has nothing to do with chilli, but everything to do with inspired cooking. Floribbean cuisine is a light and delicious marriage of fresh local ingredients, New American style and Caribbean and Asian flavours. It was perfected in the stylish restaurants and hotels of Miami Beach, but can now be found in good restaurants throughout the city, and, indeed, the state.

When eating out in Miami, keep in mind the fact that variety is the spice of life. Cuisine from Argentina, Brazil, Cuba, France, Greece, Haiti and Thailand is served in a diverse spread of eateries. Fresh fruit and vegetables are locally grown, steak is trucked in from the ranches of central Florida, fish and shellfish arrive fresh every day from the docks and adventurous eaters can sample exotic Florida specialities such as alligator meat and Everglades frogs' legs.

Stop for a meal The food-lover's day begins with breakfast, normally served between 7 and 11am. It may consist of a sticky Danish pastry and muffins; a less sugary alternative is a bagel or buttered English muffin. Late breakfast at a café table on the pavement is a popular feature along Miami Beach's Ocean Drive and in Coconut Grove, where eggs Benedict and a plate of fresh fruit accompany a leisurely session with the morning paper.

Serious lunching has become a lost art in many North American cities, but Miami's Latin and European inhabitants have ensured that it remains an important feature of their day between 11:30 and 2. However, even recent arrivals have tended to gravitate towards a lighter, healthier American eating style, and there are plenty of imaginative salads and sandwiches on restaurant menus. The snacking population grabs a double-decker bus-size Cuban sandwich, piled high with ham, pork and cheese, a burger or, alternatively, a deli sandwich. Snacking is big in Miami – everywhere there are concession stands, juice bars, delis and health-food shops.

In the evening, most Cubans eat late, but dinner is a running buffet in Miami, which starts at 5pm with cut-price 'early-bird' special menus, and lasts until the Latin restaurants and late-night cafés switch off the stove at around midnight or 1am – though many restaurants do not take orders after 10pm. There are also several 24-hour chain restaurants, usually found near busy truck routes such as US 1.

Choosing where to eat This is almost as confusing as choosing what to eat. Miami is well supplied with restaurants, bistros and cafés in every price range and a plethora of styles. There can be no doubt that the greatest concentration of dining options is found in the Art Deco District and SoBe on Miami Beach. You can dine at an art deco treasure on Ocean Drive, a 1950s-style deli or one of the many alfresco café-restaurants lining the Lincoln Road Mall. There is trendy Coconut Grove for cafés and reasonable prices; or Coral Gables, considered a gastronomic

There's no need to waste a lot of time over a meal

centre with a raft of exclusive restaurants. Or you can sample traditional Cuban cuisine amid the palm fronds of a colonial Havana-style restaurant.

Dress in Miami is casual, and it is a rarity to spot a jacket and tie, but some of the more formal hotel restaurants might frown on blue jeans.

Bayside bar in Miami

Cuban cuisine Cuban cuisine is one of the highlights of dining Miami-style. Throughout the day, Cuban sandwiches and thimbles of thick, sweet *café Cubano* keep locals on the go. In the evening, you can be certain of a lovely dining experience in one of the city's numerous Cuban restaurants.

For an early evening snack, experiment with *tapas* (a sampling of the restaurant's fare); there are several bars and restaurant lounges on Little Havana's Calle Ocho (SW 8th Street) that will make up a mixed platter of these savoury specialities for *tapas* novices to try. There is plenty of time to taste everything in a leisurely way – dining rooms in the Cuban quarter do not fill up until around 10pm.

Cuban cuisine is generally hearty and filling. Favourite menu items include *sopa de frijoles negros*, traditional black bean soup; *arroz con pollo*, roast chicken with saffron rice; *arroz con camarones*, rice with shrimps; *piccadillo*, spicy minced meat with pimento, olives and raisins; and *palomilla*, thin Cuban steaks. *Tostones*, fried green plantains, or *platanos*, ripe plantains, are popular accompaniments.

Top of the scale Sunset in Miami is thoughtfully accompanied by Happy Hour, between 5:30 and 7:30pm, which brings some of the most expensive views in town within reach of most pockets.

No mistaking what this bar is selling

NEON NIGHTS
When it was first switched on in the 1930s, Miami Beach's art deco neon lighting knocked the socks off locals and visitors. After dark, Ocean Drive is still an electrifying sight. For real magic do not miss The Crescent, 1420 Ocean Drive; The McAlpin, 1424 Ocean Drive; and The Fairmont, 1000 Collins Avenue. The Waldorf Towers, 860 Ocean Drive, has a pseudo lighthouse, and the nearby Breakwater sports an impressive ship's prow.

Nightlife and the performing arts

As evening approaches, Miami prepares for another night on the town, and cocktail shakers and conductors' batons set the pace. Miami's major performing arts venues are downtown, with outposts in Miami Beach and Coconut Grove. Miami Beach is undoubtedly the epicentre of Miami's clubland, with dozens of nightspots offering a full range of music and dance styles. The trendiest clubs can come and go in the blink of an eye, so ask around if you want to find the latest 'in' scene.

Cocktails, clubs, discothèques and shows Start off in fashionable Coconut Grove, where there are Latin, reggae and hip-hop nights at **Boheme**, *3138 Commodore Plaza* (tel: 305/448-1288); progressive, trance and house club music at **Chili Pepper**, *3399 Virginia Street* (tel: 305/442-2228); and jazz Thursday to Sunday at **Café Tu Tu Tango**, *CoCoWalk, 3015 Grand Avenue* (tel: 305/529-2222). On a more sophisticated note, **Alcazaba**, in the Hyatt Regency *Coral Gables, 50 Alhambra Plaza* (tel: 305/569-4614), summons dancers to the floor with disco, salsa and merengue.

Downtown after dark offers the more sedate pleasures of **Firehouse 4**, *1000 S Miami Avenue* (tel: 305/371-3473), a fashionable business district cigar lounge. Not far away, Miami's oldest bar, **Tobacco Road**, *626 S Miami Avenue* (tel: 305/374-1198), is famous for gritty live jazz and blues.

Celebrities and surfers stalk the sidewalk cafés, hole-in-the-wall clubs and power discos of Miami Beach's fashionable Art Deco District. **Penrod's Beach Club**, *1 Ocean Drive* (tel: 305/538-1111), reels them in with Top 40 and rock 'n' roll. Hot dance/clubbing venues include **Amnesia**, *136 Collins Avenue* (tel: 305/531-5535); **Groove Jet**, *323 23rd Street* (tel: 305/532-2002); **Level**, *1235 Washington Avenue* (tel: 305/532-1525); **Liquid**, *1439 Washington Avenue* (tel: 305/532-9154); **Crobar**, *1445 Washington Avenue* (tel: 305/531-8225); gay-friendly **Score**, *727 Lincoln Road* (tel: 305/535-1111); and celebrity-haunt **Bash**, *655 Washington Avenue* (tel: 305/538-2274).

For live jazz, check out **Jazid**, *1342 Washington Avenue* (tel: 305/673-9372), which attracts a stylish clientele from around 10:30pm onwards; and the **Van Dyke Café**, *846 Lincoln Road* (tel: 305/534-3600), which features live music nightly, from jazz to blues to Brazilian music. There are Latin sounds at **Mango's Tropical Café**, *900 Ocean Drive* (tel: 305/673-4422); and **Café Nostalgia at The Forge**, *432 41st Street* (tel: 305/695-8555), featuring Cuban musicians who fuse the traditional Havana sounds of pre-revolutionary Cuba with contemporary numbers (also in Little Havana at *2212 SW 8th Street* (tel: 305/541-2631); check programmes for both clubs in advance.

Many Miami Beach hotels offer nightly entertainment in a number of guises, including the famous **Poodle Lounge** at the Fountainebleau Hilton Resort and Towers, *4441 Collins Avenue* (tel: 305/538-2000). Under the same roof, **Club Tropigala at La Ronde** (tel: 305/672-7469) stages exotic dinner shows and revues in lavish surroundings.

It's electrifying… Ocean Drive at SoBe, the nightlife centre of the city

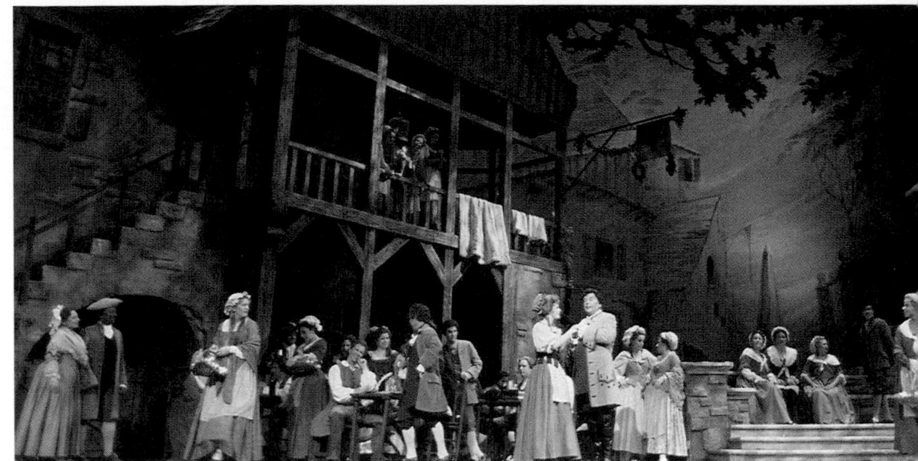

The Miami-Dade County Auditorium offers a programme of opera during the winter months

Classical music The Concert Association of Florida, *555 17th Street, Miami Beach* (tel: 305/532-3491), plays host to the annual **Prestige Series of Concerts** at the **Miami-Dade County Auditorium**, *2901 W Flagler Street* (tel: 305/547-5414). The auditorium is also home to the **Florida Grand Opera**, one of the oldest companies in the United States. The Grand also performs at the **Colony Theater**, *1040 Lincoln Road, Miami Beach* (tel: 305/674-1026). The Gusman Center Olympia Theater for the Performing Arts, *174 E Flagler* (tel: 305/374-2444), hosts the **Florida Philharmonic Orchestra** for a season of classical music and children's programmes. The young musicians of Michael Tilson Thomas's **New World Symphony** perform classical and contemporary works at the **Lincoln Theatre**, *541 Lincoln Road, Miami Beach* (tel: 305/673-3331).

Dance Former New York City Ballet principal dancer Edward Villella directs the **Miami City Ballet**, *2200 Liberty Avenue, Miami Beach* (tel: 305/532-4880), in a highly acclaimed programme of classical and contemporary choreography. And as evidence of Miami's multicultural society, flamenco flourishes at the **Ballet Flamenco La Rosa**, *555 17th Street, Miami Beach* (tel: 305/757-8475).

Film Several of Miami's shopping malls have multiscreen cinemas, including Coconut Grove's **Cocowalk 16**, *3015 Grand Avenue* (tel: 305/466-0450), **Regal Mayfair 10**, *3390 Mary Street* (tel: 305/447-9969), and **Sunset Place 24**, *5101 S.W. 72nd Street* (tel: 305/466-0450). In Miami Beach, check out the **South Beach Cinema**, *1100 Lincoln Road* (tel: 305/674-6766).

Theatre Premières, experimental productions, comedy and revues light the stage at the **Coconut Grove Playhouse**, *3500 Main Highway* (tel: 305/442-4000). The **MasterCard Broadway Series**, at the **Jackie Gleason Theater**, *1700 Washington Avenue, Miami Beach* (tel: 305/673-7300), puts on touring productions of hit Broadway shows. Also, the University of Miami's drama department stages four productions a year at the **Jerry Herman Ring Theater**, *1380 Miller Drive, Coral Gables* (tel: 305/284-3355).

LISTINGS AND TICKETS
The free *Miami New Times* covers everything from theatre and cinemas to live music, clubs and restaurants. The *Miami Herald* also has daily listings. Tickets for major local sports and entertainment events are available through Ticketmaster (*Open* Mon–Sat 10–8:30, Sun noon–5; tel: 305/358-5585).

SoBe STYLE
A 2-square-mile (5sq km) chunk at the southern tip of Miami Beach, SoBe (South Beach) is the coolest, most happening neighbourhood in the city. Small boutique hotels in art deco gems are the preferred lodging in this neck of the woods, which is a favourite haunt of visiting film stars, musicians and models. One of the most exclusive SoBe hotels is the gorgeous Delano, an Ian Schrager/Philippe Starck co-production and celebrity hang-out.

Miami Beach's art deco hotels are stylish places to stay

Accommodation

Beachfront luxury or beachfront bargain, accommodation in Miami comes in all shapes and sizes. The city currently boasts around 52,000 guest rooms in an impressive variety of hotels, motels, inns and spas. However, the first major hotel boom since the early 1980s is now under way, and a regiment of new luxury properties, including three Ritz Carltons (Key Biscayne, Miami Beach, Coconut Grove), a Four Seasons and a Mandarin Oriental, will join the ranks over the next few years, swelling the city's room capacity by a further 7,900 in developments worth over $1.4 billion.

Miami's more luxurious resorts offer a full range of recreational activities, five-star dining and spectacular views, while even the humblest motel generally provides air-conditioning, TV, telephones and a pool. Most visitors are here for the sunshine, and sunshine means the beach, so it is not surprising that Miami Beach is where most of the area's up-market hotels are found. Exclusive neighbourhoods such as Coral Gables, Key Biscayne and lively Coconut Grove also have their share of up-market accommodation, as does Downtown Miami, which features several spectacular modern hotel complexes aimed at the corporate sector, with prices pitched correspondingly high.

Miami's peak season lasts from 15 December to Easter, and even in summer, hotels can fill up over the 4th of July and Labor Day weekends.

A Greater Miami area resort tax of two to four per cent is added to hotel bills, and there is an additional six-and-a-half per cent sales tax.

Keeping down the cost Miami Beach offers the greatest choice of accommodation both in style and price range. The central, and most expensive, section of the Beach – from Lincoln Road to Surfside and Bal Harbour – is known as 'Hotel Row'. Further north, the Sunny Isles beaches front 'Motel Row', where prices are more reasonable and considerable discounts can be found during the summer season.

South of Hotel Row, the Art Deco District offers some real gems, with some rooms at moderate prices but less chance of summer discount rates. There is also good news for budget travellers, as the area's two youth hostels, the **Clay Hotel** and **Banana Bungalow Beach**, are both on Miami Beach.

There are few bed and breakfasts in the area, but some establishments are now offering this option: For a list of what is available contact **Bed and Breakfast Co., Tropical Florida**, *Box 262, Miami, FL 33243* (tel/fax: 305/661-3270); or check into the charming and historic **Miami River Inn** downtown.

There are several money-saving tips to bear in mind when choosing your accommodation. The view, for example, can add a considerable amount to the bill. Beachfront properties and ocean views may add as much as 25 to 50 per cent to the price of a room. Many hotels and motels do not charge for children under 18 sharing a room with their parents, and the excellent range of suites with separate bedroom and living areas makes this an

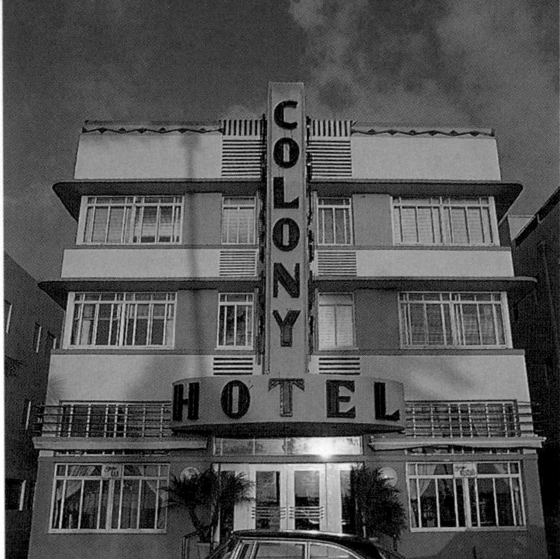

Stay at an Ocean Drive hotel for fine sea views

ideal cost-cutting arrangement. Ask about **family plans**; a minimum stay may be required. A popular option on Motel Row, **efficiencies** generally sleep 4–6 people and provide kitchenettes.

When booking accommodation, always inform the hotel of your estimated time of arrival. You may lose your room if the hotel has not been informed of a late arrival. Checkout is normally 11am.

Luxury and style If money is no object, several of Miami's finest hotels deserve a special mention. Half a mile of Miami Beach's golden shoreline is overlooked by the sweeping façade of the deluxe **Fontainebleau Hilton Resort and Towers**, a 1950s monument and a favourite of visiting celebrities. Its neighbour the **Eden Roc Resort & Spa** features a scrumptiously re-created New York deli among the marble and chandeliers. The city's newest luxury hotel is **Loews Miami Beach**, while the $64-million **Royal Palm Crowne Plaza Resort** is slated to steal its crown in the autumn of 2000. Some Art Deco District favourites are the **Cardozo**, **Delano**, **Essex House** and the luxuriously renovated **The Tides**.

In Coconut Grove, Luciano Pavarotti's split-level suite, complete with baby grand piano, is available at the **Grand Bay Hotel** when the maestro is out of town; or you can survey the bay from the rooftop pool at the all-suite **Mayfair House**.

Both the Mediterranean-style **Biltmore Hotel** and the elegant **Hotel Place St Michel** in Coral Glades were built in the 1920s. Key Biscayne's jewel is the 300-room **Sonesta Beach Resort**; out to the west of the city, sports lovers cannot get enough of **Doral Golf Resort and Spa**; and if pampering is what you're after, head for the **Fisher Island Club**, a 220-acre (90-ha) harbour island resort created as a winter retreat for William K Vanderbilt in 1925.

BILLETED AT THE BILTMORE
Crowned by an imposing Spanish-style tower, the magnificently restored Biltmore Hotel was the showpiece of George Merrick's Coral Gables development, and remains the grand dame of Miami's luxury hotels. Opened in 1926, it played host to Roosevelt, the Vanderbilts and royalty in its Jazz Age heyday before serving as a World War II veterans' hospital. Its marbled halls are supported by a veritable army of Corinthian columns, and the fabulous swimming pool measures almost 20,000 square feet (1,860sq m).

One of the restored Art Deco District hotels

Miami is sports-mad. From surf to stadium, the city's sporting calendar is packed with local and world-class events. There are plenty of opportunities for golfers, joggers, horseback riders, tennis players and watersport fanatics to follow their chosen hobbies every day of the year.

Fishing Deep-sea fishing is a major draw, but before you cast a line, check whether you need a licence. Sail fish, kingfish, dolphin, snapper, grouper and tuna are common catches. **Bill Baggs Cape Florida State Recreation Area** on Key Biscayne and **Haulover Beach Park** on Miami Beach are two popular fishing spots.

Golf The Greater Miami Convention and Visitors Bureau (see page 85) can provide information covering the two dozen or so public courses in the area. Several nine- and 18-hole courses operate year-round; green fees vary, and advance reservations are recommended in winter. **The Crandon Golf Course**, 6700 Crandon Boulevard, Key Biscayne (tel: 305/361-9129), is one of Florida's best public courses.

Golfers can also test their skills on the famed 'Blue Monster' and the new 'Great White', the southeastern US's first desert-scape golf course, a 130-acre (52-ha), par-72 redesigned by Greg Norman and opened in spring 2000 at the exclusive **Doral Golf Resort and Spa**, 4400 NW 87th Avenue (tel: 305/592-2000). The Doral hosts the Professional Golf Association's (PGA) Doral Ryder Open each spring.

Horse-racing takes place at Hialeah Race Track, Gulfstream Park Race Track and Calder Race Course in Miami

Jogging Bayside parks are numerous and popular, and many offer a fitness course, as well as scenic jogging trails. Favourites include **Haulover Beach Park**, 10800 Collins Avenue, Miami Beach (see pages 62 and 72); **Crandon Park**, 4000 Crandon Boulevard, Key Biscayne (see pages 63 and 73); **Matheson Hammock Park**, 9610 Old Cutler Road, south of Coral Gables (see page 73); and downtown's **Bayfront Park** on Biscayne Boulevard (see page 59).

Spectator sports The game that Miami has made its own is *jai alai* (pronounced *hi-ali*). Invented by Spanish Basques three centuries ago, the world's fastest game was introduced to Miami via Cuba. The pelota, or ball, is propelled at speeds of up to 175mph (280kph) with *cestas* (curved wicker slings) attached to players' hands. The betting is as furious as the play at **Miami Jai-Alai**, 3500 NW 37th Avenue (tel: 305/633-6400).

The Florida Marlins baseball team (tel: 305/626-7400) and the NFL's Miami Dolphins pack the **Pro-Player Stadium**, 2269 NW 199th Street (tel: 305/452-7000). Local NBA contenders Miami Heat moved into state-of-the-art quarters at the new bayfront American Airlines Arena, 601 Biscayne Boulevard (tel: 305/577-4328) in spring 2000. There is horse-racing at **Hialeah Park**, 2200

The Orange Bowl, home to football games and the Orange Bowl Festival

E 4th Avenue (tel: 305/885-8000); **Calder Race Course**, 21001 NW 27th Avenue (tel: 305/625-1311); and **Gulfstream Park**, 901 S Federal Highway, Hallandale (tel: 954/454-7000); and greyhound racing at **Flagler Greyhound Track**, 401 NW 38th Court (tel: 305/649-3000). Motor-racing fans should not miss the world-class **Grand Prix** of Miami, held at the **Homestead-Miami Speedway**, 1 Speedway Boulevard, Homestead (tel: 305/230-7223), each spring.

Tennis Miami's biggest tennis event is the annual springtime Ericsson Open, at the **Tennis Center at Crandon Park**, 7300 Crandon Boulevard, Key Biscayne (tel: 305/446-2200). The City of Miami Parks and Recreation Department (tel: 305/416-1308) can provide information about its three tennis centres offering top-class instruction, and 50 free first-come-first-served courts. Or contact the City of Miami Beach Parks and Recreation Department (tel: 305/673-7730), which operates the North Shore Tennis Center, and South Beach's Flamingo Park courts among others.

Watersports Virginia Key is the watersport centre of Miami, and there are plenty of facilities available. You can waterski and hire windsurfing equipment, surfboards and jet skis. Surfing is a Miami Beach speciality, with the biggest waves around **Haulover Beach** and **South Pointe Park**.

Many resort hotels offer a range of watersport facilities to non-residents as well as guests, and there are beach-front concessions offering waterskiing, wave runners and banana boat rides. Scuba diving and snorkelling excursions are arranged by **South Beach Divers**, 850 Washington Avenue, Miami Beach (tel: 305/531-6110); and **Tarpoon Lagoon**, 300 Alton Road, Suite 110, Miami Beach (tel: 305/532-1445). For swimming, see **Beaches**, pages 72–3.

The seas off Miami's coast are ideal for scuba diving

RIDING THE WAVE
In an effort to combat the appalling traffic and parking problems in the SoBe area of Miami Beach, the ELECTROWAVE Shuttle Service offers a daily two-way shuttle along Washington Avenue, between 11th and 17th streets. It operates Mon–Wed 8am–2am, Thu–Sat 8–4, Sun 10–2 and costs 25c; it includes public parking and park-and-ride locations on its route.

Policeman on the beat on Miami's streets

Practical points

Airport and transfers Miami International Airport is 8 miles (13km) west of downtown. Some overseas flights arrive at the International Satellite Building, linked to the main terminal by an automated shuttle. The airport's upper level has a currency exchange, 24-hour information desk, duty-free shops, luggage lockers, restaurants and snack-bars. There are taxis and shuttle-buses on the lower level concourse. The 15- to 20-minute taxi ride to downtown costs $18; south Miami Beach takes 25 minutes and costs around $25; north Miami Beach around $41, while 24-hour **SuperShuttle** buses provide services to all destinations within the Greater Miami area. Fares are $9 to downtown, and $11 to reach South Miami Beach and Coconut Grove (tel: 305/871-2000).

Car hire Miami's car hire agencies are based near the airport and offer free shuttle-bus transport from the terminals to the parking lots. Rates are very reasonable but advance reservations are advisable. Be prepared to queue if several international flights have just arrived. For further details, see **Travel Facts**, page 264.

Crime As in other large cities, the best advice is to be alert. Do not walk alone along dark, unpopulated streets at night; lock car doors when travelling; ask for directions at public places, such as petrol stations, rather than from passersby; keep cash in a moneybelt; and if you are asked for your wallet, don't resist.

Getting around Car hire is cheap, but Central Miami also has a very good public transport system.

By car Miami's attractions are spread over a large area, so a car makes good sense. The city is laid out on a grid system with four quadrants (NW, NE, SW and SE) divided by Miami Avenue and Flagler Street. Numbered avenues run north to south, and streets run east to west. A network of expressways makes travelling from one side of town to the other, or even around it, fast and direct. Note that parking is in short supply downtown. In Coral Gables, all the streets have names, and it is very difficult to get around without a map (pick up one at the City Hall, on Miracle Mile). Hialeah has its own grid system. Parking is difficult and expensive in its central district, but metered parking is widely available elsewhere.

By public transport More than 25,000 people use Miami-Dade County's public transport system every day. The elevated **Metromover** circuit serves a 26-block area of the downtown district. Fully automated cars operate daily between 6am and midnight (every 90 seconds in peak hours), and connect with the Metrorail at Government Center station. The **Metrorail** has 21 stops on its 21-mile (34km) journey between Kendall and Hialeah. Trains run every 20 minutes (five minutes at rush hours), daily between 6am and midnight.

Metrobus operates 63 routes around the city and suburbs Monday to Friday from 4:30am to 2:13pm; Miami's commuters use the peak-hour **Tri-Rail** service (tel: 305/836-0986). For information on all other services, tel: 305/770-3131 (6am–11pm).

By taxi Though taxis aren't cheap in Miami, they can come in handy. Miami's taxis do not cruise the streets looking for fares. Allow time to call one of the following:
Central Cab, tel: 305/532-5555
Metro Taxi, tel: 305/888-8888
Yellow Cab Company, tel: 305/444-444.

Hotel reservations The **Central Reservation Service**, *9010 SW 137th Avenue, Suite 116, Miami, FL 33186* (tel: 305/408-6100 or 800/950-0232, www.reservation-services.com), provides a free 24-hour reservation service for all hotels in Greater Miami.

Tourist information The **Greater Miami Convention and Visitors Bureau**, *701 Brickell Avenue, Suite 2700, Miami, FL 33131* (*Open* Mon–Fri 8:30–6; tel: 305/539-3063 or 800/283-2707, www.TropicoolMiami.com) publishes a glossy annual *Vacation Planner* with up-to-date information on sights and services. There are useful visitor centres at several locations. Local Chambers of Commerce (listed in the telephone directory) can also supply maps and information, including the Miami Beach Chamber of Commerce, *1920 Meridian Avenue, Miami Beach, FL 33139* (*Open* Mon–Fri 9–6, Sat–Sun 10–4; tel: 305/672-1270, www.miamibeachchamber.com).

Miami Visitor Centers *Aventura Mall, 19501 Biscayne Boulevard, Aventura* (*Open* Mon–Sat 10–9:30, Sun noon–6; tel: 305/935-4865); Bayside Marketplace, *401 Biscayne Boulevard* (*Open* daily 10–10; tel: 305/539-8070); Sears Coral Gables, *3655 SW 22nd Street* (Coral Way at Douglas Road), *Coral Gables* (*Open* Mon–Sat 9:30–9, Sun 11–6; tel: 305/460-3477).

THE DAILY NEWS
There are two daily papers printed in Greater Miami, the *Miami Herald* and its Spanish-language version *El Miami Herald*, plus another major Hispanic paper, *Diario Las Americas*. Other major papers are available at news-stands and from vending machines. The weekly free *Miami New Times* takes an uncompromising look at local issues.

Metromover, downtown's light-rail mass-transit system, is the easiest way of getting around this part of town

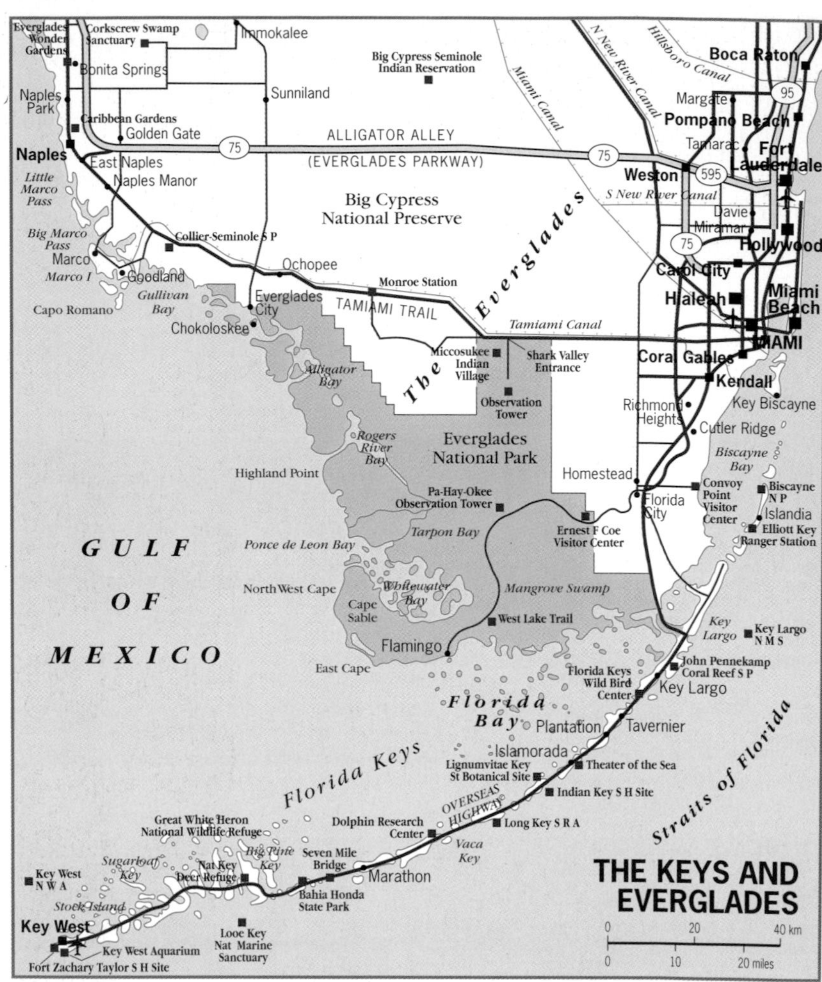

PRECIOUS TIME
A useful tip on driving in the Florida Keys: the Overseas Highway (US 1) is the only road between Key Largo and Key West. Some sections of the highway are single lane in each direction, and speed limits (maximum 55mph/88kph) are quite rigorously enforced. It is best to set aside a whole day to make the trip with stops along the way (non-stop trip around 2½ hours). Traffic on weekends and holidays can be a bumper-to-bumper nightmare.

AN HOUR'S DRIVE south of Miami, the Florida Keys angle off the peninsula in a spectacular chain of islands set in shimmering blue-green seas. This is the American Caribbean, home to tropical birds, flowers and exotic fish which dart around the only living coral reef in the Continental United States.

In the early days, pirates took over this isolated and treacherous maze of reefs and keys. Later, the sea captains and merchants of Key West profited handsomely from shipwrecks and trade on the route between the Gulf and Cuba (just 90 miles/145km to the south), and tourism arrived with Henry Flagler's 'Railroad That Went To Sea' in 1912. The railroad was destroyed by a hurricane in 1935 and replaced by the Overseas Highway (US 1), named for the 43 bridges that link the island chain from Key Largo to Key West.

This chapter is arranged in geographical order starting on the mainland with two exceptional national parks, an easy day-trip away from Miami. On the Atlantic Coast, the **Biscayne National Park** is the nation's largest aquatic

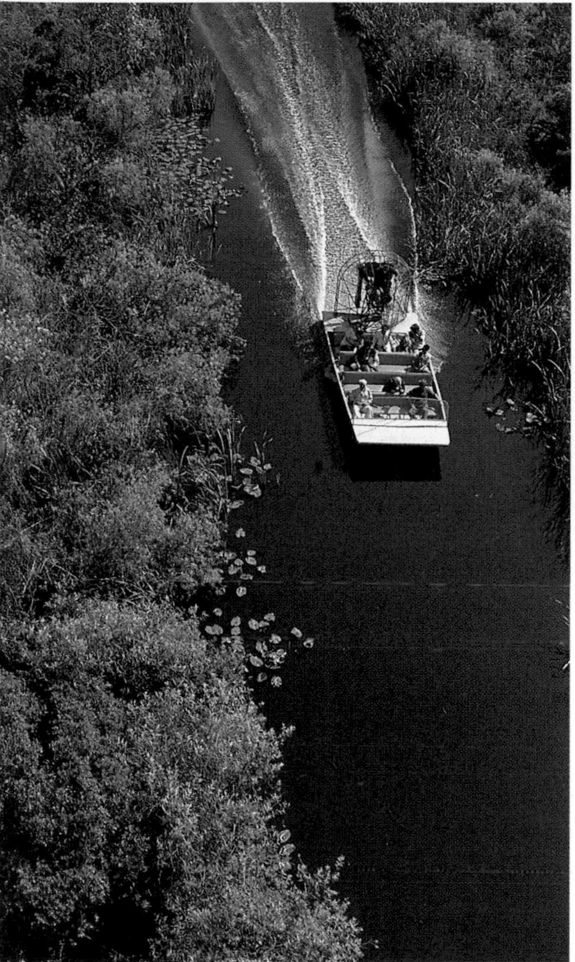

The Keys and Everglades

park and a haven for divers and snorkellers. To the west lies the **Everglades National Park**, bordering Florida Bay on the Gulf of Mexico.

Once you leave the mainland, the first stop in the Upper Keys is **Key Largo**, largest of the 42 islands and gateway to the undersea delights of the John Pennekamp Coral Reef State Park. Heading south are **Tavernier**, with a wild bird rehabilitation centre, and the sportfishing centre of **Islamorada**. **Marathon** is the hub of the Middle Keys, another diving and fishing centre with a natural history museum and restored railway workers' camp on Pigeon Key. The Lower Keys start at the southern end of Seven Mile Bridge where the beachfront **Bahia Honda State Park** makes an appealing break on the road south and **Big Pine Key** is home to the National Key Deer Drive refuge, before culminating at journey's end in funky and fun-loving **Key West**.

Roadside Mile Markers (MM) will help you navigate along US 1 from MM 126 just south of Florida City right down to Key West at MM 0.

Above: airboats skim the waterways of the Everglades

▶▶▶ REGION HIGHLIGHTS

▶▶ Big Cypress National Preserve

Oasis Ranger Station, Tamiami Trail (US 41 east of Monroe Station); tel: 941/695-2000 or 941/695-4111
Open: daily; Visitor Center daily 8:30–4:30

Big Cypress, northern neighbour to Everglades National Park, is a 2,400-square-mile (6,210sq km) wedge of wet and dry prairie, marshlands, slash pine and hardwood hammocks. Nearly one-third of the preserve is covered with cypress trees, aquatic deciduous conifers which can tolerate long periods of immersion in the swamp's seasonal high-water periods (see panel opposite). Big Cypress is a favourite home for alligators, bobcats, deer, rare black bears and a few remaining Florida panthers. Spectacular bird life includes the endangered Everglades kite, which feeds exclusively off apple snails found in the preserve.

The main drainage swamp west of Big Cypress is **Fakahatchee Strand**, which is a separate state preserve area. It contains the largest stand of native royal palms in North America and a rare concentration and variety of epiphytic orchids.

Just west of Copeland on Route 29, **Janes Memorial Scenic Drive** is a 20-mile (32km) dead-end excursion into the backwoods, where a boardwalk gives access to an impressive stand of virgin cypress. Unusual wildlife includes the mangrove fox squirrel and Everglades mink.

Road access is provided by the **Loop Road** (Route 94) from Forty Mile Bend (just west of Shark Valley) to Monroe Station, which is paved for 13 miles (21km) of its 24-mile (38km) route. There is also **Turner River Road** (Route 839), a graded dirt track running due north to Alligator Alley (note: rental-car drivers are not insured here), and hiking trails from the Oasis Ranger Station.

Big Cypress National Preserve – a contemplative view

Visitors to Florida's wet wilderness areas can explore swamps and hammocks on raised boardwalk trails

►►► Biscayne National Park

Convoy Point, SW 328th Street (9 miles east of US 1); tel: 305/230 PARK
Open: park daily 8–5:30, Visitor Center daily 8:30–5. Admission free; overnight docking fees for Boca Chita and Elliott Key
Occupying 180,000 acres (72,850 ha) along the southern portion of Biscayne Bay, 95 per cent of Biscayne National Park is under water. The remaining 5 per cent is an 18-mile (29km) chain of 44 keys, hemmed in by tangled mangroves and surrounded by the dazzling sea. Only a few of the Keys can be visited: Elliott, Boca Chita, Adams and Sand keys. Boat trips, snorkelling and scuba diving are the best ways to fully explore this fascinating underwater world. Most of the park is accessible only by boat. Boat launches are found at Homestead Bayfront Marina and at Black Point Marina. Elliott Key has a 66-berth harbour, and there are anchorages off the keys. Canoe rentals are available at Convoy Point for exploring and birdwatching along the mainland mangrove shoreline.

The brackish water trapped in the mangrove roots nurtures an enormous variety of life. Just offshore, live coral reefs teem with a multitude of creatures. Hundreds of species of fish, sponges and soft corals thrive in Biscayne Bay, and manatees frequent the warm shallows. Fishing is exceptional, with snapper, snook and barracuda among the most common catches.

The **Convoy Point Visitor Center** has a museum with exhibits on the park's cultural and natural histories, and also offers ranger-led activities. There is a ranger station and self-guided walks on Elliott Key include one along a boardwalk and another along a short nature trail. An old road runs the length of the island (7 miles/11km), and rangers lead hiking sessions during the winter months.

Offshore, **Elkhorn Reef** is a good site for inexperienced snorkellers; other popular sites include **Schooner Wreck Reef** and **Star Coral Reef**. Daily 3-hour glass-bottom boat tours and 4-hour scuba and snorkelling trips to the reefs can be booked through **Biscayne National Underwater Park Inc.** (tel: 305/230-1100), which can also arrange equipment rental for independent divers.

NOT SO BIG CYPRESSES
The 'big' in Big Cypress refers to the size of the preserve rather than the height of the cypress trees seen here. The most common variety, found in the broad belts of trees edging the wet prairies and growing on dome-shaped hammocks, is the dwarf pond cypress. Few of the mighty bald cypresses, which can grow to well over 100 feet (30m) tall, survived the Everglades logging boom of the 1930s and 1940s.

►►► Everglades National Park

Open: daily 24 hours. Admission: moderate, tickets valid for one week

The Everglades region starts at Lake Okeechobee, where a freshwater river 6 inches (15cm) deep and 50 miles (80km) wide begins to creep seaward, but the national park preserve only commences below the Tamiami Trail (US 41), extending south to the tip of the peninsula and west to the Gulf of Mexico. The best time to visit is the winter dry season, when low water levels make wildlife spotting easier, as animals and birds concentrate around the deeper pools and sloughs for food. In spring, temperatures rise uncomfortably and during the summer wet season, as water levels rise, wildlife ranges further afield and bloodthirsty clouds of mosquitoes descend.

The main Visitor Center, west of Homestead, is the park's most popular access point. Walking trails off the road between the centre and Flamingo on Florida Bay explore the six different ecosystems which constitute the Everglades' overall habitat – the Anhinga and Gumbo Limbo Trails are favourites. Check ranger schedules, and follow the trails with an experienced guide.

Tram tours depart daily from the northern **Shark Valley** entrance on a 15-mile (24km) circuit which is also open to hikers and cyclists. To the west, the **Gulf Coast Ranger Station** provides back-country camping permits and access to the Ten Thousand Islands.

Entrances and information centres

Ernest F Coe Visitor Center/Park Headquarters, 10 miles (16km) southwest of Florida City and Homestead via SR 9336 (*Open* daily 8–5; tel: 305/242-7700). The centre presents a 15-minute introductory film on the ecology of the park at regular intervals and offers free information brochures and park activity schedules, including details of boat tours, guided walks and canoe hire. Near by, the **Royal Palm Visitor Center** is the starting point for several ranger-guided

Raised hammocks provide island footholds for a variety of native trees and plants in the Everglades wetlands

walks, and **Flamingo Visitor Center** provides information on accommodation, camping, sightseeing cruises, charter fishing boats and bicycle hire. **Shark Valley/Northern Entrance** (*Open* daily 8:30–5:30; tel: 305/221-8776), 35 miles (56km) west of downtown Miami via Tamiami Trail (U.S. 41). Year-round tram tour departures daily (schedules vary seasonally so reservations recommended, tel: 305/221-8455), nature trail and bicycle hire.

Gulf Coast Visitor Center/Western Entrance (*Open* daily in winter 7:30–5; reduced opening hours mid-Apr–mid-Nov; tel: 941/695-3311). Near Everglades City, 80 miles (128km) west of Miami on CR 29 via Tamiami Trail (US 41). A Ranger Station offering marine and shore life displays, maps, information about boat tours and canoe hire.

A mangrove, the only tree that can extract fresh water from salt water

General information

Accommodations There are 103 rooms and 24 cottages at **Flamingo Lodge**, 1 Flamingo Lodge Highway, Flamingo, FL 33034-6798 (tel: 941/695-3101 or 1-800/600-3813).
Boating Excellent on Florida Bay and in the Ten Thousand Islands; canoe trails around Flamingo and Everglades City. Boat and canoe hire from **Flamingo Marina** (tel: 941/695-3101) and **Everglades National Park Boat Tours**, Gulf Coast Visitor Center (tel: 941/695-2591).
Camping Official campgrounds are available at Flamingo, Long Pine Key and Chekika (near Homestead). Permits must be obtained from ranger stations for overnight stays in the 48 back country sites around the park.

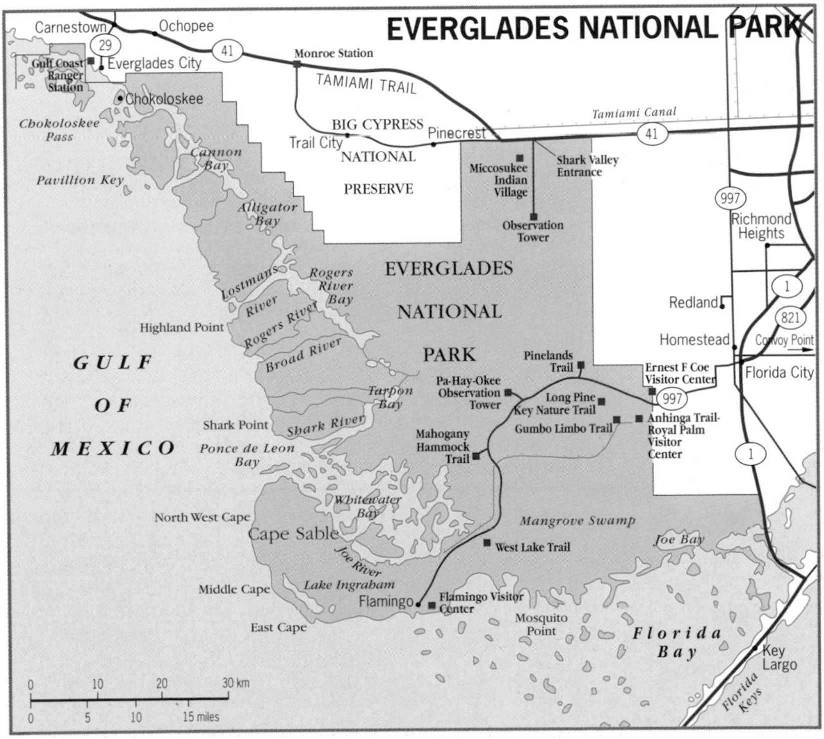

EVERGLADES NATIONAL PARK

Carnestown
Ochopee
29
41
Gulf Coast Ranger Station
Everglades City
Monroe Station
TAMIAMI TRAIL
Chokoloskee
Chokoloskee Pass
BIG CYPRESS NATIONAL PRESERVE
Trail City
Pinecrest
Tamiami Canal
41
Cannon Bay
Pavillion Key
Miccosukee Indian Village
Shark Valley Entrance
997
Alligator Bay
Observation Tower
Richmond Heights
Lostmans River
Rogers River Bay
Rogers River
EVERGLADES NATIONAL PARK
1
Redland
821
Highland Point
Broad River
Homestead
Convoy Point
GULF OF MEXICO
Pinelands Trail
Ernest F Coe Visitor Center
Florida City
Pa-Hay-Okee Observation Tower
Tarpon Bay
997
Long Pine Key Nature Trail
Shark Point
Shark River
Gumbo Limbo Trail
Anhinga Trail-Royal Palm Visitor Center
Mahogany Hammock Trail
Ponce de Leon Bay
1
Whitewater Bay
North West Cape
Cape Sable
Mangrove Swamp
West Lake Trail
Joe Bay
Joe River
Lake Ingraham
Middle Cape
Flamingo
Flamingo Visitor Center
East Cape
Mosquito Point
Florida Bay
Key Largo
Florida Keys
0 10 20 30 km
0 5 10 15 miles

'The miracle of light pours over the green and brown expanse of sawgrass and of water, shining and slow-moving below, grass and water, that is the meaning and central feature of the Everglades ... It is a river of grass.' Marjorie Stoneman Douglas, The Everglades: River of Grass *(1947).*

FRIEND OF THE EVERGLADES
A month before the Everglades National Park was dedicated by President Truman in December 1947, Marjorie Stoneman Douglas (1890–1998) published *The Everglades: River of Grass*. With a single phrase she transformed many people's perception of the Everglades from pestilential swamp to a living entity with a vital role to play in the ecology of southern Florida.

A founding member of the Friends of the Everglades campaign in 1969, she became a leading lobbyist for conservation during her 80s and 90s from her home of more than 70 years in Miami's Coconut Grove. Stoneman Douglas' autobiography, *Voice of the River*, with John Rothchild, is a fascinating account of an eventful life, and her collections of short stories paint a vivid portrait of Florida in the 1920s and 1930s.

Native Americans called the Everglades region *Pa-Hay Okee*, 'grassy waters'; it is an apt description. Vast and mysterious, a carpet of waterlogged sawgrass punctuated by cypress swamps and hardwood hammocks, the Everglades stretch to the horizon, criss-crossed by secretive waterways. Many Floridians once saw the Everglades as a challenge to be overcome, tamed, drained and reclaimed into 'useful' land. But the region is a perfectly balanced ecosystem, and its unique habitat supports myriad species of native flora and fauna and aquatic creatures. The Everglades' subtropical climate is the key to its success. There are two distinct seasons – the summer rains, followed by the winter dry period. This ancient pattern of deluge and drought is essential to the well-being of the entire region.

Seasonal variations The shorter days of October and November herald the start of the dry season in southern Florida. As the waters recede in the back country, animals and birds congregate and feed around the remaining deep-water sloughs (large pools). This is the mating season, but if water levels are too low and there is insufficient food, mating will not occur. When the rains begin in May and June, the withered brown sawgrass pushes up new shoots and algae and plankton flourish around its roots. Mosquito larvae, tadpoles and small fish start filling out the lower end of the food chain, and animals and birds disperse from dry season refuges to rear their young. Water is the Everglades' lifeblood, and in the past, the summer downpours would overflow from Lake Okeechobee, flood the prairies and move towards the sea at around half a mile (0.8km) a day. Eventually, the invisible 50-mile-wide (80km) river would discharge into Florida Bay.

Disappearing water Ever since Governor Napoleon Bonaparte Broward launched his campaign to drain the Everglades in 1905, the 'river of grass' has been under threat. The completion of the Tamiami Trail in 1928 allowed lumber barons to log the Everglades' cypress hammocks; they were followed in the 1940s by oil explorers. By 1948, the natural flow of water from Lake Okeechobee was effectively harnessed by a 1,400-mile (2,250km) network of levees and canals controlled by engineers and business interests. Ranchers to the north drained tracts of wet prairie for pasture, and contractors along the East Coast claimed vast acreages of land for housing and industrial development. Agriculture, in particular, posed a two-fold threat by siphoning off huge amounts of precious water and polluting run-off with high

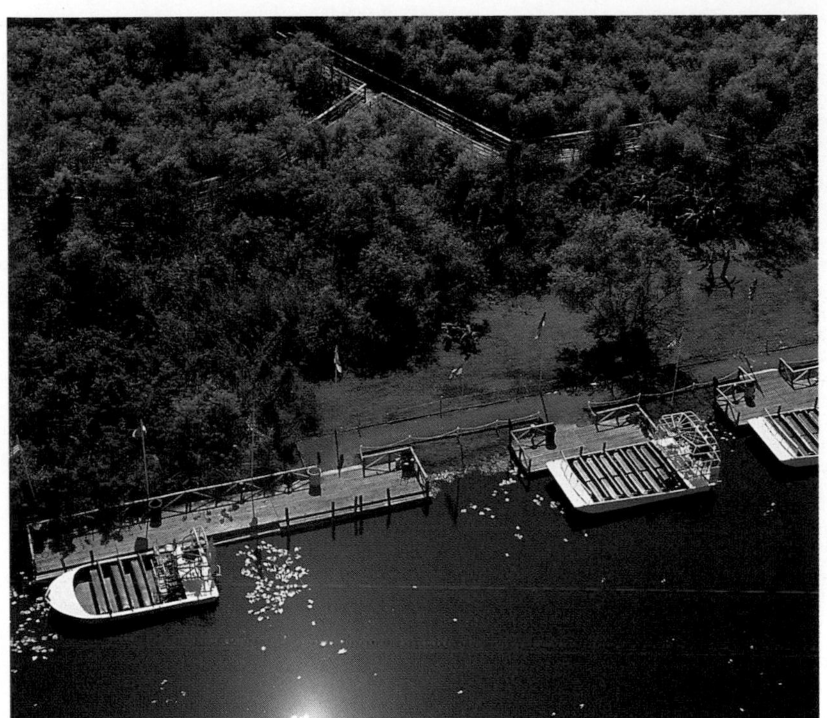

Boats for touring the Everglades

levels of phosphates and nitrates. Heavy demand for fresh water from cities such as Miami puts further pressure on supplies. Where once 800 billion gallons of water flowed through the Everglades annually, today this has dwindled to some 100 billion gallons.

Wildlife in peril Another pressing reason to preserve the Everglades is its treasury of plant and animal life. Some 2,000 diverse plant species, around 45 of which are found nowhere else in the world, rely on the sunlight and rainfall of southern Florida. The dazzling flocks of snowy egrets and pink-feathered roseate spoonbills recorded by celebrated naturalist and painter John James Audubon in 1832 have dwindled to just a handful. Wood storks, herons, bald eagles, ospreys, the Everglades mink, the Florida panther, manatees, American crocodiles and green sea turtles are also threatened.

Signs of change There are some signs of a positive change in attitudes toward the Everglades and its problems. Environmental pressure groups and government agencies are joining forces to tackle some of the major issues, from flood control to conservation. The 1989 Everglades National Park Protection and Expansion Law directed the Army Corps of Engineers to dismantle part of South Florida's flood-control canal system and restore areas of wetlands, and the Everglades Forever Act requires agricultural areas to dramatically reduce fertilizer run-off, among other vital measures. There is still much to be done but there is at least a chance the Everglades will last forever.

THE WILDERNESS WATERWAY

This 99-mile (160km) inland boating trail between Flamingo and Everglades City is a real back-country adventure. The trip can be made by canoe in 8–10 days (hire available in Everglades City) or by small outboard craft up to 18 feet (5m) in length (6–8 hours). Numbered markers indicate the route along narrow channels between mangrove forest and dozens of islands. Free back-country camping permits are required for overnight stops.

UNDERWATER SHRINE
The 9-foot-tall (2.7m), 4,000-pound (1,810kg) bronze *Christ of the Deep* statue at the John Pennekamp Coral Reef State Park is a copy of a famous Italian submarine sculpture, *Christ of the Abysses*. A gift to the Underwater Society of America, it has become one of the most photographed sites in the world. It is also a favourite location for underwater weddings.

The Upper Keys

►►► Key Largo

Across Blackwater Sound, 30-mile-long (48km) Key Largo (*largo* means long in Spanish) is the largest of the Keys, and achieved widespread fame as the setting of the 1948 screen classic *Key Largo*, with Humphrey Bogart and Lauren Bacall. Film buffs on the nostalgia trail can see the original steel-hulled *African Queen*, moored by the Holiday Inn at MM 100, which starred alongside Bogart and Katharine Hepburn in 1951.

Key Largo's present-day claim to fame lies in the spectacular John Pennekamp Coral Reef State Park and Florida Keys National Marine Sanctuary (see below), where some of the nation's premier diving sites attract thousands of visitors every year. More than 25 local dive outfits arrange daily excursions, and hire out equipment.

In November, Key Largo's **Harry Harris Park** plays host to the annual **Island Jubilee**, a nine-day festival of special events with music, food and crafts stalls, off US 1 at MM 92.6.

Accommodation in Key Largo is plentiful and varied; advance reservations are advisable in winter and at weekends.

John Pennekamp Coral Reef State Park, *MM 102.5* (*Open daily 8am–dusk, Visitor Center 8–5. Admission: inexpensive*; tel: 305/451-1202) America's first underwater park and the adjoining **Florida Keys National Marine Sanctuary** total some 178 nautical square miles of the Atlantic Ocean. Warmed by the Gulf Stream, the coral reefs and seagrass beds support more than 500 species of fish, 55 varieties of coral, and around 27 types of gorgonians, or marine life forms such as sea anemones. It is a fabulous undersea world which is a major attraction for scuba divers and snorkellers. Non-swimmers can enjoy the excellent aquariums and displays in the Visitor Center, and the glass-bottom boat trips to the main reef areas.

Looking out over the underwater world of the John Pennekamp Coral Reef State Park

Coral reefs are built by polyps, primitive soft-bodied relatives of the sea anemone and jellyfish, which secrete limestone to form an exterior skeleton. They cannot survive at temperatures below 68°F (20°C).

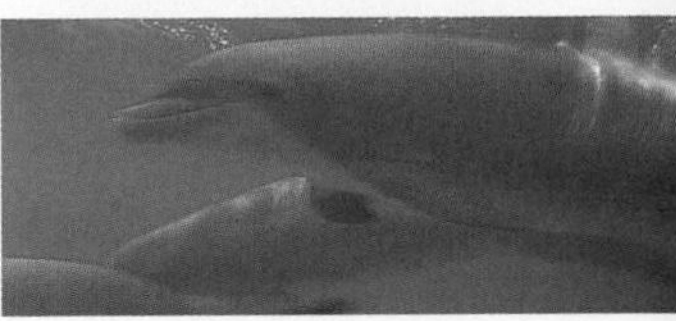

Polyps feed on tiny phytoplankton which they snare with stinging cells on their tentacles, and they also receive oxygen and nutrients from algae. In return, the algae extract carbon dioxide for photosynthesis and give coral its colours. Hard coral grows slowly as each generation builds on the skeletal deposits of its ancestors. A large brain coral can take several centuries to build; branching coral advances at a rate of only 3 inches (7cm) a year.

Inner reefs Known as patch reefs, inner reefs develop in calm shallow waters. Inner reefs comprise the more delicate coral formations, such as the sea fan, mountain star and the unnervingly lifelike brain coral. Angelfish, wrasse, tang, damsels, butterfly fish and spiny lobster are some of the more colourful inshore residents; further out, barracuda and shark cruise around massive outcrops of staghorn and elkhorn coral. Every nook and cranny of a coral reef is a potential hiding place for camouflaged moray eels, who dart out from murky crevices to snap up passing fish.

Milleflora dichotoma: *fire coral*

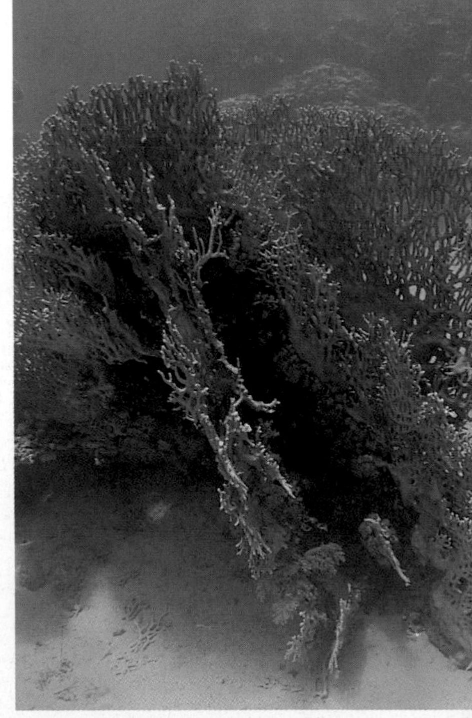

A friendly habitat Corals are functional as well as beautiful. They form a vital breakwater, diffusing the destructive force of storm-whipped seas, and provide a safe anchorage for molluscs, sea anemones, barnacles and sponges. Colourful parrot fish graze on coral, biting off chunks with their powerful beaks and grinding it up to extract polyps and algae. Fish nibbling on corals produce more than 2½ tons of sand per acre annually. The sea grasses which grow on the sandy ocean floor are a source of food for turtles, manatees and thousands of other marine plant and animal species.

Threats to the system The delicate ecosystem of a coral reef is easily damaged. Boat anchors, propellers and careless divers are an obvious threat. More insidious is the chemical run-off from the mainland and drifting oil from deep-sea shipping lanes. Pollution and sediment from dredging operations can smother living coral polyps, destroy the lower end of the food chain, and, as a result, gradually threaten the entire population of the reef.

WHEN IS A CONCH NOT A CONCH?
Conch (pronounced 'conk') is a rubbery mollusc often used by Key chefs for conch fritters, chowder and conch ceviche, cured with fresh Key lime juice. But a conch is also a native Keys resident. You become an honorary conch when you have lived in the Keys for seven years or more.

UNDERWATER PHOTOGRAPHY
Amateur photographers should not be afraid to try their skill under water to record the beauties of a coral reef. As well as purpose-built underwater cameras, waterproof cases are sold which will protect most types of normal cameras, and even video cameras, for depths of up to 35 feet (10m). The best time to shoot below the surface is between 10 and 2, when the sunlight is strongest; at depths below 10–20 feet (3–6m) use a flash. For the best results, get close to the subject and, if possible, use a wide-angled lens.

There are several popular diving sites in the park, some with underwater wrecks to explore. They include **Molasses Reef**, with its network of tunnels and towering coral formations; **French Reef** with its Christmas Tree Cave; the **Benwood Wreck**, a freighter torpedoed in 1942; **Grecian Rocks**; and the *Christ of the Deep* statue submerged under 25 feet (8m) of water at **Dry Rocks**. There are several daily dive-boat departures.

Other facilities, such as windsurfer, sailboat and canoe hire, are available from the sandy beach area; scuba gear hire and snorkelling trips can be arranged through the dive shop.

A campground is also available (information and reservations: P.O. Box 1560, Key Largo, FL 33037).

Maritime Museum of the Florida Keys, *MM 102.5 (Open* Mon–Sat 10–4. *Admission: inexpensive;* tel: 305/451-6444) This museum depicts the history of local shipwrecks through salvaged treasure, reconstructed wreck sites and preserved artefacts. Some of the more notable exhibits were culled from a fleet of treasure ships wrecked by a hurricane in 1715. Items on display include gold Mexican escudos, counterfeit coins, magnificent costume jewellery and various items of glassware and pottery. Treasure-hunting maps and books are on sale.

Dolphins Plus, *off US 1 at MM 100* (*Open* daily, call for schedules. *Admission: programmes expensive, observers moderate*; tel: 305/451-1993) Divers in the Key Largo area often have tales to tell of encounters with playful bottlenose dolphins. There are also several marine research facilities in the Keys that offer a chance to swim with these friendly and intelligent creatures. One of them is low-key Dolphins Plus, which offers two dolphin encounter programmes. Observers can watch the proceedings and attend the pre-swim orientation seminar exploring the marvels and myths attached to the dolphin. Participants in the encounter sessions must know how to use a mask and fins. For information and advance reservations: P.O. Box 2728, Key Largo, FL 33037 (www.dolphinsplus.com; email: info@dolphinsplus.com).

Florida Keys Wild Bird Center, *MM 93.6*, Tavernier (*Open* daily dawn–dusk. *Admission: donation*; tel: 305/852-4486) A rehabilitation facility and sanctuary for injured birds unable to return to the wild, the centre offers a great opportunity to get a really close look at native birdlife, from peregrine falcons and osprey to pelicans, cormorants and gulls. The enclosures flank boardwalk trails through forest hammocks, wetlands and mangrove swamp areas to the shore, where a short nature trail leads to birdwatching hides overlooking a salt pond where roseate spoonbills, herons and stilts come to feed.

▶ Islamorada

Named *islas moradas* (purple isles) by the Spanish, Islamorada is a collection of pine-fringed islands, including Windley and Upper and Lower Matecumbe Keys. Rumour has it that early explorers found great concentrations of *Janthina janthina*, a violet sea snail, here – hence the town's name. Others believe the name came from the beautiful orchid trees. Today, Islamorada is chiefly known as a sportfishing centre with a pedigree dating back to the day when author and avid fisherman Zane Grey persuaded Henry Flagler to convert his Long Key railroad camp into a fishing lodge.

Indian Key State Historic Site and Lignumvitae Key State Botanical Site, *access by private boat, by ferry or kayak from Robbie's Marina, MM 78.5;* tel: 305/664-9814. A brace of offshore islands that make a popular day out. On the Atlantic side, Indian Key was once a county-seat town and base for early 19th-century shipwreck salvagers, known as wreckers, until a Native American attack wiped out the settlement in 1840. Botanist Dr Henry Perrine was one of the victims and his plants now grow wild among the ruins which are explored on ranger-led walks (Thu–Mon 9 and 1. *Admission: inexpensive;* tel: 305/664-4815).

Lignumvitae Key is on the bayside, and is a rare preserve of virgin tropical forest surrounding the 1919 **Matheson House**, built by a wealthy Miami chemist as a holiday retreat. (There are ranger-led tours Thu–Mon at 10 and 2. *Admission: inexpensive;* tel: 305/664-4815).

Theater of the Sea, *MM 84.5* (*Open* daily 9:30–4. *Admission: expensive;* tel: 305/664-2431) The world's second oldest marine park, created in pools and lagoons formed by Flagler's railroad excavations, this is a popular stop on the Overseas Highway. Tours will acquaint you with all kinds of underwater creatures from sea urchins to sharks. You can also take a 'bottomless' boat ride, swim with dolphins and watch a sea lion and dolphin show. Call ahead for **Dolphin Adventure-Swim** reservations.

FANTASTIC FOSSILS

Windley Key is one of the highest islets in the Florida Keys chain and when Henry Flagler's railroad workers began quarrying the ancient limestone reef they discovered a fantastic treasury of fossilised corals in the rock. Visitors can now explore the quarry and take rubbings of the petrified reef creatures at the Windley Key Fossil Reef State Geological Site, MM 85.5 (*Open* Thu–Mon 8–5. *Admission: inexpensive;* tel: 305/664-2540).

All together now…one of the popular sea lion shows at Theater of the Sea

Shrimp boats in the Middle Keys

The Middle Keys

The Middle Keys stretch southwest from the 2½-mile Long Key Bridge, to the famous Seven Mile Bridge, beyond Marathon. Moving down the chain in north–south order, **Conch Key** has a rustic fishing dock, and its picturesque cluster of whitewashed cottages is deservedly popular with photographers. Neighbouring **Duck Key** once thrived as a salt producer. Though **Grassy Key** is not particularly verdant, its **Dolphin Research Center**, *MM 59* (*Open* daily 9–4; reservations, tel: 305/289-1121) offers more dolphin encounters; and **Crawl Key** was named for the turtle cages, or kraals, used to store live turtles until they were made into soup or jewellery in the days before preservation. Capital of the Middle Keys, **Marathon** is a well-developed small town with an airport, shopping malls, a marina, golf course and public beach, plus a wide range of accommodation, campgrounds and trailer parks. An interesting stop here is the **Pigeon Key National Historic District**, reached via the Old Seven Mile Bridge, which also serves as a fishing pier.

►► **Museums of Crane Point Hammock**, *MM 50.5, Marathon* (*Open* Mon–Sat 9–5, Sun noon–5. *Admission: moderate*; tel: 305/743-9100) This woodland museum complex has a well-presented overview of the natural history of the Keys. User-friendly displays explain local geology, geography, history and wildlife; exhibits include a Skylab photograph of the region, reef dioramas and tales of shipwrecks at sea. An outdoor area is specially designed for children, with touch tanks, iguanas and a playroom. A mile-long (1.5km) nature trail explores the surrounding **Crane Point Hammock**, which supports a wide range of tropical vegetation and ten endangered animal and plant species. Among the mangroves, palms and hardwood trees, a 19th-century Bahamanian coach house has been restored, the latest link in a chain of evidence which indicates this site has also been inhabited by pre-Columbian and prehistoric Native American peoples.

PIGEON KEY CAMP
Tucked beneath the Old Seven Mile Bridge, which used to link the Middle and Lower Keys, the Pigeon Key National Historic District (*Open* daily 9–5. *Admission: moderate*; tel: 305/743-5999) was once a camp for construction workers building Henry Flagler's Overseas Railway. The 5-acre (2-ha) island is accessible by tram (from 10am), or on foot across a 2.2-mile (3.5km) section of the bridge. A self-guided walking tour (call ahead for guided tour schedules) explores various 19th-century buildings, one of which houses a small museum.

The Lower Keys

The magnificent **Seven Mile Bridge** marks the transition from the Middle to the Lower Keys. Built in 1982, the present structure is actually 110 feet (33m) short of 7 miles (11km), and affords dazzling views of the bay, the ocean and the islands. Beaches are a rarity on the Keys, but just south of the bridge, Bahia Honda State Park is fringed by beautiful white sandy beaches. A large area of **Big Pine Key** has been declared a preservation area for the endangered Key deer (see page 101). Here, the speed limit on the main road drops to 45mph (72kph), 35mph (56kph) after dark, in an effort to protect any of the tiny deer who wander away from the refuge. In the middle of the refuge, Blue Hole is the largest body of fresh water in the Keys. Accessible from Big Pine, Little Torch, Ramrod and Summerland keys, the Looe Key National Marine Sanctuary (see page 101) is another diver's delight. **Cudjoe Key** is the home of the US government's zeppelin look-alike *Fat Albert*, which hovers aloft watching for illegal drug traffickers.

Bahia Honda State Park, *MM 37* (*Open* daily 8–dusk. *Admission: inexpensive;* tel: 305/872-2353) Bahia Honda, from the Spanish 'deep bay', fronts on to the Looe Key National Marine Sanctuary. Stop off for a swim or a picnic – the sandy shore was ranked among the top one per cent of the nation's beaches in a recent survey. There are snorkelling tours and dive shop rentals; pelicans, egrets, herons and terns are frequently spotted; and several rare plants dot the nature trail. Also fishing, bicycle hire, a boat ramp and a campsite.

PERKY BAT TOWER
When Righter C Perky set up a fishing camp on Sugarloaf Key in 1929, the mosquitoes were such a menace that something had to be done. Mr Perky racked his brains and finally hit upon a cunning plan: he imported a colony of insect-eating bats and released them into a purpose-built tower. But the ungrateful creatures ignored their new home and swiftly disappeared, leaving Perky's quirky bat tower down a dirt track just past the Sugarloaf Lodge at MM 17.

There's good swimming and good views of the Old Seven Mile Bridge to be had at Bahia Honda

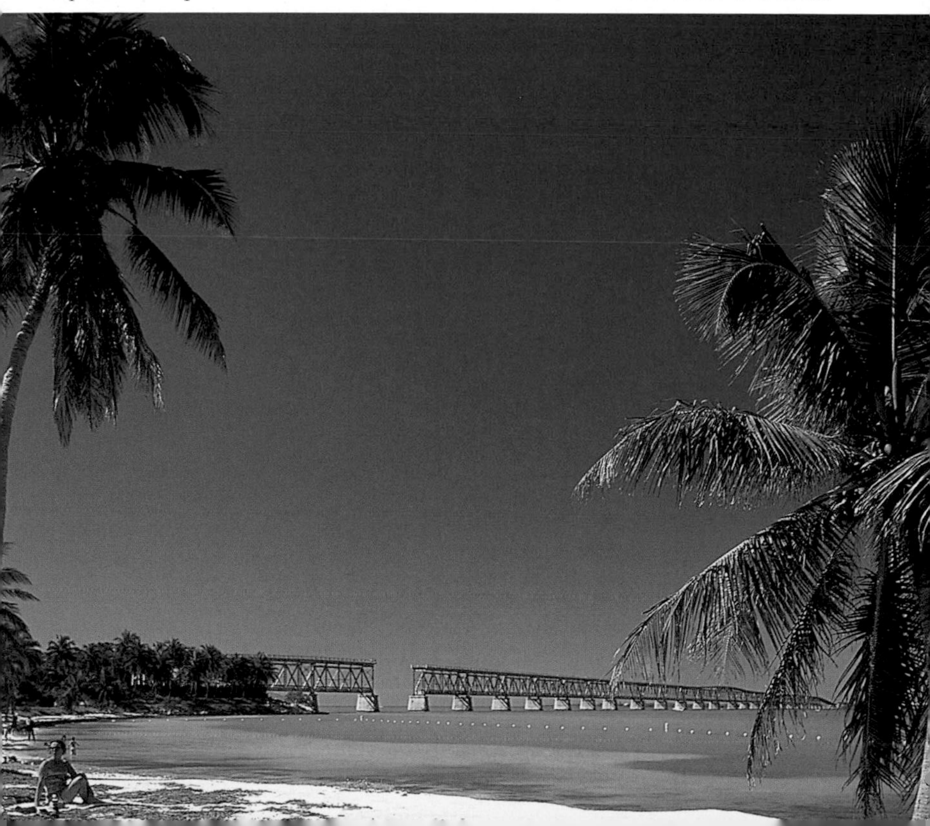

Walk

Exploring Key West

Start on Front Street, at the head of Whitehead Street, outside the imposing red-brick façade of the 1891 Old Custom House.

The former customs building has been restored to house the changing exhibitions of the **Key West Museum of Art & History**. Opposite is the **Mel Fisher Maritime Museum**, a stone's throw away from **Audubon House**.

Turn right on Front Street for the Truman Annex, entering the leafy residential quarter through a pair of gateposts.

Straight ahead is the **Harry S Truman Little White House**, where the president once made the most of Key West's relaxing informality. Stop off for one of the regular tours.

Turn left and leave the Annex, crossing Whitehead Street on to Caroline Street. On the corner is the first office of Pan American Airways, whose Flight No 1 from Key West to Cuba took off on 28 October, 1927.

A few paces down the road, the **Heritage House Museum & Robert Frost Cottage**, 401 Caroline, is housed in a traditional Key West home dating from 1832. The interior is furnished with a marvellous array of antiques and artefacts gathered by seven generations of the Porter family. Poet Robert Frost used to winter in the garden cottage. Another lovely house further down the street is the **Curry Mansion Inn**, 501 Caroline Street.

At Simonton Street, take a quick detour to the left for a visit to **The T-Shirt Factory**, 316 Simonton. Then continue on Caroline past a collection of handsome historic homes framed by mature trees, frangipani and bougainvillaea.

Caroline Street continues on to the Historic Seaport district, where a boutique has become the last in a succession of businesses to occupy the 1868 **Red Doors Building**, 800 Caroline Street, which has functioned as a cigar factory, ships' chandlery and shrimpers' bar in its colorful past. Next door, **Pepe's**, 801 Caroline Street, claims to be the oldest eating house in the Keys, and is a great place to pause for a cold drink or snack. Across the parking lot, **Flagler Station Over-Sea Railway Historeum**, 900 Caroline Street, makes an interesting stop for railroad and local history enthusiasts.

The Historic Seaport Boardwalk follows the waterfront back to Front Street.

Period furnishings in the nursery of Audubon House, a shrine to wildlife artist John James Audubon

►►► **Looe Key National Marine Sanctuary** *6½ miles (10.5km) off Big Pine Key at MM 27.5* This oceanside marine preserve is one of the most popular diving sites along the Keys. It surrounds part of a coral reef and several different undersea habitats, from sea-grass beds and patch reefs to sand flats. Clear waters and moderate sea conditions make for great snorkelling on the surface, while the wide range of depths within the park makes it equally exciting for beginners and experienced divers (see panel). In addition to the reef, there are wrecks to explore, including British frigate HMS *Looe*, which struck the reef and sank in 1744.

► **National Key Deer Refuge and Blue Hole**, *Big Pine Key, 1½ miles (2.5km) west at MM 33.5* An estimated 300 Key deer remain on Big Pine Key and the 16 islands that surround it, but dozens are killed by drivers every year. Just 24 to 28 inches (60–70cm) high, Key deer are the smallest sub-species of the Virginia white-tailed deer. The Bambi-like creatures mate in the autumn, giving birth to tiny fawns weighing only 2–4 pounds (1–2kg) at birth in spring. You can look for traces of antler velvet in late August and early September. The deer feed off native plants and berries, and although they can tolerate a small amount of salt water in their diet, fresh water is essential – feeding them is strictly prohibited (there is a $250 penalty for doing so).

There is a short nature trail, and the best time to spot deer is early in the morning and in the evening. The ranger knows from day to day where the best place to see them is.

Blue Hole (*Open daily 8–dusk*) is an old limestone quarry at the heart of the Key Deer Refuge. Material for most of the roads on Big Pine Key was removed from here, and the quarry's freshwater supply is vital to the Key deer's survival. Although some salt water seeps into the lower levels of Blue Hole, freshwater species which thrive happily in its depths include bass, blue gills, mosquito fish and alligators. Herons, cormorants, ducks, moorhens and ospreys constitute Blue Hole's varied bird life.

LOOE KEY ACCESS

A number of local diving and charter operators offer trips to the marine sanctuary. Among them are Looe Key Reef Resort and Dive Center, MM 27.5, Big Pine Key (tel: 305/872-2215; www.diveflakeys.com; e-mail: looekeydiv@aol.com); and Paradise Divers, MM 39, Sunshine Key Resort & Marina (tel: 305/872-1114; www.paradivers.com; e-mail: paradivers@aol.com). For snorkel and glass-bottom boat trips, contact Strike Zone Charters, MM 29.5, Big Pine Key (tel: 305/872-9863 or 1-800/654-9560).

There are only around 300 Key deer left on Big Pine Key and the surrounding islands

Unusual souvenirs for sale on Duval Street

KEY WEST ARCHITECTURE

Local 'conch' architecture was introduced to Key West by Bahamian settlers in the early 19th century. Houses were built from imported hardwoods or salvaged lumber and set on coral rock piles out of danger from flooding; roofs were designed to channel rainwater into cisterns. During the Classical Revival period, symmetrical façades adorned with columns, pediments and gables were all the rage, and many houses still display decorative gingerbread detailing. Windows and doors were protected from sun and rain by wooden louvred blinds, which together with other local adaptations developed into a distinctive vernacular style.

►►► Key West

The southernmost point in the Continental United States, Key West is an intriguing blend of laid-back locals and international sunseekers, quiet, leafy backstreets and tourist kitsch.

Pirates and wreckers laid the foundations of the town, and by the 1890s Key West had developed into the wealthiest city in Florida. Sponge-diving and cigar-making were already flourishing industries, when in 1912, tourism arrived via Henry Flagler's $50 million railroad.

After the devastating hurricane of 1935, Key West was saved by the intervention of the Florida Emergency Relief Administration, which replaced the railroad with tarmac and launched an ambitious plan to turn the city into a resort for authors and artists. Ernest Hemingway was already here, and it did not take long for a colony of artists to spring up alongside the revitalised tourist industry.

To get a feel for Key West, jump aboard one of the frequent trolley or miniature train tours which circulate around town. Alternatively, you could hire a bicycle. Along **Duval Street**, the heart of downtown, visiting cruise passengers plunder the boutiques, bars and eateries, including Hemingway's favourite watering hole, **Sloppy Joe's**, 201 Duval.

Take a stroll around the waterfront **Historic Seaport**, and do not miss sunset at **Mallory Square** – the ultimate Key West experience, for which half the population seems to turn up.

Audubon House and Gardens, *205 Whitehead Street* (*Open* daily 9:30–5. *Admission: moderate*; tel: 305/294-2116) This handsome house was built by prosperous wrecker John H Geiger in 1830. Self-guided audio tours explore the Geigers' home from top to bottom, and every room is beautifully furnished in period style with numerous examples of John James Audubon's splendid bird illustrations (see panel opposite). Upstairs a fine arts gallery sells original hand-painted Audubon lithographs costing from a few hundred dollars to a couple of thousand. After the tour, take time to wander around the enchanting tropical garden.

Curry Mansion Inn, *511 Caroline Street* (*Open* tours, daily 10–5. *Admission: inexpensive*; tel: 305/294-5349) Home of an early Florida millionaire, William Curry, who made his fortune in the wrecking and lumber businesses, this is one of the loveliest buildings in town and now functions as a bed and breakfast, but opens for tours. A portion of the original homestead erected in 1855 is at the rear. Milton Curry added the gracious façade in 1899. The house has been exquisitely furnished with period antiques, Tiffany glass, patchwork quilts on brass beds and a pool table in the attic, and there are great views of the surrounding area from the roof.

East Martello Museum and Art Gallery, *3501 S Roosevelt Boulevard* (*Open* daily 9:30–5. *Admission: moderate;* tel: 305/296-3913) During the 1840s, the US Army began work on a series of coastal defences to protect Key West, including downtown Fort Zachary Taylor (see below) and two Martello towers. The East Tower, the only remaining example of its type on the eastern seaboard, houses an eclectic little local history museum which focuses on local industries, including Henry Flagler's railroad and a welter of nautical memorabilia.

Climb to the top of the citadel for the views. The building also contains Stanley Papio's amusing scrap-iron folk art. A separate gallery displays Mario Sánchez's colourful carved and painted local street scenes.

Fort Zachary Taylor State Historic Site, *Truman Annex (entrance at the west end of Southard Street. Open* daily 8–dusk. *Guided tours* at noon and 2pm. *Admission: inexpensive*; tel: 305/292-6713) Founded in 1845, this fort took 21 years to complete. Although most of Florida supported the Confederacy, the fort was controlled by Union forces during the Civil War.

Today the grounds offer a sizeable public beach, barbecue grills and picnic tables. A small museum traces the fort's history, and excavations have uncovered a buried arsenal comprising the largest collection of Civil War cannons in the United States.

FORT JEFFERSON

The largest coastal fortress in the United States encircles the island of Garden Key in the Dry Tortugas, 60 miles (96km) west of Key West. Fort Jefferson was founded in 1851. Its 8-foot-thick (2.5m) walls rise 50 feet (15m) high with three gun tiers, and its 70-foot-wide (21m) moat was once patrolled by sharks and barracudas. The fort is accessible by ferry (a full-day excursion) and by boat or seaplane from Key West. The plane trip is spectacular. On arrival you can enjoy a sandy beach, diving and watch turtles and birds.

ARTIST AND ORNITHOLOGIST EXTRAORDINAIRE

John James Audubon, the son of a French planter, was born in Haiti in 1785. To escape the Napoleonic draft, he moved into a family property in Pennsylvania and began travelling extensively to record native bird life. The result was the famous series of engravings, *Birds of America*. During a trip to Florida in 1832, Audubon recorded 18 new species of birds and worked in the gardens of John Geiger's Key West home.

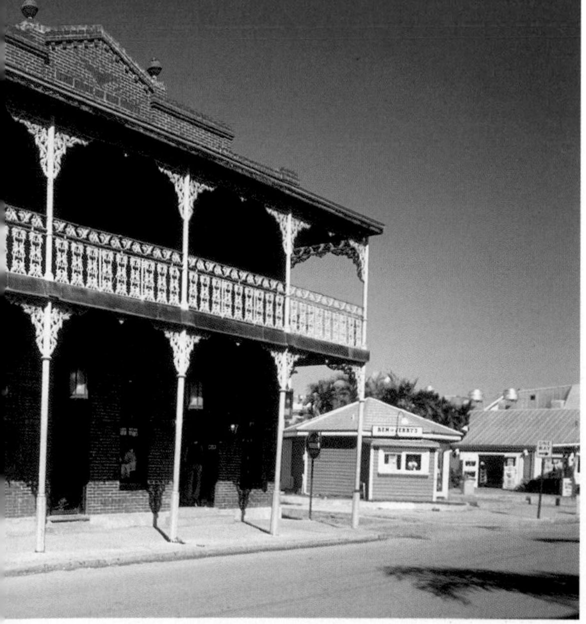

Typical southern architecture in Key West

When novelist John Dos Passos rode Henry Flagler's railroad into Key West in the 1920s, he later described it in glowing terms, saying it was 'one of the most exhilarating experiences of my life; coming into Key West was like floating into a dream'.

It was mainly Dos Passos' recommendation that lured Ernest Hemingway to Key West in 1928 and marked the beginning of a long and fruitful association between Key West and many leading 20th-century American writers.

Fishing and booze When Hemingway arrived in Key West with his second wife, Pauline, he joined the local seafaring community with enthusiasm. A turn-of-the-20th-century boomtown, Key West was on the decline. Its population had dropped from 22,000 in the town's heyday to around 10,000, and the stream of winter tourists had dried up with the 1929 stock market crash. Fortunately for 'Papa' Hemingway, Prohibition meant nothing in Key West. Cuban rum enhanced fishermen's tales of mighty marlin, tarpon and wily bonefish, and lent local bars an alluring pioneer flavour. Hemingway's fishing trips became legendary. One of his favourite fishing cronies, Joe Russell, was also the proprietor of Sloppy Joe's bar.

A writer's retreat: the lounge in Hemingway's house

A place to write Pauline's uncle bought the house at 907 Whitehead Street (see page 105) as a belated wedding present for the couple in 1931. In between trips abroad, Hemingway returned here to write *For Whom the Bell Tolls, A Farewell to Arms, The Snows of Kilimanjaro* and *Death in the Afternoon*, among others. The three stories that make up *To Have and Have Not* are his only fiction with an American setting. In 1936, Hemingway met journalist Martha Gellhorn in Sloppy Joe's. She would become his third wife and influence his move to Cuba in the 1940s.

A literary haven The Florida Emergency Relief Administration's post-hurricane scheme to attract promising writers to Key West was a wild success: ten Pulitzer Prizes have been awarded to a succession of visiting and resident writers. In the late 1930s, poet Elizabeth Bishop spent a brief sojourn in Key West; Robert Frost, Gore Vidal, and Kurt Vonnegut Jr all enjoyed a respite from northern winters in the town; and playwright Tennessee Williams lived near Duncan and Leon streets from 1949 until his death in 1983.

Hemingway House, *907 Whitehead Street* (*Open* daily 9–5, last tour at 5. *Admission: moderate*; tel: 305/294-1136) Ernest Hemingway acquired this mid-19th-century Spanish Colonial-style house in 1931. He and his second wife, Pauline, decorated the interior with a mixture of furnishings and mementos gathered on trips to Spain, Africa and Cuba, and Hemingway penned several novels and short stories in an airy study above the carriage house. Regular guided tours provide a wealth of interesting detail and anecdotes about Hemingway. An extensive colony of cats, introduced to the homestead by the writer, still has the run of the house and gardens. Look out for their enormous feet – some of them have as many as eight toes – a genetic hiccup that attracted Hemingway's attention when he adopted his first feline from a passing sea captain.

Key West Aquarium, *1 Whitehead Street* (*Open* daily 10–6. *Admission: moderate*; tel: 305/296-2051) Hundreds of brightly coloured tropical fish and other sea creatures are on display here in exhibits that will make you an expert on Florida's marine life. In addition to a huge coastal mangrove display tank, various smaller glass-fronted aquariums line the walls. There is a touch tank, tours and shark-feeding demonstrations.

FUN
Hemingway fever hits town in July, when hundreds of Ernest Hemingway look-alikes converge on Key West for the annual Hemingway Days Festival. The week-long celebration of the writer's life includes seminars, a look-alike contest, fishing competitions and storytelling. Later in the year, the October Fantasy Fest honours Halloween with a costume party, parade and a town fair. Make hotel reservations well in advance.

Marine encounters in the touch tank at the Key West Aquarium

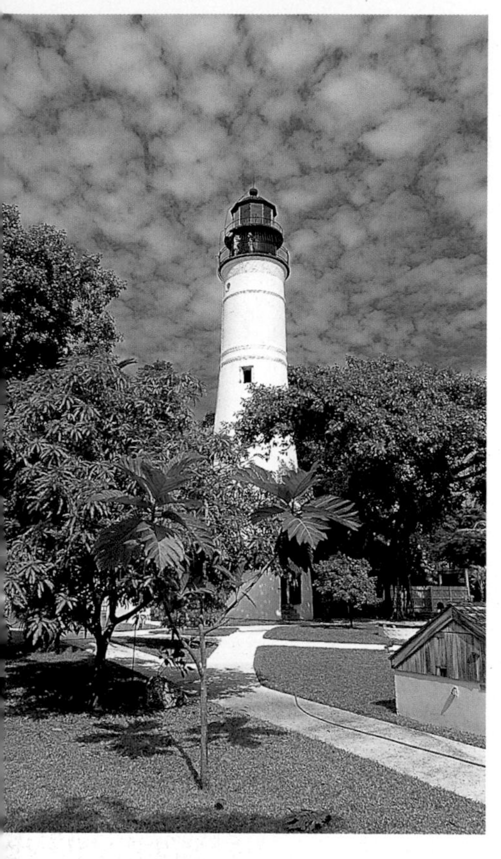

Key West Lighthouse Museum, *938 Whitehead Street (Open* daily 9:30–5. *Admission: moderate*; tel: 305/294-0012) For a bird's-eye view of Key West, look no further than the 19th-century lighthouse. It's an 88-step ascent to the viewing balcony; another ten steps lead to the light itself. At ground level, the former Keeper's Quarters, panelled with rock-solid Dade County pine, house interesting and eclectic memorabilia from past keepers, including Mary Bethel, who took over the job from her husband in 1908 and operated the station for 14 years with the help of her children.

Little White House Museum, *111 Front Street (Guided tours* daily 9–5. *Admission: moderate*; tel: 305/294-7277) Tucked away in the Truman Annex, part of an old naval station, this was President Harry S Truman's alternative White House. Truman took 11 working holidays here during his six years in office. The house dates from 1890, when it was the home of the base commander. Refurbished in 1940s style, living areas and bedrooms contain several Truman-era relics, such as his custom-made poker table with shell cases for ashtrays, and there is an excellent film presentation before the guided tour. Dwight D Eisenhower worked on his State of the Union address here in 1956.

Climb the 88 steps of the Lighthouse Museum for the superb view over historic Key West

Mallory Square Pier, *off Wall Street* Key West locals don't just watch the sun go down, they celebrate it. For this daily party, locals and visitors alike gather on the dockside at Mallory Square to watch the fiery sun slide into the Gulf of Mexico. Street entertainers roll up in force – washboard strummers and bongo players set feet tapping, and jugglers, mime artists and unicyclists show off their skills.

Mel Fisher Maritime Museum, *200 Greene Street (Open* Wed–Sun 9:30–5, Thu–Sat 9:30–6. *Admission: moderate*; tel: 305/294-2633) 'Today's the day!' is Mel Fisher's motto, and it kept him going through 16 long years of determined exploration before he finally hit the jackpot with the discovery of the Spanish galleon *Atocha* in 1985. There had been several finds in the meantime, but nothing to match the $400 million in gold, silver and jewels – the cargo that sank with the ship off the Keys in 1622. Domestic artefacts retrieved from the *Atocha* and her sister ship the *Santa Margarita* present a microcosm of 17th-century daily life, and then there is the real treasure: gold and silver tableware, emeralds from the Muzo mines of Colombia and fabulous jewellery such as a 12-foot-long (3.5m) gold wedding chain that weighs 4½ pounds (2kg) and is valued at a mere $500,000. Take in the video presentation, handle a gold bar and visit the souvenir shop, where authentic artefacts and replicas are for sale.

SHIPWRECK AHOY!

For an entertaining look at Key West's notorious wrecking era, visit the Key West Shipwreck Historeum on Mallory Square (*Open* daily 9:45–4:45. *Admission: moderate*; tel: 305/292-8990). There are displays of artefacts raised from the wreck of the *Isaac Allerton*, which sank in 1865 carrying the richest cargo of any ship of its time, as well as shows and a 65-foot (20m) observation tower with fine views of Old Town Key West and out to sea.

Mosquito Coast Island Outfitters and Kayak Guides, *1107 Duval Street* (Information and reservations, tel: 305/294-7178) A great way to get to grips with nature, this is a must for nature-lovers and outdoorsmen; experience is not necessary as instruction and easy-to-use kayaks are provided. Kayakers and all necessary equipment are transported to Geiger Key or Sugarloaf Key, where knowledgeable guides lead four- or five-hour tours into the back country, exploring mangrove islands and crystal-clear waters teeming with birds, marine life and other wildlife. Snorkelling gear is supplied for those who want to investigate coral and hard-bottom mangrove channels – be sure to bring along plenty of sun block, as well as mosquito repellent, hats, UV-protective sunglasses and waterproof camera cases.

Oldest House Museum, *322 Duval Street* (*Open* daily 10–4. *Admission: inexpensive*; tel: 305/294-9502) Built in the early 19th century, this building, which claims to be the oldest house in Key West, is a fine example of early Key West architecture, with its distinctive maritime flavour. The interior is panelled with horizontal planks reminiscent of a ship's hull, while furnishings and artefacts trace the history of the one-time owner of the house, Captain Francis B Watlington. The original outdoor kitchen is the last of its kind in the Keys.

I TOLD YOU I WAS SICK
Between Olivia and Angela streets, Key West City Cemetery is a surprising repository of local humour. As well as a litany of quirky nicknames, there are some irreverent epitaphs such as B P Robert's 'I told you I was sick', and one honest widow's revenge: 'At least I know where he's sleeping tonight'. If it all looks a little disorganised, blame the local bedrock, which has left several stone caskets resting above ground. The shortage of space means that an estimated 100,000 people have been buried in the 15,000 plots.

Looking out across the Keys over a shimmering blue-green sea from Cotton Key

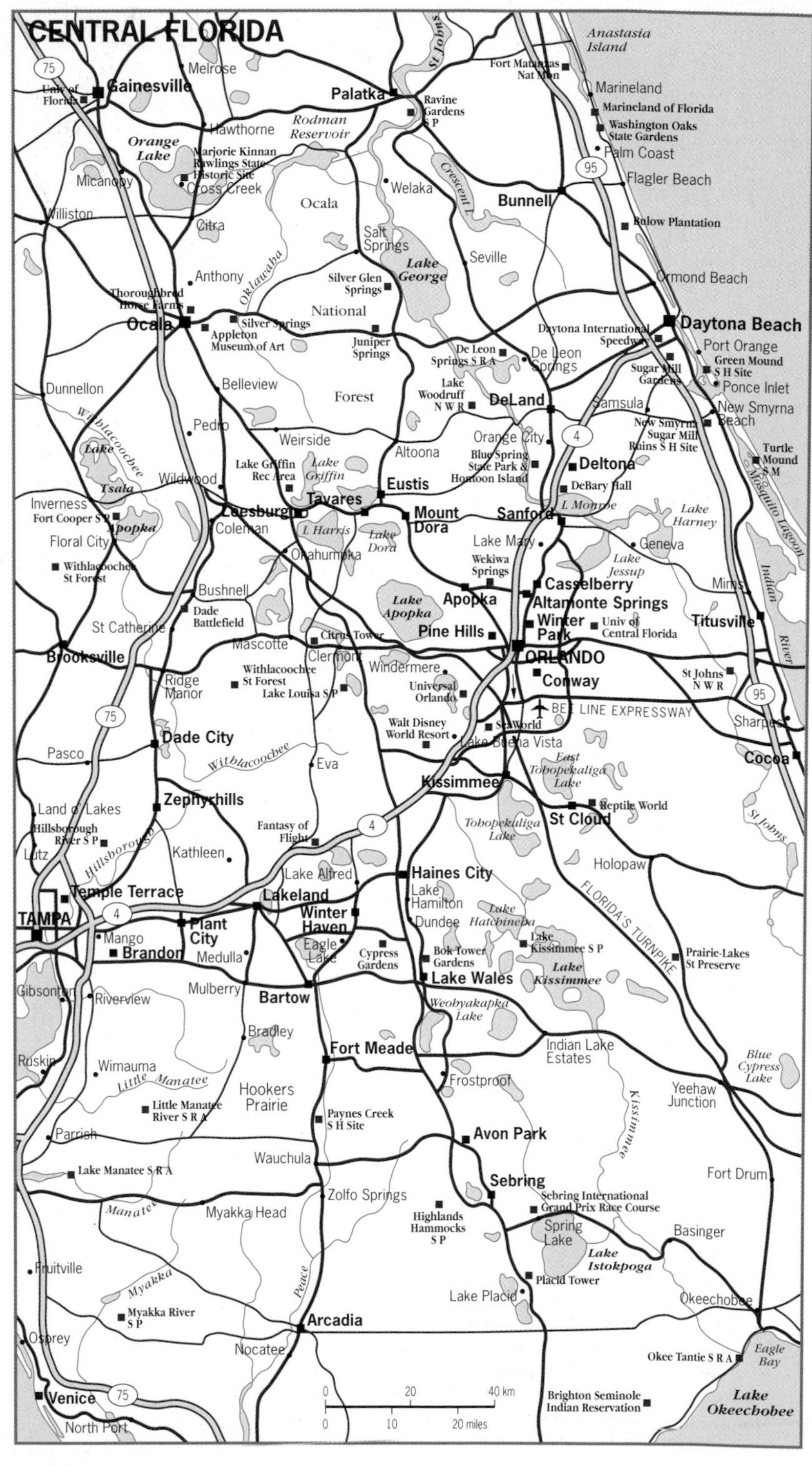
CENTRAL FLORIDA
Anastasia Island
Fort Matanzas Nat Mon
Melrose
Gainesville
Univ of Florida
Palatka
Ravine Gardens S P
Marineland
Marineland of Florida
Washington Oaks State Gardens
Palm Coast
Flagler Beach
Hawthorne
Rodman Reservoir
Orange Lake
Marjorie Kinnan Rawlings State Historic Site
Cross Creek
Micanopy
Welaka
Crescent L
Bunnell
Ocala
Williston
Citra
Salt Springs
Bulow Plantation
Lake George
Seville
Oklawaha
Anthony
Silver Glen Springs
Ormond Beach
Thoroughbred Horse Farms
National
Ocala
Silver Springs
Appleton Museum of Art
Juniper Springs
Daytona International Speedway
Daytona Beach
De Leon Springs S R A
De Leon Springs
Port Orange
Sugar Mill Gardens
Green Mound S H Site
Ponce Inlet
Dunnellon
Belleview
Forest
Lake Woodruff N W R
DeLand
Samsula
New Smyrna Beach
New Smyrna Sugar Mill Ruins S H Site
Withlacoochee
Pedro
Weirside
Orange City
Lake
Altoona
Blue Spring State Park & Hontoon Island
Deltona
Turtle Mound S M
Mosquito Lagoon
Tsala
Wildwood
Lake Griffin Rec Area
Lake Griffin
Eustis
DeBary Hall
Inverness
Fort Cooper S P
Apopka
Leesburg
Tavares
Mount Dora
Sanford
L Monroe
Lake Harney
Floral City
Coleman
L Harris
Lake Dora
Lake Mary
Geneva
Withlacoochee St Forest
Okahumpka
Wekiwa Springs
Lake Jessup
Casselberry
Mims
Indian River
Bushnell
Lake Apopka
Apopka
Altamonte Springs
Dade Battlefield
Winter Park
Univ of Central Florida
Titusville
St Catherine
Pine Hills
Citrus Tower
Mascotte
Clermont
Brooksville
ORLANDO
Windermere
Ridge Manor
Withlacoochee St Forest
Lake Louisa S P
Universal Orlando
Conway
St Johns N W R
BEE LINE EXPRESSWAY
Walt Disney World Resort
SeaWorld
Sharpes
Dade City
Lake Buena Vista
Pasco
Withlacoochee
Eva
East Tohopekaliga Lake
Cocoa
Kissimmee
Zephyrhills
Reptile World
Land o' Lakes
Fantasy of Flight
Tohopekaliga Lake
St Cloud
St Johns
Hillsborough River S P
Hillsborough
Lutz
Kathleen
Holopaw
Lake Alfred
Haines City
Temple Terrace
Lakeland
Lake Hamilton
FLORIDA'S TURNPIKE
TAMPA
Winter Haven
Plant City
Dundee
Lake Hatchineha
Mango
Eagle Lake
Lake Kissimmee S P
Brandon
Medulla
Cypress Gardens
Bok Tower Gardens
Prairie-Lakes St Preserve
Lake Wales
Lake Kissimmee
Gibsonton
Mulberry
Bartow
Riverview
Weohyakapka Lake
Bradley
Fort Meade
Indian Lake Estates
Blue Cypress Lake
Ruskin
Wimauma
Little Manatee
Frostproof
Hookers Prairie
Kissimmee
Yeehaw Junction
Little Manatee River S R A
Paynes Creek S H Site
Parrish
Avon Park
Wauchula
Lake Manatee S R A
Sebring
Fort Drum
Zolfo Springs
Sebring International Grand Prix Race Course
Manatee
Myakka Head
Highlands Hammocks S P
Spring Lake
Basinger
Lake Istokpoga
Fruitville
Peace
Placid Tower
Myakka
Lake Placid
Okeechobee
Myakka River S P
Arcadia
Osprey
Nocatee
Okee Tantie S R A
Eagle Bay
Venice
Brighton Seminole Indian Reservation
Lake Okeechobee
North Port
0
20
40 km
0
10
20 miles
75
95
4

Central Florida

CANE FIELDS AND CITRUS GROVES, cartoon characters and cowboys – Central Florida has it all, yet most visitors come for one thing only. Orlando is Central Florida's first city. Settled as a fortress during the Seminole Wars, it developed into a relatively prosperous citrus and cattle town ringed with lakes, and earned its nickname, the City Beautiful. When Walt Disney selected Florida as the location for his second theme park in the 1960s, Orlando was the perfect site, with year-round good weather and good transport and communication links close to huge tracts of undeveloped land.

Today, Walt Disney World® Resort is the world's biggest tourist destination, attracting millions of visitors every year. There has been an inevitable onslaught of tourist-related industries and tacky spin-offs, notably in **Kissimmee**, a small town-turned-sprawling-budget-dormitory at Disney's back door, a half-hour drive south of Orlando. However, it is surprisingly easy to leave the theme parks and find tranquillity in a state park or sophistication in the attractive suburb of **Winter Park**. Orlando is also within easy reach of both the east and west Florida coasts: **Kennedy Space Center** (pages 192–3) is an hour's drive east; while the Gulf of Mexico, **Tampa** (pages 226–33) and **St Petersburg** (pages 216–19) lie 90 minutes west.

Citrus country stretches west and south of Orlando. Here, **Lake Wales** is renowned among the faithful for its simple, devout annual Passion Play, and there are two marvellous gardens near by: Bok Tower Gardens, and Cypress Gardens, which incorporates a distinctly kitsch theme park element, near Winter Haven. **Arcadia**, 65 miles (104km) west of Okeechobee City, is in the heart of cattle country. Façades straight out of a Western movie line the main drag, and there are wall-to-wall blue jeans and Stetsons during the All-Florida Championship Rodeo. A vital link in the Everglades ecosystem, expansive **Lake Okeechobee** has been dangerously tamed, but it is still a haven for birdwatchers and fishermen.

North of Orlando is **Ocala**, surrounded by lush countryside and thoroughbred stud farms.A fine art museum is on the edge of town, which is bordered by the vast expanses of Ocala National Forest. Rolling hills and ranches encircle historic **Gainesville**, a college town that has hardly been touched by tourism. Enthusiastic sports fans flock here to support the University of Florida football team, the mighty Gators.

Top: a heart-stopping Kongfrontation at Universal Studios in Orlando

REGION HIGHLIGHTS

▶ Arcadia

Take a detour off Route 70 for a look at this sleepy cattle town. Past the imposing **De Soto County Courthouse**, downtown **Oak Street** has been restored, and there are some lovely old houses beyond the shopping district. If you want to stock up on genuine cowboy outfits, such as Resistol and Stetson headgear, cowboy boots, belts and ladies' leather Annie-Get-Yer-Gun skirts, visit **Eli's Western Stores**, on Highway 70 East.

North on Route 17, **Peace River** is a shallow waterway where **Canoe Outpost** (tel: 941/494-1215) rents out water-sports equipment. On Route 72, just east of Sarasota, is **Myakka River State Park**. One of the state's largest parks, at 35,000 acres (14,165 ha), the wilderness preserve can be explored on foot, on horseback, by tram or by boat trips on the Myakka River as it flows through the park. Cottontail rabbits, deer, alligators and red-shouldered hawks all make their home in the varied terrain.

▶ Gainesville

Surrounded by cattle ranches, stud farms and Florida-style rolling hills, Gainesville is home to the University of Florida. On the attractive, tree-shaded university campus, the **Florida Museum of Natural History**, Hull Road at SW 34th Street (*Open* Mon–Sat 10–5, Sun 1–5. *Admission free*; tel: 352/846-2967) presents a 12-foot (3.5m) mammoth skeleton, together with bronze casts of a sabre-toothed tiger and giant upright sloth, as well as a full-scale Florida limestone cave exhibit. Well presented displays and interactive stations present visitors with a wide variety of Florida's ecological and cultural experiences.

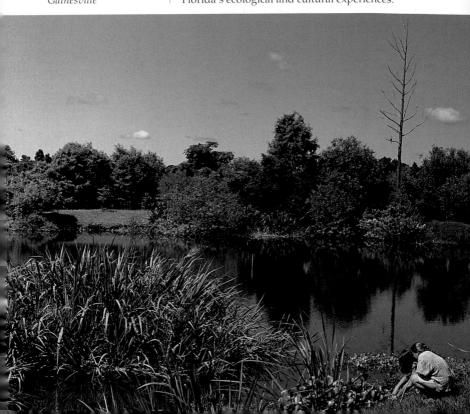

Lake Alice, near Gainesville

The neighbouring **Samuel P Harn Museum of Art** (*Open* Tue–Fri 11–5, Sat 10–5, Sun 1–5. *Admission free*; tel: 352/392-9826) is a dramatic campus feature with a fine semi-permanent collection of American, Oceanic, African and pre-Columbian art, plus contemporary works.

On the outskirts of town, the scenic and unusual **Devil's Millhopper State Geological Site**, 4732 Millhopper Road (*Open* daily 9–dusk. *Admission: inexpensive*; tel: 352/955-2008), is a 120-foot-deep (36m) sinkhole (caused by natural subsidence) festooned with lush plants and giant ferns, which are cooled by a dozen little waterfalls.

The lovely **Kanapaha Botanical Gardens**, 4700 SW 58th Drive, off Archer Road (*Open* Mon, Tue, Fri 9–5, Wed, Sat, Sun 9–dusk. *Admission: inexpensive*; tel: 352/372-4981), meander across a sloping 62-acre (25-ha) lakeside site where a profusion of azaleas and camellias blooms each spring. There are forest and desert areas, bamboo groves and a colourful hummingbird garden.

▶▶ Lake Wales

North of Lake Wales, it is worth making a short detour west to **Chalet Suzanne**, on ALT 27 (Cannery *Open* Mon–Fri 9–4; tel: 863/676-6011), a rambling country hotel-restaurant with craft shops and a home-made soup business. It is not just any old soup – this soup is so popular that it even accompanied the crew of *Apollo 15* to the moon in 1973.

A few miles south, do not miss beautiful **Bok Tower Gardens**, CR 17-A (*Open* daily 8–6. *Admission: moderate*; tel: 863/676-1408). Created by Dutch-born philanthropist Edward W Bok in the 1920s, these peaceful woodland gardens spread over the gentle slopes of Iron Mountain, the highest point on the Florida peninsula at a modest 298 feet (90m). Visitors are invited to explore the 157-acre (63-ha) spread on winding footpaths with spectacular views of the massed springtime blooms of azaleas, camellias, magnolias and ferns, shaded by slender palms, pines, and oaks. The centre-piece is a 205-foot (62m) pink and gray marble and coquina tower, boasting a 57-bell carillon which chimes every half hour from 10, with a full recital daily at 3. A programme of special events includes Moonlight Recitals and an International Carillon Festival (February). An additional highlight of a visit is **Pinewood House**, a romantic Mediterranean Revival villa built in 1931. Named for the splendid pine trees on the Great Lawn, the house is surrounded by landscaped gardens inspired by an eclectic combination of formal Italian-style plantings and a burgeoning English walled garden of the type perfected by doyenne of the English country house garden, Gertrude Jeckyll.

▶ Micanopy

Once named Wanton, but now as decorous as they come, this lovely little town offers a tantalising glimpse of Old Florida. Handsome Victorian homes and giant shady live oak trees line Cholokka Boulevard as it makes its way into the town centre, where the old red-brick shopfronts now harbour a selection of antiques and collectables dealers. The town was the first white settlement in Alachua County when it was founded on the site of a former Timuca Native American village in 1821, and the name Micanopy

CROSS CREEK

In 1928, New York author Marjorie Kinnan Rawlings moved to Cross Creek, a quiet rural community, where she bought a small homestead and settled down to learn about backwoods Cracker life. The fruits of her labours were a series of evocative novellas, including *The Yearling*, which won her a Pulitzer Prize. Her home, the Marjorie Kinnan Rawlings State Historic Site, lies 21 miles (33km) southeast of Gainesville on CR 325 (*Open* daily 9–5. Tours inexpensive; tel: 352/466-3672). It has been preserved just as she left it, with an ancient typewriter on the porch, rum by the fireplace and tinned food on the shelves.

was adopted in honour of a Native American chief. Many of the town's early residents were buried in the quiet, moss-carpeted cemetery off Seminary Avenue.

▶ Mount Dora

On the shores of Lake Dora, 20 miles (32km) northeast of Orlando, this picturesque small town was founded on a low rise overlooking the waterfront by Northern settlers in the 1870s. The oldest surviving building is the **Lakeside Inn**, dating from 1883, where President Calvin Coolidge once stayed, and there are many lovely old buildings. Mount Dora is also a favourite haunt of antiques collectors. The Chamber of Commerce, 341 Alexander Street, has walking maps of the restored downtown shopping and antiques district, and neighbouring Victorian mansions. One of the finest is the impressive 1893 Queen Anne-style **Donnelly House**, on Donnelly Street, a riot of fancy ironwork and gingerbread decoration, gables, balconies and steeply pitched roofs with a cupola.

Mount Dora was initially known as Royellou, a made-up name derived from the three children of the local postmaster, Roy, Ella, and Louis Tremain. Just off Fifth Avenue, Mount Dora's main street, the **Royellou Museum**, Royellou Lane (*Open* Thu–Sun 1–4. *Admission: inexpensive*; tel: 352/383-5228) displays local history exhibits in the old Town Fire Station.

Down on the shores of Lake Dora, there is boat and bicycle hire available in Gilbert Park, close to Grantham Point with its red and white-painted mini lighthouse. **Palm Island Park** has a nature trail and boardwalks for a close-up look at water birds and the occasional alligator or otter.

Mount Dora also prides itself on a busy calendar of events throughout the year which range from the February Art Festival through April's Sailing regatta to the charming Christmas Lighting when more than 100,000 tiny lights illuminate the downtown area.

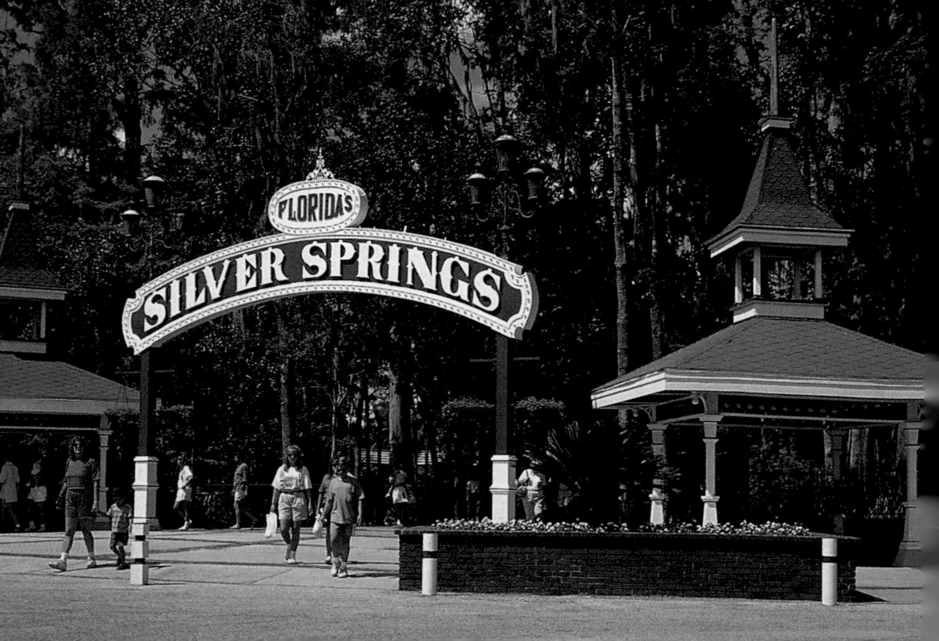

Silver Springs near Ocala has the largest group of artesian wells in the world

►► Ocala

Marion County's 600-plus thoroughbred horse farms are home to almost 58,000 horses. Every road to Ocala is lined with miles of white-painted railings and grassy paddocks, where a glossy equine fortune grazes peacefully in the shade of spreading live oaks. For information about local farm visits and the region's busy calendar of equestrian events, check with the Chamber of Commerce, 110 E. Silver Springs Boulevard (tel: 352/629-8051).

A popular family day out just east of town, **Silver Springs** can lay claim to being 'Florida's Original Attraction'. In 1878, local entrepreneur Hullum Jones launched an ingenious idea when he installed a glass viewing box in the flat bottom of a dugout canoe offering tourists a fish's-eye view of the head of the world's largest artesian spring formation. Glass-bottom boat rides with sightings of freshwater fish and turtles as well as ancient fossils remain a favourite pastime, and cruises explore the peaceful, tree-shaded Silver River. Other diversions include Jeep safaris in the backwoods with animal encounter opportunities such as the Panther Prowl, home to rare Florida panthers, and an alligator swamp, plus a variety of animal shows and demonstrations and a summer season weekend concert programme. The wave pool and water flumes of the adjacent **Wild Waters** family water park prove particularly inviting on a hot day.

On a completely different tack, **Don Garlits' Automotive Attractions**, 13700 SW 16th Avenue (*Open* daily 9–5. *Admission: moderate*; tel: 352/245-8661) feature mean drag racing machines and classic cars.

On the cultural front, the **Appleton Museum of Art**, 4333 E Silver Springs Boulevard (7 miles/11km east of I–75. *Open* Tue–Sat 10–4:30, Sun 1–5. *Admission: inexpensive*; tel: 352/236-7100), is a most unusual regional art museum. The stunning Italian travertine marble museum building houses exhibits from Ancient Greek and Etruscan pottery to African ceremonial masks, intricate Japanese ivories, Chinese jade and Tiffany lamps.

Stretching east from Ocala to the St Johns River, the **Ocala National Forest** is a giant woodland playground for hikers, birders, fishermen and canoeists. In addition to a terrific choice of walking trails and short boardwalk excursions, there are lakes and streams with excellent bass fishing, sailing and watersports opportunities; the canoe trails are among the best in the state.

► Okeechobee

Right down at the southern edge of the central region, **Lake Okeechobee** is the second largest expanse of fresh water in the United States, covering an area of 750 square miles (1,940sq km). It is possible to drive around the entire lake, with stops on the eastern side at **Port Mayaca** and at **Pahokee State Recreation Area** for picnicking, camping and boat hire. The lake is popular with birdwatchers and with fishermen on the trail of largemouth bass, which can be seen (stuffed) on many a wall. The southern end of the lake is sugar country, where the vast **Belle Glade mill** produces some 2,000 tons of raw sugar daily. **Clewiston** is a sugar town with a sideline in cabbage palms. Along the northwest lakeshore, the road traverses **Brighton Seminole Indian Reservation**.

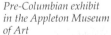

Pre-Columbian exhibit in the Appleton Museum of Art

PLANE SPOTTING
Aviation buffs will enjoy a couple of attractions close to Orlando. Fantasy of Flight, SR 559, Polk City (I–4; Exit 21), showcases wartime fighter planes and vintage classics (*Open* daily 9–5. *Admission: moderate*; tel: 863/984-3500). The Flying Tigers Warbird Restoration Museum, 231 Hoagland Boulevard, Kissimmee, features aircraft and memorabilia from World War II and the Korean War (*Open* Mon–Sat 9–5:30, Sun 9–5. *Admission: moderate*; tel: 407/933-1942).

ORLANDO Orlando, the land of theme parks, also offers a number of other attractions, from historical and science museums to botanical gardens, water parks and themed restaurants. Take time out for a stroll by lovely downtown **Lake Eola** with its remarkable fountain or a boat trip on Kissimmee's Lake Tohopekaliga, renowned for its birdlife (see page 116). There is accommodation to suit every pocket; look out for especially good deals in the Kissimmee area.

Orlando's International Drive Resort Area (off I–4) is the main tourism, shopping, and transportation hub. There is a helpful Visitor Information Center at the Gala Center, 8723 International Drive at Austrian Row (*Open* daily 8–7; tel: 407/363-5872), which sells discounted admission tickets to many local attractions and theme parks. A handy trolley service, the **I-Ride**, operates shuttles the length of International Drive (I-Drive) between SeaWorld in the south and the Belz Factory outlet mall (every 5–10 minutes, daily 7am–midnight).

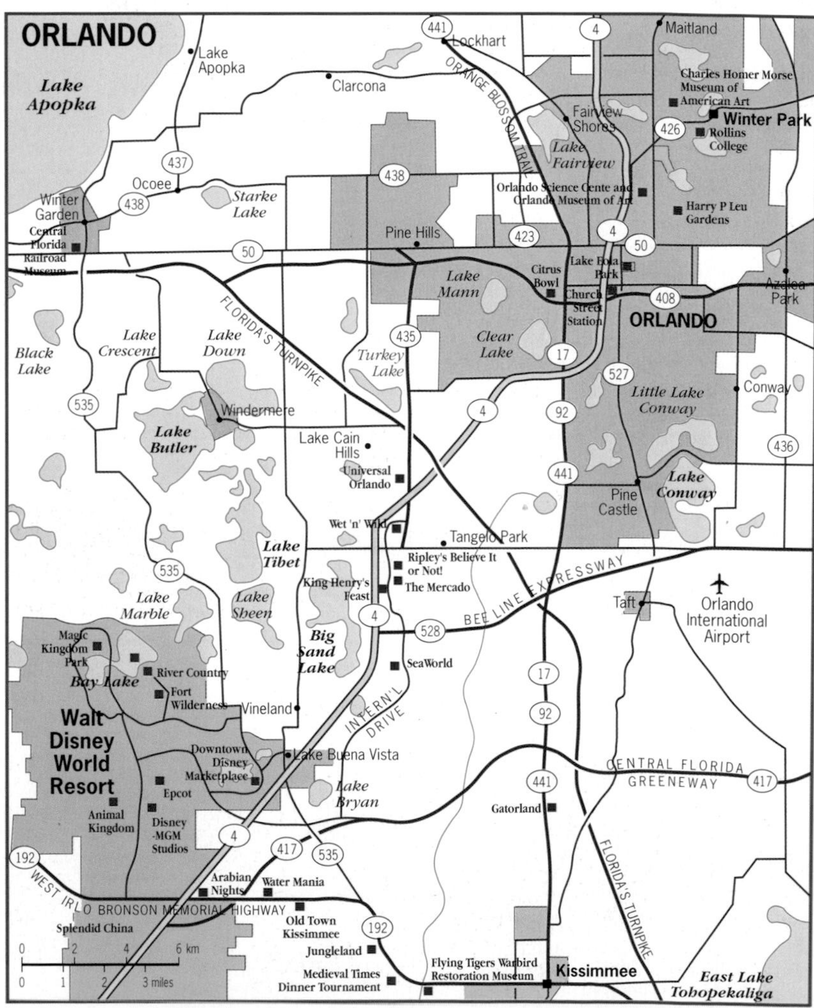

►► Church Street Station Complex

129 W Church Street (I-4/Exit 36); tel: 407/422-2434
Open: Sun–Thu 11am–1am, Fri–Sat 11am–2am, live shows from 7:15pm. Admission free until 5pm, then expensive, but admission covers all shows

Centre-piece of the rejuvenated downtown Orlando historic district, the Church Street Station Complex offers a complete shopping, dining and entertainment complex. It includes a Victorian-style shopping mall, themed restaurants, a food court, showrooms featuring a Dixieland jazz revue, country music and rock 'n roll classics, as well as a discothèque. In addition there are daytime Historical Tours (daily 11–3) and horse-and-carriage rides.

►► Gatorland

14501 S Orange Blossom Trail (US 441); tel: 407/855-5496
Open: daily 8–dusk. Admission: expensive

Just north of Kissimmee, a monster alligator jaw marks the entrance to 55 acres (22 ha) of pens and pools teeming with alligators and a breeding marsh area which can be observed safely from a raised boardwalk. There are daily alligator shows in the 'Wrestlin' Stadium'. Other attractions include Florida crocodiles and caimans, a selection of venomous snakes, and native snapping and soft-shelled turtles.

►► Harry P Leu Gardens

1920 N Forest Avenue; tel: 407/246-2620
Open: daily 9–5. Admission: inexpensive

Fifty-six acres (22ha) of lush gardens in the heart of Orlando are just the place for a quiet stroll. Take time to explore the camellia and azalea woods, the ornamental flowering-tree garden, sweet-scented Mary Jane's Rose Garden and the native wetland garden down by Lake Rowena. The floral clock is a popular attraction, as is the Orchid Conservatory, and there are tours of **Leu House**, a carefully restored turn-of-the-20th-century farmhouse. The gardens are also a popular venue for weddings.

Eat, shop and be entertained at Orlando's Church Street Station complex

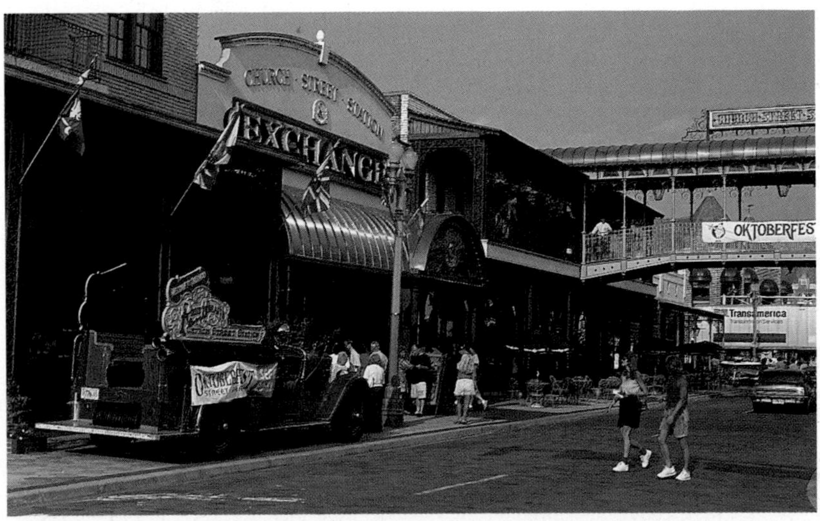

Scaly resident at Gatorland

LOCH HAVEN PARK MUSEUMS
Loch Haven Park is also home to the Orlando Museum of Art (*Open* Tue–Sat 9–5, Sun noon–5. *Admission: inexpensive*; tel: 407/896-4231), containing notable collections of pre-Columbian art and works by leading 19th- and 20th-century American artists.

RIPLEY'S BELIEVE IT OR NOT! MUSEUM
From the strange to the bizzare to the barely credible, exhibits at this museum-cum-freak-show set out to lift the lid on some of life's little oddities. Amongst the interactive exhibits, holograms, and illusion, this is the place to find authentic shrunken heads, chunks of the Berlin Wall and video nasties of truly revolting feats of human endurance. Kids love it.
8201 International Drive; tel: 407/351-5803
Open: daily 9am–1am. Admission: expensive.

▶ Kissimmee

Kissimmee is a popular vacation base south of Orlando and a few minutes from Walt Disney World. The centre of town, **Broadway**, still has historic shopfronts and there are cattle auctions at the Livestock Market on Wednesdays. Down by Lake Tohopekaliga (better known as Lake Toho), boats and fishing tackle can be hired from **Lake Toho Marina**, 101 Lakeshore Boulevard, and **Aquatic Wonders Boat Tours** depart for 2-hour nature safaris and bass fishing trips (tel: 407/846-2814).

Between I–4 and the town centre, US 192 is known as Irlo Bronson Memorial Highway. To help visitors find their way around, there are numbered guide markers (#) set approximately a mile apart: the 'Tourist Trap Trail'. Heading east from I–4, the landmark waterslides of **Water Mania**, 6073 W Irlo Bronson (#8. *Admission: expensive*; tel: 407/396-2626) are easy to spot. **Old Town, Kissimmee**, 5770 W Irlo Bronson (#9), is a period-style mall with shops, eateries and vintage Ferris wheel. **Jungleland Zoo**, 4580 W Irlo Bronson (#14. *Open* daily 9–6. *Admission: expensive*; tel: 407/396-1012), features big cats, exotic birds and monkeys alongside the obligatory gators. **Green Meadows Petting Farm**, 1368 S Poinciana Boulevard (*Open* daily 9:30–5:30. *Admission: expensive*; tel: 407/846-0770), offers hayrides, 200 farm animals, pony rides and cow-milking lessons, and is a big hit with small children. West of I–4, **Splendid China**, 3000 Splendid China Boulevard (#4. *Open* daily 9:30–7. *Admission: expensive*; tel: 407/396-7111), has 60 superbly detailed scale models of China's best-known scenic, cultural, and historic sites.

▶▶ Orlando Science Center

777 E. Princeton Street, Loch Haven Park (I–4/Exit 43); tel: 407/514-2000
Open: Tue–Thu (and school holiday Mon) 9–5, Fri and Sat 9–9, Sun noon–5. Admission: moderate

This impressive complex is crowned by an observatory and anchored by the CineDome, an eight-storey domed cinema designed to showcase large-format films, planetarium presentations and 3-D laser light shows. The complex has plenty of hands-on exhibits, plus live science demonstrations, such as Bodyworks.

►►► SeaWorld® Orlando

7007 SeaWorld Drive; tel: 407/363-2200
Open: daily 9–7, extended in summer. Admission: expensive
This is one of the world's largest and most popular marine-life parks. It is huge – 200 acres (80ha) in all, divided among a variety of different features, including marine stadiums, lagoons, aquariums, botanical gardens, restaurants and cafés – and it deserves a whole day. There are a couple of rides, but most of the attractions are walk-by viewing areas or shows, so queues are rare.

The park is laid out around a central lagoon, used for daytime waterskiing and aquabatic displays and the night-time laser and firework shows. Favourite stops include **The Shamu Adventure** killer whale show; the wacky Clyde and Seamore Take Pirate Island performance in the **Sea Lion and Otter Stadium**; and the rocky shores of **Pacific Point Preserve**, a naturalistic setting for California sea lions and seals. The **Wild Arctic** polar experience and the **Penguin Encounter** deliberately manufacture freezing conditions in order to provide a suitable habitat for their inmates, which include polar bears, beluga whales and penguins. **Manatees: The Last Generation?** investigates the plight of Florida's endangered sea cows; and **Terrors of the Deep** provides a scary cast of barracudas, sharks and razor-toothed moray eels which can be viewed from a plexiglass tunnel through the shark tank.

SeaWorld is also home to the **Kraken**, a mega sea serpent-design roller coaster. The park's other thrill ride is **Journey to Atlantis**, which takes visitors on a trip to the lost world, combining high-speed water ride and roller coaster elements with state-of-the-art special effects.

►► Wet 'n Wild

6200 International Drive
Open: daily from 9 in summer (10 in winter). Call for schedules, tel: 407/351-1800 or 800/992-9453. Admission: expensive
One of the liveliest areas here is the **Kids' Park** water playground, which gives younger visitors their turn on scaled-down versions of adult rides such as **Mach 5**: The 'grown-ups' version features 2,500 (760m) feet of twists and turns. Nerves of steel are required for the **Bomb Bay**, a near free-fall drop down to a 76-foot (23m) slide; multi-passenger rides include the interactive **Hydra Fighter**; and check out the **Fuji Flyer** speed toboggan adventure. Or cram into the **Bubba Tub** for a giant inner-tube ride.

►► WonderWorks

*Pointe*Orlando, 9067 International Drive; tel: 407/351-8800*
Open: daily 10am–11pm (extended on holidays)
Admission: expensive
It is hard to miss this eye-catching attraction that seems to be disappearing upside down into a Florida sinkhole. Once inside, things are none too straightforward either, with dozens of interactive games, virtual reality experiences and earthquake and hurricane simulators. One particularly apt diversion is the design-your-own roller coaster exhibit which you then get to 'ride'.

SHOP TILL YOU DROP
Around South Orlando's International Drive there are some amazing bargains to be had. An attraction in its own right, Belz Factory Outlet, 5401 W Oakridge Road, houses 170 outlet stores selling discounted fashions, electronics, books and toiletries. This is the place to pick up Disney character T-shirts at prices around *three-quarters* less than in official Disney shops. Traditional malls include The Mercado, 8445 International Drive, and Pointe*Orlando at 9101 International Drive; the 250-store Florida Mall, 8001 S Orange Blossom Trail; and the Orlando Fashion Square Mall, 3201 E Colonial Drive.

DISCOVERY COVE
Interactive marine adventures are the speciality of SeaWorld's sister park, *Discovery Cove, 6000 Discovery Cove Way* (tel: 407/370-1280 or 877/4-DISCOVERY). Admission is limited to 1,000 guests per day by advance reservation only and covers a whole day of water-based activities, plus lunch. Chief thrill is the Dolphin Lagoon, where guests can swim with Atlantic bottlenose dolphins. There is the Tropical River waterway which meanders past a sandy beach area and an underwater cave to an aviary housing exotic birds from around the world, swimming and snorkelling in the Coral Reef pool, and stingray encounters in the Ray Lagoon.

CITYWALK
Universal's 30-acre (12-ha) shopping, dining and entertainment complex offers something for everyone. Speciality shops run the gamut from fossils, cigars, sportswear and silver jewellery to Glow!, a store selling things that, well, glow. There is a Hard Rock Café and Hard Rock Live Orlando, a 2,200-capacity performance venue, plus jazz, reggae and Motown spots. Or you can chill out Keys-style at Jimmy Buffett's Margaritaville. Racing fans can dine out amid motor memorabilia at the NASCAR Café; Pat O'Brien's re-creates the legendary New Orleans watering hole, complete with dueling pianos; and the Universal Cineplex has 20 screens showing the latest box-office hits.

CityJazz, Universal Studios CityWalk

►►► Universal Studios Orlando

1000 Universal Studios Plaza (I-4/Exit 29 or 30-B); tel: 407/363-8000 or 1-888-U-ESCAPE
Open: daily, check schedules. Admission: expensive. One-day one-park ticket, or both parks with a 2- or 3-Day Escape Pass
The umbrella title for Universal's Florida theme park and resort complex, Universal Studios Orlando now covers the original **Universal Studios** park (see below), the **Islands of Adventure** park (see pages 120–1) opened in 1999, **CityWalk** (see panel), and a growing portfolio of on-site hotels. Though Disney has the higher profile, Universal is a clear winner in the eyes of many visitors to Orlando. Both the Universal parks are strong on rides and ideally suited to teen and adult visitors in search of serious thrills and fun.

UNIVERSAL STUDIOS FLORIDA
A movie-oriented theme park grafted on to working film and television production studios, Universal Studios invites guests to 'ride the movies' on a 444-acre (180-ha) site divided into six themed districts, covering the Deco and palm trees of Hollywood, to Fisherman's Wharf meets New England San Francisco/Amity.

Hollywood Heading up the clutch of popular diversions in the Hollywood section is the absolutely unmissable **Terminator 2:3-D Battle Across Time™**, a $24-million 3-D adventure scenario that reunites the original *Terminator 2* team in an electrifying combination of new film footage, special effects and live action. The **Gory, Gruesome & Grotesque Horror Make-Up Show** reprises revolting oozy bits from favourite movie monsters. On a brighter note, **Lucy: A Tribute℠** presents memorabilia from the life and works of that zany redhead, Lucille Ball.

New York This is just the place for a **Kongfrontation®** with one mean 35-foot-high (10m), 13,000-pound (5,900kg) ape who smashes up Manhattan while passengers in an aerial tram lurch past exploding fireballs, flying debris and old banana-breath's giant paws. Derived from a cinema favourite of the 1990s, **TWISTER®...Ride It Out®** re-creates the power of a five-storey-high cyclone; while **The Blues Brothers** show brings back Jake and Elwood to perform a selection of their hottest hits.

Production Central Stop off here for high jinks with the cartoon characters of **The Funtastic World of Hanna-Barbera™**. This entertaining but bumpy simulator ride rattles through Stone Age Bedrock and Scooby Doo's haunted mansion on the trail of Dick Dastardly and Muttley as they attempt to kidnap little Elroy Jetson. Check out the latest show schedule at **Stage 54**, where *The Flintstones in Viva Rock Vegas* may still be in town; while **Alfred Hitchcock: The Art of Making Movies** offers a 40-minute celluloid encounter with the master of suspense himself. Guests touring **Nickelodeon Studios®**, production centre of the popular children's TV network, get to test out new games, visit the Gak Kitchen to learn about slime production, and may be able to attend the recording of a show.

San Francisco/Amity You can ride a San Francisco subway train into **Earthquake®: The Big One** and experience fire, flood and crashing masonry in an earthquake experience that rates 8.3 on the Richter Scale. A gentle sightseeing cruise with Amity Boat Tours turns into something altogether snappier with an appearance by that notorious 32-foot (10m) mechanical white shark in the corny, but enduringly popular, **JAWS®** ride. And there are two rollicking shows near by in **Beetlejuice's Rock 'n Roll Graveyard Revue™**, and action-packed **The Wild, Wild, Wild West Stunt Show℠**.

Woody Woodpecker's Kidzone A special area dedicated to scaled-down rides, shows and games for young children (see panel).

World Expo Here you'll find two great thrill rides, one a Universal classic and the other the new kid on the block. First up is **Back To The Future The Ride®**, a four-minute, 21-jigowatt blast in Doc Brown's back-up DeLorean, rescuing civilisation as we know it from the awful Biff. Unveiled in 1993, this remains one of the most ambitious theme-park rides ever created. Universal's latest thriller is the interactive **MEN IN BLACK™ Alien Attack™**, where guests fight it out with alien invaders through the streets of New York in an all-out battle for the security of the planet. Also in the area is **E.T. Adventure®**. Adventures probably don't get much tamer than this cute 'flying bicycle' ride complete with an E.T. in a basket on every handlebar, but it's great entertainment.

KIDS' STUFF

Families with young children may need to make several forays to Woody Woodpecker's KidZone℠. Here tots can sing along with the purple dinosaur in A Day In the Park With Barney™, follow in the footsteps of a cheeky monkey in the Curious George Goes To Town℠ water-based interactive play area (bring dry clothes), explore Fievel's Playland® and take a ride on Woody Woodpecker's Nuthouse Coaster℠. For a well-needed time-out, take a break at the Animal Actors Stage®, where trained dogs, chimps and birds show off their tricks in an excellent live performance.

Cyborg from Terminator 2:3-D

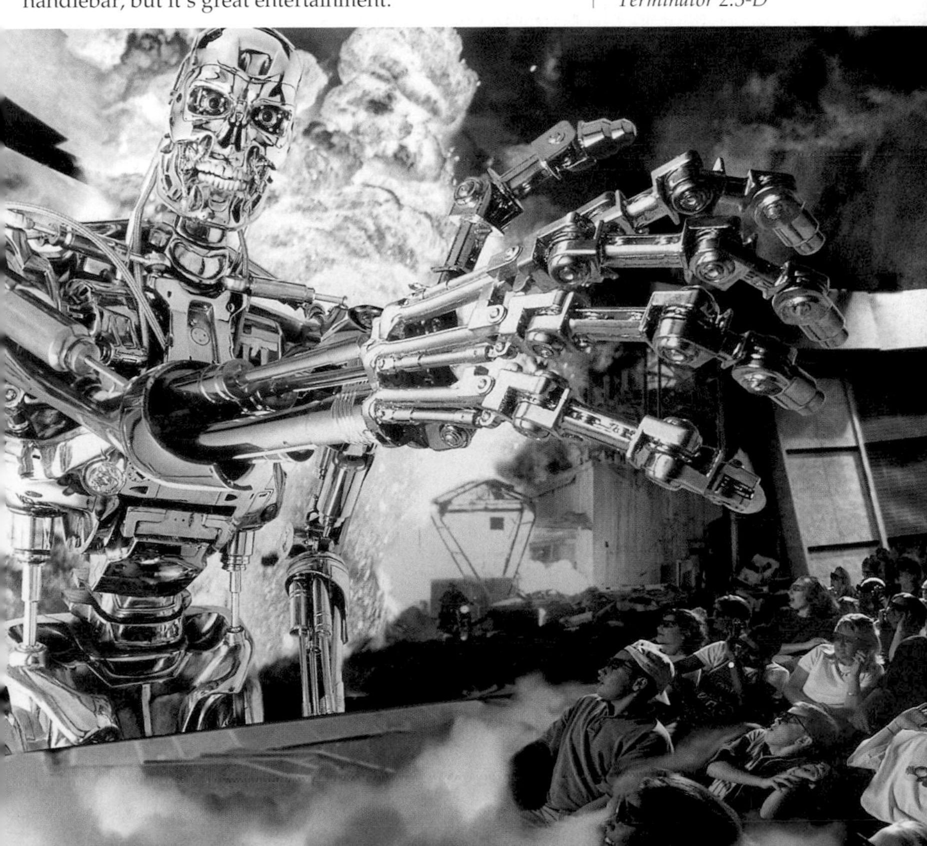

AMAZING ROBOTICS
Inspired by Steven Spielberg's *Jurassic Park* – to date one of the most successful films of all time – the special effects wizards at Universal have employed state-of-the-art technology to create the amazing robotic creatures featured in the various Jurassic Park district attractions. As well as incredibly realistic and fluid movements, the creatures' lifelike responses include blinks, muscle flinches and, in the case of the lurking Spitters, some pretty accurate spitting at passing guests.

Face to face with a T-Rex at the Jurassic Park River Adventure℠

UNIVERSAL STUDIOS ISLANDS OF ADVENTURE
A larger-than-life, primary-coloured cartoon world straight out of the comics (and blockbuster movie *Jurassic Park*), Islands of Adventure is hailed as the world's most technologically advanced theme park. There is an additional feather in the park's elaborate and distinctly wacky cap, too: it boasts producer/director Steven Spielberg as its creative consultant. Like its sister park, Universal Studios Orlando, Islands of Adventure is arranged into themed 'islands' around a central lagoon, known as the Inland Sea. Guests arrive in the souk-like Port of Entry and travel from island to island via boats or footbridges.

Jurassic Park® The **Jurassic Park River Adventure℠** is the big one here and one of the top rides in the park. A raft trip through lush dinosaur habitats harbouring remarkably lifelike robotic creatures (see panel) goes dramatically wrong when the T-Rex gets loose, and there is an 85-foot (25m) plunge down a long, fast, steep water descent. Back on *terra firma*, **Triceratops Encounter℠** allows guests to get a close look at a 'live' 10-foot-high (3m) 'animatronic' Triceratops undergoing its bi-annual check-up with a Jurassic Park vet; the interactive **Jurassic Park Discovery Center℠** encourages guests to scan a dinosaur egg, create their own dinosaur and watch a 'real' raptor hatching in the shadow of a skeletal T-Rex. Head for the **Camp Jurassic℠** adventure play area for more dino encounters and the chance to ride the **Pteranodon Flyers®** aerial runway.

Lost Continent™ A fantasy lost world combining elements of medieval dungeons-and-dragons sorcery, the Holy Land crusades and Ancient Greece, the Lost Continent's entertaining offerings are equally eclectic. Roller coaster fans should join the queues for **Dueling Dragons®** (see panel opposite), while children can enjoy the scaled-down **Flying Unicorn℠** coaster as it speeds through a mystical forest scenario. The entrance to **Poseidon's Fury: Escape From the Lost City℠** is marked by the crumbling ruins of the sea god's statue before a chilly walk-through adventure to Atlantis. Visitors pass through a whirling 17,500-gallon (79,550-litre) water tunnel for a fiery encounter between Poseidon and Zeus. There are plenty more fire and water effects, plus great stunts in the action-packed **The Eighth Voyage of Sindbad℠** show.

Marvel Super Hero Island™ Laid out beneath the landmark green aerial spaghetti of the **Incredible Hulk Coaster℠** (see panel), join the ranks of comic strip super heroes in experiencing the three other mega rides grouped here. A tour of the *Daily Bugle* offices leads into **The Amazing Adventures of Spider-Man℠** and an epic combination of rides, 3-D film action and special effects as the goodies battle the baddies for control of the Statue of Liberty. Meanwhile, the twin towers of **Doctor Doom's Fearfall®** set the scene for a rocketing 200-foot (60m) trip to the top and back down at terrific speeds. By comparison, **Storm Force℠**, an indoor attraction starring super heroine Storm in a thunderous special effects spectacular, is a walk in the park.

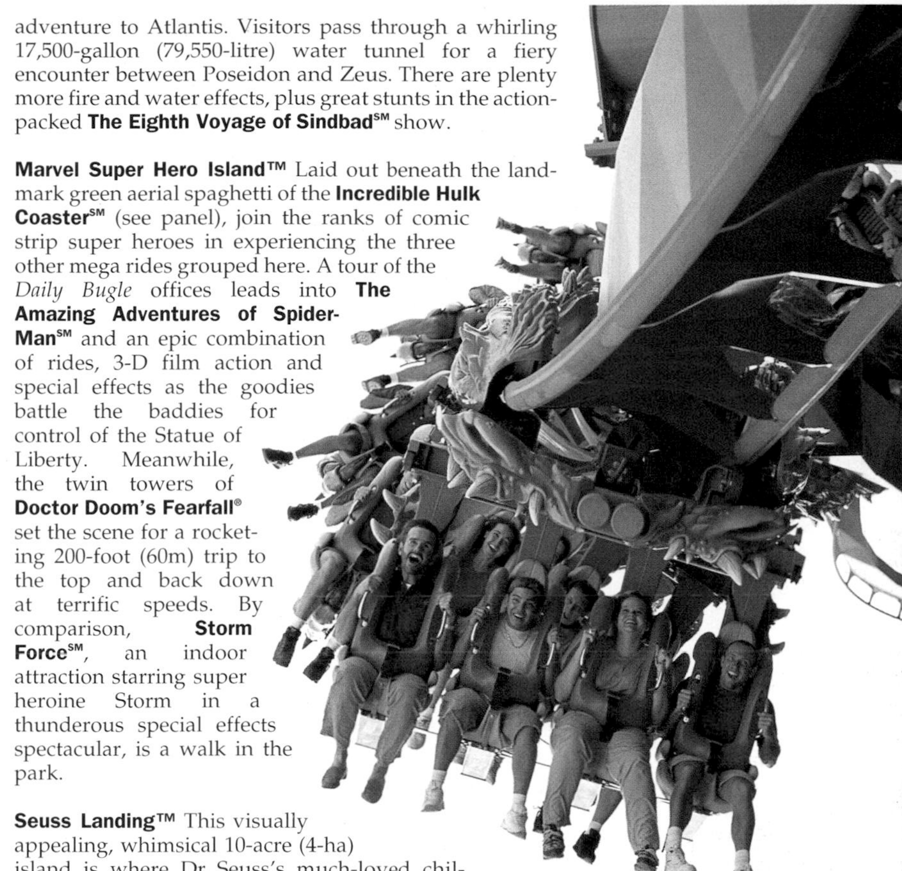

Dueling Dragons

Seuss Landing™ This visually appealing, whimsical 10-acre (4-ha) island is where Dr Seuss's much-loved children's book characters are brought to life. The elaborate **Caro-Seuss-el™** sports 54 colourful character mounts with state-of-the-art interactive animation features, while the gently entertaining **One Fish Two Fish Red Fish Blue Fish™** ride features Seussian-style, two-passenger fish that must be guided along to a special tune to avoid a soaking from 'squirt posts' dotted about the course. Kids can let off steam in the **If I Ran The Zoo™** interactive playland, where Toe Tickle stations allow junior guests to tickle the toes of giggling Seussian creatures; and don't miss a journey on a moving sofa through the classic tale of **The Cat In the Hat™** as Thing 1 and Thing 2 wreak havoc when they come to play while Mum's away.

Toon Lagoon™ First take a stroll down **Comic Strip Lane**, with its giant cartoon cut-outs, then hop aboard **Popeye & Bluto's Bilge-Rat Barges℠** for a white-water raft ride (and a guaranteed soaking) which includes a kitschy-horror encounter with an 18-foot-tall (5.5m) octopus brandishing 12-foot-long (3.5m) tentacles. **Me Ship, The Olive℠** is a family-friendly interactive play area set on board Popeye's three-story boat. And in **Dudley Do-Right's Ripsaw Falls℠**, a rip-roaring log flume ride follows the 1960s Canadian Mountie character on a wet and wild rescue attempt to save his gal.

COASTING TO NEW HEIGHTS

At Islands of Adventure, Universal has raised the highly competitive world of roller coaster design to new heights. Dueling Dragons offers two entirely different rides (Fire and Ice) over intertwined tracks which appear to be on a collision course; riders are slammed through a camelback, double helix and compound inversion. The Incredible Hulk Coaster blasts riders from zero to 40mph (64kph) in two seconds, with the same thrust as a US Air Force F-16 fighter jet, and follows up with a weightless, zero-G heartline inversion, seven roll-overs and two plunges into subterranean enclosures.

SAVE TIME WITH A FASTPASS
Save time waiting for the most popular rides in all four Disney theme parks with a FASTPASS. Pop your regular park ticket into the FASTPASS machine at the rides offering this complimentary service and you will receive a designated ride time with no need to queue up. The FASTPASS allows a one-hour window from the time printed on the ticket. At the allotted time, just present yourself at the FASTPASS entrance with your ticket and sail straight through. Each member of a party must get his or her ticket authorised by the FASTPASS machine, and you can only have one FASTPASS running at any one time, ie you must have used (or exceeded the time allocation for) one FASTPASS before you can collect another.

▶▶▶ Walt Disney World Resort

It is another world – there's no doubt about it. The Walt Disney World Resort is vast and completely self-contained: a 30,500-acre (12,340-ha) site housing four major theme parks, three water parks, 27 resorts, lakeside beaches, shopping, nightlife and entertainment areas, and enough good times to last a lifetime. Mickey Mouse is out to play, and the whole world (so it seems in peak season) has followed suit. Young and old can happily exchange the everyday for the pure fantasy of **Magic Kingdom**, the futuristic vision and international flavours of **Epcot**, a sprinkling of stardust in the Tinseltown setting of **Disney-MGM Studios**, and the wildlife and exotic landscapes of **Disney's Animal Kingdom**.

Admission Daily One Day/One Park admission tickets are valid for one park only on the stated day. For longer-stay guests, multi-day tickets offer greater flexibility.

The **5-Day Park Hopper Plus Pass** covers a) unlimited admission to any combination of major theme parks for the duration of the ticket, b) use of the WDW Resort transport system and c) a choice of two entries to Disney's water parks, Pleasure Island, or standard admission to Disney's Wide World of Sports Complex.

The **7-Day Park Hopper Plus Pass** covers all of the above, but a choice of four entries under category c). Unused days never expire and can be used on a future visit.

WDW Resort guests can purchase the **Disney Unlimited Magic Pass with Flex Feature**, which provides admission to all Disney's theme parks, water parks and entertainment zones for the duration of their stay.

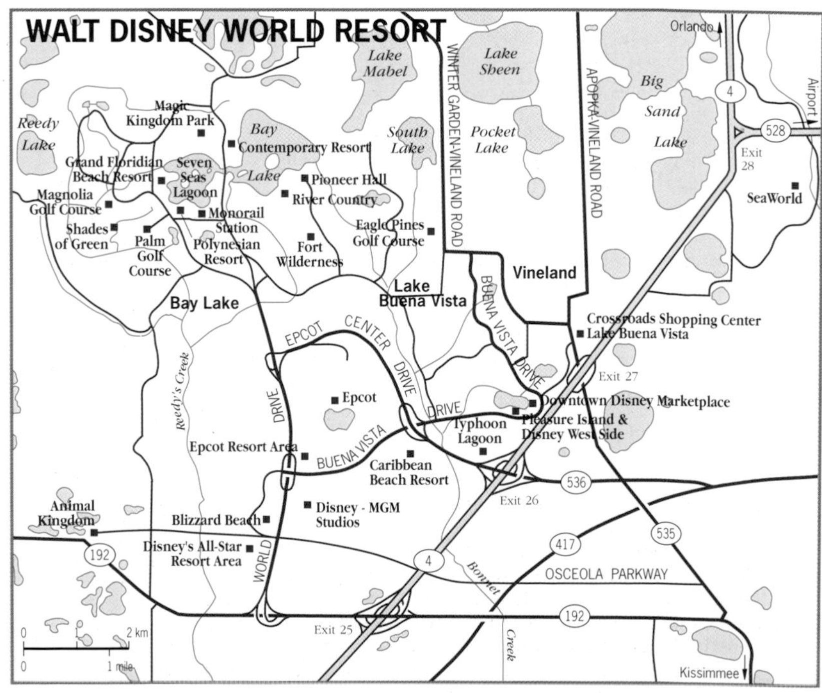

Tracking down Africa's wildlife with Kilimanjaro Safaris

Information and reservations For general information in advance, request an informative *Vacation Guide* from Walt Disney World Guest Information, Box 1000, Lake Buena Vista, FL 32830-1000 (tel: 407/824-4321). Hotel, campground, show and ticket reservations can be made through Central Reservations (tel: 407/W-DISNEY). Dinner reservations can be made up to 60 days in advance (tel: 407/939-3463).

When to go If you want to avoid WDW Resort's busiest periods, the best times to visit are from September to early November, on either side of the Easter holiday peak period, and from the Easter peak until early June. If you visit during holiday periods, expect big crowds and long waiting times in all the theme parks.

DISNEY'S ANIMAL KINGDOM

Disney's latest theme park showcases more than 200 animal species in magnificently re-created naturalistic habitats, and combines its zoological role with a strong eco-educational message. From **The Oasis** entry point, the park is laid out in five themed districts linked by bridges to the central Safari Village.

Africa In the African-inspired Harambe Village even the ice-creams come with an imprint of Simba's paw, and this is the start point for some serious wildlife spotting with **Kilimanjaro Safaris**. This safari lorry journey through the African veldt reveals lions, giraffes, wildebeest, rhinos and more. Along the leafy **Pangani Forest Exploration Trail** there is a close-up look at hippos and meerkats, and a wonderfully lush and misty gorilla habitat. The **Wildlife Express to Conservation Station** is a train ride around the 'backlot', where the animals take a break from their public duties. At **Conservation Station** itself, peek into the veterinary suite and hatchery and learn how the conservation battle continues on behalf of endangered creatures from Siberian tigers to bluefin tuna.

Asia An imaginatively re-created rain forest is the setting for this attractive rural village scenario, complete with rickshaws and ornately hand-painted and decorated Indian lorries. The **Maharajah Jungle Trek** takes visitors on a stroll around 'ancient' temple ruins, past a bat colony, tapirs and tigers and through aviaries where the heliconias, hibiscus and flowering orchid trees are as gorgeous as the birds. If it is time to cool down, head for

PARK TIPS I

- It really does pay to make an early start at Disney's Animal Kingdom, as the animals are more active in the cooler part of the day.
- A character breakfast buffet with Mickey Mouse, Goofy, Pluto and Donald Duck is served daily at Donald's Breakfastosaurus in DinoLand USA.
- Make use of the FAST-PASS system (see panel, page 122) for Kilimanjaro Safaris, Kali River Rapids and DINOSAUR.
- Information on behind-the-scenes educational programmes is available from Guest Relations in The Oasis (or tel: 407/WDW-TOUR).

CAMP DISNEY
Camp Disney offers a variety of half-day, youth-oriented activities (tel: 407/827-4800). In the 7–10 age group, there is a Critter Trek in the wilderness areas of the Walt Disney World Resort, while Broadway Bound features a dance audition experience, singing, costumes, make-up and a trip to a Disney production to watch the various elements brought together in a live show. For 11–15s, Animation Magic explores the animation process and The Magic Behind The Show goes backstage to meet cast members in Magic Kingdom.

the white-water rafting thrills of **Kali River Rapids**, and thunder down the Chakranadi River past bamboo tunnels, giant boulders and pumping water jets. Or take the weight off your feet at the **Flights of Wonder** bird show, where trained birds of prey display their incredible prowess overhead.

Camp Minnie-Mickey This Frontier-style stockade is great for small children, with character-greeting areas inhabited by the likes of Mickey, Minnie and Goofy, and characters from *The Lion King* and *The Jungle Book*, plus a couple of shows. **Pocahontas and Her Forest Friends** is aimed firmly at junior visitors, with plenty of cute animals included in the show. There is something for everyone at **Festival of The Lion King**, a high-energy song, dance and acrobatic spectacular featuring specialist acts such as fire-jugglers and stilt-walkers.

DinoLand USA A large *Brachiosaurus* skeleton, known as the Oldengate Bridge, spans the entrance to DinoLand USA, where things get distinctly prehistoric. **DINOSAUR** is the big ride here, travelling back in time for a last look at the dinosaur era before the meteorites strike. The audience's mission is to bring back a live dinosaur and there are all sorts of thrills, spills and meteorite showers along the way, from 'animatronic' dino thrills to the real thing, as genuine paleontologists demonstrate their work with dinosaur remains and answer questions in the **Fossil Preparation Lab**. The hangar-like exhibition space of **Dinosaur Jubilee** is used to display towering casts of dinosaur skeletons, fossilised dino eggs, claws and even coprolites (that's dung to the uninitiated). Kids can clamber, slither and crawl around the jumble of boulders and bones that make up **The Boneyard** playground; and **Tarzan Rocks!** unites Tarzan, Jane, Terk and a cast of jungle gymnasts in a high-energy acrobatic rock show.

Safari Village The hub of Disney's Animal Kingdom complex, Safari Village's centre-piece is **The Tree of Life**, a 145-foot-tall (44m) symbol for the park, adorned with 325

Festival of The Lion King, Camp Minnie-Mickey

animals carved into its twisting branches, roots and giant trunk. **Safari Village Trails** meander around the giant tree past enclosures housing lemurs and capybaras. Another gentle trail with close-up views of animal carvings and tropical plantings leads into the tree's root system and a theatre where Pik and Hopper from the movie *A Bug's Life* return to star in **It's Tough to be a Bug!**, an entertaining (and frequently surprising) 3-D insect's-eye view of the world. Not recommended for anybody, particularly small children, with a fear of creepy-crawlies.

DINING TIPS
A favourite stop for a quick lunch in Future World is the Sunshine Season Food Fair, a food court in The Land pavilion.

DISNEY-MGM STUDIOS

From the tips of the Mickey Mouse ears perched on the water tower to the shops and eateries of Hollywood Boulevard, Disney-MGM Studios celebrates the movies. Guest Relations, on Hollywood Boulevard, provides a dining reservations service.

Backlot Tour This ride is a must, but try to get here first thing in the morning or later in the afternoon. Before boarding the backlot tram, there is a visit to the splash tank and an opportunity to discover how special effects are created for movies with images of the sea. Then sit back for the ride through the wardrobe, props and special effects departments, and a side trip to Catastrophe Canyon to witness special effects in action (passengers on the left may get wet).

Backstage Pass A walk-through tour that kicks off with an introduction to animatronic animals, from cute puppies to incredibly realistic sheep used in the movie *101 Dalmatians*. Volunteers help illustrate 'bluescreen' editing techniques, which mix live action with previously filmed footage. Guests then continue past Production Sound Stages containing sets from recent and current film and TV productions. The tour winds up in a storeroom packed with costumes, props and detailed designers' sketches and models for *101 Dalmatians*.

The Great Movie Ride Housed in a full-scale replica of Mann's Chinese Theater in Hollywood, Audio-Animatronics figures do their best to re-create great moments from film classics, such as Gene Kelly getting drenched in *Singin' in the Rain* and Bogie and Bergman in *Casablanca*. Though there's commendable attention to detail, this is a disappointing ride.

Jim Henson's Muppet*Vision 3D Kermit, Miss Piggy, Fozzie Bear, Gonzo and the Electric Mayhem Band strut their stuff with the help of sensational special effects and 3-D film wizardry. A huge hit with kids.

Hollywood Boulevard A pastiche of the 1930s and 1940s 'Hollywood that never was and always will be'. Shopping is the name of the game along the boulevard. Star-struck cinema buffs can pick up authentic memorabilia from Sid Cahuenga's One-of-a-Kind – at a price.

Honey, I Shrunk the Kids Movie Set Adventure This imaginative adventure play area is equipped with giant apparatus that dwarfs the kids, who can also frolic in cooling water jets.

VISITORS WITH DISABILITIES
Special parking areas and 'handicap vans' with platforms for loading wheelchairs are provided on request. A WDW *Guidebook for Guests with Disabilities* details additional facilities and makes helpful suggestions.

PARK TIPS II

• Use the FASTPASS system (see panel, page 122) for the Rock 'n' Roller Coaster Starring Aerosmith, The Twilight Zone Tower of Terror, Voyage of The Little Mermaid and Indiana Jones Epic Stunt Spectacular.

• Disney-MGM Studios offers several more shows than those listed here. Check the free park guides available at the entrance for details and schedules.

• There is a daily afternoon parade on Hollywood Boulevard; and the spectacular night-time Fantasmic! firework show in the Hollywood Hills Amphitheater.

• Disney-MGM Studios' rides are not particularly suitable for young children. The shows fare rather better and the Honey, I Shrunk the Kids playground is a good place to let off steam.

GREEN THUMBS

Plant lovers who want more after the greenhouse boat tour at The Land pavilion can sign up for an hour-long Behind the Seeds guided walk, which explores the futuristic greenhouses in more depth. Make reservations for the tours, which depart every hour from 10:30 to 4:30, at the Green Thumb gift store (*Admission moderate*).

Indiana Jones Epic Stunt Spectacular! Plenty of fire, brimstone and death-defying live stunt work in this intriguing look at the tricks of the trade. Volunteers from the audience take part in scenes from *Raiders of the Lost Ark;* the rest of the crowd feels the heat of the explosive finale.

Magic of Disney Animation Hugely popular, this fascinating walk through the Animation Building lays bare every stage of the animation process. From the sidesplitting introduction to animation basics, right through to the final presentation in the **Disney Classics Theater**, this is one of the best attractions in Walt Disney World Resort.

Rock 'n' Roller Coaster Starring Aerosmith Fronted by a giant red electric guitar, this roller coaster takes the form of a motorized dash across town to catch an Aerosmith concert. Mega thrills and sound track by the old rockers themselves.

Sounds Dangerous Join funnyman Drew Carey in a pilot for a new investigative TV show and spend most of the time in the dark experiencing the action through sound alone. Take a trip to the barber, or hear a swarm of killer bees on the loose. Highly recommended.

Star Tours Hang on to your seats for this bone-shaking trip through space in an out-of-control Starspeeder vehicle on loan from *Star Wars* travel agent duo R2D2 and C3-PO.

Theater of the Stars Check showtimes to find out what's on (*Beauty and the Beast – Live on Stage* is a long-running favourite) in this handsome Sunset Boulevard covered theatre, which stages all-singing, all-dancing Broadway-style musical productions. Naturally, Disney characters take the various roles, and it is all a lot of fun.

The Twilight Zone™ Tower of Terror A nightmarish visit to the 199-foot (60m) Hollywood Tower Hotel culminates in a thrilling adventure in the elevator shaft.

Voyage of The Little Mermaid Ariel's undersea adventures brought to life in a cute combination of animation, live performances and puppetry, with lasers and other special effects for good measure.

EPCOT

This was Walt Disney's greatest dream. Inspired by his vision of an 'experimental prototype community of tomorrow', Epcot is divided into two separate 'worlds'.

Future World explores the role of communications, transport, agriculture and energy, and delves into the realms of the imagination.

World Showcase tackles the world around us, re-creating the sights and smells of far-off places, such as Britain and Beijing, all bathed in uncharacteristic Florida sunshine. Here the culture of 11 nations has been transposed to specially designed pavilions which have themed shops and restaurants. With nearly 70 shops, World Showcase is a veritable international shopping mall.

The high-speed Rock 'n' Roller Coaster Featuring Aerosmith

Future World

Imagination! If it is possible, the new **Journey Into Your Imagination** ride is even less engaging than its predecessor, but there is fun to be had in the interactive ImageWorks area and the 3-D film misadventure *Honey, I Shrunk the Audience*.

Innoventions A much more successful update of these twin pavilions has resulted in a colourful, fully interactive and child-friendly look at how science and technology influence and improve our lives.

The Land Food, glorious food, is under the microscope on a boat trip through experimental greenhouses (see panel opposite); upstairs the **Circle of Life Theater** presents an entertaining eco-conscious film.

Living Seas An illuminating study of man and the sea. The 5.7 million gallon (25,912,000-litre) central aquarium is home to more than 2,700 tropical fish, as well as sharks, dolphins and manatees.

Spaceship Earth Housed in Epcot's trademark 180-foot-tall (55m) silver geosphere, this ride spirals 18 storeys through the development of earthling communications, before releasing its captive audience into the interactive computer-video wonderland of the **A.T.&T. Global Neighborhood**.

Test Track High-speed motor racing action in the longest, fastest ride ever created by the Walt Disney Imagineers.

Wonders of Life Ricochet through the bloodstream on the **Body Wars** ride, or experience a day in the life of a 12-year-old boy in **Cranium Command**.

PARK TIPS III

- There are two FASTPASS (see panel, page 122) attractions at Epcot: the popular Test Track ride and Honey, I Shrunk the Audience.
- Dining out in one of the international restaurants in World Showcase is a major attraction. Reservations can be made in advance (tel: 407/939-3463), or through Guest Relations at the entrance to the park or in Spaceship Earth.
- A host of international entertainment, from music and Japanese drumming to acrobatics, takes place around the World Showcase 'villages' throughout the day. Check the free map and guide for details.
- The World Showcase Lagoon at the centre of the park is the setting for dramatic nightly fireworks and laser shows (check schedules).

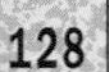

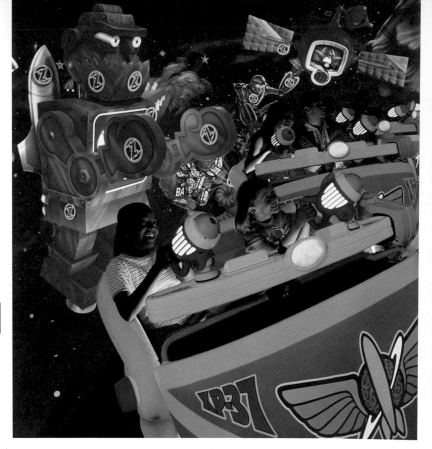

Buzz Lightyear's Space Ranger Spin transports guests to the playful world of 'Toy Story'

Universe of Energy Not-to-be-missed journey back in time to the dinosaur era on the trail of fossil fuels. Ellen DeGeneres stars alongside realistic dinosaurs and terrific big-screen effects.

World Showcase

American Adventure A generously proportioned Georgian-style building houses a 30-minute Audio-Animatronics show which celebrates the 'spirit of America' from the Pilgrim Fathers to John Wayne. Attractive souvenirs from **Heritage Manor Gifts**.

Canada A Rocky Mountain, a totem pole and a flourish of native trees precede the CircleVision 360-degree presentation, *O Canada!* Buy lumberjack shirts and maple syrup from **Northwest Mercantile**.

China A curtain of bamboo and the colourful **Gate of the Golden Sun** front a dazzling world of ornate green and gold curved roofs, carp-filled lily ponds and one of the Showcase's top features, **Wonders of China**, a CircleVision 360-degree journey through China.

France *Belle Époque* Paris in the shadow of an Eiffel Tower (to scale): a Pont des Arts-esque bridge, a sidewalk café, a poster-plastered kiosk and a deliciously scented bakery. Very chic shopping (fragrances, cosmetics, wine) and some serious cuisine at **Les Chefs de France**.

Germany Fairy-tale façades, oompah music, red geraniums, lederhosen and a pungent and unmistakable whiff of sauerkraut from the **Biergarten Restaurant** all add up to a very convincing scene.

Italy Venice's **St Mark's Square** and the **Doge's Palace** re-created in extraordinary detail. Enjoy the fine piazza, then try the pasta at **L'Originale Alfredo di Roma Ristorante**.

Japan The Japanese pavilion is a vision of tiered pagoda roofs, bonsai, monkey-puzzle trees and elegant music and dance demonstrations. Galleries exhibit Japanese arts, crafts and mechanical toys.

Mexico Take the **El Río del Tiempo** (River of Time) boat trip and visit a re-created **Mayan Temple**, then enjoy the music provided by the sombreroed mariachi bands on the lakeshore.

Morocco Wander around the bazaar and take time to admire the cool, tiled courtyards of the **Medina** (Old City). Constructed by Moroccan artisans, this is one of the most impressive buildings in the Showcase.

Norway Take ***Maelstrom***, a Viking longboat ride into Norse history and the land of the midnight sun. The Norway pavilion's craft shop is well-stocked with trolls and toys, and the bakery makes a good snack stop.

United Kingdom Half-timbered façades, old red telephone boxes and warm beer in a traditional pub are just the ticket, but Anne Hathaway's Cottage taken over by a tea shop? It's just not cricket!

MAGIC KINGDOM

The first of the Walt Disney World Resort parks to open (in 1971), the 100-acre (40-ha) Magic Kingdom site is based on the original Disneyland design. Mickey Mouse reigns over singing bears, pirates, Cinderella and a host of fun-loving characters from the magical world of Disney cartoons. Maps and information are available from **City Hall** at the start of Main Street U.S.A., near the entrance. It's easy to navigate and much easier if you arrive early, since queues will be significantly longer by mid-morning.

Adventureland Outlandish African Colonial-Middle Eastern-Moorish architecture, exotic plants and tropical juice bars take second place to the action-packed fun offered here. Explore the roomy, vine-covered **Swiss Family Treehouse**, perched in the boughs of a gigantic concrete, steel and plastic banyan tree; then hop aboard a launch at the last outpost river landing for a steamy **Jungle Cruise** down the Nile and into the Amazon jungle. **Pirates of the Caribbean** is a favourite ride in Adventureland; it is a rollicking encounter with one-eyed buccaneers, treasure troves and a sighting of the world's first raid by pirates under the influence of Audio-Animatronics. Crooning flowers and chattering totem poles join assorted Audio-Animatronics feathered friends for a Tropical Serenade in **The Enchanted Tiki Room**. The show itself lasts about nine minutes, and is a must for small children.

Fantasyland In the style of the Brothers Grimm, Disney classics centred around **Cinderella Castle** include **Cinderella's Golden Carousel**, the **Mad Tea Party**, **Dumbo the Flying Elephant** and **Peter Pan's Flight**. **The Many Adventures of Winnie the Pooh** takes a cuddly, honey-laden trip to the Hundred Acre Wood to visit Pooh, Piglet,

PARK TIPS IV

- Use the FASTPASS system (see panel, page 122) for Adventureland's Jungle Cruise, The Many Adventures of Winnie the Pooh, Buzz Lightyear's Space Ranger Spin, Space Mountain and Splash Mountain.
- Keys to the Kingdom is a fascinating 4-hour, behind-the-scenes tour of the park which takes guests backstage and beneath the Magic Kingdom (minimum age 16; additional charge). For information and reservations (up to six weeks in advance), tel: 407/939-8687.
- The daily Disney's Magical Moments Parade on Main Street U.S.A. (popular with under 8s) at 3pm is a good time to sneak on to some of the more popular rides.
- The night-time Fantasy in the Sky fireworks displays are amazing; so is the Main Street Electrical Parade. Check with City Hall for show times.

SINCE 1971 WALT DISNEY WORLD RESORT HAS ...
– welcomed more than 500 million visitors
– planted 25 million flowering annuals and 100,000 trees
– clocked up enough monorail journeys to equal the equivalent of 25 round-trips to the moon
– sold 35 million souvenir T-shirts
– found an estimated 1.5 million pairs of lost sunglasses.

Owl and Eeyore. On a hot day, make tracks for **Ariel's Grotto**, where kids can cool off amongst the bouncing water jets and pose for photos with, and collect autographs from, the famous mermaid. Other diversions include the ride-through **Snow White's Scary Adventures**, which stars the wicked queen and could well frighten little children; the **Legend of The Lion King** involves some highly skillful puppetry; and hundreds of song-and-dance dolls in national costume entertain at **It's a Small World**. This is the obvious place to raid the toy shop, though never at discount prices.

Frontierland Here you will find boardwalks and the **Frontierland Shootin' Arcade**; plenty of hootin', hollerin' and belly-laughing entertainment in the hilarious **Country Bear Jamboree**. There is also a runaway mine train charging down **Big Thunder Mountain**. **Splash Mountain** is a hair-raising experience: a log flume ride with a 47-degree drop and speeds of nearly 40mph (64kph) with a very wet finale. A raft-ride away, wooded **Tom Sawyer Island** offers a fort-stockade Mystery Mine Shaft to explore; or take to the water with **Mike Fink Keelboats**.

Liberty Square In the 19th century, while half the US was whooping it up in the local **Diamond Horseshoe Saloon Revue** in Frontierland, complete with high-stepping dance-hall belles, the other half built gracious colonial-style homes, embroidered flags and made great pickles. Brush up on American history with a presentation featuring Audio-Animatronics presidents in the **Hall of Presidents** (less impressive to children than their parents). There is a relaxing cruise through history on a sternwheel steamer at **Liberty Belle Riverboats**. The most popular ride in this land is the **Haunted Mansion**. After gravestone humour has provided a diversion from waiting in line, sidle past creepy greeters, take time to check out the horror wallpaper and climb aboard a doom buggy. Although the start is unimpressive, the trailing cobwebs and shrieking holograms ensure that this soon develops into a memorably kitschy ghost-train ride.

Main Street U.S.A. This is the hub of the Magic Kingdom from which the other lands radiate, and **Cinderella Castle** (see page 129) is its focus. With more than a hint of mad King Ludwig of Bavaria's turreted folly Neuschwanstein, this 180-foot (60m) steel and fibreglass fantasy castle encapsulates the park's storybook allure.

Main Street re-creates a pristine Victorian village of 'olde worlde' shopfronts and colour-coordinated floral displays, barbershop quartets, ice-cream parlors and hot dog stands with striped awnings. The shops are real and sell gifts, bric-à-brac and fancy foodstuffs. The scent of freshly baked croissants and cookies from the **Bake Shop** makes it hard to concentrate, but do not hurry away too soon.

Other diversions include barbershop quartet serenades and concerts in Town Square, and for a gentle circuit of the Magic Kingdom domain take a trip on the **Walt Disney World Railroad**, which departs from the station near the main entrance and stops in Frontierland and Mickey's Toontown Fair.

Fireworks over Cinderella Castle

Mickey's Toontown Fair A popular photo-stop with its colourful, outsize attractions and Disney topiary, Toontown offers a rare opportunity to visit the world's most famous mouse 'at home'. Take a stroll around **Mickey's Country House** and **Minnie's Country House**, then catch up with favourite Disney cartoon characters at the **Toontown Hall of Fame**. There is watery fun at the **Donald's Boat** play area, where hot tots can work off some energy, while the **Barnstormer at Goofy's Wiseacres Farm** is a scaled-down roller coaster.

Tomorrowland Fantasy-oriented Tomorrowland offers a full complement of escapist rides and antagonistic aliens. **The ExtraTERRORestrial Alien Encounter** is a prime example. This sensory chiller, designed with the help of George Lucas, really does raise the hairs on the back of your neck, with a combination of special effects, suggestion and short periods of total darkness. For light relief, visit **The Timekeeper**, hosted by a jocular robot and his flighty sidekicks, which whisks you back and forth through time to meet famous inventors and visionaries in Circle Vision 360°.

Buzz Lightyear's Space Ranger Spin blasts off from Star Command Headquarters on an interactive mission to defeat the evil Zurg and his minions for passengers get to test their laser shooting skills.

That old favourite, **Space Mountain**, a terrific roller coaster, rockets through the darkness past meteors and shooting stars. This is a rough ride, so batten down the hatches and take off your glasses. If there's no queue when you're done, do it again.

Goodyear's **Tomorrowland Speedway** is also popular: its mini racing cars race around four 2,260-foot (690m) tracks, good for kids only. You can ride a rocket at **Astro Orbiter**; play video games galore at the **Tomorrowland Arcade**; take in variety shows at **Galaxy Palace Theater**; and sit through the shamelessly nostalgic **Carousel of Progress**, a celebration of 20th-century domestic developments.

MORE ENTERTAINMENT AT DISNEY'S BOARDWALK
A waterfront dining and entertainment district in the Epcot Resorts area, Disney's BoardWalk re-creates 1940s Atlantic City with a collection of shops, restaurants and nightspots, including a sports bar, the ESPN Club (tel: 407/939-1177). After dark, guests can sing along and admire the duelling-pianos routine at Jellyrolls (minimum age 21, tel: 407/560-8770).

CHARACTER DINING
Dining with Disney cartoon characters is a memorable treat for both the young and the young at heart. Try Donald's Breakfastosaurus in Disney's Animal Kingdom; Hollywood & Vine at Disney-MGM Studios; the Garden Grill, in The Land pavilion at Epcot; and several locations at the Magic Kingdom, including The Crystal Palace Buffet. Different characters show up in different places; pick your character and plan accordingly. Reservations are advised for these and other Disney resort character dining locations (tel: 407/939-4363).

RAVE REVUES
There is never a spare seat in the house for the rollicking Hoop-Dee-Doo Musical Revue dinner show at Fort Wilderness. This is family entertainment at its best, and reservations for the three daily shows (5, 7:15, and 9:30pm) should be made at least several months in advance. Enjoy the verve and energy of the Pioneer Hall Players along with the generous barbecue-style banquet of ribs, chicken, corn on the cob and strawberry short-cake which arrives at intervals during the two-hour show. To book seats, write to or telephone Central Reservations.

Other WDW Resort attractions include these:

Blizzard Beach

Disney's third water park takes its inspiration from Florida's first (and last) imaginary ski resort. The slopes of towering **Mount Gushmore** feature waterborne slalom courses, toboggan and water-sled runs, chair lifts with skis and sun umbrellas, and **Teamboat Springs**, the world's longest family white-water ride. From the 120-foot-high (36m) **Summit Plummet** 'ski jump' tower, there is a 60mph (96kph) plunge down a speed slide; or you can take the slightly shorter and less severe **Slush Gusher**. There is also **Melt-Away Bay** pool; **Cross Country Creek**, which makes a circuit of the entire park (you float in inner tubes); and scaled-down **Tike's Peak**, for kids.

Open daily 10am–5pm, longer in summer and on holidays. For schedules, (tel: 407/824-4321). Admission is included with Park Hopper Plus passes.

Downtown Disney

WDW Resort's mega shopping, dining and entertainment district on the shores of Lake Buena Vista, Downtown Disney is divided into three parts. Moving from right to left along the waterfront, first up is **Marketplace** (a shopping area) with its landmark steaming volcano housing the Rainforest Café. Here, you can raid World of Disney, the largest Disney merchandise store on earth, sample a variety of restaurants and gawk at the feats of creativity displayed at the LEGO Imagination Center®. In Downtown Disney's mid-section, **Pleasure Island** is WDW Resort's Nightlife Central (see opposite).

At the far end of the complex, **West Side** is home to an assortment of shops, including a Virgin Megastore, the House of Blues® live music and dining operation with a concert venue next door (information, tel: 407/934-7781), plus, on the restaurant front, Planet Hollywood®, Wolfgang Puck® Café and Gloria Estefan's Bongos Cuban Café™. For sheer entertainment, there is a 24-screen cinema, and a purpose-built theatre to house the Cirque du Soleil®'s stunning high-energy acrobatic and dance productions (reservations, tel: 407/939-7600). Another key element to the West Side is DisneyQuest®, a five-storey indoor interactive theme park packed with techno wizardry and virtual fun.

(*Open* daily. General stores 9:30am–11pm. Restaurants for lunch and dinner. *Admission free* for dining only in one of the restaurants, otherwise there's a charge.)

Fort Wilderness

The official WDW Resort campground with some 784 campsites and 408 wilderness homes, Fort Wilderness is also an activities centre, though use of many of the facilities is restricted to guests who are staying in WDW Resort-owned properties.

Sailboats, pedal boats and little Water Sprites can be rented from the Bay Lake marina. Daily fishing excursions are arranged on the lake, and anglers can try their luck on the canals around the camp's domain. There are bicycle and canoe hire, jogging circuits, horseback trail rides, basketball, tennis and volleyball facilities.

Evening entertainment includes the **Hoop-Dee-Doo Musical Revue** (see panel opposite); a **Campfire Program** with a sing-along; and Disney cartoons and films.

Pleasure Island

Connected to the rest of Downtown Disney by footbridges, Pleasure Island is WDW Resort's offshore home of late-night entertainment, though its shops and restaurants are open all day. The island harbours eight clubs offering a whole range of musical styles, discos and comedy, plus the West End Stage which occasionally lures top-name talent to the Disney empire, and a New Year's Eve party every night from 11:45.

Pleasure Island's musical line-up kicks off with the **BET SoundStage™ Club** serving up the hottest R&B and hip hop around. For smooth jazz (and more than a touch of R&B), head for the **PI Jazz Company**. On the dance front, **Mannequins Dance Palace** does the high-tech thing to

Blizzard Beach's Summit Plummet

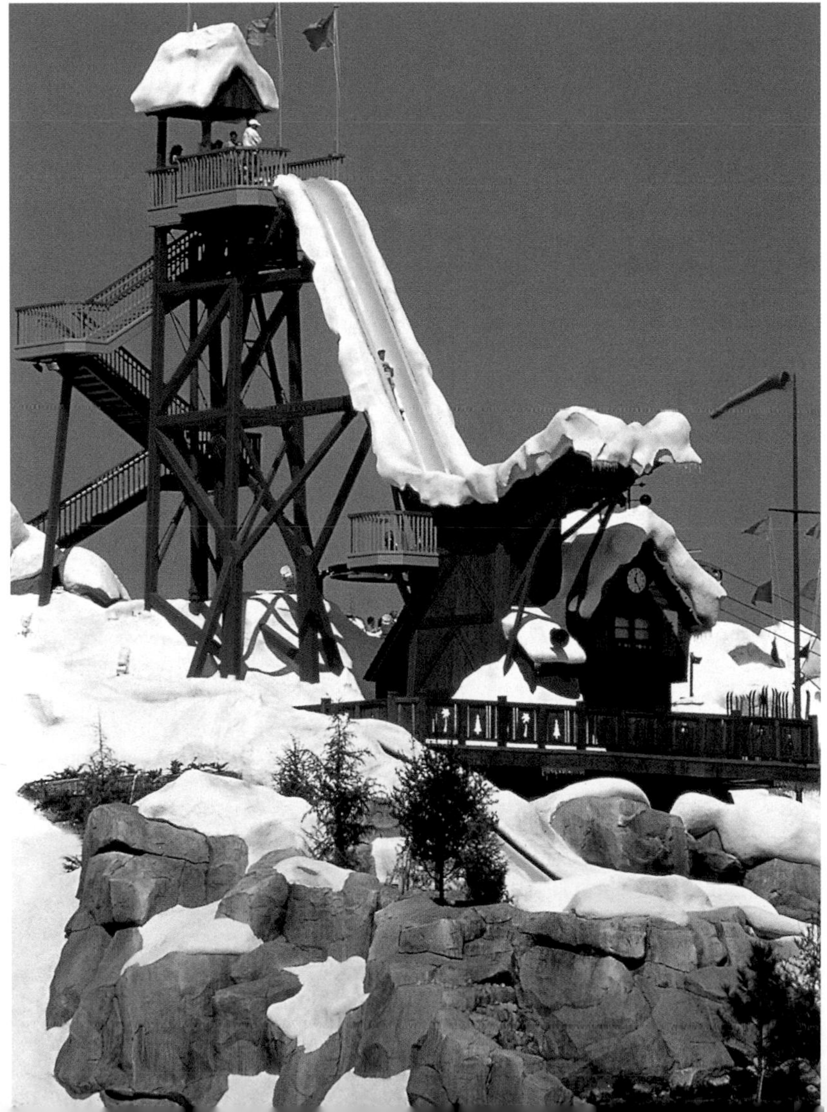

SPORTING DISNEY
It began with the Walt Disney World Marathon and Indy 200 races in January, and now Disney's Wide World of Sports Complex hosts a packed calendar of top sporting events throughout the year. The 200-acre (80-ha) site features a 7,500-seat baseball and softball park (where the Atlanta Braves move right in each year for spring training), as well as tennis and indoor and outdoor sports facilities for more than 30 sports.

SCENIC BOAT TOURS
Winter Park sits on the shores of Lake Osceola, one of a chain of six small freshwater lakes linked by narrow, leafy canals, navigable by small craft. At the foot of Morse Boulevard, Scenic Boat Tours (*Open* daily 10–4) operates hour-long sight-seeing trips on Lake Osceola, Lake Virginia, and Lake Maitland, affording fine views of the neighbourhood's most impressive waterfront homes and occasional wildlife-spotting as added extras.

Top 40 hits; pack your bell-bottoms for 70s-style dancing at **8Trax**; grab gingham and a Stetson for line dancing at the **Wildhorse Saloon**®; while all-time rock classics get an airing at the **Rock 'N' Roll Beach Club**.

When it's time to chill out, there are zany stories at the exotic-nostalgic **Adventurer's Club**. Or let the funny men (and women) take the strain at the **Comedy Warehouse**.

(*Open* daily. Shops 10am–1am, restaurants 11:30am–midnight, clubs 7pm–2am. *Admission: expensive* (covered by Park Hopper Plus Passes), including all clubs. Under 18s must be accompanied by an adult; minimum age 21 at BET SoundStage and Mannequins Dance Palace.)

River Country

The smallest of WDW Resort's three water parks, River Country occupies a corner of Bay Lake that has been transformed into an adventure-packed 'swimmin' hole' complete with a separate chlorinated swimming pool. Bay Cove has been fitted with rope swings, a ship's boom and assorted other constructions from which to jump, dive and generally splash down.

The **Whoop 'n' Holler Hollow** area of River County has two corkscrew flume rides for high-speed waterbatics; two water slides provide a brief flurry of foaming water and then dump their contents in the pool with an unceremonious splash.

For something a little less traumatic, try **White Water Rapids**. Despite its ominous title, this tube ride makes its descent in a series of curvaceous chutes and pools, which slow the ride down somewhat. On the other hand, there is always a nice, flat, dry piece of sandy beach where you can recover. In summer, River Country can be extremely busy; go in late afternoon.

(*Open* daily 10–5; extended in summer and on holidays. For schedules, tel: 407/824-4321. Admission is included with Park Hopper Plus passes.)

Typhoon Lagoon

This area features typhoon-ravaged tropical landscaping and a vast lagoon as a centre-piece, with 4-foot (1.2m) waves which crash on to the surrounding broad beach every 90 seconds. **Castaway Creek** describes a lazy 2,100-foot (640m) tube ride around the lagoon – it takes about 25 minutes. There are places to stop along the route and a dripping rain-forest section. Scale Mount Mayday for a dare on **Humunga Kowabunga** – two 214-foot (65m) water slides which send willing victims rocketing down the mountainside and through a series of caves at speeds of anything up to 25mph (40kph). Three storm slides take a less hair-raising route down to pools around the lagoon. There are also three white-water raft adventures.

Hire fins and a mask to explore **Shark Reef**. This salt-water coral-reef environment is teeming with exotic marine life, including odd-looking but harmless nurse sharks. Children (aged two to five) enjoy **Ketchakiddie Creek**'s scaled-down slides, geysers and fountains, and **SS *Squirt***, the interactive tugboat.

(*Open* daily 10–5, later in summer and on holidays. For schedules, tel: 407/824-4321. Admission is included with Park Hopper Plus passes.)

►► Winter Haven/Cypress Gardens

Near the unassuming town of Winter Haven lies Florida's oldest continuously operating theme park – **Cypress Gardens**, S Lake Summit Drive/SR 540 (*Open* daily 9:30–5; extended during special events. *Admission: expensive*; tel: 1-800/282-2123). The original botanical gardens, founded in the 1930s, have matured into a lush and colourful spectacle on the shores of Lake Eloise. Here you will find giant cypresses, masses of bougainvillaea and water lily pads the size of picnic tables. The formal gardens are renowned for their wonderfully kitschy displays and horticultural festivals, such as the two million multi-coloured chrysanthemums amassed for November's **Mum Festival**, and the Christmas poinsettia display.

The 220-acre (90-ha) site offers plenty of non-horticultural diversions, from boat trips and a water-ski show on the lake to the park's trademark crinolined Southern Belles who grace the grounds. There are animal enclosures and discovery shows in the **Nature's Way** area, a butterfly conservatory, and homage to *Gone With the Wind* variety shows and **Island in the Sky**, Kodak's 153-foot (46.5m) revolving observation platform.

►► Winter Park

Founded as a winter resort just north of Orlando at the turn of the 20th century, Winter Park is a delightful full- or half-day excursion away from the teeming theme parks. Around the compact town centre, there is excellent shopping along Park Avenue.

The **Charles Hosmer Morse Museum of American Art**, 445 Park Avenue North (*Open* Tue–Sat 9:30–4, Sun 1–4. *Admission: inexpensive*; tel: 407/645-5311), has a superb collection of Tiffany glass, much of it rescued from a fire at Louis Comfort Tiffany's home on Long Island. Stained-glass windows filled with roses and fruit-and-vegetable 'still lifes' are shown alongside jewellery, lampshades and 'drapery' glass (which is folded when soft). Other art nouveau artists with work on display include Lalique, Emile Gallé and Maxfield Parrish.

CAMPUS DELIGHT

Don't miss a stroll around the pastoral campus of Rollins College (Holt Avenue, Winter Park). By the entrance, a Walk of Fame features stones from the birthplaces and homes of famous people. There is a Spanish Mediterranean-style College Chapel and the Cornell Fine Arts Museum, which houses collections of European Old Masters, 19th-century American paintings, sculpture, modern prints and graphics, and Native American artefacts (*Open* Tue–Fri 10–5; Sat and Sun 1–5. *Admission free*; tel: 407/646-2526).

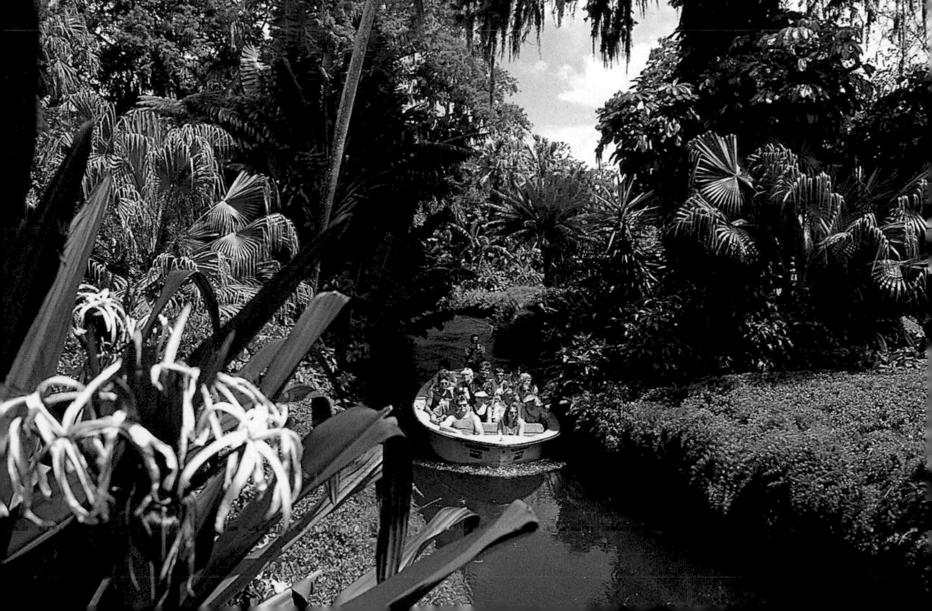

An English-looking corner of Cypress Gardens

Sun, sea, sand and palm trees on the Gold Coast

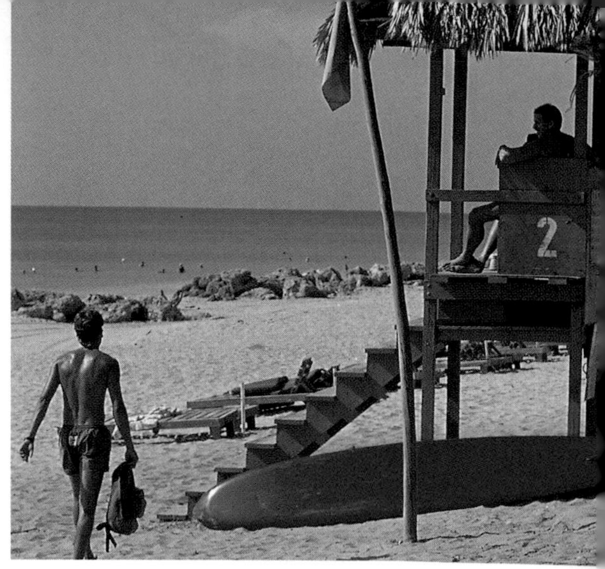

GOLD COAST

0 10 km
0 10 miles
Jonathan Dickinson S P
Blowing Rocks Beach
Tequesta
Jupiter Inlet
95
Jupiter
North Palm Beach
Juno Beach
Palm Beach Gardens
J D MacArthur Beach S P
Riviera Beach
Palm Beach Shores
West Palm Beach
Flagler Museum
Palm Beach
Haverhill
Norton Museum of Art
Lake Worth
Palm Springs
Lantana
Lantana Park
Boynton Beach
FLORIDA'S TURNPIKE
Ocean Ridge
Gulf Stream
Delray Beach
Morikami Museum
Highland Beach
Spanish River Park
Red Reef Park
Boca Raton
Hillsboro Canal
South Beach Park
Deerfield Beach
Margate
Butterfly World
Lighthouse Point
Pompano Beach
Tamarac
95
Hugh Taylor Birch S R A
Oakland Park
FORT LAUDERDALE
John U Lloyd Beach S R A
Flamingo Gardens
Davie
Dania
Hollywood
See Drive Page 153

GOLDEN SUN, GOLDEN SAND and golden opportunities are the stuff the Gold Coast is made of. A holiday mecca and rich man's retreat, it spreads its wares along a narrow coastal strip between two very different cities bordered by the Atlantic Ocean and the Everglades.

At the southern extreme, **Fort Lauderdale**, a high-rise success story built on a maze of inner-city canals carved from the swamps is one of the fastest growing cities in the state. A few minutes' drive from the glittering downtown skyscrapers and arts and entertainment districts, Fort Lauderdale beach is lined with swanky resort hotels, condominiums, beachfront motels and a minor miracle – 180 acres (72 ha) of natural preserve fronting the shore. To the south is **Port Everglades**, the second largest cruise port in the world, while the city's marinas harbour 44,000 yachts and sportfishing vessels. Fort Lauderdale is expanding west and reclaiming land with a rapacious enthusiasm that is turning small country towns like horse-mad Davie into suburban satellites.

Davie is the Gold Coast's very own Wild West show. While surfers are riding the Atlantic rollers, the residents of Davie are more likely to be testing their skills at steer wrestling or bronco-riding at the Thursday night rodeo.

Head north of Fort Lauderdale, and more than a dozen oceanside communities stretch out along A1A, fronted by a strip of golden sand. **Pompano Beach** is a noted sportfishing centre named for the fish which frequent its shores. At **Deerfield Beach**, there is a chance to explore an unspoiled oasis of coastal hammock, where armadillos can be seen trotting across the nature trail.

Then there is **Boca Raton**, with its superb beach parks and small but excellent Museum of Art. 'Pretty in pink' is the motto of this exclusive community, where elegant villas are painted to resemble strawberry ice cream; polo is the name of the game, and shopping is best left to the professionals. Palm Beach architect Addison Mizner planned to build the 'Greatest Resort in the World' here, but was cheated of his dream by the collapse of the 1920s land boom. Although Mizner managed to

complete only one hotel, the town has honoured its founder with a wealth of Mediterranean-inspired architecture in the same style – painted with oceans of pastel pink, naturally – and it is well worth a visit. For a change of pace, **Delray Beach** is a good place to collect shells and has a hidden treasure in its peaceful Japanese gardens and Museum of Japanese Settlement on the Gold Coast.

The Gold Coast's other main focal point, the island community of **Palm Beach**, is not expanding anywhere. This spectacularly wealthy enclave is notoriously insular. Railroad king Henry Flagler founded West Palm Beach on the mainland specifically to keep the riff-raff out of his exclusive resort, and that is the way the present-day residents intend to keep it, even though most of them only visit for three months of the year. An hour's drive north of Fort Lauderdale by car, Palm Beach is light years away in style. While the *nouveaux riches* of the former are charging about on their yachts, the seriously rich of the latter are planning charity croquet tournaments and packing picnic baskets for the polo game.

Palm Beach wins all the landscaping points, but **West Palm Beach** is not without its attractions, and it is the place to look for an affordable hotel. Its Norton Gallery of Art is a must for culture vultures; the Clematis Street shopping and dining district is a major attraction day and night; and polo, African safari and Everglades adventures are all to be enjoyed in the vicinity. **Juno** and **Jupiter** sound like Space Coast satellites, but turtle-watching is more common than stargazing in these relaxed beach communities at the northern end of the Gold Coast.

Sport is big on the Gold Coast. As well as spectator sports like polo, jai alai and greyhound racing, there are superb tennis and golf facilities throughout the area. If you're interested in sport, you should investigate the excellent resort packages offered, with particularly competitive rates available during the summer. Traditional off-season accommodation savings are a major attraction, and senior citizens will also find special deals.

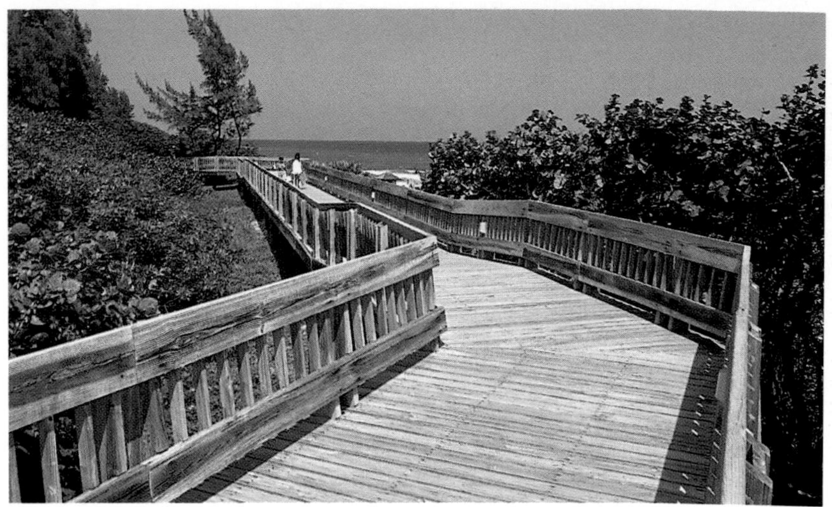

Boardwalk in Boca Raton's oceanfront Red Reef Park

►►► REGION HIGHLIGHTS

CARTOON CAPERS

Relocated from New York, the International Museum of Cartoon Art cheers up Boca Raton's Mizner Park complex (*Open* Tue–Sat 10–6, Sun noon–6). Founded by Mort Walker, creator of *Beetle Bailey*, it is the only museum in the world devoted to cartoon art. Changing displays draw on collections of more than 160,000 original drawings and 10,000 books, with work by Walt Disney, Charles Schultz and Charles Dana Gibson.

►►► Boca Raton

Boca Raton's name dates back to the Spanish explorers, who called it a 'rat's mouth' for the razor-sharp rocks guarding the bay. During the 1920s land boom, Addison Mizner gathered a coterie of blue-chip backers, including the Vanderbilts and Elizabeth Arden, to launch a luxury 16,000-acre (6,475-ha) project which was to be an American Venice. He built a collection of pretty Mediterranean-style houses in the exclusive Old Floresta neighbourhood, off Palmetto Park Road. The superb Cloister Inn was also completed (now the swish **Boca Raton Resort and Club**), but the project collapsed along with the boom, though Boca's wealth of pink Mediterranean-inspired architecture is still very much in keeping with Mizner's plan.

Boca Raton is booming again. The 'Winter Capital of Polo' is well supplied with elegant shopping malls, restaurants and golf, as well as drama, musicals and revues at the **Caldwell Theatre**, tel: 561/241-7432, and 5 miles (8km) of superb ocean beaches. Special events include a springtime explosion of activity with February's **Boca Raton Museum of Art Festival**, which attracts artists from near and far, and the jazzy **Meet Me Downtown** event in March, a free arts and crafts show and festival.

Boca Raton Museum of Art, *801 W Palmetto Park Road* (*Open* Tue, Thu–Fri 10–4, Wed 10–8, Sat–Sun 12–4. *Admission: inexpensive, free Wed*; tel: 561/392-2500) Well worth a stop for art lovers, this small museum has a well-earned reputation for intelligently themed exhibitions which change every six weeks or so. The reason for the continual turn-round is lack of space for a permanent collection which numbers around 3,000 pieces, from works by Andy Warhol and David Hockney to African and pre-Columbian artefacts. However, as of spring 2001, the museum should be able to reveal the full extent of its treasures when it moves to palatial new quarters adjacent to Mizner Park. Until then, the only permanent exhibit is the **Mayers Collection** featuring drawings, sketches and minor works by late 19th- and early 20th-century artists including Picasso, Matisse, Seurat, Degas and Modigliani, among others.

Children's Museum of Boca Raton, *498 Crawford Road (off Palmetto Park Road)* (*Open* Tue–Sat noon–4. *Admission: inexpensive*; tel: 561/368-6875) The museum occupies an octogenarian cottage, thought to be the oldest wooden structure in Boca Raton. It is a great rainy day option or a treat for children, who will enjoy a couple of hours play-acting in the grocery shop and the bank, and digging up fossils and artefacts in the Archeologists' Room.

Mizner Park, *Mizner Boulevard* (tel: 561/362-0606) This Mizner-inspired shopping, dining and entertainment complex is one of the largest pink extravanganzas to emerge in Boca Raton. This is where art galleries, jewellers, bespoke shoemakers and boutiques cater for the rich and the less rich, and it is a great free show for browsers. There are shaded benches where you can relax while surveying the scene, cinemas, an open-air amphitheatre, and the **International Museum of Cartoon Art** (see panel, and page 138), which has a spectacular collection of original cartoons, plus more than 1,000 hours of animated videotapes. There is also a wide choice of restaurants.

Red Reef Park, *1111 N Ocean Boulevard (A1A)* (*Open* park daily 8am–10pm, Gumbo Limbo Mon–Sat 9–4, Sun noon–4. *Admission free*; tel: 561/338-1473) Straddling A1A, the 67-acre (27-ha) park offers almost a mile of pristine oceanfront beach bordered by a dense strip of palms, palmettos, sea grapes and Australian pines. You can snorkel around offshore reef formations, or in an artificial reef area. Picnic facilities with barbecue grills are provided, and there is a golf course and plenty of parking (moderate). Surf fishing is a favourite pastime.

About 20 acres (8 ha) of the park have been set aside for the **Gumbo Limbo Nature Center**, which encourages visitors to learn a little more about their surroundings. Across A1A from the beach is a visitor centre with interpretive

GRAPE HARVEST

The sea grape is a native, saltwater-tolerant shrub which grows naturally in coastal hammocks and along beaches in the southern part of the state. Early settlers used the distinctive round, leathery leaves as emergency notepaper, as plates and even as headgear. The fruit was harvested to make wine and jelly, and the flowers rank in importance with those of black mangroves as nectar-producers for honey. The sea grape is now protected.

Pink is the theme in elegant Boca Raton

The old wooden cottage which houses the Children's Museum of Boca Raton

POLO
Played on a 10-acre (4-ha) field between four-man teams, polo requires speed, stamina and considerable skill – most of which is provided by the strong, agile polo ponies. Matches are divided into six chukkers (periods) of seven minutes each, and need a referee and two mounted umpires to keep up with the action. A team's all-important handicap is calculated on the ability ratings of its members, from a low of one to a high of ten.

displays, touch tanks and saltwater aquariums for turtles. A boardwalk trail has been laid out through the tropical hardwood hammock, leading to a 40-foot (12m) observation tower, and there are regular Saturday morning guided activities (call ahead for schedules and charges) which range from beachcombing with an eagle-eyed expert to exploring the many and varied examples of native flora and fauna which inhabit the preserve. From May through July, night-time turtle walks take place on the beach (call to make reservations).

Royal Palm Polo Sports Club, *18000 Jog Road* Every spring, polo players from all over the world converge on the Gold Coast, when Boca Raton's Royal Palm, one of the region's major clubs, plays host to the annual USPA $50,000 International Cup Finals at the end of March (see panel). Games are also played every Sunday at the club from January to mid-April at 1 and 3.

For general admission and box seats, pay at the grounds; for advance reservations for tailgate parking, tel: 561/994-1876. Free non-spectactor parking areas are provided.

South Beach Park, *400 N Ocean Boulevard (A1A)* (*Open* daily) This is another lovely section of beach, but less developed than popular Red Reef and Spanish River. Walkways cut through the dense coastal undergrowth; lifeguards patrol 9–5; good swimming and some snorkelling.

Spanish River Park, *3001 N Ocean Boulevard* (*Open* daily) Boca Raton's 95-acre (38-ha) city park occupies both sides of A1A, with three tunnels linking the parking areas to a 1,850-foot (560m) strip of sun-soaked beachfront. Nature trails explore an undeveloped natural hammock and woodland preserve, and picnickers will find plenty of tables and barbecue grills. Bicycle tracks and a boat dock are provided, and there is good fishing on the Intracoastal Waterway. A two-level observation tower gives impressive views of the park, the coast and the town.

Addison Mizner was a somewhat unlikely candidate for the title of most influential architectural stylist in south Florida. This 280-pound (127kg) ex-prize fighter and retired miner rolled into Palm Beach in 1918, and today is credited with introducing the 1920s vogue for Spanish-style architecture.

Everglades Club Addison Mizner's first venture, the Everglades Club in Palm Beach, was a collaboration with Paris Singer, scion of the sewing machine fortune. Intended as a convalescent home for World War I veterans, it bears a strong resemblance to a Spanish monastery with its battery of medieval turrets and wrought-iron curlicues. The end of the war saw it swiftly redesignated as a private club, which it remains today. The club's eye-catching design was an instant hit, spawning a host of imitations, and its architect was signed up immediately to build winter residences for wealthy Philadelphia socialites – Stotesburys, Vanderbilts and Wanamakers.

Spain in the New World Mizner studied the Old World architecture of South America and traced it back to its roots in Spain. Conscious of the broad blue Florida sky as the only backdrop for his designs, he created bold pastel outlines and incorporated elegant courtyards surrounded by cool arcades. Red barrel roof tiles topped second-storey galleries, fountains played into tiled pools and decorative mosaic murals added a Roman-Mediterranean touch. Interiors had lofty vaulted ceilings with exposed beams hewn from mature pecky cypress. Buying trips furnished his creations with the trappings of Old Spain, and Mizner also set up local factories to reproduce ironwork, tiles, and furniture – the accessories for his buildings – in the correct Mediterranean style.

End of a dream In 1925, with the land boom in full swing, Mizner embarked on a lavish scheme to transform 16,000 acres (6,475 ha) around Boca Raton into a dream resort. 'I am the Greatest Resort in the World,' proclaimed the boastful advertisements, and they netted \$2 million worth of contracts on the first day of sales. Six months later, the boom was over, a devastating hurricane and a trail of dirty deals had caused the project to be renamed 'Beaucoup Rotten', and Mizner was penniless.

One enduring memorial to Mizner's fantasy resort is his \$1¼ million Cloister Inn (now the Boca Raton Resort and Club), believed to be the most expensive 100-room hotel built in its time – and a famous local landmark.

OLD FROM NEW
The pecky cypress has a pitted, streaky appearance; when attacked with wire brushes, blow torches and acids, then stained, it looks suitably antique.

Mizner Park, a place for up-market shopping and people-watching

LEARNING THE ROPES
There are five standard rodeo events (see Davie), and most of them are over pretty quickly. It helps to know a couple of the finer points, such as the rule that forbids saddle bronc riders from touching the saddle, the horse or themselves with their free hand. Bull riders must stay on for a minimum of eight seconds. And just to confuse the uninitiated, steer-wrestling is also known as 'bulldogging'.

Cattlemen's skills and Western fashions get a regular airing at Davie's rodeos

►► Broward County

Ah-Tah-Thi-Ki Museum, *Big Cypress Reservation (I-75 west to Exit 14; 17 miles/27km north on CR 833 to W Boundary Road)* (*Open* Tue–Sun 9–5. *Admission: moderate*; tel: 941/902-1113) This museum offers an insight into Seminole culture through artefacts, dioramas depicting traditional pursuits and crafts, and a film presentation. The museum's name translates to 'a place to learn, a place to remember', and keeps its motto with a living village area where Seminole crafts and cooking are still practised.

A couple of miles north, the **Billie Swamp Safari Wildlife Park** offers Everglades airboat and swamp buggy rides daily (tel: 941/983-6101).

Butterfly World, *3600 W Sample Road, Coconut Creek* (*Open* Mon–Sat 9–5, Sun 1–5. *Admission: expensive*; tel: 954/977-4400) Located southwest of Deerfield Beach and the Florida Turnpike, this attraction provides an unusual opportunity to be dazzled by the insect world. On a 3-acre site (1.2-ha) , some 2,000 butterflies from more than 100 species flit around huge screened enclosures such as the dramatic 30-foot-high (9m) Tropical Rain Forest Aviary equipped with observation decks, waterfalls, ponds and tunnels. Visitors can look in at the laboratory where thousands of larvae and pupae are visible at various stages of development, explore peaceful water gardens and displays of butterfly-attracting plants; a hummingbird aviary; and an **Insectarium and Museum**.

Davie A mere 10 miles (16km) from downtown Fort Lauderdale, Davie is another world. It would be unfair to call Davie a one-horse town, because it boasts enough hitching posts to secure the 7th Cavalry. This is definitely a town with horses on the brain, where even McDonald's got the idea loud and clear: the restaurant provides a 'ride-through' service for locals who believe in taking their food at a gallop. To complete the picture, the local town hall boasts swinging saloon doors and a bristling display of imported cacti.

The 5,000-seat **Davie Rodeo Arena**, *6591 SW 45th Street* (tel: 954/384-7075), is the scene of much of the town's horse-based activity. It provides live action in the 'Jackpot Rodeo' every Thursday night at 8, and a championship rodeo event on the fourth weekend of every month. Steer-wrestling, calf-roping, bareback riding and bronc- and bull-riding all find a place on the programme, and no self-respecting cowboy should miss the **Florida State Championship Rodeo**, which takes place every autumn (see box, page 23).

Everglades Holiday Park and Campground, *21940 Griffin Road* (*Open* daily 9–5; tel: 954/434-8111) On the eastern edge of the vast Everglades swamplands which stretch across the state to the Gulf of Mexico, the park allows a brief Glades experience, complete with alligator shows and airboat rides. Powered by aircraft propellers, these metal-frame contraptions zip across the shallow marshes, giving a ringside seat for viewing all the weird and wonderful native flora and fauna. Boat rentals are available.

Flamingo Gardens, *3750 Flamingo Road (north off Griffin Road)* (*Open* daily 9:30–5:30. *Admission: moderate*; tel: 954/473-2955) There is a bit of everything at this popular attraction. A tram ride explores the 60-acre (24-ha) site, which was one of the county's earliest citrus groves. In addition to the glossy citrus trees, there are botanical gardens where bromeliads and orchids flourish among the tropical scenery, and rare gingers and heliconias make an impressive display.

Wildlife exhibits run the gamut from alligators, crocodiles, monkeys and otters to birds of prey and a brilliantly coloured array of exotic birds including the flamingos who give the park its name. Other attractions include a pioneer homestead and a children's petting zoo.

► Deerfield Beach

Just a mile south of Boca Raton's city limits, Deerfield Beach is one of the few remaining strips of Gold Coast shoreline still of interest to shell seekers, but its best-kept secret is **Deerfield Island Park** (*Open* 8–dusk). Only accessible by boat, the island sits in the middle of the Intracoastal Waterway at its junction with the Hillsboro Canal. There is a free boat service from the dock at the end of Riverview Road (off Route 810 by the Chamber of Commerce) on Wednesdays and Saturdays. A stone's throw from the hurly-burly of A1A and the coastal developments, this little pocket of virgin wilderness offers two beautiful nature trails with a chance to see armadillos and grey foxes in the wild. The Coquina Trail parallels the Intracoastal Waterway to a rocky bluff, while the Mangrove Trail is a raised boardwalk through areas of black, red and white mangroves and around a wooded swamp.

HOLLYWOOD NATURAL

Just south of Fort Lauderdale, the $50-million Anne Kolb Nature Center and Marina, West Lake Park, 751 Sheridan Street, Hollywood (*Open* daily 8:30–5:30. *Admission: inexpensive*; tel: 954/926-2410), offers an entertaining back-to-nature experience. There is a 1,500-acre (605-ha) wetland mangrove forest habitat for ibis and herons, with an observation tower, walking, canoe and bicycle trails and narrated boat tours from the marina.

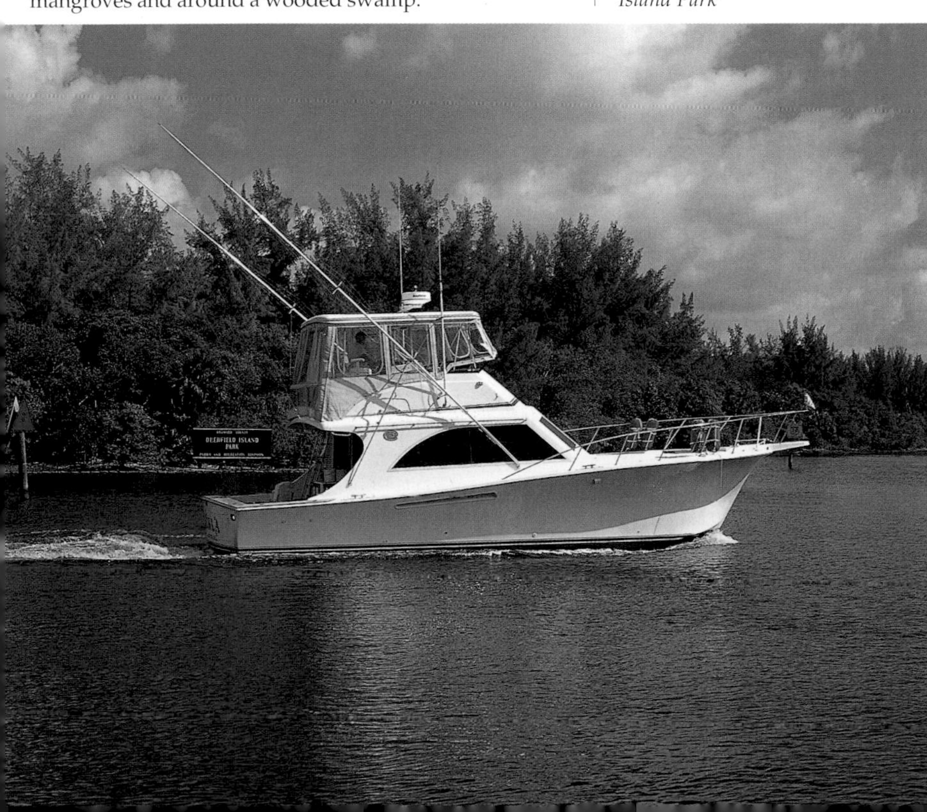

Getting away from it all by boat at Deerfield Island Park

►► Delray Beach

The earliest residents of this pleasant seaside town in the south of Palm Beach County were artists and craftsmen, and the Yamato Colony of Japanese pineapple farmers. Flagler's railroad stopped in town, and the old Ocean City Lumber Company site is being developed into a shopping and dining district behind **Atlantic Avenue**, Delray's main thoroughfare.

A one-mile (1.5km) section of downtown Atlantic Avenue has emerged as a popular visitor attraction. Its palm tree-lined pavements front an appealing collection of galleries, boutiques, speciality shops, and restaurants, and there is live music several times a week in a variety of clubs and bars. At the west end of the shops, the **Old School Square** (see panel) has been restored as a cultural arts centre. There are also visits to the **Cason Cottage** (call for schedules, tel: 561/243-0223) on NE First Street, just across from the Crest Theatre. This typical Florida-style wooden cottage dates from 1915, and is furnished with period antiques.

Morikami Museum and Japanese Gardens, 4000 Morikami Park Road (*Open* Tue–Sun 10–5. *Admission: moderate*; tel: 561/495-0233) These tranquil gardens are developing into one of the largest Japanese gardens in the US. Set amid lakes, pine forest and bonsai areas, waterfalls and lawns, the complex offers fascinating insights into Japanese art and traditions. The museum's collections include antique netsuke carvings, contemporary prints, musical instruments and folk crafts, such as origami (paper folding). You can learn about the tea ceremony and the ancient Japanese skill of bonsai culture (growing dwarf trees).

If possible, try to time your visit so that you can attend one of the four traditional Japanese seasonal festivals celebrated here: **Hatsume Fair** (February), **Bon Festival** (August), **Bunka No Hi** (November) and **Japanese New Year** (December/ January).

OLD SCHOOL SQUARE

Bordering Atlantic Avenue are three buildings set around this lawned complex which is now a National Historic Site. Whitewashed and smartly trimmed in aquamarine, the 1913 former Elementary School today is a showcase for the Cornell Museum of Art & History's changing exhibitions of works by national and local artists (for schedules, tel: 561/243-7198). The adjacent 1925 High School building has been transformed into the Crest Theatre, while the former gymnasium is a community hall.

Popular and stylish cafés line the beachfront of Delray Beach

Hitting the beach is an important ingredient of any Florida holiday, and although the Gold Coast was named for the Spanish treasure lost off its shores not its golden strands, visitors will still find beaches of every description, including wilderness beaches, along its coastline.

Fort Lauderdale area Even in downtown Fort Lauderdale, it's possible to relax on the beach. The **Hugh Taylor Birch State Recreation Area** is surrounded by a further 3½ miles (5.5km) of city beach, though the backdrop is a series of high-rise hotels and condominiums. A short distance south of Fort Lauderdale, **Hollywood Beach** (on Route A1A) is a beautiful stretch of golden sand and swaying palm trees. It runs into leafy **North Beach Park**, which has shady picnic areas, an observation tower and sea-turtle tanks. The quietest municipal beach in the area is little **Dania Beach**, off Oak Street. **John U Lloyd Beach State Recreation Area** has a coastal hammock nature trail (it may be possible to spot manatees in winter), and you can fish along the Intracoastal Waterway. **Pompano Beach**, with its fishing pier, is north of Fort Lauderdale, and there is **Deerfield Beach** (see page 143), which is a good spot for beachcombing.

Boca Raton area The first of the Boca Raton beaches, driving north, is **South Inlet Park**. It's the most secluded, good for peace and quiet during the week. Next up, **South Beach Park** (see page 140) is relatively undeveloped – in fact, it is positively backward compared with neighbouring **Red Reef Park** (see page 139), which has a golf course and nature centre across A1A. **Spanish River Park** (see page 140) is another family-oriented beach park with nature and bicycle trails. **Delray Beach** (see page 144) is good for shells, and there is a great little beach at **Lantana Park** en route to Palm Beach.

Palm Beach area A narrow 6-mile (9km) strip of sand borders the ocean at Palm Beach and parking can be a nightmare. For truly spectacular seashore head north to **John D MacArthur Beach State Park** (see page 157), which is a favourite nesting ground for sea turtles in summer. Continue north to **Juno Beach** (see page 158) for equally stunning beaches, though parking can be tricky here. **Blowing Rocks Beach** on Jupiter Island is not a good place to swim as it is rocky and dangerous, but the scenery is marvellous; venture on to **Jupiter Beach Park** for excellent swimming and walks along the shore.

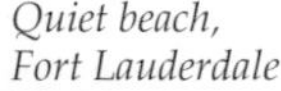

Quiet beach, Fort Lauderdale

CULTURAL CENTER
The magnificent $55-million Broward Center for the Performing Arts at 201 SW Fifth Avenue provides world-class facilities for opera, theatre, ballet, Broadway musicals and symphony and rock concerts. Artists as diverse as Itzhak Perlman, Marvin Hamlisch, Liza Minelli and Branford Marsalis have made appearances. The Parker Playhouse, 707 NE Eighth Street, also stages top-of-the-line Broadway productions.

►►► Fort Lauderdale

One of the most popular warm-weather destinations in the US, Fort Lauderdale also prides itself on being the 'Yachting Capital of the World' and the 'Venice of America' (300 miles/480km of navigable waterways). Less appealing is the nickname 'Fort Liquordale', from the days when rum runners kept the town generously supplied with liquor during Prohibition. In the 1950s, droves of college students on spring break revived the Liquordale image and inspired the 1960 beach blanket movie *Where the Boys Are*, until the harassed city fathers introduced legislation which effectively banished the student invasion in 1985. Fort Lauderdale breathed a sigh of relief as it got on with the job of promoting itself as a year-round family tourism destination.

Early days Fort Lauderdale's first known white settler was Charles Lewis, who created a plantation by the New River in 1793. Later, Major William Lauderdale came south to establish a small fort, the first of three, for the protection of local settlers during the Second Seminole War in 1838. Ohio steelworker Frank Stranahan was next on the scene. He set up an overnight camp for the Bay Biscayne Stage Line at Tarpon Bend in 1893 and founded the settlement by establishing the trading post.

For a few years, his main customers were the Seminoles, who traded pelts, alligator hides and egret plumes for provisions. The arrival of Henry Flagler's East Coast Railroad in 1896 created a mini boom. Soon there were enough children to justify having a schoolteacher, Ivy Cromartie, who later married Stranahan. Other local communities also sprang up – tomato-farming Danes congregated in **Dania**, Swedes settled in **Hallandale** and Georgians and North Carolinians migrated to **Pompano**.

Intracoastal yacht off Fort Lauderdale

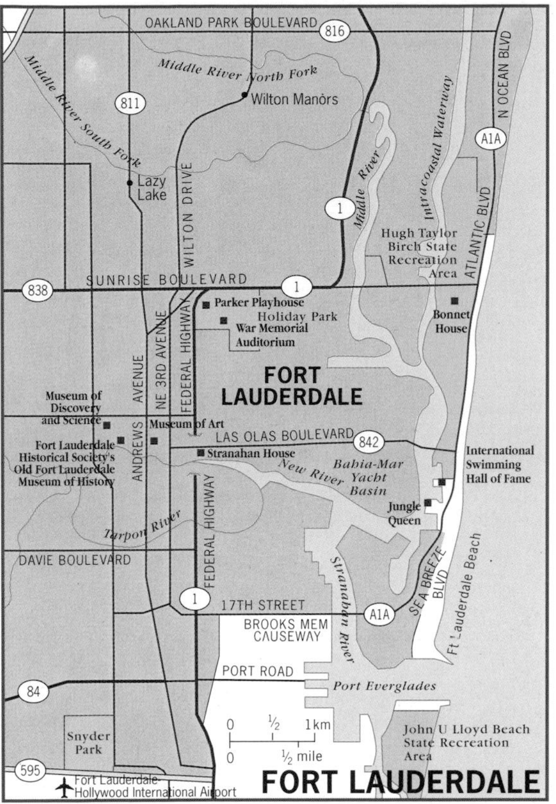

In 1906, Florida's governor, Napoleon Bonaparte Broward, launched his much-vaunted plan to drain the Everglades, and the Roaring Twenties heralded a massive programme of land reclamation. Near by, **Hollywood-by-the-Sea** was founded by developer Joseph Young, who was also the visionary behind **Port Everglades**.

Today, Greater Fort Lauderdale is experiencing a resurgence in tourism, development and population growth on a scale not seen since the 1920s Land Boom. Several billion dollars have been poured into an urban redesign programme that extends from the renovation and expansion of the international airport to the beautification of the beachfront and the completion of the downtown **Riverwalk**, which links the city's past and future as it follows the course of the New River from historic **Stranahan House** to the state-of-the-art **Broward Center for the Performing Arts**. Fort Lauderdale is now a lively, sophisticated year-round resort.

On the accommodation front, there are around 29,000 hotel rooms; they come in all prices, ranges and styles, from deluxe resorts to great-value beachfront motels. Free Tuk Tuk Trolley services operate between the beaches and the attractive shopping and dining district on fashionable Las Olas Boulevard – and do not miss the opportunity to cruise Fort Lauderdale's 'Venice' and ride in a water taxi: a fun and practical form of transport.

CROWD PLEASERS
In early May, Fort Lauderdale's popular Air & Sea Show, one of the largest air shows in the world, draws huge crowds with demonstrations by the US Air Force, a concert on the beach and night-time fireworks displays. The Beethoven By The Beach classical music festival in July is another big hit. In October, the Convention Center plays host to the Fort Lauderdale International Boat Show, attracting hordes of yachties.

WHAT'S NEW
Just south of Fort Lauderdale, the IGFA Fishing Hall of Fame & Museum (*Open* daily 10–6, Wed 10–8. *Admission: moderate*; tel: 954/922-4212) in Dania has been drawing the crowds. Part of the state-of-the-art World Fishing Center, it provides heaps of hands-on fun and virtual sportfishing experiences, as well as artefacts, special exhibitions, a kids' discovery room and outdoor marina.

ACT OF GOD
Sailing off Fort Lauderdale during a storm in the 1890s, millionaire Chicago attorney Hugh Taylor Birch was blown ashore. Taking his lucky escape as a sign from God, he promptly bought up a 3-mile (5km) stretch of the oceanfront for $3,000. Today, the Hugh Taylor Birch State Recreation Area (see page 150) and the Bonnet House estate, which was a wedding gift to Birch's daughter Helen (Frederic Bartlett's second wife), are the last remnants of Old Florida on the coast between Miami and Palm Beach.

Bonnet House, *900 N Birch Road* (*Guided tours* Wed–Fri 10–1:30, Sat–Sun noon–2:30. *Admission: moderate*; tel: 954/563-5393) Bonnet House, named for the yellow Everglades water lilies which flourish on the 35-acre (14-ha) beachfront site, is the legacy of two artists – Frederic Clay Bartlett and his third wife, Evelyn. In 1919, eschewing the Mediterranean influences of Mizner, Bartlett designed a gracious two-storey plantation house around a luxurious central garden courtyard that was intended to promote an indoor-outdoor lifestyle. Broad verandas and outdoor walkways overlook the informally landscaped gardens, which can be explored with a native trail map.

The spacious, airy ground floor (tours) is decorated with the results of successful beachcombing expeditions, antiques discovered on his European travels, and a veritable menagerie of animal and bird woodcarvings and carousel beasts as well as Frederic Bartlett's artwork—murals, frescoes, canvases. Evelyn Bartlett was a talented artist, and her paintings hang in a small gallery, while the orchid house was her special preserve.

Fort Lauderdale Historical Society's Old Fort Lauderdale Museum of History, *219 SW 2nd Avenue* (*Open* Tue–Fri and Sun noon–5, Sat 10–5. *Admission: inexpensive*; tel: 954/463-4431) Housed in the 1905 New River Inn, Fort Lauderdale's first hotel on the banks of the New River, the museum is the cornerstone of the Old Fort Lauderdale Historic District. The city's history is retold through documents such as pioneer Frank Stranahan's merchant license, period photographs, landscape paintings and dozens of artefacts including Seminole crafts and Addison Mizner's architectural plans. The photographs in particular form a fascinating record of an era of change from 1920 to 1948 as the New River marshes were transformed into today's criss-cross pattern of reclaimed land and canals.

Just down the street there is another small piece of history in the museum's **King-Cromartie House**, *229 SW 2nd Avenue* (*Open* for tours Sat noon, 1, 2, 3). This typical 1907 pioneer home is furnished as it would have been in 1915.

Fort Lauderdale claims to be the 'Yachting Capital of the World'

Built on reclaimed Everglades marshland, Fort Lauderdale bears the proud title of 'Venice of America'. However, with more than 300 miles (480km) of navigable inland waterways, Fort Lauderdale and Broward County actually outstrip Venice by a long way.

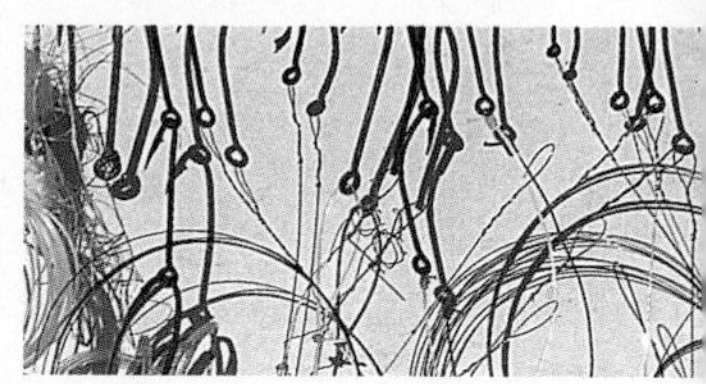

It all began with Governor Napoleon Bonaparte Broward, who won his political ticket on a promise to drain the Everglades for agricultural land. In 1906, true to his promise, he began a dredging programme on the New River at Sailboat Bend, employing settlers who had worked on the Panama Canal. The veterans of Panama called the first settlement on reclaimed land Zona, later to be renamed **Davie** after a local cattle baron.

In 1912, the North New River Canal reached Lake Okeechobee, creating a brief fad for cross-state steamboat cruises to Fort Myers, but heavy silt closed the canal in 1921. In the same year, Messrs M A Hortt, R E Dye and Thomas N Stilwell, inspired by Carl Fisher's Miami Beach land reclamation project, dreamed up a landfill operation for a stretch of mangrove swampland between the New River and the Intracoastal Waterway. They christened it Idlewyld, and it now forms part of downtown Fort Lauderdale.

Building an American Venice Idlewyld's success was the cue for seed-store merchant and real-estate investor Charlie Rodes to enter the arena. Using a Venetian land-building technique known as 'finger-islanding', he dredged a series of parallel canals from central Las Olas Boulevard towards the river, and created narrow peninsulas with landfill from the channels. Each peninsula had a central dead-end road with waterfront plots on either side, and this grid of exclusive little fingers of land was called the Venetian Isles. It remains the most sought-after real estate in the city.

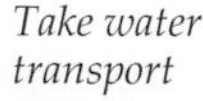

Take water transport

Sightseeing Forget the car – the best way to explore Fort Lauderdale's prime waterfrontage is by boat. Take a 90-minute Riverfront Cruise from Las Olas Riverfront (daily every two hours 10:30–8:30; tel: 954/267-3699) for a view of stately mansions, mega yachts and Port Everglades, or take to the canals with the city's water taxi service. Taxis provide pick-up services for several hotels, restaurants and sights, including Stranahan House, the Museum of Discovery and Science and the Galleria Mall (allow 10 minutes). One-way fares are expensive, all-day passes are better value. Multi-journey passes are valid for 20 trips. For information and bookings, tel: 954/467-6677.

Get away from the city bustle in Hugh Taylor Birch State Recreation Area

Hugh Taylor Birch State Recreation Area, *3109 E Sunrise Boulevard* (*Open* daily 8am–dusk. *Admission: inexpensive*; tel: 954/564-4521) Fort Lauderdale residents and visitors have reason to be grateful to Hugh Taylor Birch, who provided them with 180 acres (72ha) of city centre parkland. A green oasis sandwiched between the seafront hotels of Atlantic Boulevard and the Intracoastal Waterway, the park is the ideal antidote to life in the city, with walking trails, picnic areas, canoe hire, boating, a fitness course and an underpass to a section of ocean beach. A 1¾-mile (3km) circuit around the park can be walked, jogged or driven. The **Beach Hammock Trail** leads off into the natural hammock and mangrove areas.

The area provides a haven for wildlife, as well as humans. There are around 524 species of plants and trees in the park, such as gumbo limbo, Australian pines, mangroves and strangler figs. Butterflies, raccoons, squirrels, marsh rabbits and owls can be spotted by eagle-eyed explorers, and wading birds frequent the lagoon and shores of the Intracoastal Waterway. This is also a good fishing spot.

Near the entrance, a visitor centre housed in Birch's final residence provides a brief introduction to the park's history, flora and fauna, along with a short film and exhibits.

International Swimming Hall of Fame, *501 Seabreeze Boulevard* (*Open* Mon–Fri 9–7, Sat–Sun 9–5. *Admission: moderate*, under-12s free; tel: 954/462-6536) Do you remember Mark Spitz and his Olympic gold medals? Did you know that the legendary Johnny Weissmuller was an Olympic champion swimmer before he became the star of the *Tarzan* films? In addition to celebrating the feats of Olympic heroes, the Hall of Fame exhibits technical equipment used in professional racing, historical data and records, and even swimwear – from old woolen bathing suits to sleek modern racing gear.

The state-of-the-art neighbouring **Aquatic Complex** has two Olympic pools and diving facilities for those who want to create records of their own.

THE INTRACOASTAL WATERWAY

Florida's Intracoastal Waterway is part of a coastal boating route which runs parallel to the Atlantic Ocean and north to Chesapeake Bay in Maryland. The first section of the Intracoastal Waterway was dredged in the 1880s from pre-existing natural waterways. It ran from St Augustine to Daytona. By 1935, the channel ran the length of the state: A minimum 100 feet (30m) wide and 8 feet (2.5m) deep, it is maintained by the US Army Corps of Engineers.

Jungle Queen, *Bahia Mar Yachting Center, 801 Seabreeze Boulevard (A1A) (Open* daily. *Admission: expensive*; tel: 954/462-5596) The Jungle Queen riverboats provide an unusual form of transport and are a great way to explore the city and its environs. Three-hour narrated sightseeing cruises depart twice a day (at 10 and 2), and travel up the New River through downtown and into the edge of the Everglades. En route, the boats pass Fort Lauderdale's most exclusive neighbourhoods, and stop at a re-created Native American village to watch alligator- wrestling bouts.

You can also take a day trip to Miami (call for schedules), or sail up the New River on the four-hour **Barbecue Ribs and Shrimp Dinner Cruise** (daily at 7:30pm), which docks at an island for an all-you-can-eat spread and a vaudeville revue.

Museum of Art, *1 E Las Olas Boulevard* (*Open* Tue 10–9, Wed–Sat 10–5, Sun noon–5. *Admission: moderate*; tel: 954/525-5500) Designed by Edward Larabee Barnes and opened in 1986, this modern museum showcases its extensive collections of 19th- and 20th-century American and European art. Of particular note are works by the post-war CoBrA group, a collection of artists from Denmark, Belgium and Holland, whose title derives from the initial letters of their respective capitals, Copenhagen, Brussels and Amsterdam. There are also collections of African and pre-Columbian artefacts, and changing exhibitions which focus on specific periods and art forms. During September and October, the gallery displays the pick of entries for the M Allen Hortt Memorial Competition, south Florida's most prestigious art prize. Souvenir hunters can enjoy browsing through the museum store for great cards, posters, art books and handcrafted jewellery.

WHAT TO SEE IN DANIA

There is little trace of Dania's turn-of-the-20th century Danish origins, but this beachside community has a treasure in the acclaimed Graves Museum of Archaeology & Natural History, 481 S Federal Highway (*Open* Tue–Sat 10–6, Sun noon–6. *Admission: moderate*; tel: 954/925-7770). Local exhibits focus on the Tequesta tribe of south Florida. There are also Greco-Roman, Egyptian and South American artefacts, and a section on marine archaeology. Other Dania attractions include the 100-plus shops of Dania's Antique Row; and John U Lloyd Beach State Recreation Area (see page 145).

An easy way of seeing the sights

TEQUESTA TRACES
When Major Lauderdale founded the fort which bears his name, he chose a piece of high ground that was actually five Tequesta Native American mounds on the banks of the New River. There is evidence that the Tequestas inhabited the region between Miami and Pompano Beach some 3,000 years ago. They moved between permanent settlements on the coast and Everglades encampments, and lived off a diet of seafood, palm nuts, palmetto berries, venison and turtle and manatee meat.

Museum of Discovery and Science, *401 SW Second Street* (*Open* Mon–Sat 10–5, Sun noon–6. *Admission: moderate*; tel: 954/467-6637) Located in downtown's arts and sciences district, this museum is a favourite with kids. It is packed from floor to ceiling with more than 200 hands-on exhibits. On the ground floor, the walk-through Florida EcoScapes area contains one of the largest Atlantic Coast aquariums in the US, baby gators, turtles and a bat cave among a series of cleverly simulated natural habitats (such as a see-through beehive which you can also walk into). The innovative and colourful games area in the Discovery Center provides entertainment for little ones.

On the upper level, dozens of interactive displays cast an educational but fun look at health, sound and myriad gadgets, from a game of virtual volleyball to computer programming. SpaceBase is a particular favourite where space freaks can jump on the **Manned Maneuvering Unit** space ride – but be warned, this is not recommended for the weak of stomach. There's also a 3-D IMAX cinema with a five-storey-high screen, a museum café and the inevitable shop.

Riverwalk, *one block west of Andrews Avenue and one block south of Broward Boulevard* (tel: 954/522-6556) River frontage is prime real estate in Fort Lauderdale, but general access has always been limited in the past. The Riverwalk development has changed all this by providing a delightful stretch of downtown pedestrian footpath along the New River, which extends from Stranahan House to the historic Old Fort Lauderdale district and on to the Broward Center for the Performing Arts. Landscaped with lush tropical trees, native plants and winding walkways, Riverwalk provides a welcome interlude, with its outdoor cafés, picnic tables in gazebos and park benches for relaxing. There are free brunch jazz sessions on the first Sunday of each month.

The latest addition to Riverwalk's attractions is **Las Olas Riverfront**, a major shopping, dining and entertainment complex with water's edge views and filled with speciality shops, pavement cafés, bookshops and restaurants. New River cruises depart from the wharf.

Dolphins can be seen in the waters around Florida

Drive

Fort Lauderdale to the Palm Beaches

See map on page 136.

Two main routes run the length of Florida's east coast: the fast I–95 and the seaside route A1A. Palm Beach makes an excellent day trip from Fort Lauderdale, and a good way to see more of the area is to take a gentle drive up A1A. The trip back via I–95 can be undertaken in less than an hour later in the day.

From the intersection with Sunrise Boulevard, drive north on Atlantic Boulevard (A1A) for 7 miles (11km) to Pompano Beach.

Pompano Beach is acclaimed as the 'Swordfish Capital of the World', with a list of record catches just as long as one of those fishermen's tales. Its 1,080-foot (330m) **Municipal Pier** is a popular spot with anglers, and during winter there is a well-supplied Farmers' Market.

The Intracoastal Waterway appears to the left at Hillsboro (2 miles/3km); to the right, luxuriant greenery conceals wealthy beachfront villas.

If it is Wednesday or Saturday and there is time to spare, the intersection with **Route 810** at **Deerfield Beach** is the cue to turn left for the boat service to **Deerfield Island Park**, a 56-acre (22-ha) natural preserve on the Intracoastal Waterway (see page 143).

Continue on A1A for a short distance to the intersection with Camino Real at Boca Raton.

Founded by 1920s architect and developer Addison Mizner, **Boca Raton** is well worth a detour off the A1A for a taste of its palm-fringed elegance (see pages 138–40).

Turn left on to Camino Real and follow the old canal route past the deluxe Boca Raton Resort and Club to the intersection with Federal Highway; turn right. At Palmetto Park Road is Mizner Park, a Mediterranean-style shopping, dining and entertainment complex, and one of Boca's top attractions. Turn right here and rejoin A1A opposite South Beach Park (see page 140), along a stretch of tree-lined roadside which continues most of the way to Highland Beach and Delray Beach (8 miles/13km).

An unusual detour at **Delray Beach** is the **Morikami Museum and Japanese Gardens** (see page 144). To get the best out of the gardens, follow the nature trails, but take it slowly. Take time to appreciate the subtle harmony of Japanese style.

A1A continues up the coast to Palm Beach. After 16 miles (25km) the road divides: both A1A and the right-hand fork, South Ocean Boulevard, intersect Royal Palm Way, which crosses the Intracoastal Waterway to West Palm Beach and I–95.

You can get away from it all

The Gold Coast does not earn the name from its miles of sandy beaches, its millionaire residents, or its year-round sunshine. The gold in question comes from the sea.

AIR MYSTERY
The likelihood of discovering a new wreck is pretty remote, but that is not to say it is impossible. One unexpected find by treasure hunters was a clutch of five World War II Avenger aircraft in some 700 feet (210m) of water 10 miles (16km) from Fort Lauderdale's beach. The discovery prompted speculation that the 'Lost Squadron' of Bermuda Triangle fame had been located finally, but the Avengers were from a different flight group, so the mystery continues.

Spanish treasure During the 17th and 18th centuries, Spanish treasure fleets laden with bounty from the New World started the journey homeward hugging the south Florida coastline. Their efforts to avoid offshore storms were often to no avail, and many vessels were tossed on to the reefs or sunk with their priceless cargoes of gold, silver and precious stones and a corresponding loss of life.

One of the most notable losses was the sinking of 11 vessels off the aptly named Treasure Coast between Vero Beach and Fort Pierce, north of Palm Beach, on the night of 30 July, 1715. The Spanish began their own salvage operation immediately, and it continued for some years; more recently the renowned Florida marine-treasure specialists Real Eight and Treasure Salvors Inc have made a more comprehensive sweep.

Natural reefs The needle-sharp underwater rock formations that plagued the Spanish off the Gold Coast are the upper reaches of south Florida's three-tiered network of natural reefs, which extend 220 miles (354km) northwards from the Florida Keys. This is the largest natural reef area in North America, and it is home to a magnificent variety of marine life: fish, lobsters, snails, sponges, jellyfish and sea anemones. Viewed through goggles, the reef can look like a fantasy landscape.

Coral-reef scuba diving

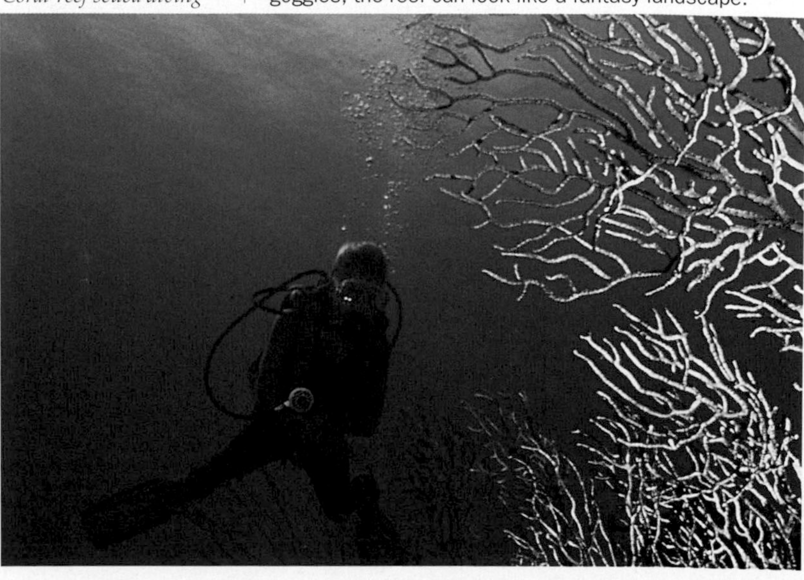

Costumes, utensils, period photographs and information panels illustrate pioneer life along the Loxahatchee River in this well-designed small museum. Other topics covered in the museum include Flagler's railroad, shipwrecks and native Seminole life accompanied by displays of carved bone tools, hammer heads, ornaments and clothing, as well as a collection of authentic, thatched chickee huts on the grounds. The natural hammock area around the museum is laid out with boardwalk trails and interpretive displays, and there is also the Tindall House – Palm Beach County's oldest-known Cracker home dating from 1892.

The museum has two other properties: a small historical museum in the restored, red-brick, 105-foot (32m) **Jupiter Lighthouse** (*Open* Sun–Wed 10–4), which was designed by General Mead who later led the Union forces at the Battle of Gettysburg, and completed in1860; and **Dubois House**, *19075 Dubois Road* (*Guided tours* Wed and Sun 1–4), a typical pioneer home built on top of a Native American shell mound in the late 1890s.

▶ Jupiter Island

Turn off A1A on to Route 707 for Jupiter Inlet Colony at the southern tip of the island and the town of Jupiter Island to the north.

These two elite residential communities have attracted the likes of Jacqueline Kennedy (who came here after President John F Kennedy's assassination in 1963), George Bush's mother and singer Perry Como – who forgot to mention that his 'little bit of heaven' was rather richer and more secluded than ordinary old downtown Jupiter on the mainland.

Blowing Rocks Preserve, *Route 707* (*Open* daily 6–5. *Admission: donation*; tel: 561/744-6668) Get here early to find a parking space and explore the preserve before the crowds arrive. Your visit should be timed to coincide with high tide, when the preserve really lives up to its name as fountains of spray are punched up through blowholes in limestone outcrops along the rocky shoreline.

A hardwood hammock borders the sand dunes, where sea grapes, palmetto and cabbage palms combine with colourful, hardy wildflowers and saltwater-resistant sea oats to anchor the sand. Woodpeckers and warblers, pelicans and osprey can all be seen. No swimming.

TURTLE TIMES

Between May and August, hundreds of female sea turtles make an annual pilgrimage to Florida's southeast coast, where they come ashore to lay their eggs in the sand. It is thought the females return to nest on the same beach on which they hatched. Loggerhead, green and leatherback turtles all frequent the Florida shores. The leatherback is the most distinctive – capable of growing up to 6½ feet (2m) in length and weighing 1,300 pounds (590kg). It doesn't have a hard shell.

Royal tern, seen around the coast

Henry Morrison Flagler was born in Hopewell, New York, on 2 January, 1830. The son of a struggling Presbyterian minister, he left home at the age of 14 and sought work with relatives in Ohio; by 1852, he was a partner in their grain and distillery business.

When a venture into the profitable Michigan salt industry was wiped out by the Civil War, Flagler moved to Cleveland, where he recouped his fortunes and made the acquaintance of John D Rockefeller, owner of a small oil company. In 1867, Flagler and an Englishman, Samuel Andrews, became Rockefeller's partners. Together they launched an American legend, the Standard Oil Company, in 1870.

The East Coast Railroad Flagler originally visited Florida in the early 1880s with his first wife. After her death, he married again (there would be three wives in all) and honeymooned with his new bride in St Augustine. The old-world charm of the city (founded by the Spanish in the 1560s), the winter sunshine and the enormous development potential captured Flagler's imagination. He chose young architects John M Carrère and Thomas Hastings to design a fabulous Spanish/Moorish-style hotel, the Ponce de León, which opened in St Augustine in 1888. To save his customers the indignity of abandoning their comfortable Pullman cars at Jacksonville, taking a ferry across the St Johns River and roughing it on the rickety local railroad, Flagler bought up the existing railroad, converted it to standard gauge, and built a rail bridge over the river.

Now committed to his vision of creating an American Riviera along Florida's east coast, Flagler began building hotels and buying out local railroads, extending his line down to Titusville and Cocoa in 1893 and Palm Beach in 1894. Then in 1896 Miami pioneer Julia Tuttle convinced him that he should continue the line to Miami.

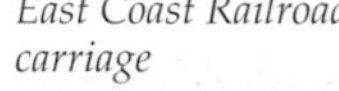

East Coast Railroad carriage

A dream fulfilled The greatest challenge was still to come – the 156-mile (250km) engineering feat that took Flagler's railroad down the Florida Keys. Three thousand workmen toiled for more than seven years to carve a path through marsh and jungle, built bridges and viaducts, and connected islands and hundreds of coral reefs until the first official train made the journey into Key West on 22 January, 1912. Flagler was on board and announced: 'Now I can die happy; my dream is fulfilled.' He died on 20 May, 1913.

▶▶▶ Palm Beach

Palm Beach has been cited as 'an example of what God would do if He had money'. And this magnificently manicured, palm-fringed, and exclusive enclave is all about serious money. It owes its fortunes to a typical Gold Coast occurrence – a shipwreck. In 1878, a Spanish brigantine, the aptly named *Providencia*, foundered off the coast with a cargo of 20,000 coconuts. A handful of settlers planted the coconuts, named the settlement after them, and the resulting swathe of tropical palms inspired Henry Flagler to create an elite winter resort here, marked by the opening of the Royal Poinciana Hotel in 1894, since demolished (see panel).

The Mizner vision In 1918, Addison Mizner arrived in town with a vision of his own. The former miner launched his career with the Spanish Revival-style **Everglades Club** on Worth Avenue. Prone to omitting such tiresome necessities as kitchens from his house plans, Mizner was in his element when designing public spaces. The 300 block of **Worth Avenue**, one of the world's most exclusive shopping streets, is a typical Mizner creation of elegant boutiques, decorated with a sprinkling of outdoor staircases, decorative wrought ironwork, tropical shrubs and vines. This is where the rich and famous gather for lunch during the winter season in between cruising the famous name stores (see page 171).

Palm Beach practicalities Anyone can visit Palm Beach, but to feel at home on Worth Avenue or to slip into The Breakers for a cocktail, it helps to dress up. Car parking is hard to come by, and the Palm Beach traffic police are tireless. Meters are limited to one or two hours, but Whitehall has its own parking area.

A GRAND RESORT
Henry Flagler drew the cream of American society to Palm Beach. Princelings and presidents were entertained at Whitehall, Flagler's magnificent 'seaside cottage'. Others flocked to his Royal Poinciana hotel, once the largest resort hotel in the world, and possibly the biggest wooden structure ever built. Today, the grandest hotel in town is The Breakers, 1 S County Road, a fabulously ornate 1926 Italianate marvel and not to be missed. For a glimpse of Palm Beach's most impressive private residences, head for South Ocean Boulevard, nicknamed 'Mansion Row'. The biggest property of all is Mar-a-Lago (No 1000), now an exclusive private club.

The suitably palm-shaded entrance road to Palm Beach

MAINTAINING STANDARDS
The battle to keep Palm Beach exclusive and genteel, started by its founder Henry Flagler, continues unabated. A series of municipal bylaws ban washing a car in public, hanging out a washing line and – horror of horrors – jogging bare-chested.

WALK SMALL
Flagler had the builders construct the frescoed ceiling of the Marble Hall in the Whitehall mansion 8 feet (2.5m) lower than the original designs, so he would 'feel at home'.

Henry Morrison Flagler's magnificent Whitehall mansion

Bethesda-by-the-Sea Church, *141 S County Road* (*Open* daily 8–5. *Admission free*; tel: 561/655-4554) Built in 1927, southeast Florida's first Protestant church is a little gem of Spanish-Gothic restraint amid the opulence. It has some lovely stained-glass windows. Behind the church, take a stroll around the formal plantings of the quiet **Cluett Memorial Gardens**.

Henry Morrison Flagler Museum, *Coconut Row* (*Open* Tue–Sat 10–5, Sun noon–5. *Admission: moderate*; tel: 561/655-2833) The Whitehall mansion, Henry Flagler's wedding present to his third wife, Mary Lily Kenan, was designed by John M Carrère and Thomas Hastings, architects of Flagler's grandiose Ponce de León Hotel in St Augustine. The classic two-storey villa near Lake Worth took just 18 months to build and cost around $2.5 million. It is now a museum. The interior is a monument to historic European styles, and has some 55 lavishly decorated rooms crammed with paintings, porcelain and antiques, most of which are originals from Flagler's time.

Portraits of Flagler and his granddaughter, Jean Flagler Matthews, who rescued the building from demolition in 1959, hang in the impressive Marble Hall where the guided tours begin, passing from the Italian Renaissance Library to Mary Flagler's opulent Music Room, with its acreage of highly polished parquet and French windows to the South Porch, a favourite setting for her musical tea parties. The magnificent Louis XV-style ballroom was designed to spill out into the courtyard. Renaissance France was the inspiration for the superb dining room. Take time to admire the extraordinary detail of the coffered ceiling created with gilded woodcarvings inset with dainty papier-mâché. Of the bedrooms, the English Arts and Crafts Movement chamber was a novel addition, and the combination of matching wallpaper and fabric in the Yellow Roses Room was also an innovation.

Beachside houses in the wealthy town of Palm Beach

As befitted a champion of train travel, Henry Flagler had his own railroad carriage, *The Rambler*, which has come to rest in the garden. It has been immaculately restored to its original glory with the help of photographs from the Flagler era. Oak-panelled, plumply upholstered and fitted with carpets and chandeliers, it even boasts a copper-lined shower and a tiny private kitchen with a wood-burning stove, a sink and an icebox for preparing refreshments en route.

Palm Beach Bicycle Trail Cycling is a great way to explore Palm Beach and take a leisurely look at some of the more imposing mansions. Most of the streets are shaded by outsized palms, and the terrain is flat as a pancake – this is Florida, after all. The official breezy cycle trail parallels Lake Worth, opposite the mainland.

You can venture further afield to South Ocean Boulevard and along the ocean side of the island. Many local hotels loan bicycles to their guests, and cycles can also be hired from the **Palm Beach Bicycle Shop**, *223 Sunrise Avenue* (*Open* Mon–Sat 9–5, Sun 10–5; tel: 561/659-4583). The shop also supplies a cycle trail map, showing a route that runs parallel to the Intracoastal Waterway and loops round to the beachfront and Worth Avenue.

Society of Four Arts Gardens, *Four Arts Plaza off Royal Palm Way* (*Open* Mon–Sat 10–5, Sun 2–5. *Admission free*; tel: 561/655-7226) This venerable cultural institution has a series of beautiful enclosed gardens, filled with plants, trees and the odd carp pond. The focus is the **Philip Hulitar Sculpture Garden**, with its contemporary exhibits. The center itself has an art gallery (Dec to mid-Apr) which plays host to changing exhibitions, a library, plus a theatre with a music and dance programme.

BEACH BREAKS

There are a couple of access points to the shore in Palm Beach. The diminutive Mid-Town Beach, 400 S Ocean Boulevard, is found opposite the eastern end of Worth Avenue. For a more expansive stretch of sand, head south to Phipps Ocean Park, 2145 S Ocean Boulevard, which has a handful of picnic tables and barbecue grills, as well as the historic 1886 Little Red Schoolhouse.

As befits one of the world's top holiday destinations, the Gold Coast does not just rely on its miles of sandy beach to occupy visitors. Sports enthusiasts can easily indulge in their favourite pursuits, from golf and tennis to sportfishing or polo.

JAI ALAI
Introduced to Miami by Cuban immigrants, this fast and furious spectator sport (see page 82) is featured at one Gold Coast site: Dania Jai-Alai, 301 E Dania Beach Boulevard/A1A (Games daily Tue–Sat at noon and 7:15pm, Sun at 1pm. *Admission: inexpensive*; tel: 954/920-1511). Games last 15 minutes with a 10-minute break in between – used by spectators to place complicated bets – and there are a dozen or so games each evening.

Jai alai, Cuban-style pelota

Armchair sports fans will have a field day too, with the frenetic excitement of jai alai (see panel), excellent polo, baseball courtesy of the Florida Marlins, plus hockey action from the NHL's Florida Panthers at the National Car Rental Center, 1 Panther Parkway, Sunrise (tel: 954/835-8326). Spring training sees the St Louis Cardinals and the Montreal Expos at the Roger Dean Stadium, 4751 Main Street, Jupiter (tel: 561/775-1818) in north Palm Beach County.

Golf Palm Beach County boasts more than 145 public and private golf courses, while Greater Fort Lauderdale can offer more than 50.

In the Fort Lauderdale area several top resorts offer all-inclusive golfing packages, including **Bonaventure Country Club**, tel: 954/389-2100; and **Palm Aire Country Club and Golf Academy** in Pompano Beach, tel: 954/974-7699. For notable non-residential courses, try **Deer Creek**, Deerfield Beach, tel: 954/421-5550; **Inverrary Country Club**, Lauderhill, tel: 954/733-7550; and the public **Pompano Beach Municipal Golf Course**, tel: 954/781-0426. Around Boca Raton, there is the **Boca Raton Municipal Golf Course**, tel: 561/483-6100, and oceanfront **Red Reef Executive Golf Course**, tel: 561/391-5014. West Palm Beach has Fazio-designed **Emerald Dunes**, tel: 561/684-4653, and 45 championship holes at the **Palm Beach Polo, Golf and Country Club**, tel: 561/798-7000. For both golf and tennis, try the excellent **PGA National Resort and Spa**, tel: 561/627-2000.

Polo It should be no surprise that the Gold Coast is the winter home of this princely pastime; the good news is that it does not cost a fortune to watch. The season runs from December/January into April and attracts a host of celebrity fans, which makes star-spotting almost as riveting as the polo action itself. For a look at both, check out the weekend action at **Royal Palm Polo Sports Club**, 18000 Jog Road, Boca Raton, tel: 561/994-1876, and **Palm Beach Polo, Golf and Country Club**, 11199 Polo Club Road, Wellington, tel: 561/798-7000. Teams of four horses and riders compete during six 7-minute

chukkers (periods). If the teams are tied at 3:30, the game continues until one side wins.

Sportfishing is a popular pastime in Florida

Sportfishing Fort Lauderdale's **Bahia Mar Marina**, 801 Seabreeze Boulevard, tel: 954/764-2233; and **Pier 66 Marina**, 2301 SE 17th Street, tel: 954/728-3572, are packed with charter fishing boats. But the top fishing spot is probably Pompano Beach, where the **Hillsboro Inlet Charter Fleet**, 2629 N Riverside Drive, tel: 954/943-8222, operates about a dozen charter vessels on the trail of marlin, pompano, shark and sailfish.

Tennis With inspiration in the form of local legend Chrissie Evert, tennis fans will find facilities galore, with 550 local courts in the Fort Lauderdale area. Try the **Jimmy Evert Tennis Center at Holiday Park**, tel: 954/761-5378; or contact the **City of Fort Lauderdale Parks and Recreation Department**, tel: 954/761-5000. Boca Raton has some distinctly stylish courts. Try the **Boca Del Mar Tennis and Golf Club**, tel: 561/392-8118; **Boca Pointe Racquet Club**, tel: 561/391-5100, ext 65; or **Memorial Park**, tel: 561/393-7978. In West Palm Beach, there is **Gaines Park Tennis Center**, tel: 561/659-0735, or ask advice from the **Palm Beach Recreation Department**, tel: 561/964-4420.

You're never far from a good golf course in Florida

West Palm Beach, once Palm Beach's poor relation, is now an important business centre

▶▶▶ West Palm Beach

If Palm Beach was born with the proverbial silver spoon in its mouth, West Palm Beach was the poor relation. The workers and the commercial and industrial services required to keep Henry Flagler's elite resort running smoothly were conveniently housed out of sight across the Intracoastal Waterway. However, it was West Palm Beach that became the administrative seat of Palm Beach County when it was created in 1909, and West Palm has developed as a business center for law, accounting and brokerage firms, while building a new reputation for computer and electronics manufacturing.

Downtown West Palm Beach is currently undergoing a massive redevelopment programme which began with the stunning Raymond F Kravis Center for the Performing Arts and the revitalisation of the Clematis Street shopping, dining and entertainment district. The $350-million CityPlace retail and entertainment complex is the focus of the western end of downtown, together with a new opera house scheduled to open in time for the 2001–2002 season. And if that were not enough, an exciting Fine Arts District is taking shape with a gallery row just south of Clematis.

Beyond downtown, West Palm Beach's attractions are spread widely, particularly to the west of the city. To the north, Riviera Beach is the departure point for water taxi trips out to Peanut Island, and the water taxis also offer scenic cruises with additional departures from the busy **Sailfish Marina** complex (tel: 561/775-2628) on Palm Beach Shores, across the Intracoastal Waterway.

Sailfish Marina has one of the largest charter fishing fleets in the area and anglers will find plenty of action around the Palm Beaches. Sportfishing charters are available from Boynton Beach, Lantana and Riviera Beach, as well as from Palm Beach Shores.

Avid fishermen can try their luck at the fish camps out at Lake Okeechobee, the headwater of the Everglades which is teeming with largemouth bass, or, closer to home, Lake Worth, which is renowned for its fishing, particularly bass.

ALL THE FUN OF THE FAIR

West Palm Beach has the lion's share of festivals. January sees the South Florida Fair, a two-week-long event combining agricultural exhibits, live entertainment and rides and games out at the Fairground. Meanwhile, February brings the Palm Beach International Film Festival, culminating in an awards gala at the Raymond F Kravis Center. The four-day Sunfest in April–May is one of the region's biggest events, with nonstop jazz, arts and crafts, food stands, puppet shows, dance demonstrations and more.

Arthur R Marshall Loxahatchee National Wildlife Refuge, *off US 441/SR 7 (west of Boynton Beach)* (*Open* daily 6am–dusk, visitor centre 9–4. *Admission: inexpensive*; tel: 561/734-8303) The closest entrance to the Everglades from the Palm Beaches, this 220-square-mile (570sq km) sawgrass and hammock preserve is a haven for an impressive variety of native wildlife, and has a wilderness canoe trail on the Loxahatchee River, a federally designated Wild and Scenic River. From the visitor centre, a boardwalk trail extends above an area of cypress swamp, where there is a chance to spot alligators; the marshland trail leads to a 20-foot (6m) look-out tower above a pond which is frequented by herons and other waterfowl.

Lion Country Safari, *W. Southern Boulevard (SR 80 at US 441/98 West)* (*Open* daily 9:30–5:30. *Admission: expensive*; tel: 561/793-1084) For a fun family day out, visit this 500-acre (200-ha) African wildlife park, complete with elephants, rhinos, bison, wildebeest, giraffes and chimps, as well as lions. The park opened in 1967 as the nation's first drive-through 'cageless' zoo, and the 1,000-plus animals are now well established. Though it is not the Serengeti, the brilliant Florida sunshine is a good substitute for the real thing.

After the drive, the **Safari World Amusement Park** offers a further chance for animal encounters and fairground rides. Enjoy a cruise on the *Safari Queen* or navigate a pedalboat around the lagoon, with its monkey islands and flamingo colony. You can meet a llama in the petting zoo, see alligators and snakes in the reptile park, walk the nature trail and delight in recent arrivals in the animal nursery.

Mounts Botanical Gardens, *531 N Military Trail* (*Open* Mon–Sat 8:30–4:30, Sun 1–5. *Admission: donation*; tel: 561/233-1749) These pretty gardens are a hidden treat. The 14-acre (5.5-ha) grassy plot has fruit groves, rare and flowering trees, and butterfly, herb and rose gardens, as well as colourful herbaceous borders and a central lily pond with a miniature rain forest section. There are guided tours on Saturday at 11am and Sunday at 2:30pm.

Norton Museum of Art, *1451 S Olive Avenue* (*Open* Tue–Sat 10–5, Sun 1–5. *Admission: moderate*; tel: 561/832-5194) An outstanding gallery founded by Chicago industrialist Ralph H Norton in 1941, the Norton's extensive collections are divided into four main areas. The most important of these is the **French Collection**, broadly representative of the late 19th- to early 20th-century Impressionist and Post-Impressionist era, with works by Monet, Matisse, Pissarro and Renoir, as well as Chagall, Dufy and Picasso.

Echoing its European counterpart, the **American Collection** includes works by Ernest Lawson, John Sloan, Winslow Homer, Edward Hopper, Georgia O'Keefe and Jackson Pollock. Bronzes, jade carvings, Buddhist sculpture and peerless ceramics occupy a gallery devoted to the **Chinese Collection**, and the fine **Sculpture Collection** embellishes an attractively landscaped patio garden with works by Degas, Henry Moore, Maillol and Duane Hanson.

NIGHTLIFE FOR NOTHING

Palm Beach County is streets ahead on the free outdoor entertainment front. On Thursday evenings year-round Clematis by Night brings live music and food stalls to the Clematis Street district in downtown West Palm Beach. Boca Raton's Mizner Park complex features the occasional Music in the Park series; while Art & Jazz on the Avenue livens up Delray Beach's Atlantic Avenue every Thursday evening during the winter season, switching to Summer Nights on Fridays in summer.

SCULPTURE SPECIAL
A few blocks south of the Norton Gallery are the Ann Norton Sculpture Gardens at 253 Barcelona Road (*Open* Tue–Sat 10–4. *Admission: inexpensive*; tel: 561/832-5328). The 3-acre (1.2-ha) gardens are devoted to the work of Ralph H Norton's wife, Ann Weaver. Her sculptures have been beautifully arranged against a luxuriant backdrop of native plants (many specifically chosen for their popularity with wild birds), and 300 varieties of palm trees. You can see small sculpture pieces in wood and marble in Norton's former studio.

The museum's reputation enables it to obtain some of the best travelling art shows circulating the United States, and there is a varied exhibition programme which highlights established artists and new discoveries.

Palm Beach Polo, Golf and Country Club, *11199 Polo Club Road, Wellington* (tel: 561/798-7000) On a Sunday afternoon in winter, everybody who is anybody in Palm Beach County packs a picnic basket and heads for the polo ground. The Palm Beach Polo, Golf and Country Club is one of the world's classiest polo venues, where international teams such as Les Diables Bleus compete in front of crowds which have included Dustin Hoffman, Calvin Klein, Sylvester Stallone and Larry Hagman in their ranks.

Polo is not the only spectator sport offered at the club. A 125-acre (50-ha) landscaped equestrian complex hosts the annual **Winter Equestrian Festival** and a wide range of other events which traditionally includes a World Cup qualifying competition. Meanwhile, golfers can take up the challenge of 45 championship holes devised by some of the top names in the golfing world.

Above: polo, a Palm Beach speciality
Left: striking sculpture in the Norton Museum of Art

Palm Beach Zoo at Dreher Park, *1301 Summit Boulevard* (*Open* daily 9–5. *Admission: moderate*; tel: 561/533-0887) This modest parkland setting is home to some 500 animals and birds from 100 different native and exotic species. Among the miscellaneous reptiles, a petting zoo and a small collection of butterflies, a sinuous Florida panther (on the endangered list) steals the show. A state-of-the-art tiger exhibit complete with jungle-style special effects is under construction and animal encounter programmes are scheduled throughout the day.

Peanut Island, *water taxi access from Riviera Beach* (*Admission free*; tel: 561/966-6600) A 79-acre (32-ha) sand island created in 1918, Peanut is being transformed into a country park with boat docks, a fishing pier, trails and a campsite. An unusual feature is the Kennedy Bomb Shelter constructed for the president in 1961 during the Cuban missile crisis. There are also plans for a maritime museum.

South Florida Science Museum, *4801 Dreher Trail North* (*Open* Mon–Thu 10–5, Fri 10–10, Sat 10–6, Sun noon–6. *Admission: moderate*; tel: 561/832-1988) Together with the zoo (above), this provides a terrific children's day out, with lots of hands-on exhibits, flashes, crackles and surprises. Adults who never grasped the basics, let alone the principles of physics, can learn more in an hour of chasing after a seven year old here than they did in their entire school careers. All the usual skeletons and dioramas are on display, but take a break to wander through the tropical Native Plant Center. The Light and Sight Hall unleashes the true spirit of investigation, with numerous hands-on exhibits.

The **Aldrin Planetarium**, at the heart of the museum complex, takes spectators on a fascinating journey through the universe. Weekend laser concerts are another popular feature, and the 16-inch (40cm) Newtonian Reflector telescope in the Gibson Observatory is one of the largest in the state.

MORE ATTRACTIONS FOR KIDS

Boomers Family Recreation Center, 3100 Airport Road, Boca Raton (tel: 561/347-1888), has go-karts, bumper boats and miniature golf. Rapids Water Park, 6566 N Military Trail, West Palm Beach (tel: 561/842-8756), is a good place to cool off. The Children's Science Explorium, 300 S Military Trail, Boca Raton (tel: 561/347-3913), offers plenty of hands-on fun; and the Sports Immortals Museum, 6830 N Federal Highway, Boca Raton (tel: 561/997-2575), is a fascinating rainy-day option for sports fans.

Some years ago, when a worldwide survey discovered that the single most popular holiday pursuit is shopping, the Gold Coast took note. Department stores, discount malls, designer boutiques and flea markets abound – shopaholics should be issued a health warning ... and several pairs of walking shoes.

Fort Lauderdale Downtown Fort Lauderdale's finest shopping street is chic **Las Olas Boulevard**, a delightfully landscaped district of pretty designer boutiques, art and antique galleries, and a choice of elegant little café-restaurants that are just the ticket for recuperating after a tough morning scrutinising price tags.

The new **Las Olas Riverfront** shopping and entertainment complex is also worth investigating, as is **The Galleria**, on E Sunrise Boulevard near the beach, which features 150 shops and restaurants, including Nieman Marcus, Jordan Marsh and Saks Fifth Avenue, Brooks Brothers, Polo/Ralph Lauren, and the Disney Store.

Head west of downtown to the Plantation district, where the cool marble and granite precincts of the **Fashion Mall of Plantation**, 321 N University Drive, offer a further 100 shops anchored by Macy's and Lord & Taylor. Lord & Taylor also has a **Clearance Center** near by which features the store's off-season merchandise at greatly reduced prices; periodic sales knock a further 40–50 per cent off already discounted price tags.

A delightful shopping haven in Palm Beach

Dedicated bargain hunters should make the trek out to **Sawgrass Mills**, 12801 W Sunrise Boulevard (9 miles/14km west of town), the world's largest designer outlet mall, with more than 270 manufacturers and retail outlets, plus brand-name discounters who slash prices on designer brands by up to 70 per cent. Levi's, Kenneth Cole, Brooks Brothers, Off 5th Saks Fifth Avenue and Ann Taylor all have discount stores, and there are electrical goods, toiletries, books, toys and fashions at amazing prices. But the fun does not stop there. In The Oasis area, shoppers can take a break at a Hard Rock Café, a cinema or GameWorks.

Another bargain-basement shopping opportunity is the 80-acre (32-ha) **Fort Lauderdale $wap Shop**, 3291 W Sunrise Boulevard, which also has a farmers' market with local produce, fairground rides and daily circus performances.

For specialist shopping, Dania's **Antiques Row**, on US 1, is a great place to browse for china, glass, furniture, silverware and jewellery.

Shopping along Worth Avenue, Palm Beach

Boca Raton Shopping is a way of life in Boca Raton, as is the colour pink. **Royal Palm Plaza**, N Federal Highway at Palmetto Park Road, has been nicknamed 'Pink Plaza' for the strawberry-ice-cream hue of its Spanish-style stucco buildings. Eighty boutiques, gift shops and speciality shops are ranged around elegantly landscaped courtyards and ornate fountains.

A stone's throw away, a delicate shade of salmon-pink distinguishes **Mizner Park** (see page 139), with its fine array of shops and restaurants. On the women's fashion front there is a Banana Republic, and Nicole Miller has her own boutique. Reluctant shoppers can take refuge in Liberties Fine Books & Music, which provides easy chairs for book browsers. Fashionable **Town Center Mall**, 6000 W. Glades Road, has lured the likes of Louis Vuitton and Laura Ashley to join Bloomingdale's and Saks Fifth Avenue in its Mediterranean-inspired complex, which numbers 180-plus shops and an array of fine dining options. Heading north, Delray Beach's **Atlantic Avenue** is an attractive downtown shopping district with a range of speciality shops, boutiques, antiques and cafés; and art lovers may like to check out **Lake Worth**, which is rapidly building a reputation as an artists' enclave served by several interesting galleries.

Palm Beaches One of the world's most exclusive shopping streets, **Worth Avenue**, is in Palm Beach. Glittering with style, sophistication and a richly appointed branch of the fabulous New York jeweler Tiffany's, it derives much of its charm from the landscaped pavements and Mediterranean-style architecture designed by Addison Mizner more than 70 years ago. Along the street, around the courtyards, and down narrow pedestrian passageways, some 200 speciality shops, a new Neiman Marcus department store, art galleries and gourmet restaurants cater to a rarified clientele (for West Palm Beach, see panel).

AND THERE'S MORE ...
Moving from the historic to the relatively recent, West Palm Beach's most impressive shopping extravaganza is the **Gardens Mall**, PGA Boulevard. Beneath a glass atrium, 180 shops and restaurants fill the complex, including big department stores such as Bloomingdale's and Saks Fifth Avenue. **Palm Beach Mall**, Palm Beach Lakes Boulevard, is another tasteful collection of skylights, shrubs, department stores and boutiques. Downtown, **Clematis Street** is awash with fashion and speciality shops, and the **CityPlace** development will add even more choice.

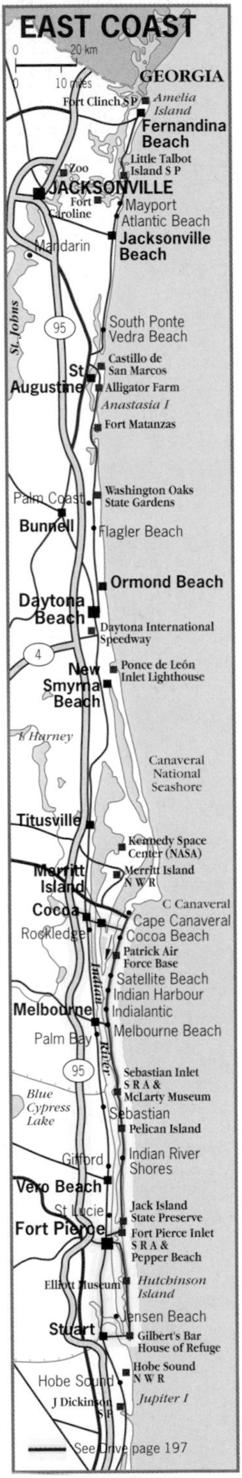

EAST COAST

See Drive page 197

THE EAST COAST covers an area north from the top of the Gold Coast to the border with Georgia. It is a 300-mile (480km) stretch of the mainland, largely protected by a string of lush barrier islands. Here, the Floridas of past and present are juxtaposed in a series of historic old towns and modern summer season beach resorts, ancient Native American shell mounds and 21st-century space wizardry.

The East Coast is where it all began, when Spanish explorer Juan Ponce de León stepped ashore near present-day St Augustine in 1513. This area now calls itself the 'First Coast', and includes Jacksonville, on the St Johns River, where French Huguenots established a settlement in 1564. Upon learning of the French settlers, Philip II of Spain dispatched his lieutenant Pedro Menéndez de Avilés to teach the French a lesson, and a brutal massacre of the shipwrecked French at Matanzas Bay ('Bay of Slaughter') left the Spanish to claim the territory by the founding of St Augustine in 1565. Though at the time the mosquito-infested swamps of the East Coast were of little value, St Augustine was a strategic link in the maritime defense of Spanish treasure fleets and a prime target of English attacks. The town was razed by Sir Francis Drake in 1586, was attacked again in 1702, and the English actually moved in for 20 years in 1763.

WAR AND TOURISTS By the early 19th century, sugar, citrus and indigo plantations were starting to appear around Indian River and the Halifax River (as the Intracoastal Waterway is known near Fort Pierce and Daytona Beach, respectively), but the outbreak of the Seminole Wars, followed by the Civil War, led many settlers to abandon their plantations. Business picked up again in the 1870s, when the first trickle of tourists drifted down to the railhead at Jacksonville and continued south by boat down the St Johns River or along the coast to St Augustine, Ormond Beach and Rockledge.

When Standard Oil millionaire Henry Flagler determined to develop Florida's East Coast as a 'Southern Newport' winter resort for wealthy Philadelphia socialites, the trickle became a torrent, and Flagler ferried them south on his railroad and put them up in his own luxurious hotels.

JACKSONVILLE is the original gateway to Florida. A Flagler hotel (long since gone) at Atlantic Beach was the start of today's Jacksonville Beaches resort area, and the city recovered from a devastating fire in 1901 to emerge as an industrial and trading port, the insurance capital of the South, and a vibrant cultural centre. The St Johns River meanders through the city, past Jacksonville University, where composer Frederick Delius once lived on a citrus plantation, and squeezes around a narrow bend to divide the downtown district in half. Once much maligned for the stench of its wood-pulp mills near I–95, Jacksonville's attractive centre, with its Riverwalk, water taxis and neighbouring beaches now justifies a detour.

A short distance north, facing Georgia across the St Mary's River, **Amelia Island** is a charming getaway with a couple of luxury resorts and wildlife preserves as well as the historic small port of **Fernandina Beach**. Fernandina has seen eight national flags struck over its

East Coast

Left: motor racing fans pack the Daytona International Speedway, home to the famous Daytona 500

picturesque old town centre. Today it is a haven for antiques collectors and for beach lovers; it also has a busy shrimping fleet.

South of Jacksonville, **St Augustine** is the longest continually inhabited settlement in the United States. Pensacola was colonised earlier, but the settlers abandoned their encampment, and St Augustine can claim the 'Oldest House', a historic fort and a tourist park on the spot where Ponce de León is believed to have made his first footfall. The town's old Spanish Quarter is beautifully preserved, and there are beaches near by, all of which combine to make the town a pleasant stopover.

Further south, **Daytona Beach** is the 'Birthplace of Speed', where Malcolm Campbell piloted his *Bluebird* into the record books (see page 174). Driving on the beach is no longer permitted for safety reasons, and Daytona Beach is now a popular, spring break resort.

The **John F Kennedy Space Center** is not called Cape Canaveral. As the third biggest attraction in Florida, and home of America's Space Shuttle programme, it is very particular about its title, pointing out that Cape Canaveral is a lump of sand. The Kennedy Space Center is the highlight of the **Space Coast**, which also offers a choice of good-value, family-oriented resorts and amazing wildlife flourishing in the shadow of the launch pad.

The sinking of the treasure-laden Spanish Plate Fleet off Vero Beach in 1715 caused this next section of Atlantic oceanfront to be nicknamed the **Treasure Coast**. **Fort Pierce** is the largest town on the **Indian River** mainland, but the real attractions here are the relaxed resorts, golden beaches, watersports and diving opportunities.

At the close of the 19th century, entrepreneur Henry Flagler bought and enlarged a grand hotel (the Ormond) on a 23-mile (37km) stretch of beach north of Daytona. He could not have envisaged that the golden sands would become one of the world's most famous racetracks, and his hotel a pit stop for early automobile enthusiasts.

Thirty-minute guided track tours of the Daytona International Speedway World Center of Racing start at the not-to-be-missed DAYTONA USA Visitors Center, 1801 W International Speedway Boulevard (see page 176). Near by is the Klassix Auto Attraction, 2909 W International Speedway Boulevard (*Open* daily 9–6, extended hours during special events; tel: 904/252-3800), which turns the spotlight on classic cars (notably the Corvette), NASCAR and 'Days of Thunder' racing cars, vintage motorcycles and a mountain of related memorabilia.

Henry Ford, Louis Chevrolet and Harvey Firestone were all lured south by the winter sunshine, but it was R E Olds, of Oldsmobile fame, who staged the first oceanside race across the hard-packed sands of Ormond Beach in 1902. Olds and Alexander Winton clocked a mind-boggling 57mph (92km) as they tore down the beach; a year later it was more than 65mph (105kph); and by 1905 speeds had passed the 100mph (160kph) mark. In 1907, Fred Marriott recorded 197mph (316kph) in a Stanley Steamer, before crashing into the surf.

Faster and faster The original 'track' began on Ormond Beach, at Granada Avenue, and ran south for 12 miles (19km) to Daytona Beach proper. It celebrated its finest hour in 1935, when Englishman Sir Malcolm Campbell set the last land-speed record on the beach when he raced his Rolls-Royce-powered *Bluebird* to 276mph (444kph). By then, motorcycles had also joined the fray.

After a quiet few years, beach racing was back on track in the southern beach area in the 1950s, but its popularity became a problem: large crowds and construction along the seafront made it too dangerous, and the action was moved to **Daytona International Speedway**, International Speedway Boulevard, in 1959, the year of the first Daytona 500 Endurance Race. Today, the Daytona 500 is a world-class event and the most famous of eight-plus major car and motorcycle events staged annually at the high-banked, tri-oval racetrack; it's the high point of February's 16-day **Speed Weeks** extravaganza, which draws thousands of fans to America's Birthplace of Speed. A couple of weeks later, **Bike Week** brings in March the motorcycling fraternity rumbling into town.

Pit crew in action in Daytona

►► Daytona Beach

The 'World's Most Famous Beach' is 23 miles (37km) long and up to 500 feet (150m) wide. The Daytona Beach resort area, which stretches down the peninsula from Ormond Beach to Ponce Inlet, is the largest resort area on the East Coast, welcoming eight million visitors annually.

Daytona's love affair with the automobile is a historic tradition. The season starts in February, with the famous formula and stock car **Speed Weeks** at the Daytona International Speedway. Several thousand leather-clad bikers transform Main Street into a week-long chrome carnival in March's **Bike Week**, followed in April by hordes of Northern students celebrating spring break. With over 16,000 hotel rooms and self-catering apartments, Daytona Beach is well prepared for these annual gatherings.

There is no shortage of other diversions – the beach itself is a giant amusement park, and concessions cater to every type of watersport (jet skis, windsurfers, surf boards and sailboats are all widely available), while **The Boardwalk** offers amusement arcades and go-karting and there are aerial gondola rides on **Main Street Pier**. Near by is the Adventure Landing Waterpark (see panel).

For some culture, visit the impressive **Ocean Center**; the London Symphony Orchestra appears every other year at the **Peabody Auditorium**, and free beachside concerts take place at the **Bandshell** in Oceanfront Park. Natural delights include trails, boating and fishing at **Tomoka State Park**, N Beach Street; **Sugar Mill Botanical Gardens** in Port Orange; and excursions on the Halifax River Intracoastal Waterway with **A Tiny Cruise Line** (for schedules, tel: 904/226-2343).

The Casements, *25 Riverside Drive, at Granada.* (*Open* tours Mon–Fri at 10 and 2:30, Sat 10 and 11:30. *Admission: donation*; tel: 904/676-3716) Named for its casement windows, this modest clapboard house – the present-day Ormond Beach Cultural & Civic Center – was built in the early 1900s, and subsequently purchased by oil magnate John D Rockefeller in 1918. The millionaire returned here every winter until his death in 1937.

Various Rockefeller-related artefacts have been gathered here, including his wicker beach chair with its glazed portholes. There is an exhibition gallery on the ground floor, and an extraordinary collection of scouting memorabilia is crammed into the attic.

►►► REGION HIGHLIGHTS

SPLASHTACULAR!

Daytona Beach's new Adventure Landing Waterpark and Entertainment Center, 601 Earl Street (*Admission: expensive;* tel: 904/258-0071) is a splashtacular affair, with its high-energy tube rides, waterslides and a 17,000 sqare-foot wave pool (*Open* daily Memorial Day–Labor Day 10–8; Feb–May, Sat–Sun only; Sep–Oct, weather permitting). The Entertainment Center has a go-kart track, mini-golf and games arcade (*Open* Sun–Thu 10–10, Fri–Sat 10–midnight all year round).

The popular Daytona Beach resort

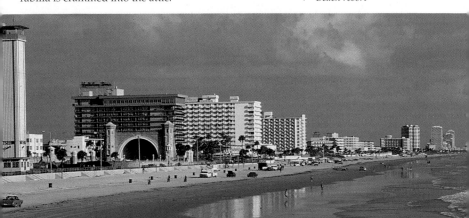

HISTORY IN THE BANK
Amateur historians will find plenty to enjoy at the Halifax Historical Museum, 252 S Beach Street, Daytona (*Open* Tue–Sat 10–4. *Admission: inexpensive*; tel: 904/255-6976), housed in a former bank. Native American artefacts here include a 600-year-old Timucuan dugout canoe. There are also Spanish relics, found in local plantation ruins, a 1909 time capsule and motor memorabilia. One of the best displays is the enchanting, marvelously detailed wooden model of the Boardwalk area as it looked in 1938.

A giant sloth, from around 130,000 years ago, in the Daytona Museum of Arts and Sciences

Museum of Arts and Sciences, *1040 Museum Boulevard* (*Open* Tue–Fri 9–4, Sat and Sun noon–5. *Admission: inexpensive*) This classy modern museum really does have something for everyone – exhibits range from a giant ground sloth skeleton to a collection of Cuban art. The 13-foot-high (4m) sloth is displayed in the prehistory section where hands-on specimen drawers offer fossils, puzzles and even a mammoth tooth and a giant ostrich egg for inspection. Elsewhere, the **Cuban Museum** records two centuries (1759–1959) of Latin American culture in vivid style, while the excellent **Dow Gallery** showcases American arts and crafts from 1640 to 1920, and there are fine collections of African and pre-Columbian artefacts. The museum is in the 60-acre (24-ha) Tuscawilla Preserve, focus of the Window on the Wood Interpretive Center.

DAYTONA USA, *1801 W International Speedway Boulevard* (*Open* daily 9–7. *Admission: expensive*; tel: 904/947-6800) Entered by replicas of Daytona International Speedway's famous under-track twin tunnels, this interactive motorsports attraction is a racing fan's heaven. Packed with hands-on activities and state-of-the-art exhibits, it is in turn a museum and a monument to the World Center of Racing. Among the highlights are Sir Malcolm Campbell's original *Bluebird V;* an interactive pit-stop challenge; and *The Daytona 500*, a spectacular film featuring in-car camera footage and behind-the-scenes action.

Ponce de León Inlet Lighthouse, *S Peninsula Drive, Ponce Inlet* (*Open* daily 10–4. *Admission: inexpensive*; tel: 904/761-1821) Set at the southern end of the Daytona peninsula, this 1887 red-brick lighthouse is now working again and affords great views up and down the coast from the top of

Nostalgic corner in the Daytona Museum of Arts and Sciences

its 203-step spiral staircase. Below is a keeper's cottage, furnished 1890s-style, a splendid 17-foot-tall (5m) Fresnel lens in a special exhibit building and a small museum of nautical memorabilia. The fishing village of Ponce Inlet is renowned for its seafood restaurants, and there are picnic areas, a marina and a beach in Lighthouse Point Park, at the end of Peninsula Drive.

▶▶▶ **Fernandina Beach** see page 183.

▶ Indian River and the Treasure Coast

One of Florida's quieter and more relaxed corners, the Indian River region is more famous for its citrus than its beaches. Indian River is the local name for the Intracoastal Waterway, which divides the mainland from the barrier island beaches of the Treasure Coast. South of Sebastian Inlet, the main business districts of chic Vero Beach and Fort Pierce and laid-back Stuart are all centred on the west (mainland) bank of the Indian River, but holiday-makers head for the modest barrier island resort annexes strung along the A1A highway.

A pioneer military outpost founded in 1838, Fort Pierce lies across from the inlet which divides the barrier islands of North and South Hutchinson, both featuring fine sandy beaches.

North of the inlet are surfing favourites **Fort Pierce Inlet State Recreation Area** and **Pepper Beach**; nature lovers should seek out well-concealed **Jack Island State Preserve** (off A1A; see page 191), a 630-acre (255-ha) mangrove island with nature trails and superb birdwatching. To the south, try **Stuart Beach**; snorkellers can explore the glassy-smooth waters around **Bathtub Reef**.

Elliott Museum, *825 NE Ocean Boulevard, Stuart* (*Open* daily 10–4. *Admission: moderate*; tel: 561/225-1961) An interesting stop on A1A, the museum is named for

THE GAMBLE PLACE

In 1907, James Gamble built himself a modest hunting lodge on Spruce Creek, just south of downtown Daytona. The comfortable Cracker-style retreat lies hidden in a 150-acre (60-ha) woodland preserve maintained by the Museum of Arts and Science. Guided tours (Wed and Sat by arrangement; tel: 904/255-0285) visit the lodge, an old citrus-packing barn and a replica of Snow White's House from the 1938 Disney film. There is also a nature trail and pontoon boat rides on the creek.

MARINE ENCOUNTER
Touch tanks, aquariums and interactive computer puzzles are all part of the Florida Oceanographic Society's Coastal Science Center, 890 NE Ocean Boulevard (A1A) Stuart (*Open* Mon–Sat 10–5, Sun noon–4. *Admission: inexpensive*; tel: 561/225-1505). There are also trails in the adjacent hammock and mangrove areas and plans for a turtle rescue facility.

VERO BEACH
A gem of a seaside community 20 miles (32km) north of Fort Pierce, Vero Beach is home to Disney's Vero Beach Resort and Dodgertown, winter home of the LA Dodgers. However, the town's real charm lies in its luxurious real estate, tree-shaded streets, sports facilities, and upmarket shopping in the boutiques and galleries lining stylish Ocean Drive. A cultural high spot is the Center for the Arts in Riverside Park, which plays host to excellent visiting exhibits.

American inventor Sterling Elliott, the man who, for example, put four wheels on a bicycle and came up with a quadricycle. Alongside some of Elliott's inventions, you will find early 20th-century domestic dioramas, a row of old-fashioned shops imported from Massachusetts and a terrific collection of rare vintage bicycles, motorcycles and cars, including a Stanley Steamer.

Gilbert's Bar House of Refuge, *301 SE MacArthur Boulevard, Stuart* (*Open* daily 10–4. *Admission: inexpensive*; tel: 561/225-1875) A mile south of the Elliott Museum, this 1875 sailors' refuge was provided by the US Life Saving Service, forerunner of the Coast Guard. The white clapboard building is the oldest house in Martin County, and the simple living quarters have been carefully restored with Victorian furnishings. There are plans for nautical museum displays.

Harbor Branch Oceanographic Institution, *5600 US 1 North, Fort Pierce* (*Open* for tours Mon–Sat at 10, noon, and 2. *Admission: inexpensive*; tel: 561/465-2400 or 800/333-4264) This is a non-profit-making research and educational facility involved in marine sciences and ocean engineering. The visitor centre shows introductory videos, together with related displays and exhibits; tours include a close-up look at working research ships and submersibles (when in port), laboratories and aquaculture facilities.

St Lucie County Historical Museum, *414 Seaway Drive, Fort Pierce* (*Open* Tue–Sat 10–4, Sun noon–4. *Admission: inexpensive*; tel: 561/462-1795) In a park at the eastern end of South Bridge, this museum provides a pleasant introduction to local history. Among the nostalgic items on display there is the restored 1907 Gardner House, a 1919 fire engine, 19th-century shops, and a reconstructed Seminole tribe encampment. You can also see military hardware from Old Fort Pierce and artifacts from Spanish shipwrecks.

Savannas Recreation Area, *1400 E Midway Road* (*Open* daily 8–dusk. *Admission: inexpensive*; tel: 561/464-7855) Close by Indian River, Florida's last intact freshwater lagoon system is preserved within the Fort Pierce city limits. The park consists of a fragile marsh and uplands ecosystem with a diverse range of both plant and animal life. Birdwatching and fishing are popular pastimes, plus there is canoe hire and a campsite.

UDT-SEAL Museum, *3300 N A1A Fort Pierce* (*Open* Tue–Sat 10–4, Sun noon–4. *Admission: inexpensive*; tel: 561/595-5845) This is a real-life adventure story featuring the US Navy's World War II Underwater Demolition Teams (UDT), and its modern-day successors, the Sea, Air and Land Teams (SEAL). In 1943, this beach area was chosen as the training site for the Navy's elite wartime frogmen, and the museum pays tribute to this usually secretive branch of the armed forces. An impressive array of military exhibits, diving equipment, demolition apparatus, weapons and photographs tells the story of the teams in graphic detail.

►►► Jacksonville

Capital of the 'First Coast' (see page 172), Jacksonville is flourishing – the 16th largest city in the United States has plenty to offer family holiday-makers, historians and visiting culture vultures.

The city's roots run deep. A party of French Huguenot soldiers and settlers, led by René de Goulaine de Laudonnière, founded **Fort Caroline**, one of the earliest European colonies in North America, on the banks of the St Johns River in 1564. The native Timucua people helped them construct a rough fort, but the Spanish did not take kindly to 'foreign' occupation of their New World territories, and ousted the French before establishing their own settlement at St Augustine, 60 miles (96km) further south.

Jacksonville was named for General Andrew Jackson and was laid out on the site of Fort Caroline around 1822. Extending to both sides of the St Johns River, it prospered as a river port and then as one of the earliest Florida tourist destinations with the arrival of the railroad. At the end of the 19th century, Henry Flagler built a hotel (which has now gone) at **Atlantic Beach**, part of Jacksonville's 15-mile (24km) stretch of sandy beachfront.

The downtown district is compact, divided by the river. To the north, the business district flows into **Jacksonville Landing** for shopping, dining and entertainment. Ferry services run shuttles from here to the south bank, where a **Riverwalk** meanders past several small museums of local and maritime history, and the fountains of **Friendship Park**. As the river curves south, it flows past the leafy residential enclave of San Marco, with its fine old homes and small speciality shopping district.

On the opposite bank, around St Johns Avenue, the attractive **Riverside/Avondale** neighbourhood is home to another pocket of up-market interior decorators, boutiques, antiques shops and restaurants. The lovely

FIT FOR THE KING

For 21 years, a suite in what is now the Jacksonville Hilton and Towers was set aside for the sole use of the legendary King of Rock and Roll, Elvis Presley. The snake-hipped one slept in it six times between 1955 and 1976. The room is now available to guests (tel: 904/398-8800).

Jacksonville: modern skyline of an historic city

RIVER JAUNTS
The St Johns River is the focal point of the city and a great sightseeing opportunity. For views of the downtown skyline, hop aboard one of the frequent water taxi services between Jacksonville Landing and the Riverwalk. More leisurely sightseeing cruises with commentaries and musical entertainment are offered by River Cruises Inc (tel: 904/396-2333) aboard their 1890s-style sternwheelers *Annabelle Lee* and *Lady St Johns*.

Cummer Museum of Art and Gardens on Riverside Avenue is a must-see. Cultural events in Jacksonville include programmes at the gloriously over-the-top **Florida Theatre** (tel: 904/355-2787). Painstakingly restored to its 1920s grandeur, it has earned a spot on the National Register of Historic Places, probably despite, rather than because of the fact that it is where Elvis Presley made his first stage appearance.

Downtown the **Times-Union Center for the Performing Arts** is one of the state's finest cultural showcases and frequent host to the highly regarded **Jacksonville Symphony Orchestra** (tel: 904/354-5547). In October, jazz lovers are treated to one of the world's largest free jazz events during the annual three-day **Jacksonville Jazz Festival**, in Metropolitan Park.

Cummer Museum of Art and Gardens, *829 Riverside Avenue* (*Open* Tue and Thu 10–9, Wed, Fri and Sat 10–5, Sun noon–5. *Admission: moderate*; tel: 904/356-6857) If you need an excuse to visit the attractive Riverside district, then this is it. One of the Cummer's greatest attractions is its lovely gardens, a mixture of formal Italian and English landscaping, wisteria arbors, a superb old live oak with a canopy spreading over 175 feet (53m) and brick paths leading down to the water's edge. The ten galleries display fine arts and antiquities from the Cummer's permanent collection of over 4,000 items, making it the largest museum in northeast Florida. Exhibits span ancient, medieval, Renaissance, baroque, rococo, Impressionist and contemporary art from Europe and America, and pre-Columbian ceramics, while there are also notable Asian collections. The Cummer also boasts the Wark Collection of 18th-century Meissen tableware, one of the largest publicly displayed collections of its kind in the world. Another new development is the hands-on education programme, where kids can have fun in the interactive Art Connections area.

On the beach at Jacksonville

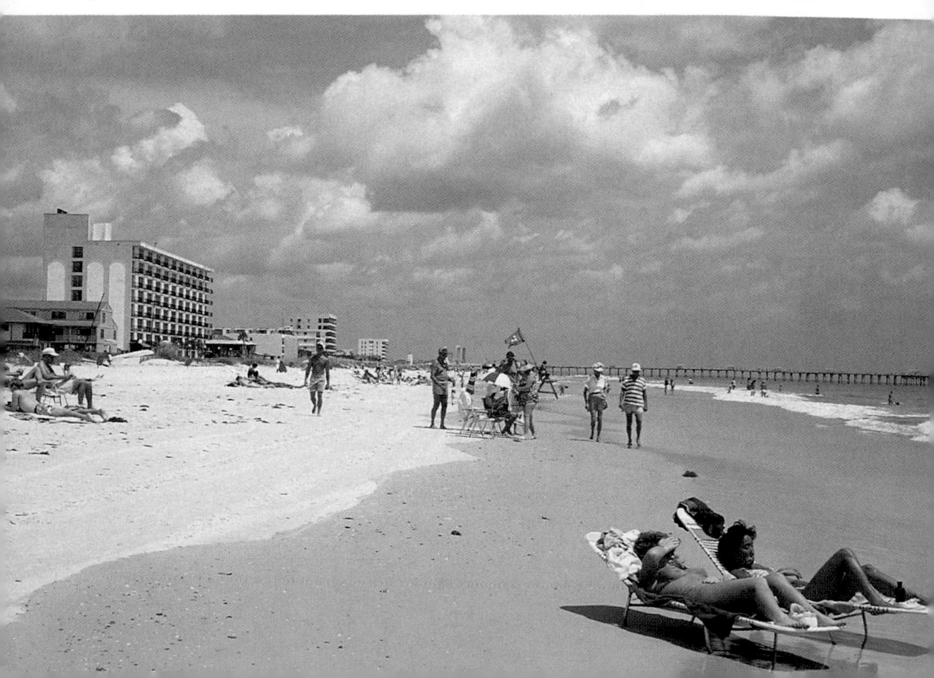

Fort Caroline National Memorial, *12713 Fort Caroline Road (off SR 10)* (*Open* daily 9–5. *Admission free*; tel: 904/641-7155) Historic site of de Laudonnière's French Huguenot colony, this park has a scale model of the original Fort Caroline, as well as three walking trails and several pleasant picnic spots. A granite marker commemorates French explorer Jean Ribaut, and it is a good place to look for bottlenose dolphins in the river.

Just southeast of Fort Caroline, the Theodore Roosevelt Area has been designated a **Timucuan Ecological and Historic Preserve**, encompassing 46,000 acres (18,615 ha) of wetlands, river systems, historic sites and several hiking trails through maritime forest and salt marsh.

Jacksonville Museum of Contemporary Art, *4160 Boulevard Center Drive* (*Open* Tue–Fri 10–4, Thu 10–10, Sat and Sun 1–5. *Admission: inexpensive*; tel: 904/398-8336) On the south side of downtown, this museum combines its role as a showcase for the latest trends in the art world with more historic permanent exhibitions. Notable collections of pre-Columbian artefacts and porcelain share the bill with contemporary graphics and photography, and there is an excellent programme of shows, lectures and workshops.

Jacksonville beaches *(12 miles/19km east via US 90/SR 10)* Jacksonville's Atlantic beaches were established as a resort area with the arrival of the railroad in the 1880s. Fifteen miles (24km) of dazzling sand, sun and fun link the three distinct beachfront districts of **Atlantic Beach**, **Neptune Beach** and **Jacksonville Beach** (together with its southern annex, **Ponte Vedra Beach**). The first two are bordered by residential communities and are somewhat quieter than the more commercial Jacksonville Beach section, which offers a full range of shopping, sports facilities and family entertainment (see panel).

The official beach season opens in April with a round of festivals and entertainment celebrating the end of the winter months. Watersports enthusiasts will find a host of beachfront surf shops hiring out surfboards and sailboards; boat hire for water-skiing and diving is also available at the beach. **Jacksonville Beach Pier**, at *6th Avenue South* (*Open* daily 6am–10pm), is a great spot for fishing and is well supplied with tackle rental and bait shops.

Jacksonville Landing, *Independent Drive* (*Shops open* Mon–Thu 10–8, Fri and Sat 10–9, Sun noon–5:30; tel: 904/353-1188) Downtown's shopping, dining and entertainment complex, the horseshoe-shaped festival marketplace sits on the northern bank of the St Johns River, below Main Street Bridge. During the day, the mall is packed with temptations from evening wear and tennis gear to speciality gifts and jewellery, in more than 65 retail shops including many well-known names. The Food Hall's wide range of restaurants and take-away joints caters to all tastes, including Japanese, Mexican and Italian, and offers generous deli sandwiches. At sunset, the Landing is transformed from a shopping mall into a live entertainment venue, with a variety of events staged in the central courtyard.

FAMILY ADVENTURES

Rain or shine, Adventure Landing, 1944 Beach Boulevard, Jacksonville Beach (*Open* daily 10am–2am. *Admission: expensive*; tel: 904/246-4386), offers family entertainment from outdoor miniature golf, batting cagers and go-karting to an indoor video arcade and laser tag.

In hot weather, the shipwreck-themed water-park is a good place to cool off – arranged around a 65-foot-tall (20m) Caribbean play village with a dozen waterslides, wave pool and 200 water-squirting nozzles for added drenching power.

Shells are a popular souvenir. You can also pick up your own from the beach, but be aware of the restrictions

The African veldt at Jacksonville Zoo

NAUTICAL MAYPORT
On the south bank of the St Johns River where it flows into the Atlantic is Mayport, one of the nation's oldest fishing communities. Famous for its seafood restaurants, the shrimp dock is dwarfed by neighbouring Mayport Naval Station (tel: 904/270-5226), the fourth largest naval base in the United States. A popular outing with children, the base offers free tours of navy vessels, which can include home-based aircraft carrier USS *John F Kennedy* (call for weekend schedules).

Jacksonville Zoological Gardens, *8605 Zoo Road (off Heckscher)* (*Open* daily 9–5. *Admission: moderate*; tel: 904/757-4462) A short drive north of the city on the interstate, Jacksonville Zoo is nearing completion of a ten-year redevelopment programme during which the majority of the old-style caged enclosures have been phased out in favour of natural habitat areas such as the African veldt exhibit and the Florida wetland area, due to open in 2001.

The 73-acre (30-ha) site is home to more than 800 animals from the warthogs, Cape buffalo and rhinos of the plains of East Africa to the porcupines and pint-sized dik-dik deer of the Okavango Trail. At Okavango Station there is a popular petting zoo with pygmy goats, dwarf zebu and donkeys. On a grander scale, stop at the aviaries and elephants, great apes and big cats. It is well worth making the effort to catch one of the well-presented animal programsme, and a miniature train ride provides welcome transport.

Kathryn A Hanna Park, *500 Wonderwood Drive* (*Open* daily 8–dusk. *Admission: inexpensive*; tel: 904/249-4700) A 450-acre (182-ha) beachfront park south of Mayport Naval Station, this is a highly recommended alternative to the main public beaches. Dunes crested with sea oats stretch for more than a mile along the shore, while behind the beach woodland hiking and bicycle trails extend throughout the nature preserve, which also encompasses more than 60 acres (24 ha) of freshwater lakes. As well as good fishing spots, there are lakeside picnic tables and barbecue grills (supplies are available from the park campers store), summer concessions, and around 300 campsites.

Museum of Science and History, *1025 Museum Circle, Southbank (Riverwalk)* (*Open* Mon–Fri 10–5, Sat 10–6, Sun 1–6. *Admission: moderate*; tel: 904/396-7062) This interest-packed museum complex offers a broad range of displays and hands-on exhibits illustrating local and natural history and the physical sciences. The first floor **Living Room** is inhabited by rescued birds and a slithery collection of native and exotic reptiles, from snakes to skinks, and there may be snapping turtles and tarantulas as well. The **Atlantic Tails: Whales, Dolphins, and Manatees of Northeast Florida** is an informative section, relating the story of five endangered marine animals native to the region. Local NFL heroes the Jacksonville Jaguars also warrant a shrine packed with memorabilia and interactive playstations.

Moving up a floor, there are hands-on science pods and a motion simulator which provides virtual explorations of the dinosaur era and the moon, while on the historical front, **The Current of Time** delves into Jacksonville's history through cleverly displayed artifacts and dioramas. There are daily displays in the **Alexander Brest Planetarium** (seating passes can be obtained from the front desk) and 3-D musical laser shows.

Children enjoy Jacksonville Zoo's miniature train

Follow this coastal route for exciting glimpses into history, views of beautiful architecture, excellent food and stunning scenery. Northeast from Jacksonville, Route A1A takes a scenic trail up the coast to historic Fernandina Beach. This makes for a great day trip, starting with a short ferry ride from Mayport as far as Fort George Island. Ferries operate daily every 30 minutes, from 6:20am (6am Mon–Fri) to 10:15pm.

The first stop is **Kingsley Plantation**, 11676 Palmetto Avenue (*Open* daily 9–5), the oldest plantation house in the state, owned by slave trader Zephaniah Kingsley from 1813 to 1839. He grew cotton, sugar cane, sweet potatoes, and citrus fruits; his 200 slaves lived in tabby cabins, made from a mixture of shells and lime, 23 of which still exist arranged in a neat row in a clearing in the woods.

Follow A1A north, along the **Buccaneer Trail**, by Little Talbot Island State Park, where 5 miles (8km) of wide sand beach, salt marshes and coastal hammock harbour bobcats, otters, marsh rabbits, water fowl and superb fishing opportunities. A causeway crosses the Nassau Sound to **Amelia Island**, named by the British in 1735 after George II's beautiful daughter. Host to legions of Spanish, French, British and Mexican invaders, the island is now a quiet resort area offering bed-and-breakfast accommodation, small hotels and deluxe resorts.

The historic town centre of **Fernandina Beach** lies on the west side of the island, with a wealth of fine Queen Anne stick-style and Victorian buildings, antiques and crafts shops, boutiques, galleries, restaurants and, alledgedly, the state's oldest continuously operated hostelry, **The Palace Saloon**, 117 Center Street. This is a good place to sample local shrimp delivered to the docks daily. The best way to explore the 50-block historic district is on foot. The **Amelia Island Museum of History**, 233 S Third Street, offers walking tours and strolls; for information, tel: 904/261-7378 or pick up a map from the Chamber of Commerce, 102 Center Street.

East of the town center, **Fort Clinch State Park** (*Open* daily 8–dusk) lies on the south bank of Cumberland Sound, the border with Georgia. Dating from 1847, the brick fortress has worn well, and park rangers, dressed in Civil War uniforms, cook, clean and take turns standing guard. There are picnic grounds, a nature trail, a beach area, a fishing pier and a campsite. (For camping information, tel: 904/277-7274.)

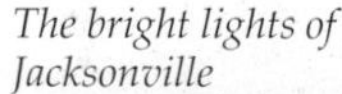

The bright lights of Jacksonville

To find Florida as it used to be, you need to take a step back from the popular coastal strip and explore an area of the state which flourished in the pre-railroad era, but has been largely overlooked for almost a century.

RIVER OF LIFE
The St Johns River has been an important landmark and highway for a very long time – there is evidence of a human presence along its banks as early as 5000 BC. Archaeological research has pieced together a picture of these early Floridians. They were tall, dark-skinned people who consumed a lot of clams and oysters (mounds of shells bear vivid testimony to this). The shells themselves were used to make tools and to hollow out wooden canoes.

Florida's largest and most important natural watercourse, the St Johns is also one of the few rivers in the United States to flow north. It rises in St Johns Marsh, 8 miles (13km) north of Fort Pierce, and flows parallel to the Atlantic coast for 250 miles (400km) or so before curving east through Jacksonville to reach the ocean.

By the time the first Europeans tried to settle Florida's east coast in the mid-16th century, Timucua Native Americans occupied the northeast corner of Florida. They helped French settlers to build a fort near the mouth of the St Johns River (which the French called the River of May), and provided them with native corn. The original site of the fort was destroyed during dredging operations in the 1880s, but a reconstruction of the rough wooden stockade based on contemporary drawings is the centrepiece of the **Fort Caroline National Memorial** on the outskirts of Jacksonville (see page 180).

A strategic gateway To control the lower St Johns River was to control the interior of Florida (and the backdoor to St Augustine), but until the 19th century, pioneer settlers generally restricted their incursions to the immediate coast. During the 1820s, however, Jacksonville was founded, and trading posts were established upriver. Lumber, sugar cane and citrus, which flourished along the fertile river banks, were shipped north, and the steamboat era brought luxurious passenger steamers south. A popular stop was the fashionable spa at **Green Cove Springs**. Its natural spring attracted the patronage of President Grover Cleveland and of chain-store magnate J C Penney.

The river is more than a mile wide as it rounds an S-bend about **Palatka**. The town was named for the

There are various ways of enjoying the river

Steamboat on the St Johns River

Native American word *pilaklikaha*, meaning 'crossing over'. Confederate troops trounced a Unionist outpost here in 1864, but this old lumber town is better known as a top bass fishing spot.

South of Palatka, the river runs through Lake George, with the vast 366,000-acre (148,120-ha) wilderness of **Ocala National Forest** spreading off to the west. Then it squeezes past the citrus centre of **De Land** (see panel).

Manatees and shell mounds French marine biologist Jacques Cousteau was lured to the St Johns River to film its endangered manatee population. One of the best places to watch these hefty sea cows is Blue Spring.

Blue Spring State Park at 2100 W French Avenue, 2 miles (3km) west of Orange City, is a popular winter resort for manatees, who escape the cooler main river to bask in the 72°F (22°C) spring from November to March. For human , there are swimming, fishing and canoeing opportunities here, as well as picnic areas, boat tours and trips to **Hontoon Island State Park**. This 1,650-acre (667-ha) island has been a boat yard, cattle ranch and settlement. The Timucua Native Americans built shell mounds, visible from the nature trail.

Sanford, 200 miles (320km) south of the St Johns River mouth at Mayport, is the last navigable stretch of the river. When steamboats ceased to ply the river, Sanford settled for growing celery and quiet obscurity. However, things are changing today, with a revival of interest in St Johns River cruises. This is the place to hop aboard a riverboat for a short narrated sightseeing trip, keeping an eye out for bald eagles, alligators, manatees and deer. For details, contact **Rivership Romance**, 433 N Palmetto Avenue, Sanford (tel: 407/321-5091 or 800/423-7401).

The St Johns continues upstream from Sanford, through Lake Harney, to its headwaters in **St Johns Marsh**. West of Cocoa and Melbourne, there are river camps and recreation areas, such as **Lone Cabbage Fish Camp** (Route 520) and **Camp Holly** (Route 192), which provide fishing and boating facilities, airboat rides and campsites.

CITRUS POWER

De Land was founded by a baking powder manufacturer, but is more notable as the scene of Chinese citrus cultivator Lue Gim Gong's experiments with cold-weather grapefruit and cherry-sized currants in the 1880s and 1890s. He succeeded in both cases.

LITERARY LANDMARK

As early tourists made their way upriver on steamboats, they passed Harriet Beecher Stowe's house on the bank at Mandarin. A famous author since the publication of *Uncle Tom's Cabin* in 1852, she was paid by the riverboat companies to sit outside on the lawn and wave to their passengers.

The Old World arts and crafts area of St Augustine

GLORIOUS GOLF
Golf is a major visitor attraction in the St Augustine area, and a handful of top professional golfers make their home here. The first golf course in St John's County was built in St Augustine in 1916. Now the centre-piece of World Golf Village, just outside town, is the World Golf Hall of Fame (*Open* daily 10–6. *Admission: moderate*; tel: 904/940-4200), which celebrates the history of the game and great players through antiques, artefacts and interactive displays. The Village boasts designer courses, a golf academy, a spa, accommodation, and dining.

▶▶▶ St Augustine

The oldest continuously occupied European settlement in the Continental United States, St Augustine is definitely 'Historyville, USA'. It was named in 1565, after the feast day of St Augustine (28 August), by Pedro Menéndez de Avilés, the Spanish governor of Florida. The settlement predates the British colony at Jamestown by 42 years and the Pilgrims by 55 years. None of the earliest buildings remain, but the 17th-century **Castillo de San Marcos** and a few early 18th-century dwellings have survived in the old Spanish Quarter. These dwellings housed Spanish soldiers garrisoned at the fort, and then British soldiers during their brief occupation of Florida from 1763 to 1783.

When the Spanish returned, they planted citrus trees, built courtyards off the narrow streets and added balconies to the simple whitewashed houses. The **Cathedral of St Augustine**, in the town center, contains the oldest written records in the United States, dating from 1594.

St Augustine was a scruffy little garrison town when the Americans finally acquired Florida in 1821. Yellow fever epidemics and the outbreak of the Seminole Wars discouraged early speculators. After the Civil War, tourists began to venture further south. A significant visitor in the early 1880s was Standard Oil millionaire Henry Flagler, who later launched his Florida resort hotel chain here with the luxurious **Ponce de León Hotel** in 1888.

Although the grand resorts have had their day – the famous hotel is now a college – tourism is still the city's prime industry. The best way to explore the old town centre is on foot, but sightseeing trams and horse-drawn carriages offer an alternative method of getting around the main sights. Across the **Bridge of Lions**, on A1A, St Augustine's beach annex provides an additional choice of restaurants and accommodation near the landmark black-and-white striped 1874 **lighthouse**.

Castillo de San Marcos, *1 Castillo Drive East* (*Open* daily 8:45–4:45. *Admission: inexpensive*; tel: 904/829-6506) St Augustine's most significant historic site, this star-shaped fortress stands on the foundations of nine previous wooden structures, the earliest dating back to 1565. The foundation stone of the present fort was laid in 1672, and it was constructed of coquina, a soft seashell 'rock',which proved a remarkably efficient defensive building material. Assailants' cannon balls simply buried themselves in the walls, so they could be dug out and re-used by the defenders. Linked by curtain walls, diamond-shaped bastions allowed cannons to set up a deadly crossfire. The fortress is surrounded by a moat with a single point of entry (the sallyport), backed up by a portcullis. Around the gun decks, long-barreled cannons and short-nosed mortars were supported by musket fire, and the central courtyard, where soldiers drilled, is enclosed by guardrooms, stores, and the powder magazine. (During 2001, a restoration programme will limit access to parts of the fort, but external living history exhibits will be increased to compensate.)

Flagler College, *74 King Street* (*Open* foyer daily 8–5, guided tours in summer every half-hour 10:30–4:30. *Admission: inexpensive*; tel: 904/823-3378) Henry M

Flagler visited St Augustine during the winter of 1883–4, and liked what he saw. He returned a year later to build the Ponce de León Hotel, a monumental Spanish/ Moorish Revival affair that now houses Flagler College. It was the first major US building to be constructed using poured concrete. The interior was decorated with imported marble, carved oak and Tiffany stained glass. An elegant courtyard leads to the foyer where an elaborately gilded and pointed cupola displays symbolic motifs representing Spain and Florida. Beyond this, the Rotunda has been transformed into a grand college dining hall.

Fountain of Youth, *11 Magnolia Avenue* (*Open* daily 9–5. *Admission: moderate*; tel: 904/829-3168) It is a matter of record that Ponce de León discovered neither legendary Bimini (see page 36), nor the source of eternal youth. But he did discover a spring: There is one in this touristy park. Archaeological digs have revealed the existence of early Timucua tribes here and evidence of Christian Native American burial grounds, but guided tours merely scratch the surface of local history. They also include a film show, a planetarium visit which reconstructs the position of the heavens as seen by Ponce de León and an opportunity to sample the famous spring water.

DRESSING UP

St Augustine residents find any excuse to dress up in period costume. In Spanish Night Watch (third Saturday in June), there is a torchlit procession through the old Spanish Quarter, with 'troops' dressed in 18th-century costume, re-enacting colonial customs. September's Menendez Landing marks the 1565 Spanish landing on the grounds of the Mission of Nombre de Dios, and the British Night Watch (first weekend in December) marks the British occupation of St Augustine with a three-day living history re-enactment.

Reconstruction of the arrival of explorer Ponce de León at the Fountain of Youth

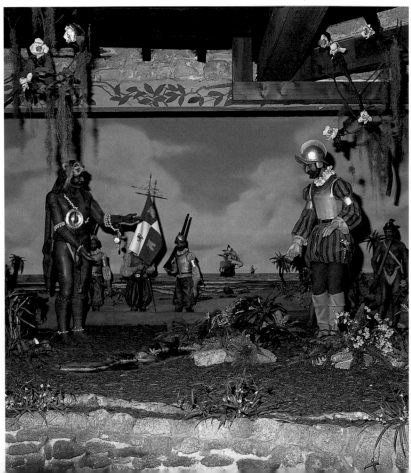

Lightner Museum, *75 King Street* (*Open* daily 9–5. *Admission: moderate*; tel: 904/824-2874) Opposite Flagler College, the Lightner displays the decorative arts collections of Chicago newspaper baron Otto C Lightner in the third of Henry Flagler's former grand hotels. (The second was the newly and beautifully restored Casa Monica Hotel across Cordova Street.)

This is a real treasure trove, best visited from top to bottom. The highlight of the collection is the glass on the second floor, featuring the largest gathering of American cut glass: On display are superb Tiffany lamps and other decorative pieces; delicate Venetian glass; and scalloped, frilled, satin-finish, coloured, and copperised glass. In the basement, the Lightner Antiques Mall occupies the impressive former swimming pool.

Oldest House, *14 St. Francis Street* (*Open* daily 9–5. *Admission: inexpensive*; tel: 904/824-2872) Also known as the Gonzalez-Alvarez house, after two former occupants – Tomas Gonzalez, an early 18th-century artilleryman, and Geronimo Alvarez, who bought the house in 1790 – this is one of the best researched and documented houses in the United States. It has a fascinating story, told with great gusto and plenty of incidental detail on the frequent guided tours.

There are traces of a crude palm-thatched wooden habitation here dating from the early 1600s. Later, sometime after the great fire of 1702, this was overlaid with a single-story coquina structure, constructed of coquina blocks made of compacted shell material quarried on Anastasia Island, shipped to the mainland site and then cemented into place with 'tabby', a mixture of lime, shells and sand.

A wooden second storey was added in the mid-18th century by Maria Peavett, the wife of an English soldier. Maria operated a successful tavern and boarding house, and her extraordinary life was the basis for the novel *Maria* by Eugenia Price (available in the gift shop). Each room in the house has been furnished in a period relevant to the building's long and colourful history. The gardens are beautiful, with deliciously cool arcades and a picnic

DOMESTIC ARRANGEMENTS
In 1821, Dr Seth Peck moved his family to St Augustine, where they took lodgings in a boarding house at 20 Aviles Street, now known as the Ximenez-Fatio House. Later, the family moved to Pena-Peck House, 143 St George Street, built for the Spanish Royal Treasurer in 1740. Both houses have been imaginatively restored and provide an intriguing insight into 19th-century domestic life.

Once a luxury Flagler hotel – the Lightner Museum

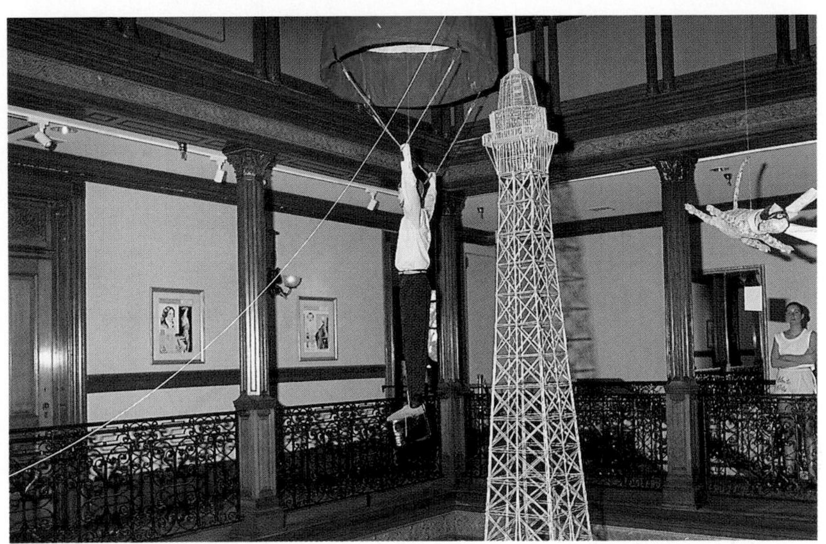

Some of the curiosities in Ripley's 'Believe it or Not!' Museum in St Augustine

area. There is also a **Museum of Florida's Army**, which displays uniforms and weaponry.

Oldest Store Museum, *4 Artillery Lane* (*Open* Mon–Sat 9–5, Sun noon–5. *Admission: inexpensive*; tel: 904/829-9729) A popular stop on St Augustine's historic trail, this 19th-century former general store is stocked from floor to ceiling with antique wares. There are more than 100,000 items on display, many of them actually found on the premises, ranging from patent medicines to decoy ducks to Edison Home Phonographs.

Old St Augustine Village, *250 St George Street, entrance on Bridge Street* (*Open* daily 9–5. *Admission: moderate*; tel: 904/823-9722) The latest addition to St Augustine's compendium of historical attractions, this restored city block will be a work in progress for some time after its autumn 2000 opening. Set around the charming, tree-shaded property are eleven historic houses ranging from the 1790 Spanish-Colonial Prince Murat House to a 1910 Colonial Revival-style home. Displays in the buildings will cover topics as varied as Cracker Culture, ornithologist John James Audubon and American decorative arts.

Ripley's Believe it or Not! Museum, *19 San Marco Avenue* (*Open* daily 9–7 or later. *Admission: moderate*; tel: 904/824-1606) Robert L Ripley was born in California in 1893, and his story is no less peculiar than most of the strange-but-true exhibits in his museums. He graduated from an early career as a cartoonist to become America's master of trivia, collecting weird and wonderful tales and artefacts from around the world. He visited some 198 countries, traveling the equivalent of 18 complete circuits of the globe. Opened in 1950, this museum was the first permanent display of his finds and includes such oddities as a shrunken head, grotesque film footage of freaky circus acts and Van Gogh masterpieces re-created in jellybeans – get the idea?

SMALLER ATTRACTIONS
St Augustine's trade in things historical extends to a host of smaller attractions, such as the creaky Oldest Wooden Schoolhouse, 14 St George Street, dating from 1763. The Old Jail, 167 San Marco Avenue, retains its 19th-century cage-like cell block. The collections on display at the Museum of Weapons and Early American History, 81C King Street, are small but fascinating.

FOOD, GLORIOUS FOOD
In 18th-century colonial St Augustine, food cooked on outdoor fires was provided by hunting, fishing and kitchen gardens, such as those in the Spanish Quarter Village. The gardens are planted with chillies, beans, aubergines, onions and pumpkins, and even the odd citrus tree which the Spanish originally imported to counter the risk of scurvy.

St Augustine Alligator Farm, *A1A (1 mile east of Bridge of Lions)* (*Open* daily 9–5. *Admission: expensive*; tel: 904/824-3337) The alligator farm is the only place in the world where all 23 species of crocodilians from around the world can be viewed. Founded in 1893, the 'World's Original Alligator Farm' has added a few interesting extras to its menagerie. There are still plenty of crowd-pulling crocodilians of all shapes and sizes, but visitors will also have the opportunity to see monkeys and tropical birds from South America, giant Galapagos tortoises and snakes from around the world. There is a boardwalk nature trail leading through the swamps, alligator and reptile shows throughout the day and a petting zoo.

Spanish Quarter Village, *Triay House, 33 St. George Street* (*Open* Sun–Thu 9–6, Fri–Sat 9–7. *Admission: moderate*; tel: 904/825-6830) Tucked away towards the City Gate end of St George Street, this is a great little living history museum. Plan to spend extra time in the buildings and gardens where costumed interpreters explain how life was lived in old St Augustine.

A group of seven historic buildings dating from the 18th century has been restored and sparsely furnished to recreate colonial life in St Augustine around the 1740s. Visitors are free to explore the grassy plot and nose around the old houses, and staff in period costumes are on hand to answer any questions and perform demonstrations. There is a blacksmith in the smithy, sweating over ancient bellows as he fashions cooking utensils and tools. The spinning demonstration includes an explanation of wool dyeing from locally available materials, such as onion skin and bark. Tours are frequent and worth waiting for.

A five-minute walk away, the **Spanish Military Hospital**, 3 Aviles Street (off the Plaza), depicts the fate of a soldier-patient in the 18th century.

Costumed bandsmen lead visitors back to St Augustine's colourful past in the restored historic Spanish Quarter

Rocketry on display

Once you've bought your tickets, the first stop is the Visitor Complex, which offers a range of exhibits and shows as well as tickets and shopping and dining opportunities. Take time to stroll around the **Rocket Garden**, with its towering collection of original manned and unmanned craft. Inspect the space hardware, models, space suits, specially prepared foodstuffs and interactive displays in the **Exploration** exhibits. Space art and the IMAX cinemas are located in the **Galaxy Center** at the northern end of the complex.

Do not miss a chance to see the stunning 35-minute **The Dream Is Alive** IMAX presentation, with seat-shuddering footage of a shuttle launch, astronauts working in space and shots of the Earth translated on to a screen five-and-a-half storeys high and 70 feet (21m) across. There are also child-friendly adventures in the **Robot Scouts** show, and the Universe Theater's **Quest for Life** show ponders the possibility of alien life beyond our planet.

Tours Two bus tours depart from the Visitor Complex. The must-do **Kennedy Space Center Tour** runs throughout the day and ventures to the heart of NASA's Florida facility to **Launch Complex 39**. Along the way, the tour passes the vast **VAB (Vehicle Assembly Building)**, one of the largest-volume structures in the world, where Space Shuttles are assembled before being rolled by monster Crawler Transporters to the launchpad. The highlight of

(Continued on page 196)

LIFT OFF
Cruised Miami Beach? Dived the Keys? Eaten alligator and done Disney? Here is a chance to sample one more Florida speciality, a Space Shuttle launch from the Kennedy Space Center. Advance information about schedules can be obtained from Florida Launch Information, Kennedy Space Center, FL 32899 (tel: 321/867-4636; www.pafb.af.mil or www.floridatoday.com/space). The limited number of launch passes allowing viewing from inside the security gates is usually booked well in advance (tel: 321/449-4444), but there are excellent vantage points along US 1 at Titusville and from Cape Canaveral City (Route A1A). Titusville permits roadside parking from 24 hours before launch time.

STAR SPOTTING
For a view of the heavens right up close, take a trip to the Astronaut Memorial Planetarium and Observatory, 1519 Clearlake Road, Cocoa (*Open* evenings, call for schedules. *Admission free*, small fee for film shows; tel: 321/634-3732). Observe the rings of Saturn and study the surface of Mars 450 million light years away. Then catch an Iwerks film presentation or a rock laser show.

A distinctive peninsula which juts out from the Florida coastline into the Atlantic, Cape Canaveral was named by Spanish sailors for the hollow reeds which grow abundantly in the area. Contrary to popular misconception, this region is by no means all given over to the space business; in fact, most of it is devoted to wilderness and wildlife.

BEYOND CANAVERAL
Away from Cape Canaveral, downtown Melbourne seems an odd place to go manatee watching, but the Crane Creek Promenade boardwalk along Melbourne Avenue (west of Front Street Park) is a prime site to spot these gentle vegetarian giants. At the Audubon Society's Turkey Creek Sanctuary in Palm Bay, a 4,000-foot (1,220m) boardwalk traverses three distinct Florida plant habitats which attract a wealth of native wildlife. There is another chance to go turtle-watching with the Sea Turtle Preservation Society (tel: 321/676-1701), which organises nesting-season walks along the coast between Satellite Beach and Spessard Holland Park.

Merritt Island is located between the cape and the mainland, marooned to east and west by the Banana and Indian rivers, and bordered to the north by Mosquito Lagoon and the **Canaveral National Seashore**. The southern portion of this island houses one of the most technologically advanced facilities in the world: the **Kennedy Space Center**. An area of 220 square miles (570sq km) in the north is given over to the **Merritt Island National Wildlife Refuge** (*Open* daily dawn–dusk). For an introduction to the wildlife and native flora found in the reserve, stop at the Visitor Center, off SR 402 (*Open* Mon–Fri 8–4:30, Sat–Sun 9–5. *Closed* Sun in May–Oct. *Admission free*; tel: 321/861-0667).

Since its emergence from the ocean around 1 million years ago, this 25-mile-long (40km) barrier island has been battered and sculpted by the elements. It has protected the coastline and has developed a wide variety of habitats which harbour around 330 species of birds, 31 kinds of mammals, 117 types of fish, and 65 kinds of amphibians and reptiles. A sad statistic is that 21 of these species are endangered, more than in any other single wildlife refuge in the whole of the United States.

Merritt Island's diverse habitats range from pocket-size freshwater lagoons to vast saltwater estuaries; brackish marshes give way to hardwood hammocks and to areas of pine flatwoods. Flourishing within the shallow marshlands, a nutritious smorgasbord of worms, snails, crabs, clams and fish attracts crocodiles and shore and wading birds. During winter, a further 23 species of migratory waterfowl take advantage of these open-water feeding grounds, while pelicans, cormorants, great blue herons, egrets and wood storks live here year-round. The well-watered hardwood hammocks provide an ideal environment for a lush backdrop of exotic bromeliads (air plants) and tropical and subtropical plants. Pileated woodpeckers, squirrels and armadillos are also common.

Walks and trails For a closer look at hammock environments, there are two walking trails off SR 402, east of the visitor center. **Oak Hammock Trail** is a half-mile stroll through a subtropical forest, with interpretive signboards along the route. The **Palm Hammock Trail** is a more interesting 2-mile (3km) hike which includes hardwood forest, cabbage palm hammocks and boardwalk sections over open marshland. Early

Watching whales – a fascinating spectacle

morning and late afternoon are the best times to undertake the **Black Point Wildlife Drive**, a 7-mile (11km) one-way circuit off SR 406. There is a series of parking areas for observing the mud flats and lagoon areas, which fairly bustle with bird activity during the height of the winter migration (January/February). A 5-mile (8km) marsh hike, the **Cruickshank Trail**, begins at Stop 8, and there is an observation tower a 5-minute walk along the trail from the car park. The optimum time to visit the park is October to April; always bring mosquito repellent.

Canaveral National Seashore Extending north for 24 miles (38km) from Merritt Island toward Daytona, this is one of Florida's few remaining areas of undeveloped coastal dunes. The preserve also contains **Mosquito Lagoon**, a shallow saltmarsh estuary with a particularly interesting variety of wildlife, reflecting its location at the point where the American temperate and tropical climates meet. Animals and birds typical to both habitats coexist around the marsh and areas of coastal forest, which are thick with oaks, cedars and wild orange trees. White-tailed deer, bobcats, raccoons and rattlesnakes hide out in the woodlands, while dolphins, manatees, osprey and roseate spoonbills enjoy the rich lagoon feeding grounds.

From May to August, the warm sandy beaches are an ideal nesting ground for female green and leatherback sea turtles. Starting in September, the original 'snowbirds' – bald eagles, warblers, even Arctic peregrine falcons – journey up to 6,000 miles (9,650km) to winter here. In early spring, migratory right whales calve offshore. There is parking and access to the seashore from **Playalinda Beach** (SR 402). Visitors should keep to official beach access points and not climb the dunes, or pick seagrasses which anchor the fragile environment. During summer, guided **turtle walks** are led by Merritt Island rangers.

CRUISE FROM CANAVERAL
The closest port to the Orlando area, Port Canaveral is booming. The growing popularity of two-destination holidays has not escaped Disney, whose two fun-packed cruise ships offer seven-day land-and-sea packages, combining a stay at Walt Disney World Resort with a cruise to the Bahamas. Other major cruise operators serving Port Canaveral include Cape Canaveral Cruise Line, Carnival Cruise Lines, Premier Cruise Lines, Royal Caribbean International and Sterling Casino Lines.

(Continued from page 193)

the tour is a visit to the spectacular $37-million **Apollo/Saturn V Center**, which you can explore for as long as you wish. In addition to the 363-foot (110m) Saturn V rocket in the main hall, there are interactive exhibits, the dramatic Firing Room Theater presentation and a re-created moon walk.

On the return trip to the Visitor Complex, there is a stop at **International Space Station Center** where components for the 21st-century space facility are made and tested. Aboard the tour bus, the recorded commentary is by James Lovell, Commander of Apollo 11.

The **Cape Canaveral Then & Now Tour** (several departures daily; check schedules) visits Cape Canaveral Air Force Station, where NASA launched its operations in 1958. The tour explores the site of the early Mercury and Gemini space projects.

US Astronaut Hall of Fame, *NASA Parkway (SR 405)* (*Open* daily 9–6, last admission 5. *Admission: expensive*; tel: 321/269-6100) A short drive from the Kennedy Space Center, the Hall of Fame, a showcase for the country's astronauts and their historic missions, is particularly user-friendly for children. Artefacts and rare video footage turn the spotlight on the men of the Mercury space programme, and there is plenty of stomach-churning fun to be had in a variety of simulators, including a full-scale replica orbiter. The complex is also home to **US Space Camp Florida** (information, tel: 800/63 SPACE), which offers live-in five-day camp programmes for young astronaut wannabes.

Valiant Air Command Warbird Museum, *Space Coast Regional Airport (SR 405), Titusville* (*Open* daily 10–6. *Admission: moderate*; tel: 321/268-1941) More than 350 vintage World War II and postwar military planes are housed here. Each March the collection comes alive for the **Valiant Air Command Warbird Airshow**, when fans can see the planes put through their paces.

The deep-water Port Canaveral

Drive

Along the East Coast

An easy day's excursion from the Space Coast, this drive follows A1A from Cocoa Beach down to the Treasure Coast around Fort Pierce.

Cocoa Beach is a bastion of 'surfie' culture and fluorescent beachwear – both in and out of the water. Just south of Cocoa Beach, **Patrick Air Force Base** borders A1A to the west for the next 5 miles (8km). There is a display of military rocketry set up outside the Technical Headquarters.

A seamless run of beach communities continues to spill down the coast: Satellite Beach, Indian Harbor, Indialantic, and Melbourne Beach, where A1A does a little signposted jig slightly inland before the road narrows. It is 14 miles (22km) from the southern city limits of Melbourne Beach to the entrance to Sebastian Inlet State Recreation Area.

This is a great place to stop off. The premier saltwater fishing location on the East Coast boasts two Atlantic jetties and a catwalk, giving access to waters teeming with bluefish, redfish, snook and Spanish mackerel. Surfers flock to a reserved beach area, and there are plenty of opportunities for snorkelling and excellent swimming off sparkling white beaches.

To visit the McLarty Museum, continue on A1A, then follow the signs.

On the site of an old Spanish salvage camp, the **McLarty Treasure Museum** (*Open* daily 10–4:30. *Admission: inexpensive*; tel: 561/589-2147) is the place to check out the history of Spanish shipwrecks off this part of the coast. There are several more beach access points carved through the thick coastal barrier of palms, oaks, sea grapes and pines.

Rejoin A1A and continue for 14 miles (22km), following signs to Vero Beach.

Vero Beach (see panel, page 178) is a wealthy resort town off A1A. The main street is **Ocean Drive**, with its exclusive shopping district and the eccentric **Driftwood Inn**.

Continue to Fort Pierce.

There is more fishing, snorkelling and swimming at **Fort Pierce Inlet State Recreation Area**. The Treasure Coast itself has several attractions such as the **Elliott Museum**, right on A1A before Stuart, and **Gilbert's Bar House of Refuge**, at the southern tip of Hutchinson Island.

A1A rejoins US 1 at Stuart.

F4-4 Fighter Race Corsair on show at Valiant Air Command Museum

REGION HIGHLIGHTS

SKILLED MARINERS
Southwest Florida was once Calusa territory. Skilled mariners and fishermen, these Native Americans ranged far and wide, sometimes venturing as far south as Cuba. Archaeologists have discovered Calusa artefact from around 5000 BC in some of the many ancient ceremonial, burial and refuse shell mounds dotted about the barrier islands and mainland back bays of the region.

LAPPED BY THE warm, translucent waters of the Gulf of Mexico, Florida's West Coast is an alluring mix of white-sand beaches, water sports, world-class museums and wildlife. Once the butt of retirement jokes, it has developed into a cosmopolitan holiday destination offering a broad range of accommodations and diversions, including areas of exceptional natural beauty.

The early Spanish explorers – Juan Ponce de León, Pánfilo de Narváez and Hernando de Soto – all stopped here, but were discouraged by warring Native Americans and steaming, insect-infested mangrove belts. Coastal navigation was perilous because of reefs and shoals. This was to the advantage of legendary 18th-century pirate Gasparilla, who was able to operate unhindered.

The US Army arrived in the 1820s, and a handful of fishing settlements began to grow along the coast. **Tampa**, the Gulf Coast's largest city, was put on the map by Henry Plant's railroad in the 1880s. Vincente Martinez Ybor and his cigar industry added the city's Cuban connection, which remains strong even today. Across the bay, **Pinellas County**, with its 28 miles (45km) of barrier-island beaches, St Petersburg, Clearwater and Largo, is Tampa's Gulf shore playground. To the north, Dunedin and **Tarpon Springs** provide a further touch of cultural diversity – Scottish and Greek, respectively – and the Manatee Coast continues up to Crystal River.

South of Tampa, **Sarasota** is a cultural capital, and is where circus king John Ringling built a fabulous estate and an Italian Renaissance-style museum to house his art collection. Sarasota's two performing arts centres feature nationally acclaimed programmes. The 'City of Palms', **Fort Myers** is renowned for being the winter home of inventor Thomas Alva Edison and for its offshore islands. The South Seas paradise of the Lee Island Coast is shell heaven for seashell seakers, and Edison earned the city its nickname by planting the first royal palms along McGregor Boulevard. At the southern end of the coastal strip, elegantly manicured **Naples** luxuriates in social circles and shopping malls worthy of Palm Beach. There are excellent golfing opportunities, too, and it is also an ideal base for excursions into the Everglades.

Fun and games on the coast: Naples Beach

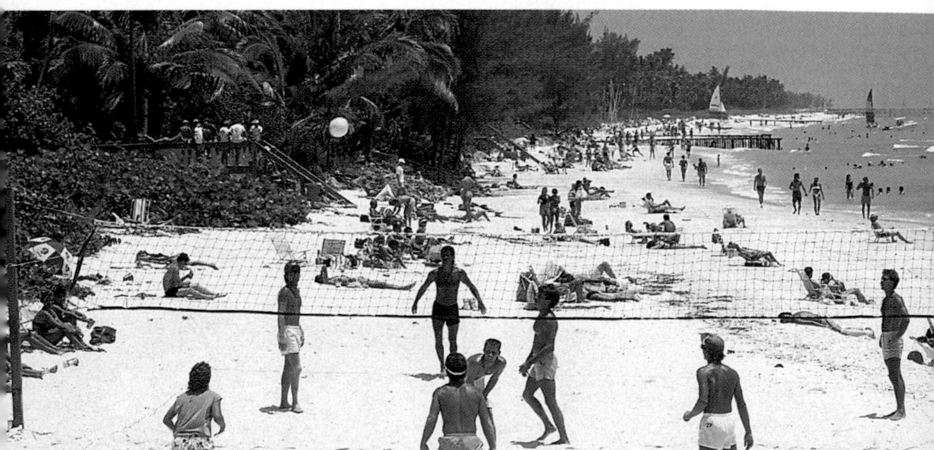

West Coast

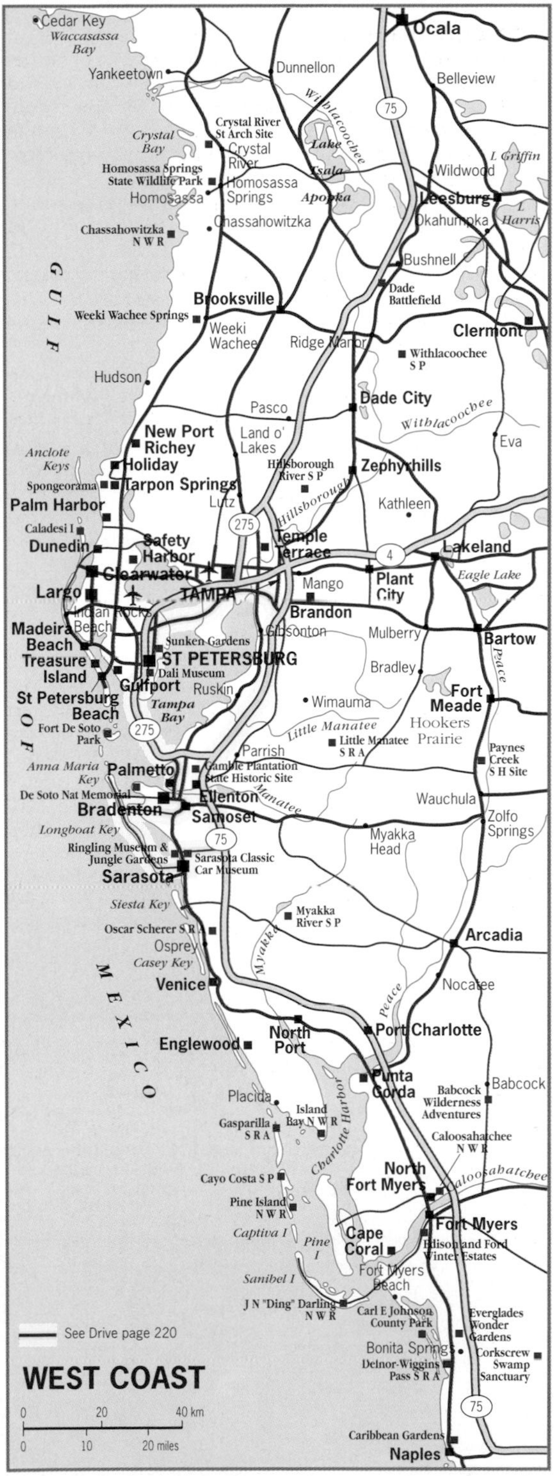

Cedar Key
Waccasassa Bay
Yankeetown
Dunnellon
Ocala
Belleview
75
Withlacoochee
Crystal River St Arch Site
Crystal Bay
Crystal River
Lake Tsala Apopka
Wildwood
L Griffin
Homosassa Springs State Wildlife Park
Homosassa
Homosassa Springs
Leesburg
L Harris
Okahumpka
Chassahowitzka
Chassahowitzka N W R
Bushnell
Dade Battlefield
GULF
Brooksville
Weeki Wachee Springs
Weeki Wachee
Ridge Manor
Clermont
Withlacoochee S P
Hudson
Pasco
Dade City
Withlacoochee
New Port Richey
Land o' Lakes
Eva
Anclote Keys
Holiday
Hillsborough River S P
Zephyrhills
Spongeorama
Tarpon Springs
Palm Harbor
Lutz
Hillsborough
Kathleen
Caladesi I
275
Dunedin
Safety Harbor
Temple Terrace
4
Lakeland
Clearwater
TAMPA
Eagle Lake
Largo
Mango
Plant City
Indian Rocks Beach
Brandon
Madeira Beach
Gibsonton
Mulberry
Bartow
Sunken Gardens
Treasure Island
ST PETERSBURG
Dali Museum
Bradley
Gulfport
Ruskin
Fort Meade
Peace
St Petersburg Beach
Wimauma
Tampa Bay
Hookers Prairie
OF
Fort De Soto Park
275
Little Manatee
Little Manatee S R A
Parrish
Paynes Creek S H Site
Anna Maria Key
Palmetto
Gamble Plantation State Historic Site
De Soto Nat Memorial
Ellenton
Manatee
Wauchula
Bradenton
Samoset
Zolfo Springs
Longboat Key
75
Myakka Head
Ringling Museum & Jungle Gardens
Sarasota Classic Car Museum
Sarasota
Siesta Key
Myakka River S P
Oscar Scherer S R A
Arcadia
Osprey
Casey Key
Myakka
MEXICO
Venice
Nocatee
Peace
North Port
Port Charlotte
Englewood
Punta Gorda
Babcock
Placida
Babcock Wilderness Adventures
Island Bay N W R
Gasparilla S R A
Charlotte Harbor
Caloosahatchee N W R
Cayo Costa S P
North Fort Myers
Caloosahatchee
Pine Island N W R
Fort Myers
Captiva I
Pine I
Cape Coral
Edison and Ford Winter Estates
Fort Myers Beach
Sanibel I
J N "Ding" Darling N W R
Carl E Johnson County Park
Everglades Wonder Gardens
Bonita Springs
Corkscrew Swamp Sanctuary
Delnor-Wiggins Pass S R A
75
Caribbean Gardens
Naples

See Drive page 220

WEST COAST

0 20 40 km
0 10 20 miles

ESTERO BAY BOAT TOURS
A fascinating introduction to local natural history, Charlie Weeks runs a one-man boat tour which combines knowledgeable commentaries with a spot of showmanship. There is not a nesting spot, manatee playground or fishing hole on the back bay which he doesn't know about, and you'll learn about Calusa Indians, too. Daily tours morning, afternoon, and dusk; call for information and schedules, tel: 941/922-2200. The Weeks' Fish Camp is 4.7 miles (7.5km) north of Bonita Springs, off US 41 at the end of Coconut Road.

▶ Bonita Springs

Sandwiched between the ever-encroaching cities of Naples and Fort Myers, Bonita occupies a rare pocket of the southwest Gulf shore, where large-scale development has been kept to a minimum. The virgin coastline of the **Carl E Johnson Country Park**, off Hickory Boulevard, is one of the few remaining stretches of natural shell beach, or take a hike around **Lovers' Key State Recreation Area**. Bonita's back bay estuary area is teeming with bird life; there also are manatees here, and the fishing is great. For after-dark entertainment the **Naples/Fort Myers Greyhound Track**, *1601 Bonita Beach Road (at Old US 41;* tel: 941/992-2411) lures in the spectators and speculators to its races.

Corkscrew Swamp Sanctuary, *Route 846 (20 miles/32km east of US 41)* (*Open:* daily 8–5; Dec–Apr from 7. *Admission: moderate*; tel: 941/348-9151) Corkscrew was once the northern tip of southwest Florida's immense Big Cypress Swamp. The 11,000-acre (4,450-ha) sanctuary preserves America's largest remaining unspoiled stand of bald cypress trees and is a unique natural wildlife habitat. The National Audubon Society recognised the area's importance in 1912, when poachers roamed the swamp slaughtering wood storks and egrets for their feathers – then much in demand as fashion accessories. Today, the swamp is one of the Society's greatest treasures and home to a large population of rare woodstorks, as well as several species of wild orchid which can be seen during the winter months. The best time to visit is early morning before the heat of the day drives the wildlife into the protective shade. (See Walk on page 215.)

Everglades Wonder Gardens, *Old US 41* (*Open* daily 9–5, last tour 4:15. *Admission: moderate*; tel: 941/992-2591)

Bonita Beach

Reeking strongly of sulphur from Bonita's springs, this is one of the original Florida attractions. Founded in 1936, it needs a coat of paint, but the selection of Everglades wonders you can see here is hard to fault, and the tour guides provide well-informed and entertaining commentaries. Meet Everglades alligators and American crocodiles, eagles, Florida panthers and black bears, as well as deer, bobcats and wild boars. There are regular otter shows and alligator feeding times, and a Calusa Indian museum.

Lovers' Key State Recreation Area, *8700 Estero Boulevard/CR 865* (*Open:* daily 8–dusk. *Admission: expensive;* tel: 941/463-4588) Encompassing two islands and a couple of uninhabited islets, this Gulf-side preserve combines recreational activities such as canoeing, biking and hiking trails, shell-collecting and fishing with bird-watching and wildlife-spotting ranging from manatees and dolphins to turtles. There are snack-bar and picnic facilities, too.

► Bradenton

Bradenton is on the southern bank of the Manatee River and makes a good starting point for a trip to west Florida's only true antebellum building, the **Gamble Mansion** at Ellenton (see page 204). Bradenton's beach lies out to the west, on **Anna Maria Key**, a really old-fashioned narrow beachfront lined with clapboard houses, fast-food and ice-cream stands, plus a few surfies who do their best to ride the relatively tame Gulf waves. A detour via the beach makes a change from the highway when travelling to or from Sarasota.

De Soto National Memorial, *75th Street* (*Open* daily 9–5. *Admission free;* tel: 941/792-0458) This memorial park commemorates Spanish explorer Hernando de Soto, who is said to have landed at this very spot in May 1539. His 600-man expedition also included 350 horses, bloodhounds and greyhounds for hunting, pigs, weapons and tons of supplies. Park rangers dress up in period costumes (Dec to Apr) and re-enact life in an early settlement. There is also a good nature trail (see Walk on page 215).

South Florida Museum and Bishop Planetarium, *201 W 10th Street* (*Open* Tue–Sat 10–5, Sun noon–5, Mon in Jan–Apr and Jul. *Admission: moderate;* tel: 941/746-4131) The museum's main attraction is Snooty, an 8-foot-long (2.5m) male manatee, who has lived here since 1949. Born in captivity at the Miami Seaquarium in 1948, Snooty is fed four times a day – some 24 heads of lettuce, 16 apples, two vitamin pills and a pineapple – and after years as a solitary bachelor has recently acquired a poolmate, Mo. The museum itself provides good dioramas of Native American life displayed together with archeological finds – a reconstruction of a midden (shell mound) and a burial mound. Upstairs, set-piece rooms run the gamut from 16th-century Spain to the Victorian era, complete with traditional crafts, costumes and collectables. The **Bishop Planetarium** presents daily astronomy shows and weekend laser light shows (Fri–Sat).

GREAT EXPECTATIONS

In 1894, Dr Cyrus Teed and followers of his eccentric religious sect, the Koreshan Unity, moved to a site near Bonita Springs, where they planned to build a city for 10 million people. At the height of its popularity, the settlement attracted around 250 inhabitants. Tours of the Koreshan State Historic Site, US 41 at Corkscrew Road, include descriptions of Teed's bizarre belief that mankind lives on the inner surface of a hollow globe containing the galaxy at its heart. The sect's commendable belief in equal rights for women was considered just as outlandish in 19th-century Florida.

HIGHLAND GAMES
Not much more than a caber's throw from Greek Tarpon Springs is a corner of Florida with strong Scottish roots. Dunedin's Hibernian links were forged in the 1860s, when Scottish merchants founded the first settlement here and gave it the Gaelic name meaning 'peaceful rest'. Each spring, the town pulls in the crowds for Highland Games, complete with bagpipes, a military tattoo and much swaggering around in kilts.

►► Clearwater and the Pinellas County Beaches

One of the Pinellas County beaches with St Petersburg to the south, Clearwater proper is on the mainland, but all the action is along Clearwater Beach on the barrier islands lining the Gulf of Mexico.

Beaches Pinellas County boasts 35 miles (56km) of coastline, most of it maintained under the public parks system. In fact, it is so well cared for that beach scientists regularly rank Clearwater Beach, Caladesi Island State Park and St Petersburg's Fort De Soto Park among the Top Ten beaches in the US.

North of Clearwater, **Honeymoon Island** and **Caladesi Island** (see page 203) are two of the last natural barrier islands on the coast with beautiful white-sand beaches. **Clearwater Beach** is reached from the mainland via the Memorial Causeway; then head south for **Sand Key**'s fabulous Gulf-shore beach; fashionably sedate **Belleair Beach** and **Belleair Shores**; **Indian Rocks Beach**, with its (2.5m) fishing pier; **Redington Shores Beach**, where the famed Suncoast Seabird Sanctuary houses around 500 rescued birds; and **Madeira Beach**, which fronts funky John's Pass Village, a shopping and dining enclave with a scenic waterfront stroll along the boardwalk. Treasure hunters be warned: **Treasure Island**, a section of beach and hotels, was just a name dreamed up as a promotional gimmick in the land-boom era, and hopes should not be raised too high.

Next stop along the shores is **St Petersburg Beach**, the busiest of them all, dominated by the vast pink outline of the 1928 Don Cesar Hotel. This land boom folly of staggering proportions was a playground for the rich and famous, from F Scott Fitzgerald to Babe Ruth. Last but not least, top-rated **Fort De Soto Park** encompasses the tip of the peninsula.

The West Coast: sun, sea and palms

Sunset over Clearwater

Caladesi Island State Park (*Open* daily 8am–dusk. *Admission: inexpensive*; tel: 727/469-5918. Information from Honeymoon Island SRA) It is just a short ferry hop to this natural barrier island, where the only inhabitants are birds, armadillos and the occasional alligator. Caladesi was once a part of a larger barrier island linked to Honeymoon Island, its neighbour to the north, but it was annexed by hurricanes in 1848 and 1921, and has remained undisturbed ever since, save for a small area of development near the dock and a ranger station. On the island, visitors will find sandy swimming beaches linked by boardwalks to picnic and changing facilities, as well as diving, shell-collecting opportunities and a 3-mile (5km) nature trail. There is boat access to the island from Clearwater and from Honeymoon Island State Recreation Area, reached by Causeway Boulevard from Dunedin.

Clearwater Marine Aquarium, *249 Windward Passage* (*Open* Mon–Fri 9–5, Sat 9–4, Sun 11–4. *Admission: moderate*; tel: 727/447-0980) Not far from Clearwater Beach, this aquarium has a dual function – as a tourist attraction, showing sea creatures in huge tanks, and as a rehabilitation unit for injured sea turtles and marine mammals such as otters. Displays focus on local marine life. Among the best are the Mangrove/Seagrass Marsh Tank, with a 55-foot-long (17m) 'Window to the Sea' tank; and Sam, the rescued bottlenose dolphin. There are also aquariums of loggerhead turtles, rays and other exotic species. The aquarium also offers two-hour Sea Life Safari Cruises with a marine biologist and guided Kayak Adventures in Clearwater Harbor and St Joseph's Sound, as well as one- to four-day Marine Life Adventures to study endangered animal and plant species.

CRUISING FROM CLEARWATER

Starlite Cruises offer several options from the Clearwater Beach Marina or from St Pete Beach. The *Starlite Princess Riverboat* offers daytime sightseeing cruises and jazz cruises (Tue, Wed, Fri, Sat), while the modern *Starlite Majesty* sets sail for dinner cruises with live entertainment (Tue–Sun). For more information and reservations, tel: 727/462-2628.

GENTLE GIANTS
The aquatic West Indian (Florida) manatee evolved from a four-footed terrestrial mammal thousands of years ago. Shaped like an Idaho potato with the face of a gentle boxer dog and a spatulate tail like a beaver's, you can still see the outline of three or four toe nails on their forelimbs. These gentle giants can grow up to 14 feet (4m) long and weigh in at over a ton, but their vegetarian diet consists of little more than aquatic grasses found in rivers and estuarine areas. When calves are born they have a pinky hue to their gray-brown skin. A healthy manatee (who avoids the propellers of power boats!) can expect to live for 50 to 60 years.

Storm clouds over the Crystal River

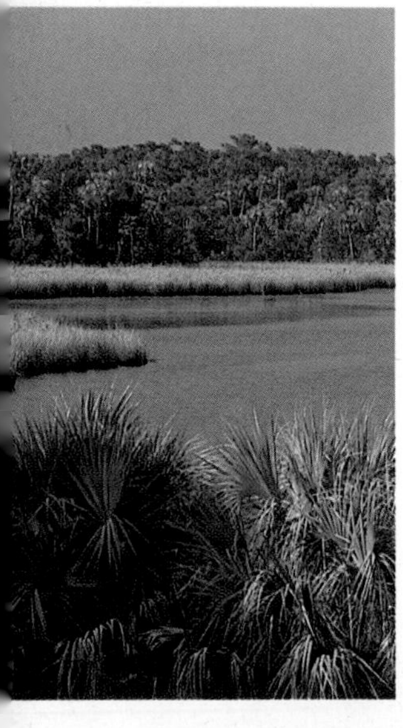

▶ Crystal River

North of Tampa on US 19

Crystal River is best known for its warm springs. More than 100 of them rise around Kings Bay and attract manatees, especially during the winter months (Dec–Mar). These vegetarian mammals can weigh up to 3,000 pounds (1,360kg), and are quite safe to swim with. For information about diving with the manatees, boat trips and canoe rentals in the **Crystal River National Wildlife Refuge**, contact the Citrus County Chamber of Commerce, at Crystal River, 28 NW US 19, tel: 352/795-3149.

Just north of the town, the **Crystal River State Archeological Site**, 3400 Museum Point North (*Open* daily 8am–dusk. *Admission: inexpensive*; tel: 352/795-3817) is one of the oldest and longest continuously inhabited Native American sites in Florida. The six-mound complex was an important ceremonial centre from around 200 BC to AD 1400; archaeologists have uncovered more than 400 graves filled with prehistoric artefacts ranging from everyday tools and weapons to a sophisticated astronomical calendar.

▶▶ Ellenton's Gamble Plantation (State Historic Site)

3708 Patten Avenue (US 301 E), Ellenton; tel: 941/723-4536
Open: Thu–Mon 9–5. Admission: inexpensive

One of southwest Florida's first settlers, Major Robert Gamble was granted the original 160-acre (65-ha) plot of land here in 1844. The estate grew to 3,500 acres (1,416 ha) along the Manatee River. Sugar-cane was refined in the plantation's mill; citrus, wild grapes and olives were shipped to New Orleans. Gamble built himself a classic two-storey antebellum mansion from tabby brick (limestone and shell blocks cemented with molasses, lime, sand, and water), with its broad verandas supported by 18 columns. To keep the house cool, he made it only one room wide and the two-foot-thick whitewashed walls are lined with loose-shuttered windows aligned to catch the breeze. Great care has been taken to maintain the authentic period interior, the house is also a memorial to Confederate secretary of state Judah P Benjamin, who took refuge here in 1865 before he escaped to England.

▶▶▶ Fort Myers and the Lee Island Coast

Thomas Alva Edison, the town's most famous winter resident, had it about right when he predicted, way back in 1914, that 'there is only one Fort Myers, and 90 million people are going to find it out'. Airport gateway to the southwest coast, Fort Myers covers a lot of ground. The historic and commercial downtown district lies on the south bank of the Caloosahatchee River, with North Fort Myers and Cape Coral across the water. Hotel-lined Fort Myers Beach is a 20-mile (32km) drive south on Estero Island. Meanwhile, life on the offshore islands and keys is still largely a *mañana* affair of palm-fringed sands, fabulous seashells, scenic boat trips and deep-sea fishing charters. Sports fishermen from across the world travel to Boca Grande for a chance to lure a mighty tarpon, while the 'Sanibel stoop' is an affliction of shell gatherers harvesting the treasures washed up on that island's white-sand beaches.

The best way to explore downtown Fort Myers is a guided **Tram Tour** (Tue–Sat 10–3). Tours depart from the Edison House and trundle around the historic district. The drivers supply a constant stream of lively anecdotes about the city's early history and residents.

Babcock Wilderness Adventures, *8000 SR 31, Punta Gorda (9½ miles/15km north of SR 78)* (*Open* Nov–Apr, 9–3; May–Oct, mornings only. *Admission: expensive*; tel: 941/489-3911 or 1-800/500-5583; reservations only) An exciting swamp-buggy ride allows a unique look around the vast 90,000-acre (36,420-ha) Babcock Crescent B Ranch. Logging baron E V Babcock bought the property in 1914 and logged the cypress swamp during the 1930s. However, he recognized the importance of the trees in the swamp-filtration process, and at the heart of the property, the clear, brown, tannin-rich waters of Telegraph Cypress Swamp – so named because telegraph wires had to be routed around it – retain an amazing display of curious 'cypress knees', protrusions around the base of the cypress tree trunk, uncluttered by weed or grass. Here, bird life and alligators thrive, and a boardwalk leads to the cougar enclosure, where native American panthers roam and breed in a natural habitat. The 32-seat swamp buggies, carved from old trucks, make a 90-minute circuit of the grounds (there is also a 10-mile/16km Off-Road Eco-Bike Tour). There are usually sightings of the ranch's bison herd, unusual crossbreed Senepol cattle and quarter horses, plus unscheduled appearances by wild hogs, turkey, deer and snakes.

FUN FOR THE YOUNG

There is plenty of fun in store for youngsters at the Imaginarium Hands-On Museum and Aquarium, 2000 Cranford Avenue (*Open* Tue–Sat 10–5; tel: 941/337-3332), where exhibits include a variety of subjects from anatomy and physics to marine biology. Kids can hop into a hurricane chamber, touch a crab, surf the Internet or dig up a fossil. In Cape Coral, Sun Splash Family WaterPark, 400 Santa Barbara Boulevard (for schedules, tel: 941/574-0557), is a good summer season cooler with water slides, inner tube rides and games; and the Children's Science Center, 2915 NE Pine Island Road (*Open* Mon–Fri 9:30–4:30, Sat and Sun noon–5; tel: 941/997-0012), is near by, with exhibits ranging from holograms to hermit crabs.

Fort Myers beach and pier

Examining the wares in Fort Myers' Shell Factory

Calusa Nature Center and Planetarium, *3450 Ortiz Avenue (north of Colonial)* (*Open* Mon–Sat 9–5, Sun 11–5. *Admission: inexpensive*; tel: 941/275-3435) Founded in 1970, on a 105-acre (42-ha) plot, the Nature Center was specifically designed with children in mind. In the reception area is a collection of snakes, tree frogs, terrapins, baby alligators and American crocodiles, as well as a selection of touchable exhibits, including seashells, rudimentary musical instruments and Native American artefacts, augmented by a group of traditional Seminole chickee huts outside. Stop off in the shade below the main building for a look at the turtle ponds housing assorted native Florida species such as snapping and mud turtles, and musk turtles who employ scent as a pungent form of defence.

Next, head for the bobcat enclosure and the centre's aviary, where the Audubon Society houses a number of its injured birds. Starting from here, there are two boardwalk trails in the swamp, cypress and pine woods, and a more taxing 2½-mile (4km) Wildlands Trail without the benefit of a boardwalk.

The 90-seat planetarium (*Admission: inexpensive*; call ahead for schedules) operates a busy programme of astronomy and laser shows.

ECHO, *17391 Durrance Road (off SR 78, east of I-75)* (*Open* tours only Tue, Fri and Sat at 10am. *Admission free*; tel: 941/543-3246) Under its full title, Educational Concerns for Hunger Organization, ECHO does not sound like much of a tourist attraction, but gardeners will find it fascinating. ECHO is a Christian ministry with a mission to fight world hunger by developing a seed bank of unusual food plants for use in the Third World and by promoting efficient recycling methods. An example of an ECHO success story is the moringa tree: its leaves make highly nutritional baby food, the pods are used as a vegetable, the root makes a horseradish substitute and the seeds can purify water overnight. Ideas developed here include space-saving gardens using plastic gutters and lightweight rooftop gardens made from soft drink cans and grass clippings to grow ginger and chillies or (without cans) radishes, lettuces and much more. Flourishing in the gardens are edible landscaping plants, such as coffee, citrus, carambola (starfruit), pepper and cashew trees;

THE SHELL FACTORY

A southwest Florida institution for more than half a century, The Shell Factory, N Tamiami Trail (US 41) North Fort Myers, claims to offer the world's largest collection of rare shells, corals, sponges and fossils from the world's oceans. Some five million shells and shell-related souvenirs are for sale, from sand dollars costing a couple of cents to pricey exotica; plus beachwear, T-shirts and manatee fridge magnets. Outdoor entertainment includes miniature golf and bumper boat rides.

and you can meet another of ECHO's special projects – the wool-free sheep.

Edison and Ford Winter Estates, *2350 McGregor Boulevard* (*Open* Mon–Sat 9–4, Sun noon–4. *Joint admission: expensive*, river cruises additional, *inexpensive*; tel: 941/334-3614) Inventor of the automatic telegraph, phonograph and incandescent lamp, Thomas Alva Edison can also be credited with 'discovering' Fort Myers. Holidaying in Florida, on his doctor's orders in 1884–5, he ventured down to this small, semitropical fishing village on the Caloosahatchee River. He loved the area so much that he eventually bought a 14-acre (5.5-ha) plot of land there. The **Edison Winter Home** was an innovation, too: its prefabricated sections were constructed in Fairfield, Maine, transported south on four schooners and erected in 1886. Edison and his second wife, Mina Miller Edison, their children and friends spent winters here until his death in 1931.

The modest house retains its original furnishings, and the surrounding gardens reveal that the wizard inventor was also an expert horticulturist.

Friends and colleagues were constantly proffering gifts of exotic plants to add to his collection (for example Henry Firestone's monstrous banyan tree), and several varieties of rubber plant and goldenrod stand as a testament to Edison's search for a domestic source of natural rubber.

Across McGregor Boulevard, lined with majestic royal palms planted by Edison, is his fully equipped laboratory. It is still lit by the original carbon-filament light bulbs that have shone for 12 hours a day ever since they were installed. The museum holds hundreds of Edison inventions, which range from talking dolls to miners' lamps, and

LAP OF LUXURY

Fort Myers' first luxury residence, the lovely Burroughs Home, 2505 First Street, was built on the banks of the Caloosahatchee River by cattle baron John Murphy in 1901, and later passed into the hands of the Burroughs family. Living history tours explore the elegantly restored Georgian Revival-style building (*Open* Dec–May, Tue–Fri 11–3; Jun–Nov, Fri only. *Admission: moderate*; tel: 941/332-6125).

Thomas Edison's laboratory, a fitting memorial to a great scientist

ALL ABOARD
The old Fort Myers–Naples railroad has been restored betwen Fort Myers and Bonita Springs, allowing the old-fashioned Seminole Gulf Railway to ply the route with sightseeing excursions, lunch and dinner tours and mystery dinner theatre outings. Trains depart from Colonial Station at the Amtel Mall, Metro Parkway, and Colonial Drive (for schedules and reservations, tel: 941/275-8487 or 800/SEM GULF).

illustrate just a handful of the 1,097 patented designs he achieved during his 84 years.

The Henry Fords visited the Edisons in 1915, and a year later bought the adjacent property, which they named Mangoes. The **Ford Winter Home**'s garage is used to display the cornerstone of the Ford fortunes: a 1914 Model-T, a 1917 Ford truck and 1929 Model A.

Fort Myers Historical Museum, *2300 Peck Street* (*Open* Tue–Sat 9–4. *Admission: moderate*; tel: 941/332-5955) The museum's collections present the history of southwest Florida in a nutshell. The story begins with Calusa Native American artefacts and continues with the founding of the fort, the Seminole Wars and events of the 20th century. The museum also displays a refurbished 1930s railway carriage, *The Esperanza*, and a recently excavated World War II P-39 bomber found in Estero Bay, as well as the Cooper collection of Depression and Carnival glassware, plus excellent scale models of trains and a gift shop.

Island hopping Many of the highlights of the Lee Island Coast are accessible only by boat. A generous sprinkling of sun-drenched islands and keys offers the promise of a day away from it all. Island hoppers can explore more than 100 offshore retreats and are given plenty of opportunities for shell-collecting, fishing or just simply lazing.

Across Pine Island Sound, home to an abundant population of playful bottlenose dolphins, **Cayo Costa State Park** is the largest barrier island in the region and one of the largest uninhabited islands in Florida, undisturbed for the past 500 years. Acres of pine forest, oak palm hammocks and gumbo limbo are fringed with deserted sandy beaches which offer excellent shell-collecting, particularly during the summer months. There is spectacular bird life and sea turtles lay their eggs here.

See exhibits of Calusa and Seminole artefacts as well as a railway carriage at the Historical Museum

Cruise under sail on the tall ship Eagle

Calusa Native Americans left their mark on **Cabbage Key** with a huge shell mound. Today's visitors are more likely to leave an autographed dollar bill pinned to the walls of the island's historic inn – built on top of the mound in 1938 by mystery writer Mary Roberts Rinehart.

North of Cabbage Key, **Gasparilla Island** on the Boca Grande Pass and a top tarpon-fishing spot, draws dozens of sportfishermen every spring. In the Gasparilla Island State Recreation Area, the **Boca Grande Lighthouse Museum and Visitor Center** (*Open* Wed–Sun 10–4; closed Aug. *Admission: inexpensive*; tel: 941/964-0060) traces the island's Native American heritage, its development as a pioneer south Florida resort and its natural history.

Nature lovers should find time for a sea kayak tour with the **Gulf Coast Kayak Company**. Guide-led trips (Tue–Sun; for reservations, tel: 941/283-1125) take a detailed look at the region's aquatic bird life, dolphins, stingrays and manatees around the coastal islands.

To get around the islands, experienced sailors will find plenty of boat-hire outfits offering everything from dinghies to motorboats. Shelling charters are available from the 'Tween Waters Inn Marina, Captiva (tel: 941/472-1051); shelling and out-island cruises are offered by **Captiva Cruises**, *South Seas Plantation, Captiva* (tel: 941/472-5300). To explore the Estero Bay Aquatic Preserve, contact **Calusa Coast Outfitters**, *Fish Tale Marina, Fort Myers Beach* (tel: 941/332-0709), who lead historical, archaeological and dolphin encounter tours around the marine/island reserve. Meanwhile **J C Cruises**, *Fort Myers Yacht Basin* (tel: 941/334-7474), ply the Gulf and take tours up the Caloosahatchee River.

Manatee Park, *SR 80 (1½ miles/2.5km east of I-75/Exit 25. Open* Apr–Sep, 8–8; Oct–Mar, 8–5. *Admission: inexpensive*, parking fee; tel: 941/432-2004) East of downtown Fort Myers, this winter season (Nov–Mar) manatee haven lies on the Orange River. During the cooler months, manatees are drawn here by the warm waters from the Florida Power & Light plant downstream. They can be viewed from riverside observation decks (call the manatee viewing update line, tel: 941/694-3537); or on a kayak tour.

SHELLING POINTERS
Here are some tips for shell seekers: Bowman's Beach on Sanibel Island is the acknowledged top spot, and Captiva Beach has piles of easily accessible washed-up shells. But both of these beaches are very popular, so why not try secluded beaches, such as Upper Captiva, Cayo Costa and neighbouring Johnson Shoals? Only accessible by boat, they are great for shell-collecting. *Remember, the law limits the collection of live shells to two per species per person per day along Lee Island Coast, except Sanibel Island where collecting live shells is completely banned.*

STATE SYMBOL
The horse conch (*Pleuroploca gigantea*), also known as the giant band shell, is Florida's official state shell symbol. The conch can grow to a size of around 24 inches (60cm) and feeds off clams in waters from a depth of 1 to 80 feet (0,3–25m). Though the conch is protected in Florida, the locals have no qualms about eating their state symbol. Imported conch is the staple filler in local chowders and appears in various guises on menus from the Panhandle to Key West.

Sanibel and Captiva Islands Linked to the mainland by a mile-long (1.5km) scenic causeway, picturesque Sanibel and Captiva could be hundreds of miles from the busy coastal highways and condominiums. In fact, this is Florida's Tahiti, a lush island paradise where, in the 18th century, pirate José Gaspar held his female captives among the purple trumpets of morning glory and brilliant hibiscus. Life is easy on the miles of sandy beaches and in the funky cafés, friendly restaurants and artsy-craftsy boutiques. Bicycle hire is the most popular way to get around here, and there are a number of low-key attractions to explore, from the 1884 lighthouse and a brace of 19th-century stilt houses on the eastern tip of Sanibel to the CROW wildlife rehabilitation centre on Sanibel–Captiva Road.

The islands' top sight is the **J N 'Ding' Darling National Wildlife Refuge**, a 5,030-acre (2,035-ha) preserve with a 5-mile (8km) scenic drive (good bird life in the mornings) and nature trails. Open-air guided tram tours, kayak excursions with a naturalist guide, and canoe, kayak and bicycle hire are available from the adjacent Tarpon Bay Recreation Area, 900 Tarpon Bay Road, Sanibel (*Open* daily. Tram tours *moderate;* call for schedules, tel: 941/472-8900). Near the Refuge, conchologists, or shell enthusiasts, will want to stop off at the informative and well-presented **Bailey–Matthews Shell Museum**, 3075 Sanibel Road (*Open* Tue–Sun 10–4. *Admission: inexpensive;* tel: 941/395-2233).

When it comes to beaches, **Bowman's Beach** is one of the best, and there is another popular sand strip at **Blind Pass** where the islands meet. **Turner Beach** is considered a prime spot for shells, and an excellent vantage point for the spectacular Gulf sunsets.

The beaches of Captiva Island attract both amateur and professional shell collectors

It starts off with one little whelk and before you know it, you have collected a small mountain of striped, speckled, spotted and striated seashells – all begging to be taken home. Shell-collecting is not a hobby in Florida, it is a fixation. Confirmed conchologists are known to hit the beach before dawn, shuffling along with the distinctive 'Sanibel stoop', armed with torches and bags full of treasures.

Several species of cockles, cones, moons and glossy olives are common and easy to collect. Cleaned up, the Atlantic moon bears an eerie resemblance to its nickname, shark's eye. Whelks, with their rounded living quarters and elegant tapered tails, are also a familiar sight on Florida beaches. Mature whelks can range from 3 or 4 inches (7.5–10cm) to 16 inches (40cm) long, depending on the variety; look for females of the species, who lay leathery chains of eggs or shell-bearing capsules.

Conches Conches come in all shapes and sizes, from the delicate hues of the pink conch to the mottled hawkwing and the strangely named 3-inch-long (7.5cm) Florida fighting conch. Sheltered bays and saltwater mangrove areas harbour the crown conch, easily identified by its single or multiple spiky 'crowns'.

Sand dollars Shuffle along a sand bar, and there will be a fortune in sand dollars. To get that shop-clean look, soak the coarse green discs in a weak bleach solution and dry them in the sun.

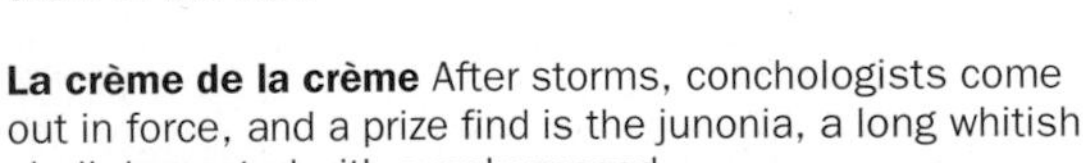

La crème de la crème After storms, conchologists come out in force, and a prize find is the junonia, a long whitish shell decorated with evenly spaced dark brown spots. The lion's paw scallop is another beauty – an exotic cousin of the common scallop with raised 'knuckles' which give it the appearance of a paw. Keep an eye out also for delicate janthina shells, home of the violet sea snail.

Only collect dead, empty shells; it's illegal to collect live shells as the species may be threatened. Only buy shells from reputable sources.

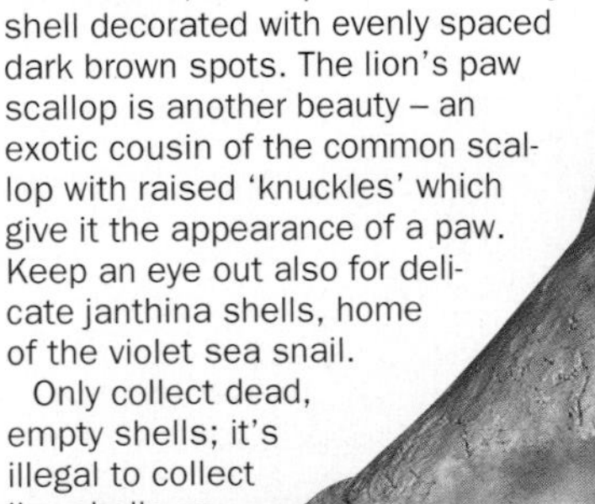

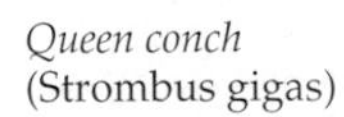

Queen conch (Strombus gigas)

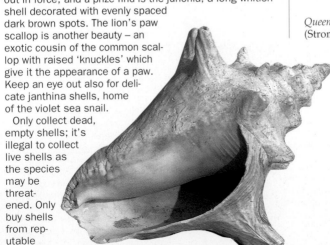

Feeding the manatees in Homosassa Springs State Wildlife Park

►► Homosassa Springs State Wildlife Park

9225 W Fishbowl Drive, Homosassa Springs (off US 19); tel: 904/352-2311

Open: daily 9–5:30; last ticket 4. Admission: moderate

Homosassa Springs has been a tourist attraction since the early 1900s, when trains travelling along what is now Fishbowl Drive stopped by the spring so that passengers could stretch their legs.

Within the wildlife park an underwater observatory provides an unrivalled view of the 45-foot-deep (14m) **Spring of 10,000 Fish**. The natural spring pumps 6 million gallons (27¼ million litres) of water to the surface every hour at a constant 72°F (22°C), and attracts as many as 34 different species of fish, both freshwater and saltwater varieties and, of course, manatees.

Explore the rest of the park on pontoon boat trips and self-guided nature trails. Look for river otters, turtles and marvellous bird life; native wildlife kept in enclosures includes black bears, bobcats and deer.

► Largo: Pinewood Cultural Park

11909 N 125th Street (between Walsingham and Ulmerton); tel: 727/582-2123

Open: Tue–Sat 10–4, Sun 1–4. Admission free

Three attractions have been brought together in this hidden away location, which is well worth seeking out. The original attraction is the beautifully presented **Pinellas County Heritage Village**. Here, some 23 historic homes, barns, a schoolhouse, railway station and shop have been rescued from around the county and re-erected, restored and in many cases furnished in period style on a 21-acre (8.5-ha) plot surrounded by pine woodlands and palmettos.

On a neighbouring site, the **Gulf Coast Museum of Art**, *12211 Walsingham Road* (*Open* Tue–Sat 10–4, Thu 10–7, Sun noon–4) hosts regular exhibitions and takes a particular interest in Florida artists. There are plans to link the two sites with the new **Florida Botanical Gardens**, an ambitious 200-acre (80-ha) scheme due for completion in 2001, which will combine 18 individually landscaped areas – from rose gardens to hammock trails.

►►► Naples

A smart and fast-developing resort city built on an appealingly small scale, Naples is rapidly earning a reputation as the Palm Beach of the Gulf. Just take a stroll down chic Fifth Avenue South or the attractively developed Third Street South shopping and historic district and you will see why. Famous for its photogenic pier, Naples also boasts lovely, sandy beaches – its sweeping Gulf beaches are just a stone's throw from the Everglades – and some 50 golf courses, up-market accommodation and fine restaurants.

For getting around, **Naples Trolley Tours** provide narrated information about more than 100 points of interest, with convenient stops along the way. On the cultural front, drop in on the **Philharmonic Center for the Arts** at 5833 Pelican Bay Boulevard (for information, tel: 941/597-1900), for a look round the sculpture gardens and galleries; and check out the varied music, theatre and dance programmes.

HISTORIC NAPLES

For a well-rounded history of the southwest region, stop off at the Collier County Museum, 3301 E Tamiami Trail (*Open* Mon–Fri 9–5. *Admission free*; tel: 941/774-8476), for displays of prehistoric fossils, Native American, Spanish and pioneer artefacts. In the downtown historic district, the 1895 Palm Cottage, 137 12th Street South (*Open* Nov–Apr, Tue–Fri, Sun 1–4; May–Oct, Fri and Sun only. *Admission: moderate*; tel: 941/261-8164), has been restored and furnished in Victorian style. A couple of blocks away, the beachfront Wilkinson House built around 1914 opened in the autumn of 2000.

Caribbean Gardens, *1590 Goodlette-Frank Road* (*Open* daily 9:30–5:30. *Admission: expensive*; tel: 941/262-5409) Go to this zoo garden in a state well supplied with the genre. It is relatively small, so not too taxing for small children, but the inhabitants range from antelopes to spider monkeys via rarities such as the Southeast Asian binturong, a little bear-cat related to the mongoose. Thoughtfully designed habitats have contributed to the animals' longevity and several successful captive breeding programmes. The stars are the big cats – cougars, lions, leopards and tigers – some of which take part in the truly amazing twice-daily show with their trusted trainer. There are 'meet the keeper' encounters, where visitors can learn more about individual animals from their carers; inexpensive zoo keys which activate audio information stations outside various exhibits; and Primate Expedition Cruises which set out (every 30 minutes) across the alligator lagoon to visit monkey colonies on wooded islets.

Naples Nature Center, *1450 Merrihue Drive* (*Open* Mon–Sat 9–4:30; Jan–Mar, Sun 1–5. *Admission: moderate*; tel: 941/262-0304) Headquarters of the Conservancy of Southwest Florida, the Center doubles as a natural science museum and a wildlife rescue and rehabilitation facility. Investigate the aviaries, aquarium and boardwalk nature trail, then hire a kayak or take one of the regular mini-boat tours.

Teddy Bear Museum Of Naples, *2511 Pine Ridge Road (east off Airport-Pulling)* (*Open* Mon, Wed–Sat 10–5, Sun 1–5. *Admission: moderate*; tel: 941/598-2711) Naples philanthropist Frances Pew Hayes opened this $2 million teddy bear museum with her own collection in 1990, and the 3,000-teddy roll call is growing all the time. Antique and brand new bears, bear dioramas, a bear theatre, and sculpted marble bears are kept in a house in the woods.

SANCTUARY ON MARCO ISLAND

Six miles (9.5km) long and 4 miles (6.5km) wide, Marco Island (14 miles/22km south of Naples) hangs off the tip of the Florida peninsula surrounded by the scattered islets of the Ten Thousand Islands. Rampant resort development has not quite ousted nature or obliterated the memory of the island's early inhabitants, the Calusa people. Ancient shell mounds can still be seen, and bald eagles are encouraged to breed in artificial nests among the hotels and apartments. The island is a sequestered sanctuary to more than 200 species of birds, a natural haven for manatees and hatching ground for loggerhead sea turtles.

Boating is the key to exploring Florida's unspoiled coastline and island wildlife sanctuaries

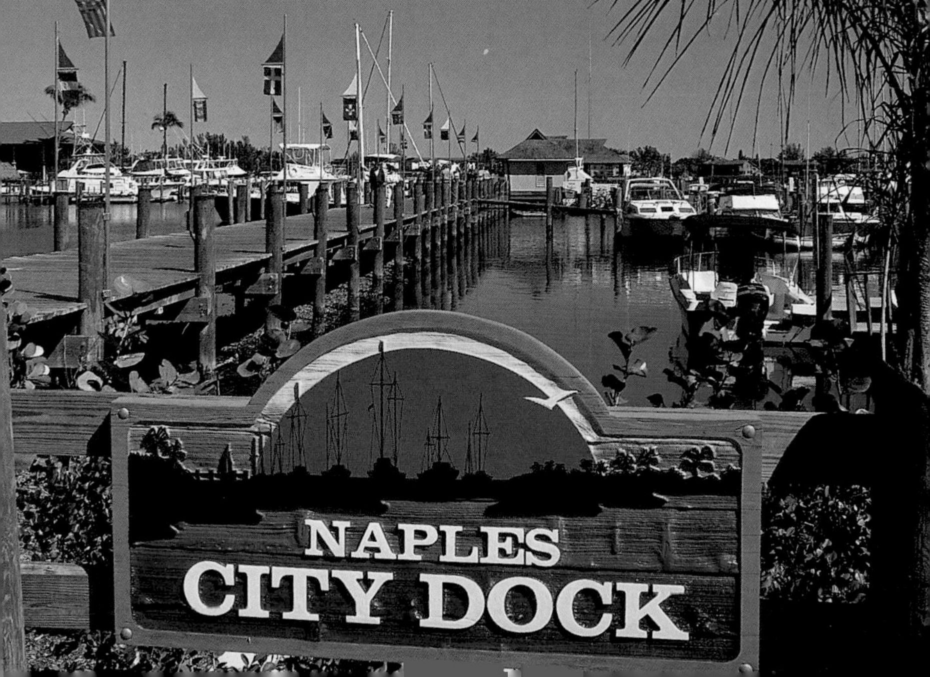

Walk

Trails in Cayo Costa State Park

Access is by boat or ferry from Sanibel, Captiva and Pine islands.

Directly south of Boca Grande, this park (*Open* daily 8am–dusk. *Admission: inexpensive*; tel: 941/964-0375) is set at the tip of Cayo Costa Island. A barrier island, Cayo Costa shelters Charlotte Harbor and Pine Island Sound from the worst ravages of the Gulf storms; it's also a major shell-collecting destination.

Between the beaches and dunes of the island's Gulf shore and the bay-side mangrove belt, there is a network of attractive short trails which explore the subtropical interior, comprising a mixture of pine flatwoods, oak palm hammocks and grassy regions dotted with palms.

The Quarantine Trail leaves from the Bayside Dock and works its way north to a picnic area on Pelican Bay. A tram from the dockside crosses the island to the Gulf coast and a Gulf Trail. Cemetery Trail runs north–south, passing the site of an old pioneer graveyard. The Pinewoods Trail and Scrub Trail run east–west, and the latter links with the Quarantine Trail on the way to the picnic site.

Walk

Collier-Seminole State Park

Tamiami Trail (US 41), 17 miles (27km) southeast of Naples.

On the northwestern edge of the Everglades, this superb park (*Open* daily 8am–dusk. *Admission: inexpensive*; tel: 941/394-3397) is frequently overlooked. Named after 1940s entrepreneur and developer Barron Collier, who first envisaged the park, and after the Seminole Native Americans who made the area their home, the park offers an introduction to the Everglades, plus fishing, canoeing and boating access to the Ten Thousand Islands in the Gulf of Mexico.

Louisiana heron

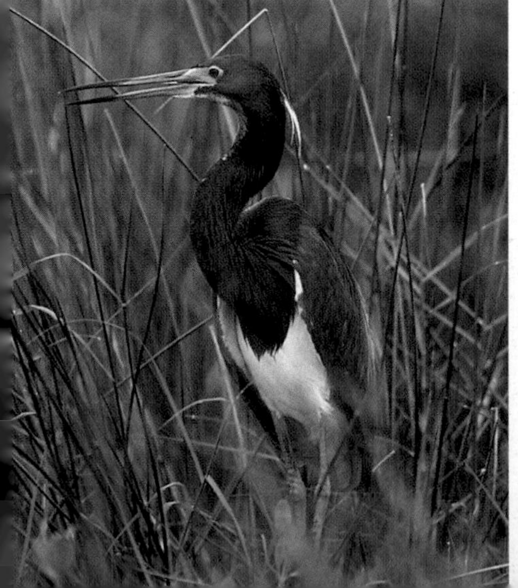

The 6½-mile (10.5km) hiking trail leaves from the boat basin and winds its way through pine flatwoods and cypress swamp.

A special feature of the park is an unusual tropical hammock (an area slightly raised above the surrounding swamp) flourishing with trees more commonly found in West Indian coastal forests and in the Yucatán, Mexico. In the woodlands, native Florida black bears and panthers keep to themselves, but wood storks, cockaded wood-peckers and mangrove fox squirrels are frequently spotted. A separate boardwalk system and observation platform overlook the salt marsh region, where bald eagles circle overhead. A word of warning: biting insects can be a problem.

Trail in Corkscrew Swamp

Route 846, Bonita Springs (20 miles/32km east off Route 41).

This 2-mile (3km) boardwalk trail, starting at the Visitor Center, covers a minute section of the sanctuary, but offers an unbeatable opportunity to explore three contrasting native habitats. Just beyond the park headquarters, a woodland area of slash pines, palmetto and occasional wax myrtle is a great place to spot woodpeckers and tiny grey flycatchers. Then a broad swathe of wet prairie reveals alligator trails and a mass of brilliant wildflowers flourishing among a sea of grasses. In the shade of the thin, silver-grey pond cypresses, look for masses of little white apple-snail eggs, the only food of the rare Everglades kite. Corkscrew's bald cypress stand is the largest in America. These impressive trees, draped in Spanish moss, are hundreds of years old. At their feet, ferns grow in abundance and bromeliads (air plants) nestle against the trunks, gathering nutrition from rainwater. Visit the central marsh in July, when it is aflame with red hibiscus; in the autumn it is a sea of primrose willow (see page 200).

Trail in De Soto National Memorial

75th Street, Bradenton.

A short half-mile (0.8km) trail, the great charm of this walk is its breezy waterside location.

Take in the Visitor Center first.

There is a 20-minute video and display of Spanish explorers' artefacts, including armour, weaponry and a model shallow-draft caravel.

Set out along the beach.

You can imagine how it seemed to the early pioneers, attacking the mangrove thickets. Along the beach, the leaves of the sea grape trees were used by the explorers as stationery. In the undergrowth, broken blocks of tabby (the settlers' version of concrete – made from sand, limestone, and shells) mark William Shaw's 1840s pioneer cottage. This area was known as Shaw Point for many years. The bayside cove is a good place to see pelicans, gulls, terns, ospreys and cormorants (see page 201).

Sentinel heron

GATEWAY TO THE SUN
For the most impressive entry to St Pete and Pinellas County, visitors arriving from the south should take the spectacular Sunshine Skyway (I–275), north of Bradenton. The nominal toll is a small price to pay for the 4-mile (6.5km) long suspension bridge, which was modelled on the Brotonne Bridge over the River Seine in France.

▶▶▶ St Petersburg

On the western shores of Tampa Bay, St Pete (as it is generally known) is the cultural centre of Pinellas County, and like neighbouring Clearwater is divided into two parts, with the downtown heart on the mainland linked by causeways to a barrier island beach. Downtown St Pete looks out over Tampa Bay behind its landmark pier and new BayWalk shopping, dining and entertainment complex, which opened in autumn 2000. Near by is the world-class Salvador Dalí Museum and several more notable cultural attractions, but for most visitors the chief draw remains the beach and the county's much-vaunted average of 361 sunny days per year; the *Guinness Book of World Records* credits St Pete with the most consecutive days of sunshine on record – some 768 during 1967–9.

Salvador Dalí Museum, *1000 S Third Street* (*Open* Mon–Sat 9:30–5:30, Sun noon–5:30. *Admission: moderate*; tel: 727/823-3767) Opened in March 1982, this museum is the permanent home of the world's largest and most comprehensive collection of Spanish surrealist Salvador Dalí's work. The collection was amassed by Cleveland industrialist A Reynolds Morse and his wife, Eleanor Reese, who first encountered Dalí's work at a travelling exhibition in 1942. A year later they purchased their first canvas, *Daddy Longlegs of the Evening ...Hope!*, the foundation stone of a collection which now numbers some 94 oil paintings, more than 200 watercolours and drawings, 1,300 graphics, plus posters, sculpture and decorative pieces. A 2,500-volume library is devoted to Dalí and surrealism.

The exhibits are displayed chronologically, starting in 1914, and chart the eccentrically mustachioed artist's

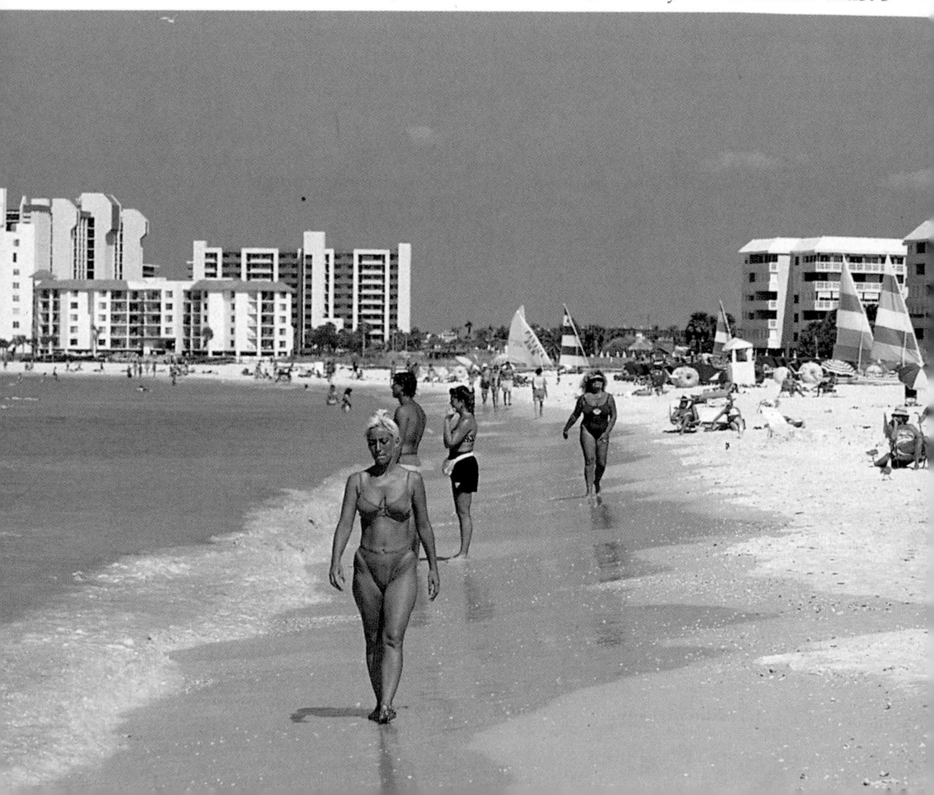

Sunshine is almost guaranteed on St Pete's beaches

development from early dabblings with Impressionism to the theatrical 1921 *Self-Portrait*, which shows a hint of things to come, to the full-blown classical period. Here Dalí's twin obsessions – religion and science – are consummately illustrated in the *Discovery of America by Christopher Columbus* (1958) and *Nature Morte Vivante* (1956), respectively. Dalí's ability to express himself in a variety of media is amply proved by the diversity of sculpture and glassware on display. There is even a hologram.

Excellent guided tours of the museum are offered throughout the day, and the gift shop provides an exhaustive range of Dalí-phernalia, from books, posters and cards to jewellery.

Florida Holocaust Museum, *55 S 5th Street* (*Open* Mon–Sat 10–4, Sun noon–4. *Admission: moderate*; tel: 727/821-8261) The third largest museum of its kind in the US, the Florida Holocaust Museum gives a moving account of the period through photographs, memorabilia, film and art exhibits. The centre-piece is a freight train carriage used to transport people to the concentration camps.

Florida International Museum, *261 N Second Avenue* (call for schedules and ticket reservations, tel: 727/822-3693) An admirably ambitious arts project, the museum has swallowed up a whole city block of downtown St Pete to house major artistic and historical exhibitions from around the world. Shows have included 'Treasures of the Czars' from Russia and 'Splendours of Ancient Egypt' from the National Museum in Cairo. It now shows 'John F Kennedy: The Exhibit' daily as a permanent display. The intention is to host a major international exhibit every year, coupled with a travelling domestic show.

Fort De Soto Park, *via Pinellas Bayway (toll)* (*Open* daily dawn–dusk. *Admission free*; tel: 727/866-2662) A welcome respite from the high-rise hotels lining the Gulf shore, this 900-acre (365-ha) park is actually made up of five islands off the southern tip of Tampa Bay. Its strategic importance led to a fort being constructed on the biggest island, Mullet Key, in 1898, but the hefty 12-inch (30cm) mortars have never fired a shot in anger. The park boasts three excellent beaches, a couple of popular fishing piers, boat ramps and picnic and camping facilities. Make sure that you wear shoes on the beach to avoid the spiky sand spurs which anchor the sand at the top of the beach.

Great Explorations, *800 NE 2nd Avenue (The Pier, 3rd Floor)* (*Open* Mon–Sat 10–8, Sun 11–6. *Admission: inexpensive*; tel: 727/821-8992) There is pure fun to be had at this splendid museum. Start your visit by creating instant images in the Phenomenal Arts section using kinetic touch or audio-activated image makers. The 90-foot (27m) Touch Tunnel, which is approached on hands and knees in the dark, is not advised for the claustrophobic, but provides a satisfyingly peculiar experience as you 'feel' your way out. In the Body Shop, active testing stations check reactions and muscle tone, and the latest diversion is the Mission Control: from the Moon to Mars launch experience.

RECREATIONAL TRAILS
For sporting types, how about a 47-mile (75km) walking, running, cycling, and in-line skating route? The Pinellas Trail follows an abandoned railway track from Gulfport in the south of the county all the way north to Tarpon Springs, linking a variety of neighbourhoods and green spaces off the main roads. Another option is the Friendship TrailBridge, a 2.6-mile (4km) route across the Old Gandy Bridge between Tampa and St Pete.

The Salvador Dalí Museum is one of St Pete's main attractions

HISTORY IN ST PETE
During the 1920s, archaeologists from the Smithsonian Institution excavated an important Native American site at Weedon Island, north of St Pete. Artefacts from Weedon and from another Native American site at Safety Harbour are on display at the St Petersburg Museum of History, 335 NE Second Avenue (*Open* Mon–Sat 10–5, Sun 1–5. *Admission: inexpensive*; tel: 727/894-1052), together with pioneer exhibits and a replica of the *Benoist*, the world's first commercial airliner, which flew from Tampa to St Pete on 1 January, 1914.

Museum of Fine Arts, *255 NE Beach Drive* (*Open* Tue–Sat 10–5, Sun 1–5. *Admission: moderate*; tel: 727/896-2667) Housed in a very attractive Mediterranean-style villa near The Pier, the museum has several notable collections, so allow enough time to do them justice. The Impressionists are well represented, as are sculptures and paintings from the 17th- and 18th-century European schools. American art from the 19th and 20th centuries includes some gorgeous Gorgia O'Keefe flower studies. Decorative arts and crafts gathered from around the world run the gauntlet from pre-Columbian artefacts, and Greek and oriental treasures, to Steuben crystal.

As well as the galleries, there are charming set-piece rooms, each of which has been carefully furnished in period style. Another treat is the photography collection. Guided tours are available, and the museum frequently plays host to special exhibitions from other collections.

The Pier, *800 NE Second Avenue* (*Open* daily, most shops open from 10–9; tel: 727/821-6164) Projecting into the bay like the superstructure of a vast turquoise-and-cream aircraft carrier, The Pier (a St Petersburg landmark) combines shopping, dining and sightseeing opportunities all in one. Its lower-deck mall houses a variety of boutiques, toy and gift shops, a tourist information point, and snack stops. Moving on up, Ybor City's famous **Columbia Restaurant** has an outpost here, serving fine Spanish-Cuban cuisine (lunch and dinner). The top-deck observation platform offers a cocktail lounge and panoramic view of downtown St Pete and the bay. There is plenty of parking, linked by a free tram service (or valet for a fee); sightseeing boat trips; fishing along the causeway; trike, roller blade, aquacycle, windsurfer, kayak and catamaran hire; plus a sunny rear-deck with bench seating which provides an excellent spot for outdoor snacking.

The upside-down pyramid of St Petersburg's Pier

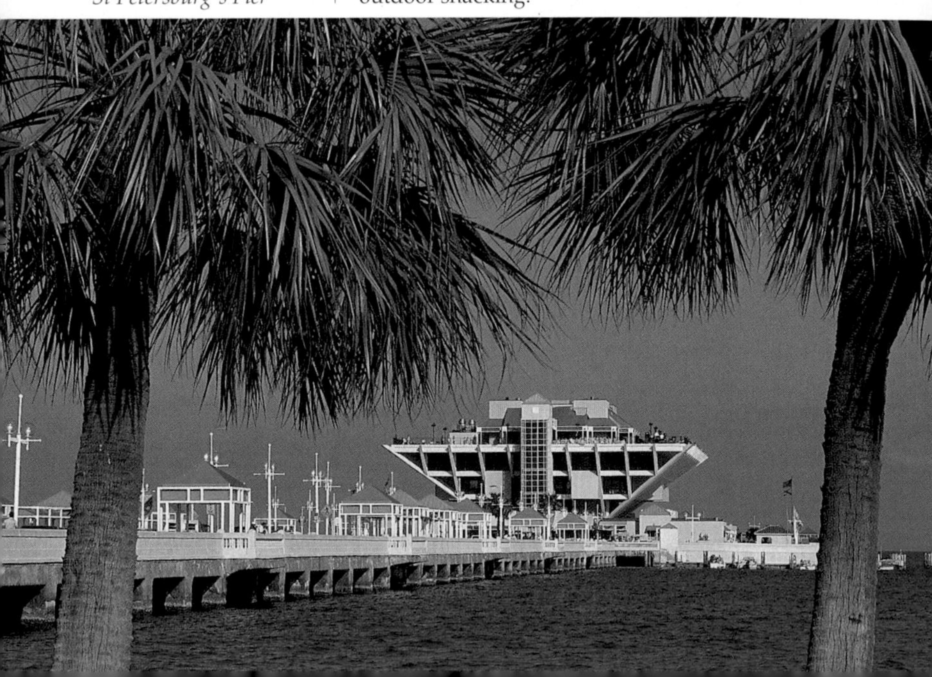

Suncoast Seabird Sanctuary, *18328 Gulf Boulevard, Indian Shores* (*Open* daily 9am–dusk. *Admission: donation*; tel: 727/391-6211) A fascinating excursion across the peninsula from downtown St Pete, the sanctuary started with a chance encounter between Ralph Heath and an injured cormorant in 1971. Heath had the bird's wing set and nursed it back to health, though Maynard, as the bird was named, would never fly again. Soon word of the 'bird doctor' spread, and injured birds were brought in from far and wide.

The aim is to release birds back into the wild unless their injuries are permanent and would affect their ability to survive. Each year the sanctuary cares for around 8,500 injured birds, of which more than 80 per cent survive. Among those figures are some 500 pelicans, most of them injured by fish hooks and nylon line. Over 180 chicks have been hatched from breeding couples, and the offspring then rejoin their fellows in the wild. Other success stories have involved great blue herons and great egrets, owls, gannets, petrels, an Arctic loon and peregrine falcons.

Feeding time at Suncoast Seabird Sanctuary

Sunken Gardens, *1825 N Fourth Street* (*Open* Wed–Sun 10–4. *Admission: inexpensive*; tel: 727/551-3100) Laid out in a former natural sinkhole, which was drained in the 1930s, this colourful profusion of exotic plant life flourishes in the rich layer of fertile soil residue. There are lush tropical corners, brilliant curtains of bougainvillaea, along with carefully landscaped contours of formal gardens, replenished with around 50,000 plants each year. The hundreds of rare and exotic blooms in the Orchid Arbor are certain to be appreciated by gardeners, and there are hour-long garden tours offered daily at 10:30 and 1:30. Additional features include a flock of flamingoes, turtle ponds and parrot show presentations, and there is also a walk-through aviary containing a butterfly garden.

Luxuriant growth in the exotic Sunken Gardens

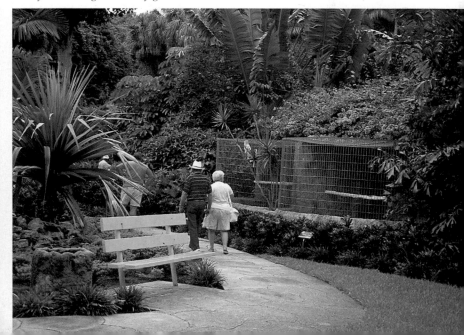

Drive

Around Tampa Bay

See map on page 199.

This full-day drive around Tampa Bay starts in downtown Tampa at the **Florida Aquarium** (see page 228). This terrific state-of-the-art complex deserves a really thorough visit, so an early start is recommended.

From the Aquarium, take the Downtown Crossway east (direction Brandon) to Exit 15-A, and join I–75 south (direction Naples) for 30 miles (48km). At Exit 43, follow signs for US 301 south to Ellenton.

On the right-hand side of the road, you will see the **Gamble Plantation State Historic Site** (see page 204). This elegant restored plantation house is one of the few remaining antebellum houses in Florida. Guided tours provide an intriguing insight into plantation life and vernacular architecture especially tailored to local Florida conditions.

Rejoin I–75 south for 12 miles (19km) to Exit 40 for Sarasota. University Parkway leads directly to the gates of the Ringling Museum (7 miles/11km) across US 41/Tamiami Trail.

The Venetian-inspired winter residence of a circus king is part of the **John and Mable Ringling Museum of Art** complex (see page 221) which occupies a fabulous site on Sarasota Bay. The museum café-restaurant makes a good lunch stop. Sarasota has several other attractions (see pages 221–5), plus sweeping barrier island beaches across the bay.

From the Ringling Museum, US 41/Tamiami Trail heads north to connect with US 19, the direct route to the Sunshine Skyway bridge and St Petersburg for downtown Tampa.

If you are heading for the barrier islands around Sarasota, take US 41/Tamiami Trail south for 3 miles (5km) and turn right for St Armands Key (SR 789 N) across the John Ringling Causeway. Follow SR 789 N up the barrier island chain.

Bradenton Beach is a good place to stop off for a swim, with its busy strip of cafés, shops and water sports concessions overlooking the Gulf.

To return to the mainland, take SR 64 to Bradenton; then rejoin US 41 N/US 19.

Spanning the entrance to Tampa Bay, the 4-mile-long (6.5km) **Sunshine Skyway** is something of an attraction in its own right. The central span is a record 1,200 feet (365m) and rises 183 feet (55m) above the water below.

From the Skyway, I–275 cuts across downtown St Petersburg for downtown Tampa.

A taste of Italy in Sarasota: the John and Mable Ringling Museum of Art

The skyline of 'culture city' Sarasota

►►► Sarasota

Once known as 'The Town the Circus Built', Sarasota is a sophisticated, cultured resort founded by early Florida pioneers in the 1840s. When a 'fine hotel' was built here in the 1880s the town prospered, attracting socialites from the North, among them John Ringling, the circus king and art lover, who installed himself in predictably flamboyant style at Ca'd'Zan, a grand waterfront mansion.

One of the great joys of Sarasota for the visitor is the compact nature of the city. From a beach hotel on Longboat or Lido Key, it is only a five-minute drive downtown and the attractive antiques district on **Palm Avenue**. Restored shop-fronts lure the collector to browse in more than 30 shops, and the **Marie Selby Gardens** are at the end of the street. There is waterfront dining and more shopping at downtown **Sarasota Quay** and shoppers should not miss Lido Key's **St Armand's Circle**. Performing arts are big news in Sarasota, with the **Asolo State Theater** blazing a trail as one of the nation's leading regional theatres; the Florida West Coast Symphony performs in the **Van Wezel Performing Arts Hall** on Sarasota Bay; and the city has its own ballet and opera companies.

John and Mable Ringling Museum of Art, *5401 Bay Shore Road* (*Open* daily 10–5:30. *Admission: moderate*; tel: 941/359-5700) Sarasota's cultural epicentre, the Ringling bayfront estate, should not be missed. On trips to Europe between 1924 and 1931, the Ringlings amassed an extraordinary collection of artwork – more than 600 paintings, plus tapestries, *objets d'art* and several tons of statuary – and Ringling constructed a magnificent Italian-style palazzo to house what remains of one of the largest and finest collections of European paintings in the United States. Ringling's particular passion was the Italian baroque period, but he also bought several notable examples of medieval and Renaissance art. He owned the largest collection of Rubens in the world, and commissioned a special gallery to show off his beloved Rubens cartoons. Surrounded by three wings of the museum, 20th-century copies of classical statuary adorn formal gardens.

SHARK TOOTH CITY

Once the winter home of the Ringling Brothers and Barnum and Bailey Circus, the quiet seaside town of Venice (20 miles/32km south of Sarasota) now rejoices in the unlikely sobriquet of 'Shark Tooth Capital of the World'. Casperson Beach, south of the airport, is a great beachcombing spot, with rewarding shell-collecting as well as a chance to gather a haul of the distinctive fossilised shark's teeth that have washed up on the shore. They range in size from one-eighth of an inch (0.3cm) up to 3 inches (7.5cm) or more. There also are nature trails and scuba diving and other water-sports opportunities.

Part of the Ringling art collection

Down on the water's edge is **Ca'd'Zan** (Venetian dialect for 'House of John'), the Ringlings' winter residence. The house is currently undergoing a major restoration. It was inspired by Mable's two favourite buildings, the Doge's Palace in Venice and the tower of P T Barnum's Old Madison Square Garden in New York. Around the main hall, 30 luxurious rooms and 14 bathrooms abut the 2½-storey atrium. The former garages have been transformed into a **Circus Museum**, where posters and memorablilia rub shoulders with sequined finery, calliopes, rare carved and painted circus wagons and cannons for launching human projectiles.

ANIMAL MAGIC
For more than 60 years, the Sarasota Jungle Gardens, 3701 Bay Shore Road (*Open* daily 9–5. *Admission: moderate*; tel: 941/355-5305), have attracted visitors to their 10-acre (4-ha) tropically landscaped site for bird shows, reptile displays and assorted animal encounters. Meet alligators and flamingoes, talented cockatoos and leopards. The Kiddie Jungle has an animal farm, tree house and jungle-themed playground. There is a regular programme of shows and a shell museum.

Marie Selby Botanical Gardens, *811 S Palm Avenue* (*Open* daily 10–5. *Admission: moderate;* tel: 941/366-5731) These glorious gardens, overlooking Sarasota Bay, were the idea of Marie Selby, who wintered in Sarasota with her Ohio oil baron husband, William. The modest house in the middle of the property was built in 1921 as a temporary residence for the Selbys until a more substantial home could be constructed. They never bothered, and the 11-acre (4.5-ha) bayfront estate was donated to the county in 1971 with a bequest and proviso that it should be laid out as a garden. Some 20,000 plants have now been introduced and 20 distinct garden areas created. Most famous is the orchid collection, but bromeliads, hibiscus and cacti grow in profusion. There is a colourful Butterfly Garden, the waterfront Baywalk and a tropical display house overflowing with exotic plants from around the world. A small Museum of Botany and Arts (same ticket) exhibiting botanical illustrations is housed in the neighbouring **Payne House**, a gracious 1935 mansion which combines all the best features of southern architecture.

Mote Marine Aquarium, *1600 Thompson Parkway* (*Open* daily 10–5. *Admission: moderate;* tel: 941/388-2451) A terrific family outing, this excellent aquarium complex offers a fascinating window on the marine world. Tanks full of gruesome puffer fish and electricity-producing stargazers grab children's attention from the start. There are outdoor touch tanks and a 135,000-gallon (613,700-litre) shark tank which houses a floating – or rather circling – population which may include lemon and nurse sharks, the hefty mottled jewfish, shoals of sardines, and the occasional tarpon. The plate-glass windows make for interesting viewing, but there is nothing quite like watching one of those predatory dorsal fins slicing through the water up on the surface. Other smaller aquaria are inhabited by seahorses, clearnose skates, octopus and more.

Take a walk through the lab area before crossing the street to the waterfront turtle hospital, aquaculture tanks and manatee sanctuary. An additional attraction is the Sea Cinema, which puts the audience into the shark's 'shoes' as it hunts for food. And call in advance for information about **Sarasota Bay Explorers** (tel: 941/388-4200), nature cruises with a naturalist on Sarasota and Roberts bays, where mangrove islands are home to pelicans, egrets and herons, and dolphins and manatees can be seen.

Sarasota Classic Car Museum, *5500 N Tamiami Trail (US 41)* (*Open* daily 9–6. *Admission: moderate*; tel: 941/355-6228) On show are 70 antique and classic cars, from the Model-T Ford to the Volkswagen Beetle via handsome Rolls-Royces, racy Corvettes and John Ringling's 1932 Pierce Arrow. The museum also displays old coin-operated arcade games and a collection of nickleodeons, pianolas, music boxes and an Edison's Home Phonograph.

ECO ENCOUNTERS

There are around 200 permanent inhabitants at the Pelican Man's Bird Sanctuary, 1708 Thompson Parkway, next to the Mote Marine Aquarium (*Open* daily 10–5. *Admission: donation*). These birds can no longer survive in the wild, but the sanctuary has successfully rehabilitated thousands of injured pelicans and other birds such as herons, hawks and owls. Birdwatchers flock to Oscar Scherer State Park, US 41 at Osprey, to look for endangered Florida scrub jays and bald eagles.

Elegant shopping at Sarasota Quay

John Nicholas Ringling was born on 30 May 1866, in MacGregor, Iowa, the sixth of seven sons raised by immigrant parents. His father, a German-born leather craftsman, and his mother, the daughter of a prosperous French weaver and vineyard owner, moved frequently around the Mid-west until they finally settled in Baraboo, Wisconsin, in 1875. Although fortunes fluctuated, the boys were given a strict Lutheran upbringing in which the qualities of honesty, dignity and pride in a job were rigorously emphasised, beliefs which would characterise the Ringling brothers' business deals.

The travelling circus During the 1870s, the newly built railroads opened up the whole country, enabling travelling entertainment acts to reach a vast new audience. Circuses were among the first to take advantage of this new way to reach the public. In 1872, entrepreneur Phineas T Barnum recognised the potential of railways and purchased a fleet of railway carriages, turning his successful freak show into the 'Great Traveling Museum, Menagerie, Caravan and Hippodrome'. Albert, Otto, Alfred and Charles Ringling launched a variety act inspired by Dan Rice's Circus in the same year. It was called the Classic and Comic Concert Company. Their brother John joined them in 1882, and two years later the Ringling Brothers Circus was formed in Baraboo.

The Ringling mansion Ca'd'Zan has more than a touch of the Doge's Palace in Venice

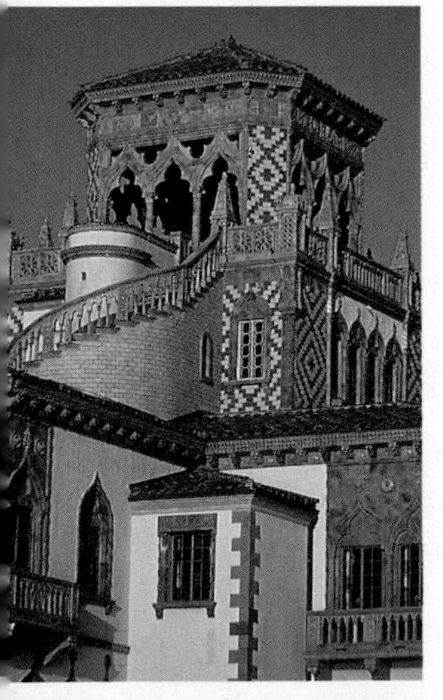

On the up Two more brothers, August and Henry, were soon added to the payroll, and responsibilities were divided. John's brains and extraordinary memory earned him the position of transport manager. In his spare time, he invested in oil, property, railways and a variety of smaller concerns. On business trips to Europe, sightseeing visits to the great European museums and palaces fuelled his interest in art. While his brothers wintered in Baraboo, John busied himself in New York and Chicago among cultured friends drawn from the ranks of artists, celebrities and politicians. By the time he first visited Sarasota in 1911, John Ringling was already a celebrity in his own right, a wealthy businessman and an imposing figure, described by a contemporary as 'tall, with the chest of a sea elephant, the chin of a prize fighter, and sensitive, artistic hands'.

The move to Sarasota John married Mable Burton, a noted Ohio beauty, in 1905. After he bought a winter property on the Sarasota bayfront in 1912, he and Mable made annual visits, often entertaining the family. Brother Charles built a marble mansion on adjacent land, now the University of South Florida's College Hall. In 1917, John began to invest in Sarasota real estate. Circus elephants occasionally helped out with the heavy work as causeways were built to link his barrier island properties to the mainland, and New York landscape architect John Watson was chosen to design the elegant St Armands Circle shopping district: 'Now Mable won't have to go to Palm Beach to shop', Ringling explained. However, other projects did not fare so well, and work on a luxurious Ritz Carlton hotel on Longboat Key was halted by the collapse of the 1920s land boom.

Mable's 'House of John' Meanwhile, Mable had been fully occupied supervising the construction of Ca'd'Zan, a Venetian Gothic-style residence of grandiose proportions, truly fit for a circus king. She personally visited the kilns where the terracotta decorations for the interior and exterior of the house were glazed, accommodated shiploads of columns, doorways, balustrades and Venetian glass windows, and approved the exuberant designs by Ziegfield Follies set artist Will Pogany for the ballroom and playroom ceilings. An 8,000-square-foot (740sq m) marble terrace extended west from the house, and an elegant dock was constructed for Mable's Venetian gondola. Christmas 1926 was celebrated in the newly completed house, and in the New Year work began on a museum to house additional treasures.

End of an era After the death of his brothers, John managed the circus alone, and in 1927 moved its winter quarters to Sarasota in an effort to boost the flagging local economy. The Ringlings had purchased Barnum & Bailey's Circus in 1906, and their last major rival, the five circuses of the American Circus Corp, were brought under Ringling's control in 1929. It was also the year that Mable died, after just three winters in her dream home. John Ringling opened his museum in 1930, but the last few years of his life were plagued by unhappiness and business disappointments. He had just $350 in his bank account when he died in 1936, and bequeathed his entire estate to the state of Florida, which finally accepted the $14 million legacy in 1946.

A LITTLE GEM
John Ringling would have been delighted with the Asolo Theater, a dazzling little rococo gem added to his estate in the 1950s. Originally built for the Palazzo Asolo in Italy, it seats 300 in a horseshoe arrangement of rising tiers of boxes, ornately decorated with pastels and gilt friezes, and lit by small lamps. It is used for concerts and lectures, and shows art-house films.

A replica of Michelangelo's David *surveys the Ringling Museum of Art*

Not a mosque, but the Henry B Plant Museum in Tampa

►► Tampa

The safe anchorage of Tampa Bay made it one of the first spots marked on early explorers' maps. In 1824, Fort Brooke was established here as a pioneer military outpost to monitor the Seminole people, and during the Civil War a steamship service was opened between Tampa and Cuba. Henry Plant's railway line rolled into the port in 1884. Two years later, Vincente Martinez Ybor moved his cigar industry from Key West to the growing megalopolis of late 19th-century Tampa. In just six years, the bayside fishing village was transformed into a boom town with more than 5,000 inhabitants. Plant lured wealthy Northerners south to winter in his fabulous **Tampa Bay Hotel**, and used his considerable connections in Washington to turn Tampa into a troop embarkation point during the 1898 Spanish-American War.

Today, downtown Tampa is the West Coast's commercial powerhouse, a glistening array of towering skyscrapers, modern shopping malls and the brilliant Florida Aquarium. But its history is never far away. Plant's dream hotel has survived and is now used as a university building, and a mile down the Crosstown Expressway, the Victorian façades and red-brick cigar factories of **Ybor City** have been developed into a popular tourist attraction.

Adventure Island, *10001 McKinley Drive* (*Open* daily late Mar–early Sep; mid-Feb–mid-Oct, weekends. *Admission: expensive*; tel: 813/987-5600) A one-day pass entitles visitors to try out all the facilities at this outdoor water park. The Rambling Bayou offers a leisurely passage through a man-made rain forest, complete with weather effects from mist to a monsoon. For more exciting watersports, have a go on the Tampa Typhoon, a 76-foot (23m) free-fall body slide, or the Gulfscream – all 210 feet (64m) of it – where sliders reach speeds of up to 25mph (40kph) . Other hot favourites are Splash Attack and the Spike Zone volleyball courts. Small children are catered for in the scaled-down Fabian's Funport area; there are also beaches, picnic areas and cafés.

There's fun for water-babies of all ages at Tampa's Adventure Island

A Bengal tiger cools off in the water at Busch Gardens

Busch Gardens, *3000 E Busch Boulevard (at 40th Street)* (*Open* daily from 9:30 (call for schedules). *Admission: expensive*; tel: 813/987-5082) Originally designed by the Anheuser-Busch Tampa Brewery for its workers, this 300-acre (120-ha) African-themed family attraction now combines more than 2,700 animals from 320 species with theme park rides, creatively landscaped grounds and live entertainment. Not surprisingly, it is one of the most popular days out in the Bay area.

At the entrance to the park, there are shows and shopping in **Morocco**, then it's off to **Crown Colony** for the cable car or Nairobi Train Station, where guests can depart for tours of the **Serengeti Plain**. This is the park's focal point, home to hippos and lions, herds of graceful gazelles, zebras and giraffes, as well as the **Edge of Africa** self-guided safari. Explore a replica of King Tut's tomb in **Egypt**, take a spin aboard the hair-raising Montu roller coaster (see panel), or hop aboard a Serengeti-bound miniature train. **Nairobi** is home to the Myombe Reserve gorilla and chimpanzee habitat and a popular Animal Nursery. To the north, there are thrill rides and shows in **Timbuktu**; bumper cars, rafting adventures and tigers in the **Congo**; flume rides aboard the Tanganyika Tidal Wave and the Stanley Falls Log Flume (this is definitely the place to cool off), and orangutans in **Stanleyville**; and a koala habitat in the **Bird Gardens**. Children have the run of **Land of the Dragons**, a colourful collection of storybook tree houses, splash zones, play areas and scaled-down rides. The latest addition to the park is **Gwazi**, you can hear the rumble of this spectacular double wooden roller coaster before you see it (see panel).

THRILLS AND SPILLS

After the Serengeti comes the really wild stuff: Busch Gardens' thrill rides are some of the mightiest movers in the business, beginning with Gwazi's duelling coasters careening over 15 hills along 7,000 feet (2,130m) of track generating up to 3.5 G and speeds of over 50mph (80kph). Egypt's Montu roller coaster conquers one of the world's largest inverted loops at 104 feet (31m). The Congo's Kumba spirals through a Cobra Roll at speeds in excess of 60mph (96kph), and Python has two 360-degree loops and a 70-foot (21m) plunge.

FESTIVALS IN TAMPA
The annual Gasparilla Festival, in early February, is Tampa's big day out. The timetable begins mid-morning when the world's only fully rigged pirate ship sets sail from Ballast Point Pier and docks downtown with a full crew of colourful 'pirates' all armed to the teeth. A victory parade sets off down Bayshore Boulevard, culminating in a vast street party. There is only about a week's breathing space before festival fever breaks out again. Fiesta Day in Ybor City sees sideshows and art, craft and food stalls line Seventh Avenue, in the evening the streets are ablaze with dozens of illuminated floats.

Piratical goings-on in Tampa's Gasparilla Festival

Downtown Tampa You will not find any priceless architectural gems or quaint backstreets in downtown Tampa, but you will find a busy, well-maintained district which has invested in quantities of public sculpture assisted by the City of Tampa Art in Public Places programme.

If you are interested in local history, start your explorations at the **Tampa Bay History Center** in the Convention Center Annex, 225 S Franklin Street (*Open* Tue–Sat 10–5, Sun 1–5. *Admission free*; tel: 813/228-0097) for a five-century overview of the Bay Area. On Tampa, at the corner of Kennedy is Charles Perry's stainless-steel sculpture *Solstice* (1985). Beyond it is George Sugerman's *Untitled* of 1988. If you are feeling in the mood for further artistic inspiration, then head for the Tampa Museum of Art (see page 231). Two of Tampa's best buildings are the art deco Woolworth's building and the ornate Tampa Theatre (see page 231), both on Franklin. You will find more art on Franklin in the shape of the *Franklin Street 1925* mural and Geoffrey Naylor's 1973 aluminum sculpture *The Family of Man*.

Florida Aquarium *701 Channelside Drive* (*Open* daily 9:30–5. *Admission: expensive*; tel: 813/273-4020) Opened in 1995, this impressive downtown aquarium traces the journey of a drop of water from its underground source to the sea through a series of Florida habitats. Self-guided tours begin in the Florida Wetlands section, a steamy re-creation of springs and streams, sawgrass marshes, swamps, hammocks and mangrove forests enclosed in a giant glass seashell. Turtles and bass, native birds and alligator hatchlings inhabit the living complement of wetland plants and trees. The creepy critters in Frights of the Forest are largely non-native, but the poison-dart frogs, vampire bats and tarantulas are a big hit with kids. In the Bays and Beaches exhibit there are seabed close-ups providing glimpses of crabs, conch, shrimp and sand dollars, among others. The highlight of the Coral Reefs Gallery is the massive 500,000-gallon (2,273,000-litre) aquarium tank with its colourful corals and darting tropical fish. Interactive diving shows are held here several times a day, and the audience can listen to the diver explaining what's what from inside the tank.

Other denizens of the deep – sharks, rays, drifting jellyfish – occupy the Offshore Gallery, and there is a family-friendly outdoor area, Explore A Shore, which has a sandy beach for digging and giant water-squirting scallops.

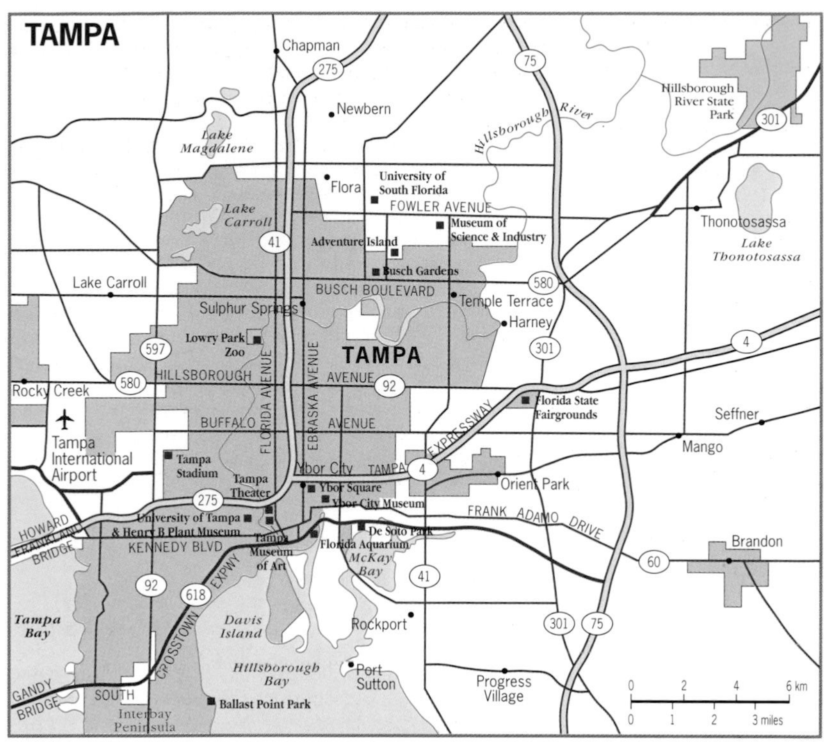

Henry B Plant Museum, *University of Tampa, 401 W Kennedy Boulevard* (*Open* Tue–Sat 10–4, Sun noon–4. *Admission: donation*; tel: 813/254-1891) There is no difficulty locating Henry B Plant's palatial Tampa Bay Hotel building, now part of the city's university campus. Visitors to the downtown district will have caught intriguing glimpses of its silver onion-domed minarets. Built in 1891, Plant's 500-room hotel was a triumph of Moorish Revival architecture, from its crescent-tipped spires to its acres of red-brick and ornamental fretwork. It is surrounded by broad verandas, wide enough to accommodate rickshaws for the guests' convenience, and was furnished with enormous quantities of antiques and art treasures collected in Europe and the Orient.

The museum occupies only a corner of one wing, but its suite of rooms, with original furnishings, recreates some of the former splendour of this extraordinary building. (You can walk through the college sections and see the former lobby and other public areas.)

Hillsborough River State Park, *15402 US 301 N (6 miles/10km southwest of Zephyr Hills)* (*Open* daily 8–dusk. *Admission: inexpensive*; tel: 813/987-6771) One of Florida's earliest state parks, opened to the public in 1938, Hillsborough lies 12 miles (19km) north of Tampa. The 2,990-acre (1,210-ha) reserve, bordering the scenic Hillsborough River, contains **Fort Foster State Historic Site**, a carefully reconstructed 1837 frontier post built during the Second Seminole War. There are weekend tours of the fort, nature trails, swimming, fishing and picnic areas.

BUY THE BUY

Shoppers will have a great time in Tampa's malls. Two of the largest are the Tampa Bay Center, Himes Avenue and Martin Luther King Jr Boulevard, and University Mall, 2200 E Fowler Avenue, while WestShore Plaza at Westshore and Kennedy boulevards is Tampa Bay's premier fashion mall with more than 100 shops and department stores. In the historic district, Old Hyde Park Village, just south of downtown at Swann and Dakota Avenues, offers up-market shops in an attractively restored setting. For antiques, collectables, cigars and craft shops, visit Ybor Square, 8th and 13th streets, in a former Ybor City cigar factory.

MOSIMAX: THE BIG ONE
A giant 10,500-square-foot (975sq m) gleaming blue bubble parked up against the Museum of Science and Industry (MOSI), the IMAX® *Dome* Theatre houses an 82-foot (25m) hemispherical movie screen specially designed to maximise the IMAX film format. This is the place to get immersed in a tropical rain forest, dive deep into the ocean on the trail of a whale or savour a moon shot from the comfort of an armchair. There are regular showings throughout the day (reservations, tel: 813/987-6000).

Lowry Park Zoo Gardens, *7530 North Boulevard* (*Open* daily 9:30–5. *Admission: moderate*; tel: 813/932-0245) A multimillion-dollar rejuvenation project launched here in the 1980s revolutionised the old city zoo, transforming it into one of the top-ranked, mid-sized zoos in the country. Pride of place goes to the **Manatee and Aquatic Center**, with its three 25,000-gallon (113,650-litre) manatee treatment tanks and emergency rescue clinic. Natural habitats have been provided for other aquatic and wetland creatures native to Florida, including alligators, snapping turtles and river otters, while the **Florida Wildlife Center** showcases Florida panthers, black bears and fox squirrels. An 18,000-square-foot (1,670sq m) **Free-Flight Aviary** houses exotic birds; orangutans, chimpanzees and lemurs hang out in **Primate World**; tigers, camels, tapirs and rhinos reside in the **Asian Domain**. Children will be enchanted by the small inhabitants of **Children's Village**, such as pygmy goats and Vietnamese pot-bellied piglets; and the **Harrell Discovery Center** provides interactive exhibits and a creepy-crawly insect zoo.

Museum of Science and Industry, *4801 E Fowler Avenue* (*Open* daily from 9am. *Admission: expensive*; tel: 813/987-6100) The southeast's largest science centre is a monster, with a Grand Lobby which manages to dwarf not one but two three-storey-high sauropod dinosaur skeletons. The museum is a sprawling scientific playground boasting some 450 hands-on exhibits, from the **Saunders Planetarium** to the mysteries of palaeontology revealed in **EarthWorks**. Experience a hair-raising encounter with a van de Graaff generator or pedal power into a light bulb, then try the **Weather Station's** hurricane chamber, simulating winds up to 74mph (120kph). The human body comes under the microscope in **The Amazing You**; there is a trip to space at the **GTE Challenger Learning Center**; and 'backwoods trails' are laid out in the grounds. Last, but by no means least, check the daily film programme in the IMAX® *Dome* Theatre (see panel).

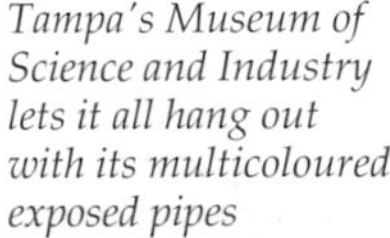

Tampa's Museum of Science and Industry lets it all hang out with its multicoloured exposed pipes

Sacred Heart Catholic Church, *509 Florida Avenue* (*Open* daily) For a taste of old Tampa buried among the downtown high-rises, walk off the beaten track for just a moment to this quiet oasis. Completed in 1905, the Romanesque-style edifice has fine stained glass, including scenes from the life of Christ.

Tampa Museum of Art, *600 North Ashley Drive (at Twiggs)* (*Open* Tue–Sat 10–5, Thu 10–8, Sun 1–5. *Admission: inexpensive*; tel: 813/274-8130) There are two main, and totally diverse, strands to this museum's collections: one is the display of 19th- to 20th-century American art; and the other is a significant holding of Greek, Roman and Etruscan antiquities. The latter collection of sculpture and elegantly decorated pottery is on permanent display, and ranges from two grotesque and remarkably contemporary-looking heads from the 2nd or 3rd century BC, to exquisite statuettes and gracefully fashioned urns and vases. The Florida Gallery showcases works by local artists, while other galleries house selected exhibits from the museum's collections of paintings, sculture, photography and works on paper. The museum also plays host to a wide-ranging programme of travelling and special exhibitions. Don't miss the waterfront terrace, which has a terrific view across the Hillsborough River to the University of Tampa's Plant Building.

Tampa Theatre, *711 Franklin Street Mall* (Occasional tours, call for schedules. *Admission: inexpensive;* tel: 813/274-8981) Modestly hailed as 'The Pride of the South', this 1926 rococo-style cinema is a weird and wonderful addition to the downtown district. Its historic façade is decorated with elegant classical reliefs, while the interior is a grotto-style, low-lit Aladdin's cave, with roughly finished walls, ornate painted ceilings and coloured floor tiles. Pillars and arches are topped with gargoyles and statuary, and there is a grand old theatre organ. In addition to all that, the old cinema still shows films.

ON THE WATER

A great way to get round downtown Tampa, the Tampa Town Ferry (Tue–Wed, Fri–Sat; tel: 813/223-1522) offers a daily passenger service between popular waterfront attractions such as the Florida Aquarium, the Convention Center and the Henry B Plant Museum at the University of Tampa, major hotels and the marina; or take a dinner cruise aboard the modern *Starlite Majesty* (Tue–Fri and Sun). Cruises depart from St Pete Beach or Clearwater Beach Marina (call for schedules; tel: 727/462-2628). If you prefer to paddle your own canoe in a stunning wilderness setting, contact Canoe Escape, 9335 E Fowler Avenue (tel: 813/986-2027), who can organise canoe hire and guided canoe trips on the Hillsborough River.

Tampa Museum of Art has displays of both ancient and modern art

UP IN SMOKE
The 110-block Ybor City historic district contains more than 1,300 significant buildings, of which more than 150 are old cigar factories which once employed nearly 13,000 people. Some 500 million cigars are still produced in Tampa annually by just 15 manufacturers with a work force of around 3,000. Annual sales are in the region of $150 million.

If it's souvenirs you're after, cigars are the obvious buy in Ybor City, and there are dozens of cigar shops to choose from. One of the most impressive is Metropolitan Cigars, 2014 E 7th Avenue (tel: 813/248-3304), which sells local and foreign-made cigars and features one of the world's largest walk-in humidors.

Cuban is the style in Ybor City

Ybor City The name Tampa means 'sticks of fire', and the city's old cigar-factory neighbourhood, Ybor (pronounced E-bor) City, is undergoing a renaissance. One of Florida's prized National Historic Landmark Districts (along with the likes of St Augustine and Pensacola), this century-old Cuban district has been polished up with replica 19th-century street lamps, restored wrought-iron balconies, cobblestone streets and an influx of artisans, boutiques and entertainment venues, all of which are designed to recapture the gaiety of its heyday.

Don Vincente Martinez Ybor moved his cigar-making operation from Key West to Tampa in 1886. Cuban workers were joined by a mixture of Italian, Spanish and German immigrants, who brought their own customs and traditions to the area, creating a vibrant, bustling community which entertained Cuban freedom fighter José Marti, Teddy Roosevelt's Rough Riders and every goodtime gal in town.

The heart of the district is La Setima (Seventh Avenue), the main shopping district, well-supplied with restaurants and cafés. This is also the nightlife strip, which comes alive after sundown, particularly on Friday and Saturday nights when the clubs are open until early morning. The new **Centro Ybor** entertainment and dining complex is set to open here, on the 1600 block. On 13th Street, Ybor's original red-brick cigar factory, with its three-storey oak and heart pine interior, has been restored and converted into another shopping and restaurant complex, **Ybor Square**. When the factory was operational, hundreds of workers (mostly men) spent long hours at the serried ranks of benches, rolling cigars by hand while a lector (reader) read novels and daily newspapers aloud to relieve the tedium.

For a look at life as it used to be lived here, visit the former bakery that houses the compact **Ybor City State Museum**, *1818 E Ninth Avenue* (*Open* daily 9–5. *Admission: inexpensive*; tel: 813/247-6323). Do not miss the furnished worker's 'shotgun' cottage a few doors down. Though

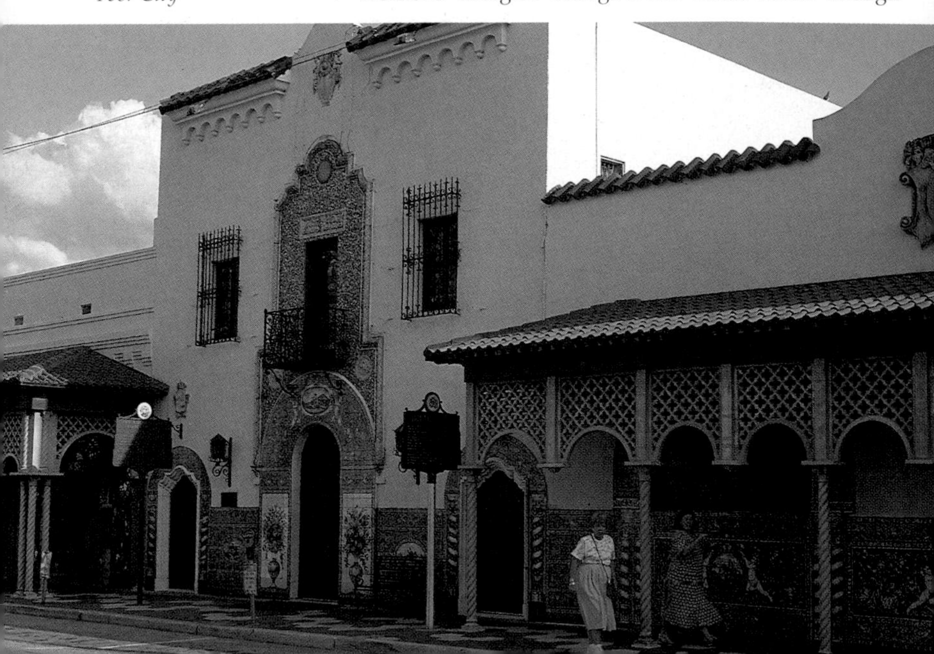

the bakery no longer bakes bread, there are plenty of opportunities to sample Cuban cuisine on Seventh Avenue. Feast on a Cuban sandwich or sample traditional fare in one of the family restaurants – a historical favourite is the 1905 **Columbia Restaurant**, on 21st Street, which is decorated with wonderfully photogenic hand-painted tiles.

There are 90-minute guided walking tours from the museum on Saturdays at 10:30am (*Admission: inexpensive*; tel: 813/248-3712). Tours and beer tastings (small charge) are also available at the **Ybor City Brewing Company**, *2205 N 20th Street* (*Open* Tue–Sat 11–3. *Admission: inexpensive*; tel: 813/242-9222), a micro-brewery in a former cigar factory.

The Old Bakery in Ybor City, Tampa

►► Tarpon Springs

And now for something completely different: a Greek sponge-fishing town on the shores of the Gulf of Mexico. A stroll down Dodecanese Boulevard to the sponge docks here is like taking a Mediterranean holiday. The aroma of freshly baked Greek pastries scents the air (there is a more pungent whiff of drying sponges when the fleet is in), and *bouzouki* music accompanies coffee and ouzo in small cafés off the main street. You should certainly sample traditional Greek delicacies, such as nut and honey *baklava*, savoury *spanakopita* (spinach), or *tiropita* (cheese) triangles wrapped in flaky filo pastry and sold in bakeries.

The Greek community arrived in the early 1900s to harvest the Gulf sponge beds. They imported their customs and culture, too; one example is **St Nicholas' Greek Orthodox Cathedral**, *N Pinellas Avenue (US 19)* (*Open* daily 9–5). The present neo-Byzantine building, dating from 1943, contains marble from the Greek pavilion's display at the 1939 New York World's Fair. Its broad nave is lined with striking stained glass, and there is a miraculous weeping statue of St Nicholas.

Back on Dodecanese Boulevard, take a 30-minute boat trip around the docks with the **St Nicholas Boat Line** (*Admision: inexpensive*; tel: 727/942-6425). Frequent daily sailings include a narrated history and demonstration of diving techniques. There are fish and other marine life from the Gulf and Caribbean at the **Tarpon Springs Aquarium** (*Open* daily 10–5. *Admission: inexpensive*; tel: 727/938-5378); while **Spongeorama** (*Open* daily 10–5. *Admission free*; tel: 727/942-3771) comprises a dusty old museum and film about the sponge industry, housed in a former wharfside factory.

The old cigar factory, the heart of Ybor City, is now a shopping and restaurant complex

► Weeki Wachee Springs

US 19 (at SR 50); tel: 1-877-GO-WEEKI or 352/596-2062
Open: daily from 10am. Admission: expensive

While the rest of the state is getting back to nature, this is one of the original Florida fantasies, a watery wonderland of make-believe, where human 'mermaids' perform Hans Christian Andersen water ballets 16 feet (5m) under water and the rain forest is nurtured by a sprinkler system. Created in 1947 by an ex-navy frogman, the mermaid shows are now part of an entertainment package which includes exotic and birds of prey shows, a petting zoo, river cruises and a pirate-themed water park.

The first Florida sponges were discovered off the shores of Key West in the mid-19th century. In 1890, property developer John K Cheyney, looking for ways to promote Tarpon Springs, found a wealth of sponges growing off the central Gulf coast and began his own small-scale 'hooking' operation. These 'hookers', or early spongers, set off in small rowing boats from a mother ship, armed with a glass-bottomed bucket to survey the seabed and long poles with hooks on the end which they used for gathering the sponges. Hooking required considerable dexterity, and the spongers were limited to shallow waters no more than 15–20 feet (4.5–6m) deep.

Arrival of the Greeks During the Spanish-American War, spongers from Key West joined the Gulf fleet, and their haul was sold at the Tarpon Springs Sponge Exchange. John Cocoris, a Greek sponge buyer from New York, travelled south to trade with Cheyney in 1905. He stayed on and soon sent for his brothers from Greece. Together they worked for Cheyney, while surreptitiously surveying the extent of the sponge beds until they were confident enough to send back to Greece for a diving team. The Greeks had already pioneered the use of diving suits and air pipes in the Mediterranean, and Cocoris' divers revolutionised the Gulf sponge industry.

By 1936, Tarpon Springs was recognised as the sponge capital of the world, and its 200-vessel fleet set sail in the traditional Phoenician-style boats built by local Greek craftsmen. They would stay out for six months at a time, curing and cleaning their catch on board as they plied the Gulf from the Keys to the Panhandle.

The sponge boat quay at Tarpon Springs

Spongeorama in Tarpon Springs

Disaster and recovery In the 1940s, a bacterial blight ripped through the Gulf sponge beds. Nothing grew for almost 20 years, until most divers had moved away, grown too old or turned to shrimping and fishing. The recovery rate was slow, and only four or five sponge boats operated during the 1970s; they had to work up to 100 miles (160km) offshore, collecting just 200 to 300 pieces per day. In 1985, Hurricane Elena swept up the Gulf coast and spent a couple of days churning up the seabed in the crook of the Panhandle. A year later, a boat belonging to one George Billiris hove to in the face of a storm, about 5 miles (8km) offshore. One of the divers went down to look at the old sponge beds and discovered ... wall-to-wall sponges. The hurricane had redistributed the larvae, and they were flourishing. In four or five days, Billiris collected 4,000 pieces of sponge, and the Gulf sponge industry was back on its feet.

What happens to the sponges? Each sponge is protected by a membrane which solidifies if it dries out. To prevent this, when the sponges are harvested, they are graded into types, piled on deck and covered with canvas. The membrane dies and decomposes over two to three days (a very smelly process), leaving the sponge skeleton, which is then cleaned with high-pressure hoses. Beaten, washed and turned constantly to remove all the dead matter, the sponges are then placed in big string bags and hung on the rigging until they are prepared for market. At auction, the sponger displays his catch in strings of 50 sponges, varying in size, but all of the same type. Wool sponges are the highest grade, followed by yellow, grass and wire varieties. A successful bid sees the sponges removed to a wholesaler's packing house, where they are bleached from grubby brown to a soft yellow colour, cut, clipped into shape with shears and then sold for one of their 1,400 commercial uses.

MARINE HARVEST
Sponge is a living multi-celled organism, one step up the evolutionary ladder from an amoeba. Sponges are hermaphrodites: they produce both male and female cells and reproduce themselves. The main requirement is firm anchorage for the larvae – rocks are ideal, but not sand. The sponge grows at a rate of about half an inch (1.25cm) in diameter each month for four to five years, then the growth rate slows, but does not stop. It can grow up to 10 feet (3m) across. Fragments left behind when a sponge is picked will grow again, and state law prohibits the harvesting of any sponge less than 5 inches (12.5cm) in diameter.

THE PANHANDLE

0 20 40 60 80 km
0 10 20 30 40 50 miles

A SOUTHERN SONGBIRD
A year-round Florida resident, the common mockingbird was chosen as the state bird in 1927. About 10 inches (25cm) in length, with a 15-inch (38cm) wingspan, grayish upper body, white underside and patches on the wings and tail, they are great songsters, singing well into the night on balmy spring evenings.

SANDWICHED BETWEEN the Gulf of Mexico, Georgia and Alabama, Florida's Panhandle extends west from the peninsula in a dark green ribbon of pine forest edged by pristine white quartz beaches. This is 'Florida with a Southern accent', where *Gone with the Wind* antebellum mansions grace historical plantations, oak-canopied roads draped with Spanish moss tunnel into the countryside, and Deep South hospitality serves up grits and throws 'all comers welcome' mullet fries.

In its early days, the region was bandied between foreign invaders like a shuttlecock. French, British and two terms of Spanish rule left a handful of fortresses,

Oyster boats off Apalachicola

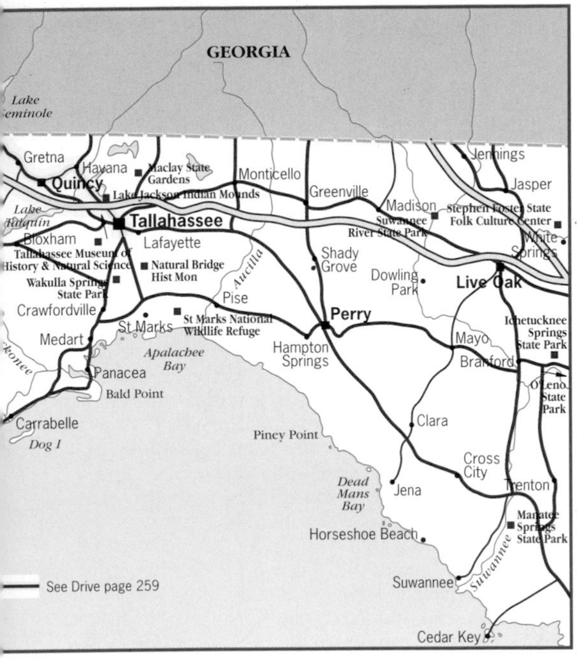

The Panhandle

foreign place names and a clutch of shipwrecks. Historic **Pensacola** was the main settlement until the 1820s, when, midpoint between Pensacola and St Augustine, **Tallahassee** was chosen as the site of the new state capital, and here it remains, an attractive small city, a stone's throw from the Georgia border.

Largely bypassed by Northern tourists fleeing south and by international visitors pouring into Orlando and Miami, the Panhandle is Florida's well-kept secret. Its fabulous beaches rank among the finest in the state (and, indeed, the nation), and now attract a far wider audience than the holiday-makers from Alabama, Georgia and Mississippi who earned the Panhandle Coast its nickname: the 'Redneck Riviera'. The Panhandle's main season is summer (May–Sep). When things become a little too hot and sticky down in the south, the northern reaches of the state welcome tourists to the well-developed mainland beaches and to the barrier islands of the **Gulf Islands National Seashore**, which preserves tracts of spectacular undeveloped shoreline in the west. The central **Emerald Coast**, named for its glassy green waters, and **Panama City Beach**, offer excellent deep-sea fishing and diving opportunities, family oriented entertainments, sport and accommodation with the emphasis on good value.

In the back-country pine forests, freshwater springs feed narrow creeks and the pristine, dark, tannin-stained rivers so favoured by canoeists. The rich coastal estuaries these rivers create are a haven for fish and birdlife, and the little town of **Apalachicola** is famous for its oyster beds. The subterranean beauty of the **Florida Caverns**, near Marianna, makes them a popular outing.

(Note: West of the Apalachicola River, the Panhandle operates on Central Standard Time, one hour behind Eastern Standard Time in the rest of Florida.)

▶▶▶ **REGION HIGHLIGHTS**

OYSTER STEW

1 pint shucked oysters
quarter cup butter
1 quart milk
salt, pepper, paprika

Drain oysters; reserve juice. Remove any shell particles. Add oysters and juice to butter; cook for three minutes, or until edges of oysters start to curl. Add milk, salt and pepper. Heat thoroughly, but do not boil. Sprinkle with paprika and serve at once.

▶▶▶ Apalachicola

If miles of fine, sandy beach, superb fishing and wildlife, historic houses and buckets of fresh oysters daily sounds like heaven, it could be named Apalachicola. This small fishing port, 60 miles (96km) southwest of Tallahassee, is a real find for a quiet break. Founded as a rivermouth customs post back in 1823, the town and its history and prosperity have long been tied to the Apalachicola River, one of Florida's largest natural waterways. As settlers further north developed plantations, so river transport increased, and thanks to 'King Cotton', Apalachicola's customs post grew to be the third largest port on the Gulf of Mexico. When the cotton bubble burst, Apalachicola turned to logging until the cypress forests were exhausted; it then hit on fishing and oystering. Mullet, pompano, mackerel, bluefish and trout were the fishermen's staples. Apalachicola's oystermen still harvest their catch by hand, prying oysters from the beds with long-handled tongs worked like scissors, from their boats.

Apalachicola's boom periods in the mid-19th and early 20th centuries produced some wonderful buildings. The crumbling cotton warehouses on the downtown docks are being restored, and the many gracious houses lining **Chestnut Avenue** (Avenue E) and the surrounding streets evoke the prosperous Victorian lifestyle once enjoyed by the town's successful merchants. The best way to see Apalachicola is on foot. There are around 200 houses dating from 1840–80, and the Chamber of Commerce, 99 Market Street (tel: 850/653-9419), provides a map of an exhaustive walking tour of the town which covers all sorts of interesting places, from the pre-1830s **Chestnut Street Cemetery**, with its memorials to the town's early settlers, yellow-fever victims and Confederate soldiers, to the **John Gorrie State Museum** (*Open* Thu–Mon 9–5. *Admission: inexpensive*; tel: 850/653-9347; see panel). A reproduction

(Continued on page 240)

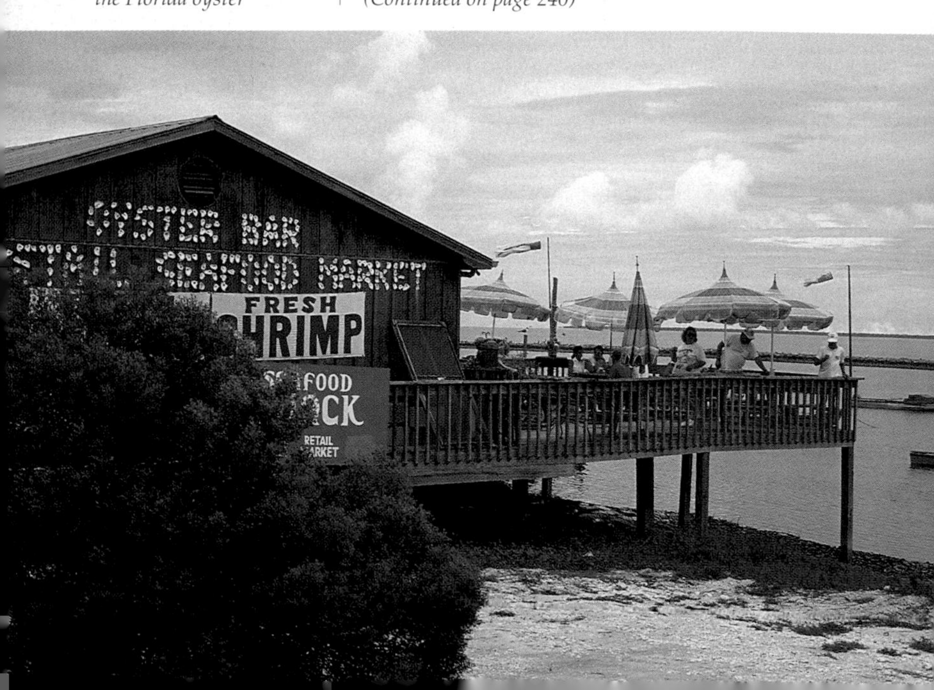

Apalachicola, source of the Florida oyster

The barrier islands off the Franklin County coast protect St George Sound, one of the most productive fishing regions on the Gulf of Mexico. Largely undeveloped – two of them are uninhabited – they are superb natural reserves.

Dog Island Situated 5 miles (8km) across the sound from Carrabelle, Dog Island has the highest sand dunes in the state. Its tiny population is linked to the mainland by a daily ferry service. Most of the island is a wildlife reserve of coastal dunes, with marsh and mangrove enclaves on the protected bayside.

St George Island The biggest of the islands (25 miles/40km long) and the most developed, St George is reached by a 4-mile (6.5km) causeway from the east bank of the Apalachicola River. The central and western parts of the island have a clutch of shops and restaurants, and a forest of weatherboard holiday homes on stilts, many of them available to rent.

Nine miles (14km) of undeveloped Gulf and bay beaches on the eastern end are protected by a state park. Here, the wind has sculpted the fine sand into miniature mountains, their ridges and hummocks crested with sea oats and scrub grasses. Waves and currents move 180,000 cubic yards of sand west along the island coast annually. Pine trees have been buried up to their crowns by these drifts, and the boardwalk trail completely disappears in places. On the Gulf shore, ghost crabs and little wading birds called sanderlings scuttle around the seashells in the surf; the back bay woodlands are full of birds, and ospreys and bald eagles ride the thermals above the fishing grounds.

St Vincent Island Nine miles (14km) offshore and part of the National Wildlife Refuge System, St Vincent is the least accessible of the barrier islands and therefore the most enticing for nature lovers. Its remarkably diverse habitats, including dunes, tidal marshes, freshwater lakes, oak ridges, pine flatwoods, magnolia and cabbage palm hammocks, attract an equally diverse cross section of wildlife. Captive breeding programmes for endangered native species, such as the red wolf, exist alongside such exotic surprises as sambar deer (originally from India), introduced by hunters in the 1920s. (There is a visitor centre in Apalachicola; for information, tel: 850/653-8808.)

LITTLE ST GEORGE ISLAND
Once part of the main island, uninhabited Little St George Island is now separated by a channel, and can only be reached by boat.

Fishing off the islands

Busy Destin marina is a top sportfishing centre

ICE MAKER
A young physician from Charleston, South Carolina, John Gorrie moved to the mosquito-infested estuary port of Apalachicola in 1833. During the next 22 years, until his death in 1855, he served as the town's mayor, postmaster, treasurer, council member, bank director and church founder, and still found time to practice medicine. Ignorant of the mosquito's role in spreading yellow fever, Gorrie and others believed that humid marsh air was to blame, and he set about devising a method of cooling and purifying the air in the sickroom. En route he invented an ice-making machine, and the concept of refrigeration and air-conditioning was born.

(Continued from page 238)

of Gorrie's original ice-making machine is the centre-piece of the interesting little one-room museum. Gorrie's tomb is found across the street at the **Trinity Episcopal Church**, which was assembled from sections shipped from New York in 1837.

Finding a quiet spot away from town is easy. **St George Island** is a short drive from downtown Apalachicola, across a 4-mile (6.5km) causeway from the fishing community of Eastpoint. Drastically developed with old Florida-style beach holiday homes in recent years, it still has several miles of magnificent white beach in the state park (see page 239). The **Apalachicola National Forest** contains **Fort Gadsden State Historic Site** (28 miles/45km northeast of Apalachicola, off SR 65), where the British once recruited Native Americans and escaped slaves to fight the white American settlers. Further east, the extensive **St Marks National Wildlife Refuge** is a winter destination for thousands of migratory birds and has some great hiking trails (see page 253).

▶▶ Cedar Key

Anchored to the mainland by a 3-mile (5km) run of island-hopping bridges, Cedar Key looks out over the Gulf of Mexico from the southern edge of Florida's Big Bend. Where the panhandle meets the pan, this former cross-state railroad terminal and logging town is one of only a handful of small settlements and fish camps which survive along the Bend's 150-mile (240km) stretch of undeveloped coastal wetlands and forest.

Cedar Key's fortunes pretty much ran out when its cedar stands were logged to extinction in the 1870s. Fishing and low-key tourism have kept the town afloat, and it is a great place to sit back and relax, go fishing or birdwatching, or take a boat trip out to island beaches in the **Cedar Keys Wildlife Refuge**. There are some fine old Victorian homes, small hotels, shopping and dining on the dock, and the landmark Island Hotel.

The little **Cedar Key Historial Society Museum**, at Second and D streets (*Open* Mon–Sat 11–5, Sun 2–5. *Admission: inexpensive*; tel: 352/543-5549), displays an eclectic range of exhibits, from fossilised tapir teeth to crab traps. You can also buy a walking map to historic houses. Thirty miles (48km) north of town is **Manatee Springs State Park** (*Open* daily 8am–dusk. *Admission: inexpensive*; tel: 352/493-6072) on the banks of the Suwannee River. It's a good place to spot manatees in winter, hire a canoe or follow a nature trail.

▶ Emerald Coast: Destin and Fort Walton Beach

The Emerald Coast unfurls in a 24-mile (38km) ribbon of shimmering white-sand beaches reaching from Fort Walton Beach in the west to the fishing village of Destin. The emphasis here is on laid-back family fun and outdoor activities, and there's shell collecting, watersports, sailing on sheltered Choctawhatchee Bay and golf to enjoy. Affordable accommodation, shopping malls, dive shops and tourist attractions are strung out along the main drag, US 98, which parallels the shore.

Destin regularly plays host to fishing tournaments and an annual Seafood Festival in October. For the largest and most elaborately equipped sportfishing charter fleet in the state, look no further than Destin's East Pass marina.

Air Force Armament Museum and Eglin Air Force Base, *14 Eglin Parkway (north of Fort Walton Beach)* The largest US Air Force base in the world, Eglin covers some 720 square miles (1,865sq km) of the mainland and rules the skies over a further 86,500 square miles (223,950sq km) of test area in the Gulf of Mexico. The base's Armaments Museum (*Open* daily 9:30–4:30. *Admission free;* tel: 850/882-4062) displays an array of lethal weaponry, from a 1903 Springfield rifle to the 6,000-rounds-per-minute GAU8, plus the 180 exhibits of the Sikes Antique Pistol Collection. The latter includes flintlock duelling pistols, six-shooters and Civil War firearms. A comprehensive aircraft collection is arranged inside and around the building.

Eden State Gardens and Mansion *Port Washington, 4 miles/6.5km northeast of Grayton Beach on SR 395* (*Open* gardens daily 8–dusk; house guided tours Thu–Mon 9–4. *Admission: inexpensive;* tel: 850/231-4214) Tucked away off a back road, this lovely two-storey southern mansion was built by mill-owner William H Wesley in 1897. Timber logged in the nearby woods was floated down the Choctawhatchee River to this site until the mill was burned down and the family sold out. The antebellum house was restored in the 1960s, filled with antiques and the gardens created. Towering, moss-draped live oaks dot the lawns and shade picnic tables down by the Choctawhatchee. This is where timber logged in the nearby woods would be sawn up in the mill and then transported by barge to Pensacola. Camellias and azaleas are in bloom from late October to May; the peak flowering season is mid-March.

FISHING SEASON

When to go for 'the big one':
Amberjack: all year.
Barracuda: Aprl–Nov.
Black/Red Grouper: all year.
Blue Marlin): May–Nov.
Jack Crevalle: May–Oct.
Red Snapper: all year.
Sailfish: Apr–Nov.
Tarpon: Apr–Nov.
Wahoo: Apr–Oct.
White Marlin: May–Dec.
But note: you need a licence for sportfishing off the Florida coast.

Fascinating hardware at the Air Force Armament Museum

The little resort of Seaside is developing a name for itself

WEDDING CAVERN
Several of the caves in Florida Caverns State Park have special names suggested by the rock formations, like the Wedding Cavern, with its glittering white 'wedding cake'. Several weddings have actually taken place here in the constantly cool temperature of 61–66°F (16–19°C).

Gulfarium, *1010 Miracle Strip Parkway (east US 98)* (*Open* Jun–Sep, daily 9–6; Oct–May, daily 9–4. *Admission: expensive*; tel: 850/243-9046) A short distance east of Fort Walton Beach, Gulfarium was one of the area's pioneering seaside attractions, founded in 1955. Shows include aquabatic entertainment from performing porpoises and sea lions. The Living Sea exhibit tank has a varied collection of sharks, stingrays, sea turtles, sinuous eels and performing scuba divers. The tropical penguin colony is a must, so are the otters. Other bird colonies include the Duck and Pelican Roost and the Geese and Swan Sanctuary.

Indian Temple Mound Museum, *139 Miracle Strip Parkway* (*Open* Jun–Aug, Mon–Sat 9–4; Sep–May, Mon–Fri 11–4, Sat 9–4. *Admission: inexpensive*; tel: 850/833-9595) This small museum, which traces 10,000 years of Native American life, is right next to a Native American ceremonial and burial mound dating from around 1400 BC. Artefacts and displays include arrowheads, fish-hooks and pottery. A re-created thatched temple has been built atop the burial mound.

▶▶ Grayton Beach

Grayton is the oldest community on the coast between Apalachicola and Pensacola. Its quiet, sandy and tree-shaded streets have been tastefully preserved. There are a couple of fine old homes, smart little boutiques, galleries and antiques shops, but Grayton's real pride and joy is **Grayton Beach State Recreation Area** (*Open* daily 8–dusk. *Admission: inexpensive*; tel: 850/231-4210). The spectacular Gulf beach fronts a 365-acre (148-ha) park, which offers great swimming, boating, nature trails and surf-fishing. There are also popular campfire interpretive programmes in summer.

A mile up Scenic Country Road 30A, the resort community of **Seaside** boosted its profile when it was chosen as the set for the 1998 Jim Carrey movie, *The Truman Show*. A fanciful re-creation of a 19th-century seaside resort complete with grand Victorian cottages, picket fences, and colourful public buildings, Seaside's neo-traditionalist approach has found many fans.

▶▶ Marianna/Florida Caverns State Park

3345 Caverns Road (off SR 167, north of Marianna); tel: 805/482-9598

Open: daily 8–dusk, frequent cave tours 9–4. Admission: inexpensive

The Florida peninsula is a vast limestone plateau, honeycombed with underground caverns, rivers and sinkholes. Most of the caverns are permanently flooded as they are below the water-table level, but at Marianna the Chipola River has cut deep into the limestone, reducing water levels and revealing a superb network of caves.

The upper-level caverns are permanently dry; the lower levels, around 65 feet (20m) below ground, fill with water during the flood season in winter. Within the caverns, stalactites, stalagmites, rimstones, flowstones and ribbon formations continue to develop – very slowly. It takes roughly 100 years for a single cubic inch of solid calcite to grow. The formations are caused by precipitation: rainwater collects carbon dioxide from the air to create a weak carbonic solution which filters through the limestone into the dry cave. There, it evaporates into a concentrated limestone solution, and speleotherms (cave formations) gradually develop. At Marianna, the formations come in two different colours: brilliant white, formed by calcium carbonate, and an orange-yellow tint, from iron oxide in the soil. Above ground, the 1,280-acre (518-ha) park offers two good nature trails, picnic areas, horse-riding, canoeing (see page 244), fishing and a swimming hole.

▶ Monticello

Named after Thomas Jefferson's Virginia mansion, Monticello was founded in 1827 at one of the highest points in the state – some 235 feet (71m) above sea level. Today, it is a quiet country town and an important agricultural centre, with historical roots which can be traced back to the cotton plantations established in the area before the town itself. In the early days, the citizens of Monticello were prosperous, reactionary and influential. Noted politicians, judges and the state's first elected governor, William D Moseley, came from the district, and local lobbyists were at the forefront of Florida's 1861 secession from the Union. During the mid-19th century, Monticello acquired a wealth of elegant Greek and Classical Revival mansions, pretty stick-style houses with gingerbread detail and needle-spired churches. Several pre-Civil War buildings have survived, and there are more than 40 registered buildings in the Historic District. At the centre of town, traffic is routed around the 1909 **Jefferson County Courthouse**, and on the southwest corner of Washington Street is the red-brick 1890 **Perkins Opera House**, which is the focus of a lively arts scene. The ornate Operatic Chamber is an ideal showcase for musical and dramatic performances. Drivers heading west on US 90 can make a pleasant back-road detour to the village of Miccosukee (12 miles/19km west of CR 59, then 5 miles/8km north), and follow **Miccosukee Road**, one of the old, oak-canopied 'cotton trail' roads back to Tallahassee.

PUCKER UP
Jefferson County celebrates its status as a watermelon growing region with an annual festival held during the last week of June. Activities include a beauty pageant, a canoe race, a parade, a golf tournament and a mess of good ol' country cookin'. The highlight has got to be the Watermelon Seed Spittin' Contest. Make a few practice runs, then prepare to pucker up and fire.

The courthouse in Monticello

There is no better way to explore the quiet backwaters of Florida than paddling a canoe. The state has 36 designated canoe trails totalling 950 miles (1,530km) of scenic waterways. The Panhandle has plenty of waterborne opportunities, from a gentle novice meander or family inner-tube rides to more challenging creek runs for experienced canoeists.

CANOE TRAILS
Officially designated canoe trails are managed as part of the Florida Recreational Trail System. For further details, contact the Office of Greenways and Trails, 3900 Commonwealth, Mail Station 795, Tallahassee, FL 32399–3000, tel: 850/488-3701.

Canoe Capital of Florida **Milton**, north of Pensacola, is the Panhandle's main canoeing centre and a good base for exploring the tannin-stained **Blackwater River** as it winds its way through the dense woodlands of the Blackwater River State Forest. Local canoe-hire operations provide equipment and shuttle services for visitors to the Blackwater, considered one of the purest sand-bottomed rivers in the world, and to **Coldwater Creek**, a pretty, freshwater stream running through the forest, 12 miles (19km) north of Milton. For real back-to-nature adventurers, there is camping in the state park.

Further east Holmes Creek, which rises in Georgia and eventually empties into Choctawhatchee Bay (sheltered by the Emerald Coast), makes for a lazy day's paddling. There is good fishing along its sandy banks and lush swamplands. The 52-mile (83km) **Chipola River Trail** starts in Florida Caverns State Park, north of Marianna. There the river flows through high limestone bluffs and caves and around a series of small rapids and shoals.

The going is rougher on the top section of narrow, twisting **Econfina Creek**, northeast of Panama City Beach, but this 22-mile (35km) trail also offers beautiful springs and gentler waters along its lower reaches.

State park facilities Four state parks and canoeing facilities abut the **Suwannee River** and its tributary, the Sante Fe. At the **Suwannee River State Park**, 20 miles (32km) east of Madison, where the much-sung-about Suwannee is joined by the Withlacoochee River, there is great canoeing country. Otters, beavers and gopher tortoises bustle about the river swamp and hardwood hammock habitats. **Ichetucknee Springs State Park**, one of the most beautiful riverfront parks in Florida, is good for tubing (floating in an inner tube) as well as canoeing, and **O'Leno State Park** marks the point where the Santa Fe resurfaces after a 3-mile (5km) journey underground. Both are close to US 441, south of Lake City.

Manatee Springs State Park, 23 miles (37km) short of the Gulf of Mexico, has 2,075 acres (840-ha) in which to canoe, fish, swim and scuba dive, as well as to spot manatees. The river swamp is alive with cypress, gum, ash and maple trees.

Canoeing camp

The Gulf Islands National Seashore stretches for a total of 150 miles (240km) across the top of the Gulf of Mexico, from Florida's Santa Rosa Island in the east to West Ship Island off the coast of Mississippi. Abundant plant and animal life flourishes in this magnificent natural reserve, and the three main habitats – dunes, marsh and woodlands – are all represented within the six areas of the Florida district: Santa Rosa, Okaloosa, Naval Live Oaks, Fort Pickens, Pensacola Forts and Perdido Key.

Naval Live Oaks Just across the bay from Pensacola, Naval Live Oaks, at Gulf Breeze (US 98), is the National Park Service headquarters and visitor centre. Natural history and historical exhibits, together with an audio-visual presentation, give an overview of the reserve, and there is plenty of helpful information.

Santa Rosa This glorious stretch of beach reserve lies east of Pensacola Beach along SR 399. Here there are miles of incredibly white sand, with not a condominium in sight.

To protect the fragile dunes, it is strictly boardwalk access only to the shore from designated parking areas. Once on the beach, there is a Day Use facility at the Navarre Beach end, with picnic shelters, toilets and a concession stand.

What else is there? The other reserve areas offer several pleasant nature trails, such as the marsh, forest and sandhill trail at **Johnson Beach** on Perdido Key. **Fort Pickens** (see page 249) offers two short and remarkably diverse trails: a quarter-mile (0.4km) dune walk and the half-mile (0.8km) Blackbird Marsh circuit in the maritime forest. On the mainland, the **Fort Barrancas** trail explores woodlands near the naval air station.

AWESOME OAKS
The 1,378-acre (557-ha) woodland park that surrounds Naval Live Oaks is dominated by majestic live oaks. It is so called because in 1828 the US government reserved great tracts of southern oak forest to be managed exclusively for shipbuilding. The heaviest of all the oaks, live oaks are also remarkably resistant to disease and decay. There are several nature trails through the forest, which is a haven for foxes, bobcats and racoons as well as reptiles, from skinks to coral snakes.

MOVING ALONG
The Panhandle's barrier islands are on the move. Littoral currents erode the fine quartz sand from the eastern tip of the islands and deposit it at the western end. Constant winds and storms rearrange the dunes ceaselessly, and the dunes' only protection are the hardy stems and elaborate root systems of the salt-spray-loving sea oats. Sea oats are a protected species along the coast: disturbing them or picking them is against the law.

DIVERS' DELIGHTS
The Gulf of Mexico's crystal-clear waters offer great diving opportunities off Panama City Beach, where wreck dive sites include the tanker *Empire Mica*, the *Grey Ghost* and the 220-foot (67m) *Chippewa*. There are several natural coral reefs, and they teem with fish, lobsters, and shellfish. Snorkellers and divers can explore the St Andrews State Park jetties, which range in depth from just 1 foot (0.3m) to 50 feet (15m). For details of diving and snorkelling trips, contact Hydrospace, Hathaway Marina, tel: 850/234-3063.

►► Panama City Beach

Fun-loving Panama City Beach is typified by its 'Miracle Strip' of neon, concrete, and candyfloss, which extends for almost 27 miles (43km) along the gleaming white Gulf beaches. Love it or loathe it, there is no disputing its distinctive flavour and wide-ranging family appeal. With 18,000 hotel rooms offering everything from secluded luxury resort accommodation to beachside motels, as well as caravan sites, there is plenty to choose from.

The beach is the city's pride and joy, and has recently been the beneficiary of the largest beach nourishment project in Florida's history. An additional 8 million cubic yards of sand have extended the shore to a width of 100 feet (30m), and dune systems have been created. Here watersports are at the top of the activities list: Snorkelling, diving, jet skiing, windsurfing, sailing and parasailing. Fishermen can go for 'the big one' on single or party charter boats or just take it easy and hang a line off one of the numerous piers and jetties. Golf is increasingly popular: There are more than 20 excellent courses within a 40-mile (65km) radius. Several sports clubs have added top-class hard-surface and clay tennis courts as well.

Meanwhile, back on 'The Strip', miniature golf courses, featuring model shipwrecks, moated castles and gaping monsters, are open from early to floodlit late, late night. Restaurants, bars, boutiques and video arcades abound, and as the sun goes down, neon snaps into action and the serious fun begins. Entertainment runs the gamut from comedy to Broadway-style musicals, from fairground thrills to beachclub discos. A notable favorite is the 1,000-seat family-oriented Ocean Opry theatre (for information and reservations, tel: 850/234-5464) and its crowd-pleasing programme of country and western classics, old-time rock 'n' roll, bluegrass and gospel music, as well as comedy shows.

Panama City Beach, with its Miracle Strip Amusement Park

Although Panama City Beach is turning into a year-round holiday destination, the main season runs from April to September; the spring break is also busy. Hotel rates are bargains during the winter months, but many attractions are closed off-season.

Gulf World, *15412 W Front Beach Road* (*Open* daily Jun–Aug 9–7. *Admission: expensive;* tel: 850/234-5271) Now expanded with the addition of a climate-controlled tropical garden and 2,000-seat Dolphin Stadium, this popular marine showcase occupies a prime location in the main beach area. Take in the parrot show, an informative underwater show and scuba demonstration and the stingray petting pool, where visitors are encouraged to feed the rays with slivers of fish held between their fingers. The rays have had their barbs removed and are therefore safe; visitors may have their own views about the moral issues raised. The dolphins can be stroked, the sharks are fed and there is lots of splashing around in the sea lion and dolphin show. After dark, the new Dolphin Stadium is the setting for a spectacular laser light show, Splash Magic, complete with music, fireworks and a dramatic patriotic salute.

Miracle Strip Amusement Park, *12000 W. Front Beach Road* (*Open* Apr–May, Fri–Sat 6pm–11:30pm; Jun–Labor Day, Sun–Fri 6pm–11:30pm, Sat 1pm–1:30am. *Admission: expensive;* tel: 805/234-5810 or 800/538-7395) Right opposite the beachside Visitor Information Center, this is northwest Florida's biggest attraction and one of the top ten in the state, with 9 acres (3.5-ha) of brash, loud, gaudy fun – swings, carousels, contests and games. Undisputed king of the park is the 2,000-foot (610m) roller coaster, rated one of the world's foremost rides by coaster aficionados. A variety of other stomach-churning rides and attractions include the 40-foot-high (12m) Sea Dragon Viking Ship, which rocks passengers up to 70 feet (20m) in the air; the Ferris wheel; the Log Flume; and the Abominable Snowman-Scrambler. There is live entertainment in summer and snack concessions and fast-food joints serve everything from pizzas and hotdogs to home-made fudge.

St Andrews State Recreation Area, *4607 State Park Lane* (*Open* daily 8–dusk. *Admission: inexpensive;* tel: 850/233-5140) On the eastern tip of Panama City Beach, this 1,063-acre (430-ha) park is one of the most popular in the state. It's also regularly included on the University of Maryland's prestigious 'best beach in the US' list. Nature trails throughout the woodlands and dunes offer plenty of opportunities to spot wild deer, racoons, alligators and seabirds, and there is a re-created turpentine still among the pine trees, near the Grand Lagoon fishing pier. Guided hiking tours are available (call for schedules), and there are summer season campfire programmes organised by park rangers. From the bayside fishing piers you can try to hook speckled trout, red fish and flounder, while bonita, pompano and Spanish and king mackerel can be caught on the Gulf side. There are picnic areas, a campsite, and boats for hire, and the park is an excellent place for young children, since man-made reefs around the jetties form a shallow play area.

SUBMARINE MAN

The small and unusual Museum of Man in the Sea, 17314 Back Beach Road (*Open* daily 9–5. *Admission: inexpensive*; tel: 850/235-4101), traces the definitive history of diving, from the earliest records to the miracles of modern science, including marine salvage and construction, archaeology and oil drilling. There are lots of dioramas, models and equipment, plus a landmark orange Sealab deep-diving capsule anchored in the car-park.

Acrobatic dolphins and sea lion shows at Gulf World

Try out the rides in Shipwreck Island Water Park, then recover in the sun

Shell Island, *ferry access from St Andrews SRA* (*Open* Apr–Oct, daily in summer, weekends only in low season. *Admission: moderate*; tel: 850/233-5140) Scheduled to become a state park in the near future, this sheller's paradise lies just off Panama City Beach. Also known as Hurricane Island, it has 7 miles (11km) of untouched shoreline shaded by a smattering of pines. Three-hour shell safaris leave from **Captain Anderson's Marina**, *5550 North Lagoon Drive* (tel: 850/234-3435 or 800/874-2415), and **Treasure Island Marina**, *3605 Thomas Drive* (tel: 850/234-7245), from April to early October. There are also glass-bottomed boat trips and dolphin-feeding excursions.

Shipwreck Island Water Park, *12000 W Front Beach* (*Open* mid-Apr–May, weekends 10:30–5; Jun–Labor Day daily 10:30–5. *Admission: expensive*; tel: 850/234-0368 or 800/538-7395) Back-to-back with the night-time Miracle Strip Amusement Park complex, Shipwreck Island is the answer to what to do during the day. There are six exotically landscaped acres of watery fun park, fully equipped with lifeguards, restaurant facilities, snack bars, sundecks, shops and free parking. Meander down the 1,600-foot (485m) Lazy River on an inner tube; check out the Ocean Motion wave pool; or try out the flumes, speed slides and 370-foot (112m) White Water Tube Ride for thrills and spills. Then settle down under a sun umbrella while the kids splash about in the thoughtfully miniaturised Tadpole Hole.

ZooWorld, *9008 Front Beach Road* (*Open* daily 9–dusk. *Admission: moderate*; tel: 850/230-1243) A small zoo set in 7.5 acres (3ha) of tropical gardens, ZooWorld has a full complement of around 350 animals, among them monkeys, bears, big cats, exotic birds, giraffes, camels, reptiles and Florida alligators. You can meet baby goats and other farm animals in the petting zoo. The zoo also takes care of 15 rare and endangered species as part of its commitment to the internationally recognized Species Survival Plan (SSP).

TEEPEES FOR TOTS

A fun outing for young children is Bay County's Junior Museum, 1731 N Jenks Avenue, in Panama City (*Open* Tue–Fri 9–4:30, Sat 10–4. *Admission: inexpensive*; tel: 850/769-6128). It adopts a hands-on approach to its science, art and nature exhibits. Children can play Native American games and explore a life-size teepee, feed chickens and ducks in a re-created pioneer homestead and investigate the nature trail.

►►► Pensacola

The second oldest city in Florida, Pensacola is proud of its history and has three fine historical districts to prove it: the **Seville Historic District**, where the first stockade was erected in 1752; **Palafox Street**, leading down to the waterfront; and 19th-century **North Hill**, with its elegant houses built by wealthy lumber merchants. Sightseeing also includes sophisticated state-of-the-art technology on display at the **National Museum of Naval Aviation**.

Across the bay, Pensacola's beaches are responsible for turning the city into a major resort – 40 miles (64km) of 99 per cent pure quartz sand. **Pensacola Beach**, on Santa Rosa Island, is lined with hotels, boutiques and cafés and is popular for watersports. To the west is **Perdido Key**, part of the Gulf Islands National Seashore; it has free showers and changing facilities in the Johnson Beach area. Or head east along SR 399 for the fabulous undeveloped dunes of the **Santa Rosa** and **Navarre beaches**.

Fort Pickens, *W Santa Rosa Island* (*Open* daily 8:30–dusk. *Admission: moderate* per car; tel: 850/934-2635) Strategically sited at the entrance to Pensacola Bay, Fort Pickens was the largest of four defensive fortresses constructed to protect the harbour in the 1800s. More than 21 million locally made bricks were transported out to the island on barges to reinforce the massive five-sided earthworks.

Originally, the fortress was surrounded by a 10-foot-deep (3m) moat, but this has since been filled in. Bastions with a broad range of firepower anchor the corners and heavy cannon once lined the wall. To the left of the sallyport (entrance) are the officers' quarters, which were used to house the captured Apache chief Geronimo. Geronimo's enforced stay (1886–8) generated the beginnings of Pensacola's tourist industry, when curious folk came to ogle at his humiliating downfall. Today, there are historic and natural history displays, beach access and a ranger station.

CITY OF FIVE FLAGS

In 1559, 500 Spanish soldiers and 1,000 colonists sailed into Pensacola Bay and established a settlement. It lasted just two years. But the Europeans were back to stay in the late 17th century, and in less than 100 years the area was controlled by Spanish, French and British interests. Those three, plus the Confederate forces of the 19th century and the forces of post-Civil War America, add up to Pensacola's nickname, the City of Five Flags.

Marine life exhibits capture the imagination of a visitor to Pensacola's Fort Pickens

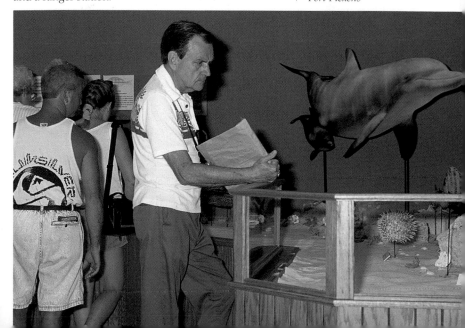

Historic Pensacola Village, *Zaragoza and Tarragona streets* (*Open* museums and restored historic houses Mon–Sat 10–4; closed Mon in winter. *Guided tours* Mon–Sat 11–1. *Admission: moderate*: combination tickets with the T T Wentworth Florida State Museum; tel: 850/595-5985) Also known as the **Seville Historic District**, this is one of three exceptional preservation districts found in Pensacola. The original street plans were laid out by the British in the mid-18th century, and were later retained by the Spanish, although the names of the streets were changed. Today, the area looks much as it would have appeared in the late 1880s. First stop is the ticket and tour office located in the **Tivoli House**, 205 E Zaragoza Street. Accompanied tours visit a selection of immaculately restored historic houses, while other village properties are open for self-guided tours.

A good place to begin a visit is at the **Museum of Commerce**, Zaragoza and Tarragona streets. A short video presentation covers Pensacola's history, and a re-created late 19th-century shopping street features a print shop and a pharmacy; and hardware, music and toy shops. Across the street, exhibits in the **Museum of Industry** illustrate Pensacola's two founding strengths, the maritime and lumber industries.

Opposite the Tivoli House are two prime examples of early architecture. **Julee Cottage** was built in 1805 and owned by renowned Pensacolan Julee Panton, a 'free woman of colour'. Its companion, the **Lavalle House** (pronounced La-va-lay), is an eye-catching affair dating from the same year. It was built by one Charles Lavalle with the specific intention of attracting French Creole lodgers – who might prefer the bright colour scheme.

Florida's oldest Protestant church, **Old Christ Church**, faces pretty, tree-shaded Seville Square. Across the street is the **Dorr House**, a beautifully restored 1870 Greek Revival building. The last of the village's official properties, **Quina House**, which was constructed in 1821, is a cosmopolitan mixture of Spanish-French Creole architecture.

There is plenty more to find with the help of the self-guided *Historical Guide to Pensacola* leaflet (obtainable from Tivoli House). Many houses have been converted into folksy law offices, and the local boutique and restaurant owners are usually delighted to regale visitors with tales of their historic surroundings.

Other local museums worth checking out are the **Pensacola Historical Museum**, housed in Old Christ Church; the **Pensacola Museum of Art**, 407 S Jefferson Street, in the former city jail; and the **T T Wentworth Florida State Museum**, on Jefferson between Government and Zaragoza streets, where local history exhibits introduce visitors to Pensacola's Colonial Archeological Trail.

National Museum of Naval Aviation, *NAS Pensacola, 1750 Radford Boulevard (via US 98)* (*Open* daily 9–5. *Admission free*; tel: 850/453-2389 or 800/327-5002) 'Top Gun fun', shrieks the slogan, and visitors are greeted at the entrance by an F14 Tom Cat – one of 130 planes, all with a tale to tell. This is indeed an amazing attraction – one of

SLAVES AND SCALPELS

Tucked behind a shopfront in the downtown business district, the Civil War Soldiers Museum, 108 S Palafox Street (*Open* Tue–Sat 10–4. *Admission: inexpensive*; tel: 850/469-1900) gives a vivid account of the origins of slavery in the US and the Civil War. A range of artefacts and photographs follows the main characters, actions and campaigns, and there is a particularly comprehensive (and gory) selection of medical equipment – the collection was established by a doctor.

the largest air and space museums in the world. For sheer scale, look at the full-size reconstruction of a World War II aircraft carrier, the USS *Cabot* in the West Wing. The model displays Corsair, Avenger and Hellcat fighters on its wooden decking, while examples of Wildcat, Dauntless and Kingfisher aircraft are locked in stationary flight overhead. The collection features aircraft from the earliest wood-and-canvas pioneer prototypes to sophisticated space gadgetry. Unwieldy flying boats, supersonic jets, moon buggies and naval aviation memorabilia all earn a place in the Hall of Fame. Video presentations deliver the excitement of flight secondhand; getting closer to the action, there is an IMAX cinema (for schedules, tel: 850/453-2024), and F-4 and A-7 jet cockpit simulators, plus a chance to take the controls of a TH-57 helicopter trainer. Guided tours with former pilots add a special insight to tales of derring-do in the skies, and a visit to the Hanger Bay restoration facility provides an intriguing opportunity to watch museum volunteers refurbish historical aircraft.

EARLY DEFENCES

Long before the US Air Force arrived to protect Pensacola Bay, Spanish colonists fortified a strategic bluff (*barranca*) overlooking the harbour entrance and later built a sunken mini-fortress. Visitors to the air station are free to explore 18th- to 19th-century Fort Barrancas and the forward artillery defences of the Advance Redoubt, signposted from the aviation museum.

Inside the National Museum of Naval Aviation

ARTISTIC LICENCE
One of America's best-loved musical storytellers, Stephen C Foster, never saw the Suwannee, or even visited Florida. Looking for a good ol' Southern name for one of his compositions, he had no compunction about tailoring the Suwannee to 'S'wanee' to fit the two-syllable cadence he needed. A prolific composer, Foster has about 200 songs to his credit, including sing-along favourite *Oh Susannah* and the lilting *Jeannie with the Light-brown Hair.*

►► Ponce de León Springs SRA

Ponce de León (off US 90, north of I–10); tel: 850/836-4281
Open: daily 8–dusk. Admission: inexpensive
When you drive across the Panhandle on a baking hot day, this is a great place to stop for a picnic and cooling swim. The park's main spring produces more than 14 million gallons (63½ million litres)of crystal-clear water daily, and some find its constant 68°F (20°C) temperature a lot more refreshing than the lukewarm waters of the Gulf. There are picnic benches and barbecue grills (bring charcoal) in the shade of pine and cypress trees, canoe hire and fishing, two self-guided nature trails and ranger-led seasonal guided walks.

►► Suwannee River

White Springs (US 41)
In 1851, composer Stephen C Foster immortalised the state's second largest river in his popular melody *Old Folks at Home*, better known as *Way Down upon the Swanee River*. It was adopted as Florida's official state song in 1935. A former spa resort 10 miles (16km) northwest of Lake City, White Springs has cashed in on the free promotion with its **Florida Folk Festival**, held here each May.

Near by, the **Stephen Foster State Folk Culture Center** (*Open* daily 8–dusk. *Admission: inexpensive*; tel: 904/397-2733) contains the remnants of the original Victorian spa, a collection of rare musical instruments and a 93-bell carillon which runs through a medley of Foster compositions. There are also summer season paddle-wheel boat excursions.

►► The ZOO

5701 Gulf Breeze Parkway (12 miles/19km east of Gulf Breeze, on US 98); tel: 850/932-2229
Open: summer, daily 9–5; rest of the year, daily 9–4
There is plenty to do at this 30-acre (12-ha) zoo, with more than 600 animals, botanical gardens, a children's petting corner and a safari train which rides around natural habitat enclosures. Take a ride on an elephant or hand feed giraffes from a purpose-built high-rise feeding station, and catch a show at the amphitheatre.

On the Suwannee River, Florida's most famous waterway

More than three-quarters of the Panhandle's state parks offer short nature walks within their preserves, but for something a little more exacting there are several longer trails. In 1979, the Florida Recreational Trails Act authorised the establishment of a network of scenic and historic trails, and there are plans to create a series of hiking routes from Pensacola across to Lake Okeechobee and from Big Cypress Swamp in southwest Florida up to the Gulf Islands National Seashore.

Rails to trails One way to create routes is to convert abandoned railroad tracks into multi-use trails, and the first of these routes to open was the **Tallahassee–St Marks Historic Railroad State Trail** in the eastern Panhandle. Once a transport corridor for cotton and other goods, the 16-mile (26km) trail starts just south of Tallahassee (off SR 363), and is now open to hikers, horse-riders, and bicyclists – it is the most popular cycling trail in Florida.

St Marks National Wildlife Refuge Within St Mark's National Wildlife Refuge on Apalachee Bay, you can choose from the half-day Ridge Trail (4½ miles/7.5km) and Stoney Bayou Trail (6 miles/10km), to the longer Otter Lake Trail (8 miles/13km) and Deep Creek Trail (12 miles/19km). The 45-mile (72km) St Marks Trail winds deep into some of the more remote areas of this vast coastal marsh and swampland reserve. It ends just east of Sopchoppy, where the Apalachicola Trail begins its 22-mile (35km) hike across four rivers into the wild regions of the Apalachicola National Forest.

Other trails For a shorter introduction to the forest, take the circular Camel Lake Trail (4 miles/6,5km) from the Camel Lake Recreation Area off SR 12 north of Wilma. West of Apalachicola, **St Joseph Peninsula State Park** is the start of the 18-mile (29km) St Joseph Peninsula Trail, which loops through the wilderness preserve. It is an excellent birdwatching area, with more than 209 species recorded. In the western Panhandle region, hikers can venture across the Blackwater State Forest on the Jackson Red Ground Trail (21 miles/34km) or sample the Sweetwater Hiking Trail, a short 4½-mile (7km) walk from the Krul Recreation Area in the middle of the forest near Munson.

A grey squirrel in the Apalachicola Forest

CEREMONIAL CENTRE
The name Tallahassee comes from the Apalachee word for 'land of the old fields' or 'abandoned villages'. Archaeological surveys of the Lake Jackson area, north of the city, have revealed evidence of a Mississippi Native American ceremonial centre dating back more than eight centuries. Spanish explorer Hernando de Soto celebrated the first Christmas Mass on the continent here in 1539.

▶▶▶ Tallahassee

By the 1820s, the hunt was on for a government seat where Florida's newly elected state legislature could meet, somewhere between the two historic centers of St Augustine and Pensacola. A scout was sent out from each city, and the two met on the hill called Tallahassee. Suggestions that the capital should shift to the growing urban and business centres in the southeast have met with rebuff, and present-day Tallahassians guard their position and history jealously.

Surrounded by gently rolling hills, forests and lakes, old plantations, and with the accents of America's Deep South, Tallahassee seems a world away from the crowded southern tourist trails. Quiet streets, lined with trees draped with Spanish moss, exude old-fashioned charm, even though they're just minutes from the bustling **Capitol Complex** at the centre of downtown.

Two major universities are based here: Florida State (FSU), with its mighty Seminoles football team, and Florida Agricultural and Mechanical (FAMU), founded in 1887. Florida's Sunshine Act made it one of the first states to insist that legislative sessions be open to the public, so a visit to the New Capitol building during the March to May sessions is a popular excursion. The nearby elegant **Governor's Mansion**, 700 N Adams Street, modelled on General Andrew Jackson's Tennessee plantation home, is open to view at the same time.

A good way to get around downtown is on the **Old Town Trolley**, which provides free services and makes frequent stops (weekdays 8–5, weekends 9–3; tel: 850/413-8200). Shopping in Tallahassee focuses on the malls along Apalachee Parkway. **Governor's Square** offers the best range of boutiques and department stores, with the bonus of an unrivalled view of the Old and New Capitol buildings from the top of the parkway heading back into town. Springtime visitors will find Tallahassee in a festive mood, with a four-week (March to April) jamboree of arts, crafts, entertainment and parades.

The Fourth of July parade in Tallahassee

Walk

Downtown Tallahassee

Start from the Old Capitol on Monroe Street at Apalachee Parkway.

Across the street, the twin granite slabs of the **Vietnam Veteran's Memorial** commemorate the 1,942 known Floridian casualties of the conflict. The **Union Bank Building**, facing Apalachee Parkway, is Florida's oldest surviving bank. This restored 1841 Federal-style edifice now houses Florida A&M's Black Archives Extension and displays.

Walk back up to Monroe; turn right.

The **Exchange Building**, 201 Monroe, is a fine example of art deco office architecture, built in 1927 and decorated with reliefs and stone griffins.

Turn left on College, then turn left again on Adams.

This attractive restored area, with its old Southern-style, neo-classical buildings, is known as the **Adams Street Commons**.

Turn right on Jefferson for two blocks to Bronough.

The **Museum of Florida History**, 500 S Bronough, is situated just across the intersection (see page 256).

Continue along Bronough to Madison, and turn left.

On the corner of Madison and Monroe, the **Jackson Square Marker** indicates the original site of downtown Tallahassee circa 1824, a village of wooden cottages and shops which stretched from Call Street to the south wing of the Old Capitol.

CRADLE AND GRAVE BRIGADE
One of Florida's Civil War actions is celebrated every spring with a re-enactment of the Battle of Natural Bridge. At the Natural Bridge Battlefield State Historic Site, 15 miles (24km) southeast of Tallahassee, volunteers dressed as Confederate and Union troops set up encampments at the site near the St Marks River and honour the Confederate victory of 3–7 March, 1865. The victory preserved Tallahassee as the only Confederate capital east of the Mississippi never to fall into Union hands during the Civil War. The victory was quite an accomplishment since the Confederate troops were largely old men and boys facing seasoned Union soldiers.
For information, tel: 850/922-6007.

The Capitol Complex in Tallahassee

A B Maclay State Gardens, *3540 Thomasville Road* (*Open* daily 8–dusk. Maclay House Jan–Apr, daily 9–5. *Admission: inexpensive*; tel: 850/487-4556) Just north of I–10, this is one of the loveliest gardens in Florida, founded by New York financier Alfred B Maclay in 1923. Maclay's creative landscaping combined native pines and oaks with a diverse selection of exotic imported species, all incorporated into a network of walks, paths, pools and lawns surrounding his house and stretching down to Lake Hall. The camellias (around 100 varieties) commence their flowering season in December, and the gardens are at the height of their beauty from January to April, when the furnished house is also open to the public. Big Pine Nature Trail winds through the woodlands around the lake, where visitors can picnic, boat and fish. Alligators and turtles have been spotted in the lake, and more than 150 species of birds and animals inhabit the woodlands.

Capitol Complex, *S Monroe (at Apalachee Parkway)* (*Open* Mon–Fri 9–4:30, Sat 10–4:30, Sun noon–4:30. *Admission free*; tel: 850/487-1902) The towering 22-storey New Capitol building (see panel opposite) may dominate Tallahassee's modest skyline, but the **Old Capitol** remains the curator of Florida's early legislative history. Time was of the essence when the original Capitol was constructed on this site in 1845. A half-century later it had to be completely remodelled by architect Frank P Milburn. Milburn's classical designs incorporated triangular tympana above the columned porticoes of the east and west entrances, which are embossed with pressed-metal reliefs of details from the state seal. Crowning the creation is a 136-foot (41m) dome with colourful stained-glass decoration. The distinctive candy-striped awnings also date from Milburn's day.

The building was further enlarged in 1923, housing the Senate Chamber at one end and the House of Representatives at the other, with the Supreme Court downstairs. The restored chambers have been furnished with authentic reproductions of the original wicker-seat armchairs, arranged in wide semicircles. In between, former offices house an excellent permanent history exhibit, illustrated with memorabilia, photographs and fascinating tales of early legislators and their times.

Museum of Florida History, *500 S Bronough Street* (*Open* Mon–Fri 9–4:30, Sat 10–4:30, Sun noon–4:30. *Admission free*; tel: 850/488-1484) Interesting and informative, this user-friendly jaunt through Florida history starts with geological relics and the skeleton of a giant prehistoric mastodon, then runs through sunken treasures salvaged from Spanish galleons and Civil War battle flags right through to the Roaring Twenties. You can go 'all aboard' a reconstructed steamboat for a 19th-century riverside view, or, in contrast, take a look at how an earlier generation set up 'tin can' holiday campsites in the first great tourist boom of the 1920s.

Park Avenue and Calhoun Street Historic Districts These gracious tree-shaded streets are lined with the homes and churches of Tallahassee's prominent 19th-century citizens. Walking tour brochures are available from the information centre in the New Capitol. Notable stops along the way include the 1830s Greek Revival-style **Columns**, *100 N Duval (at Park)*, the city's oldest surviving structure, moved from the site where it was put up by a Georgian banker, William 'Money' Wiliams. **Knott House Museum**, *301 Park* (*Open* Wed–Fri 1–4, Sat 10–4. *Admission: donation*; tel: 850/922-2459) is also known as 'The House that Rhymes' after its eccentric 1920s occupant Luella Knott, who decorated the antique furnishings with examples of her poetry, which she tied on with ribbons. It was on the steps of this house on 20 May, 1865 that General Edward McCook of the Union Army read out the Emancipation Proclamation. Also look out for the Brokaw-McDougall House, Virginia Street.

San Luis Archeological and Historic Site, *2020 Mission Road (at Ocala Road)* (*Open* Mon–Fri 9–4:30, Sat 10–4:30, Sun noon–4:30. *Admission free*; tel: 850/487-3711) This site, located on a hillside west of the downtown district, has a history as a Spanish mission and an Apalachee Native American village. So far, the digs have uncovered a wealth of archaeological relics, and the excavation work is still in progress. Recovered artefacts include pottery, weapons and jewellery.

The Spanish settlement was in existence in 1656 and contained a religious site. There also were houses built alongside a large Native American council house. The entire village was deliberately burned to the ground in 1704 to prevent it falling into British hands. There are special guided tours and events on Saturdays.

GOVERNMENT IN ACTION
The State Legislature in the New Capitol building is in session from March to May, and visitors can watch the proceedings in both chambers from viewing galleries on the sixth floor (*Open* Mon–Fri 9–11, 1–3, Sat–Sun 9–3. *Guided tours* on the hour. *Admission free*; tel: 850/413-9200). The 22nd-floor Observatory affords a panoramic view of the city, plus an exhibition gallery for mainly contemporary Floridian artists.

The Old Town Trolley

PICTORIAL HISTORY
One of 72 buildings across the United States constructed under the Works Progress Administration during the 1930s Depression years, the Old US Courthouse, 110 W Park Avenue, is well worth a quick stop for the humorous murals in its foyer. Laced with amusing detail, a series of gentle, tongue-in-cheek scenes illustrates the development of the state, from the Native Americans to the muskets and flags of the Spanish explorers and Civil War to the emancipated women golfers and sunseekers of the 1920s and 1930s.

Tallahassee Museum of History and Natural Science, *3945 Museum Drive (off Lake Bradford Road)* (*Open* Mon–Sat 9–5, Sun 12:30–5. *Admission: moderate*; tel: 850/575-8684) This excellent outdoor museum has a wide range of exhibits, from an 1880s-style Big Bend Farm to bobcats and brown bears. In a shady glade, the main farmhouse is surrounded by outbuildings, including a smithy, smokehouse and barn where farmyard animals are tended by staff in period costume. Cotton and cane grow in the garden and mules munch away in the stables.

A boardwalk trail spans a cypress swamp area on Lake Bradford and then continues around natural-habitat enclosures for alligators, Florida panthers, red foxes, skunks and white-tailed deer. The walk-through aviary provides interesting bird-spotting. A group of historic buildings includes an 1890s schoolroom, the 1850 Bellevue Plantation house and the Bethlehem Missionary Baptist Church, built in 1937 by one of Florida's first black Baptist congregations, founded in the 1850s. There are picnic and play areas as well as a gift shop.

Wakulla Springs State Park, *SR 267 at SR 61, 15 miles/24km south of Tallahassee* (*Open* daily 8–dusk. *Admission: inexpensive*; tel: 850/224-5950) At Wakulla, a state park since 1986, the freshwater springs are among the world's largest and deepest. The centre-piece of the 2,860-acre (1,160-ha) park is a pool above the main spring, which Native Americans called 'mysteries of strange water'. Some 600,000 gallons (2¾ million litres) of water per minute flow from an underground river into the 4½-acre (1.8-ha) pool, which is so astonishingly clear that even the deepest point (185 feet/56m below) is visible, as is the entrance to a subterranean cavern where mastodon bones have been discovered.

A glass-bottomed boat makes regular trips around the pool, and there are ample opportunties to see wildlife – another boat ferries passengers down the scenic Wakulla River, where deer, turtles, alligators and the abundant bird life along the riverbanks can be spotted. Nine species of herons and egrets, plus vultures, anhingas, kites and osprey nest and feed here all through the year – though the population swells dramatically during the winter migration. There is a swimming hole, nature trails, plus shaded picnic tables and barbecue grills, as well as accommodation and a restaurant.

Farming 1880s-style at the Tallahassee Museum of History and Natural Science

Drive

Into the Panhandle

See map on page 236.

This drive west into the central Panhandle from Tallahassee makes an equally good day trip or an off-interstate route halfway to Pensacola. Along the way there are opportunities for antiques shopping, discovering beautifully preserved antebellum houses, some underground exploration, picnics and a cooling swim.

Leave Tallahassee on N Monroe Street (US 27) and cross I–10. In Havana (11 miles/17km), continue one block from the intersection with SR 12 and park on Seventh Avenue.

Havana's tiny but attractive antiques district is a popular spot for browsers. Start at the Cannery, an old factory building given over to antiques dealers and artists' studios and galleries. Shops and indoor markets on Main Street offer easily portable mementos, such as vintage posters and *Time* magazines.

Retrace your route to SR 12 at Ninth Avenue; turn right (west). At the first traffic light in Quincy (11 miles/17km), turn left on Madison. The red-brick Chamber of Commerce is on the corner.

Explore **Quincy**'s elegant antebellum heritage on foot, with the Chamber of Commerce's excellent brochure *A Tour of Historic Quincy*. Founded in 1828, Quincy's fortunes were built on tobacco and on the Quincy State Bank's far-sighted investment in the fledgling Coca-Cola Company.

By the courthouse, turn right on US 90 (west) for 20 miles (32km).

The next landmark is **Chattahoochee**, which has a panoramic view of the central region's pine and oak forests. The **Apalachicola River** marks the change to Central Time (turn your watch back one hour). On **Victory Bridge**, look north for a view of the 6,130-foot (1,868m) **Jim Woodruff Hydroelectric Dam**, built in the late 1950s. This is a great fishing spot and a watersports centre. For a closer look, there is an observation point off to the right (2 miles/3km from Chattahoochee).

In Marianna (25 miles/40km from Chattahoochee), follow signs for the Florida Caverns.

Florida Caverns State Park reveals the very foundations of the state in a series of magnificent limestone caves cut into the plateau (see page 242).

Back at US 90, day trippers can head back to Tallahassee via the fast I–10 (turn left on US 90 and follow signs to the interstate). For Pensacola, turn right on US 90.

One last stop en route to Pensacola is a refreshing swim at **Ponce de León Springs State Recreation Area** (47 miles/75km). (See page 252.)

I–10 is just one mile from Ponce de León.

On the Apalachicola River

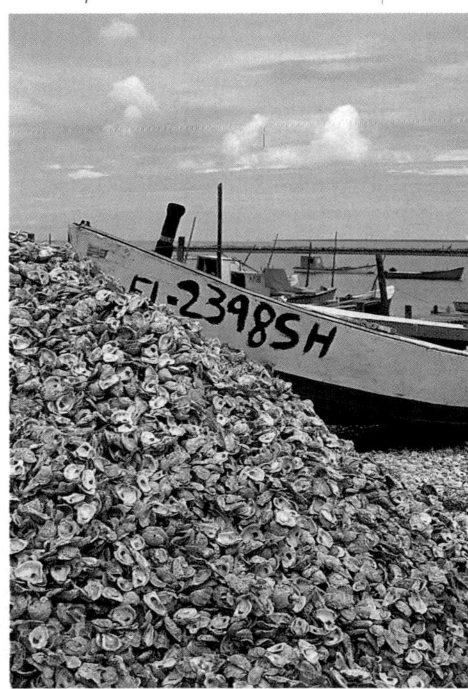

Arriving

Air routes Most North American airlines operate regular scheduled services to Florida from numerous destinations within the US and Canada.

The only direct scheduled flights from the UK are London to Miami and Orlando, though several airlines and tour operators offer direct charter flights and one-stop services from regional airports such as Luton, Manchester and Glasgow. From Eire, there are one-stop flights ex-Dublin.

One-stop flights are also available from New Zealand ex-Auckland; two-stop flights ex-Sydney, Melbourne and Brisbane from Australia.

Entry requirements UK, Irish, Australian and New Zealand residents with return or onward tickets on a business or holiday trip lasting less than 90 days no longer require a visa. Holders of full valid passports can fill out a visa waiver form issued by travel agents or at check-in to be handed to US immigration control on arrival.

Customs declarations must be filled in by all travellers arriving from outside the US. Fresh foods, agricultural products, items from Cuba, Cambodia, North Korea and Vietnam, obscene materials, lottery tickets (even though Florida has a lottery), chocolate liqueurs and pre-Columbian art will be confiscated on arrival.

Illegal drug smuggling is treated with severity, and penalties are harsh. There is no limit on currency brought into the US, but amounts exceeding US$5,000 (or their foreign equivalent) must be declared.

Duty-free customs allowances on arrival permit persons of 18 and over to import 200 cigarettes and 100 cigars (*not* Cuban); at 21 or over add one litre of drinking alcohol for personal use.

Ground transport Some hotels provide airport transfers, while car rental companies operate shuttle services to their parking lots. Otherwise there are local bus services, and a plentiful supply of taxis. Taxis are often worth the added expense for speed and convenience, and fares to downtown areas are usually reasonable. (For fuller details of transport into Miami, see page 84).

Major Florida airports
Daytona Beach (tel: 904/248-8030)
Fort Lauderdale (tel: 954/359-6100)
Jacksonville (tel: 904/741-2000)
Key West (tel: 305/296-7223)
Miami (tel: 305/876-7862)
Orlando (tel: 407/825 3887)
Palm Beach (tel: 561/471-7400)
Panama City–Bay County (tel: 850/763-6751)
St Petersburg/Clearwater (tel: 727/531-1451)
Southwest Florida/Fort Myers (tel: 941/768-1000)
Tampa (tel: 813/870-8700)

Camping

Camping is popular in Florida. There are privately run campgrounds, plus resort, national and state parks offering camping opportunities throughout the state. Facilities range from elaborate 'pull thru's' designed for RVs (recreational vehicles) to rustic backwoods campsites for hikers. Many campgrounds offer on-site trailer and tent hire, but it is advisable to make reservations in advance, particularly during the winter months.

The *Florida Camping Directory* lists some 200 member sites around the state together with information about their RV and camping facilities, plus listings covering on-site amenities such as pools, shopping and children's playgrounds. For a copy of the directory, contact the **Florida Association of RV Parks & Campgrounds**, 1340 Dickers Drive, Tallahassee, FL 32303 (tel: 850/562-7151). For information about camping in the state's parks, contact the **Florida Department of Environmental Protection**, Division of Recreation and Parks, Mail Station 535, 3900 Commonwealth Boulevard, Tallahassee, FL 32399-3000 (tel: 850/488-9872).

A popular option is to hire an RV from a local rental company. **Cruise America**, 5801 NW 151st Street, Miami Lakes (tel: 305/591-7511 or

Travel Facts

800/327-7799) provide local and one-way motorhome and van rentals from several gateway destinations within Florida. Services include airport transfers.

Children

Florida's informal lifestyle is a gift for families on the move. Many resorts and facilities make a special point of catering for the family market.

Hotels in every price bracket frequently offer free lodging for children up to 18 sharing a room with their parents, so look out for bargains.

Babies' and children's items such as baby foods and high factor sunblock are readily available at any grocery store or pharmacy. Larger theme parks provide a range of child services from changing rooms with all the requisite toiletries to strollers (pushchairs). While on the subject of theme parks, do take advantage of the child name tags often available at park information offices. Lost children can be speedily reunited with their family if the authorities know who to contact.

Perhaps the greatest danger to young children is the sun. Its rays can burn tender skin within a few minutes. If children are going to be exposed to the sunlight for any length of time, and that means sightseeing not just swimming and bathing, cover them liberally with sunscreen. Hats are essential for small children, while older, fashion-conscious young can generally be induced to cover up with a baseball cap.

Climate

Florida winters, especially in the southern part of the state, are normally mild. Except in the northern regions, winter temperatures seldom drop below freezing; snow is a rare event anywhere in Florida. The shoulder seasons of spring and autumn generally provide the best weather of all, ideal for sightseeing and sports. Summer days can be real scorchers. The early part of the summer is typically hot and dry. As summer progresses, high humidity and a pattern of almost daily afternoon thunderstorms sets in.

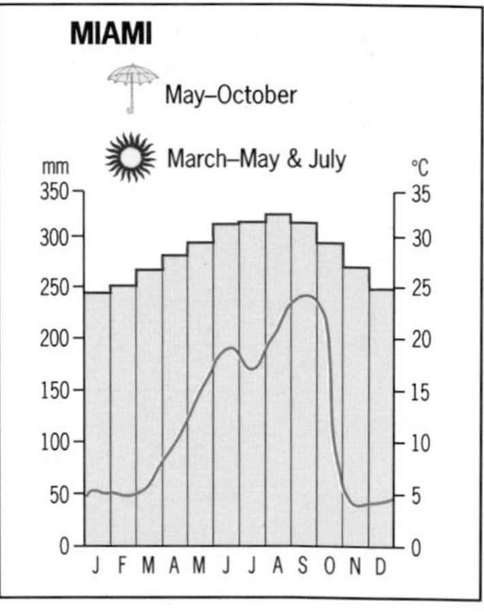

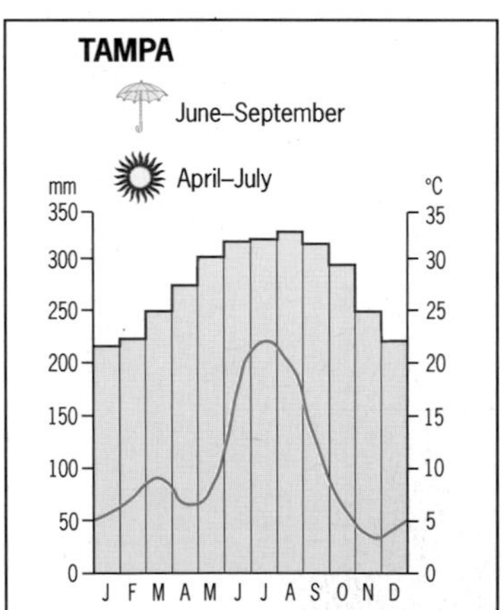

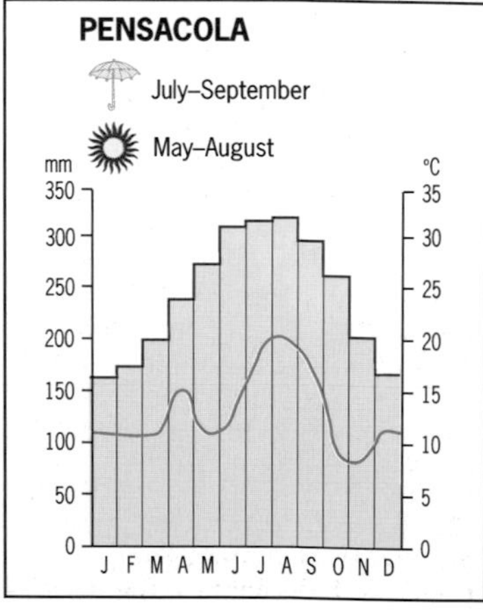

Crime

For the most part, Florida is as safe as anywhere in the world. Its notorious reputation is largely based on a handful of trouble spots such as the Overtown and Liberty City districts of Miami. These are definitely to be avoided. As in many cities, there are certain other areas which may be unsuitable for lone travellers, particularly women, and especially at night. Rather than take a chance, ask at hotel or motel desks if there are parts of the city which should not be visited for safety reasons, and follow this advice. When in doubt about an area do not explore alone; take a cab instead of walking.

Car travellers should take a few simple precautions which should prevent most problems.

- Consider a mobile phone rental if you are hiring a car. Most of the national operators offer this option.
- Keep the doors locked when driving through unfamiliar areas.
- Ignore any attempts by civilians (including hitch-hikers) to flag the car down.
- Lock all the doors and the boot when parking the car, and ensure packages, cameras and other valuables are out of sight.

In the event of an accident, find a well-lit telephone – petrol stations, shops or diners are recommended – and dial 911. This call is free, even at pay telephones, and will connect with law enforcement agencies within seconds.

Travellers with disabilities

Facilities for people with disabilities are widespread in the US, and Florida is no exception. Public buildings are required to have some form of access for the wheelchair-bound, and many public buses are now supplied with wheelchair lifts. Copies of the helpful brochure, *Florida Planning Companion for People*, can be obtained from the Florida Governor's Alliance, 345 S Magnolia Drive, Suite D-11, Tallahassee, FL 32301 (tel: 850/487-2223 or 850/847-2222 T.D.D., and local telephone directories list support groups for people with disabilities. The visually impaired, travelling with guide dogs, will find it relatively easy to take their dogs into attractions.

Most attractions accept visitors with disabilities, though viewing may be somewhat restricted and access to certain rides impossible or forbidden for safety reasons. Generally, efforts are made to provide tips, assistance and wheelchairs for visitors with disabilities.

Walt Disney World offers a useful *Guidebook for Guests with Disabilities*, and transport services are equipped with motorised platforms. Tours and specially equipped hotel rooms are available and should be booked well in advance. Avis, Hertz and National car rentals have a limited number of hand-controlled cars available. Again, early reservations are a must.

Useful contacts

Information about individual and group tours for travellers with disabilities is available from The Society for the Advancement of Travel for the Handicapped (tel: 212/447-7284; the Travel Information Service (tel: 215/456-9600); and members of Mobility International U.S.A. (tel: 503/343-1284).

Immigration laws covering the entry qualifications for mentally handicapped travellers to the US should be checked out in advance

Hollywood Boulevard, WDW

with a travel agent or directly with the US Embassy before departure.

Drinking

The sale and consumption of alcohol in bars, restaurants, stores and other public places is restricted to adults aged 21 and over. It is also illegal to have an opened can or bottle of an alcoholic beverage in a car.

Driving

Hiring a car Car hire in Florida is cheaper than anywhere else in the US. Car hire companies are located throughout the state, with concessions at major airports and some hotels. Car hire companies operating in Florida include:

Alamo, tel: 800/327-9633
Avis, tel: 800/331-1212
Budget, tel: 800/527-0700
Dollar, tel: 800/800-4000
Hertz, tel: 800/654-3131
National Interrent, tel: 800/227-7368
Thrifty, tel: 800/367 2277

The minimum age limit for a driver's licence in Florida is 16; the minimum car hire limit is 21, though many companies impose the limit at 25. Arranging car hire in advance can prevent the latter restriction from ruining a holiday. Additions to the basic hire charge include CDW (Collision Damage Waiver), which covers damage to the vehicle, and a small state tax; both of these are charged on a daily basis. Full insurance is also available. Credit cards are the preferred method of payment, otherwise a large cash deposit will be required. Major airlines and tour companies offer a wide range of good value fly-drive packages which conveniently tie up all these details in advance.

In general, foreign nationals can drive and hire a car in the US for a period of up to one year with a valid full driver's licence from their country of origin, provided they have held it for one year.

Before setting off in an unfamiliar rented car, check all the systems. Power steering is common even in the lowest range cars; be aware of central locking; and beware of automatic seat-belts which pinion unsuspecting drivers and front seat passengers to their seats as the doors shut.

Sunshine Skyway, Tampa

Fuel Gas (petrol) is cheap. It is sold by the US gallon (3¾ litres), and hire cars generally run on unleaded gas available in three grades. At many self-service gas stations it is necessary to pay first (or leave a credit card with the cashier) to release the pump.

Rules and regulations

- Driving is on the right.
- Speed limits on interstate roads and highways are set at 55mph (88kph), with some exceptions where the limit is raised to 65mph (105kph). In built-up areas limits vary between 20 and 40mph (32–64kph).
- In Florida it is legal to turn right on a red light unless posted otherwise. The car must come to a complete halt before turning. In built-up areas avoid the right-hand lane unless intending to turn right.
- Parking can be a problem. Look for designated metered parking places or find a car park. Illegally parked vehicles are ticketed and/or towed away with remarkable alacrity.

Electricity

The electrical current in the US is 110 volts AC; most sockets are designed for two-pronged plugs. Most

European visitors will need an adaptor for their electrical appliances; these can be purchased from some electrical goods stores, or ask at the front desk of large tourist hotels.

Emergencies
Dial: 911
Emergency help is easily summoned in the US by the use of this single number. An operator or despatcher will connect calls to the appropriate emergency service including the police and fire departments, ambulance and medical services. To ensure the emergency services arrive as quickly as possible, give accurate directions including the street name and nearest cross-section together with any further details to assist them.

On interstate highways, call boxes have been installed every quarter to half mile. These boxes allow callers to alert police, ambulance and mechanical services without dialling 911.

Etiquette
In general Floridians are so laid back and welcoming it is difficult to imagine how to offend them. Certainly the dress code for restaurants and social gatherings is informal to a degree, but this does not apply on the beach. Topless sun-bathing for women is actually illegal, though allowances are made for bare-breasted visitors on certain sections of the beach in more risqué resort areas such as Miami. Do not try this around the hotel swimming pool, or on a family beach in the Panhandle. Check out local reaction with a discreet enquiry at the hotel.

Smokers in Florida will find the atmosphere a lot more friendly than in health-crazed California. Some restaurants, particularly of the family variety, will provide both smoking areas for addicts of the weed and non-smoking areas. Cinemas, public transport, elevators and most public buildings are smoke-free zones.

Health
There is no national health system to provide medical cover for foreign citizens visiting the US, and private health care is exorbitantly expensive. Therefore, it is vital for foreign travellers to arrange health insurance before they leave home. Travel agents and tour companies can provide information and arrange a policy. Keep all insurance documents in a safe place.

For minor ailments, pharmacies (drugstores) are plentiful and usually open between 9 and 9; most larger towns and cities have walk-in medical and dental clinics listed in the telephone directory.

Sunburn is a common complaint, and a chronic case of it is agony. So do not underestimate the sun's power reflected off sand and sea.

- Use plenty of sunscreen.
- Wear a hat.
- Restrict the time you spend in the sun, at least on the first few days.
- Drink plenty (not alcohol, which is dehydrating).

Hitch-hiking
The best advice is not to do it, and do not pick up hitch-hikers either. In legal terms, hitch-hiking is forbidden on toll roads and interstates, and throughout the Florida Keys.

Lost property
For lost property in hotels, check with the front desk or hotel security. Cab companies and public transport telephone numbers are listed in local telephone directories.

Lost or stolen travellers' cheques and credit cards should be reported to the issuing company immediately (keep a list of the numbers) and to the police.

The police should also be informed of lost travel documents, and it is advisable to obtain a police report about valuable items for insurance claims.

Maps
Car hire companies supply basic maps, but for extensive touring it is a good idea to pick up large-scale maps, such as the Rand McNally series, from a bookshop. (If you are lost in a city, it may help to remember that most cities' **avenues** run north–south and **streets** east–west.)

CONVERSION CHARTS

FROM	TO	MULTIPLY BY
Inches	Centimetres	2.54
Centimetres	Inches	0.3937
Feet	Metres	0.3048
Metres	Feet	3.2810
Yards	Metres	0.9144
Metres	Yards	1.0940
Miles	Kilometres	1.6090
Kilometres	Miles	0.6214
Acres	Hectares	0.4047
Hectares	Acres	2.4710
Gallons	Litres	4.5460
Litres	Gallons	0.2200
Ounces	Grams	28.35
Grams	Ounces	0.0353
Pounds	Grams	453.6
Grams	Pounds	0.0022
Pounds	Kilograms	0.4536
Kilograms	Pounds	2.205
Tons	Tonnes	1.0160
Tonnes	Tons	0.9842

MEN'S SUITS

UK	36	38	40	42	44	46	48
Rest of Europe	46	48	50	52	54	56	58
US	36	38	40	42	44	46	48

DRESS SIZES

UK	8	10	12	14	16	18
France	36	38	40	42	44	46
Italy	38	40	42	44	46	48
Rest of Europe	34	36	38	40	42	44
US	6	8	10	12	14	16

MEN'S SHIRTS

UK	14	14.5	15	15.5	16	16.5	17
Rest of Europe	36	37	38	39/40	41	42	43
US	14	14.5	15	15.5	16	16.5	17

MEN'S SHOES

UK	7	7.5	8.5	9.5	10.5	11
Rest of Europe	41	42	43	44	45	46
US	8	8.5	9.5	10.5	11.5	12

WOMEN'S SHOES

UK	4.5	5	5.5	6	6.5	7
Rest of Europe	38	38	39	39	40	41
US	6	6.5	7	7.5	8	8.5

Chambers of Commerce and local visitor information centres publish and distribute local maps, walking tour brochures, and information on bicycle routes. State and national parks issue maps of scenic drives, hiking routes and interpretive trails on admission.

Visit Florida will provide state maps on application to its head office in Tallahassee or at its offices abroad (see **Tourist information**, page 269).

Media

Newspapers Most Florida communities produce weekly bulletins, while the main cities all have their own daily newspapers such as the *Miami Herald*, *Orlando Sentinel*, *Tampa Tribune* and Jacksonville's *Florida Times-Union*. The national daily *USA Today* is widely available from self-service news bins in every town; the *New York Times* and *Wall Street Journal* can be found at news-stands. A small selection of foreign newspapers may be available in tourist areas.

Television and radio There is hardly a motel or hotel room in the state without a television, though chi-chi bed and breakfasts tend not to permit them amongst the Victoriana. The least sophisticated offer no less than six to eight channels; if a hotel shells out for cable stations such as HBO or Cinemax, the choice increases dramatically. Among the main stations are CNN for continuous news reports, and ESPN for sports.

Radio stations abound with a wide range of formats such as hard or soft rock, easy listening and country-and-western, broken up by news, weather bulletins and commercials.

Money matters

Foreign visitors should invest in US dollar travellers' cheques. Foreign currency is extremely difficult to exchange throughout the US. US travellers' cheques and major credit cards (American Express, Carte Blanche, Diners Club, MasterCard, Visa) can be used for most transactions from buying gas to paying restaurant bills.

For non-US visitors here is a rundown on the currency. The dollar is divided into 100 cents. Dollar bills are all green ($1, 5, 10, 20, 50, 100) so look carefully before spending; coins are half a dollar (50 cents), a quarter (25 cents), a dime (10 cents), a nickel (5 cents), and one cent.

Local taxes, which vary throughout the state, are levied on a range of items including clothes, books, sightseeing attractions, restaurant meals and accommodation. The tax may not appear on the price tag.

National holidays
New Year's Day 1 January
Martin Luther King's Birthday 15 January
President's Day February (third Monday)
Good Friday
Memorial Day May (last Monday)
Independence Day 4 July
Labor Day September (first Monday)
Columbus Day October (second Monday)
Veterans' Day 11 November
Thanksgiving November (fourth Thursday)
Christmas Day 25 December

Opening hours
Banks: Monday to Thursday 9–3, Friday 9–5.
Drugstores: daily 9–9, some are open 24 hours.
Offices: Monday to Friday 8 or 9–5 or 6.
Shops: Supermarkets, Monday to Saturday 8–9, Sunday 8–7; some are open 24 hours; downtown, Monday to Friday 10–6, Saturday 10–1 or 6; malls, Monday to Saturday 10–9, Sunday 10–6.

Organised tours
With Florida's many miles of coastline and proximity to offshore islands, the most obvious opportunity for touring is taking a cruise. These range from two-hour cruises to week-long (or longer) trips to the Bahamas, the Caribbean, and beyond.

Many of these longer trips depart from Miami, but shorter excursions – one-day, half-day or evening cruises – depart from many places in the state. A few of the shorter trips offer casino gambling on board. For information about local cruises, contact the Visitors and Convention Bureau where you are staying.

Street bar, Miami

Places of worship
Most communities have churches of several denominations. Contact the local Chamber of Commerce.

Police
Law enforcement in the US is divided into three main jurisdictions: **City Police** within the urban areas; the **Sheriff** outside the city limits; and the **Highway Patrol**, who handle traffic accidents and offences beyond the city limits. Other agencies also deal with specific areas of law enforcement such as drugs and major criminal investigations.

In an emergency dial **911** for all services. Non-emergency police numbers are listed in local telephone directories.

Post offices
Post office hours vary, but in most places are 9 to 4.30 or 5 on weekdays. Some are open on Saturday mornings. Postage stamps may be purchased at hotels and drugstores as well as post offices. Keep small change for stamp machines.

US Mail boxes are blue bins on legs on the sidewalk.

Public transport
The most popular method of transport on the ground is, without

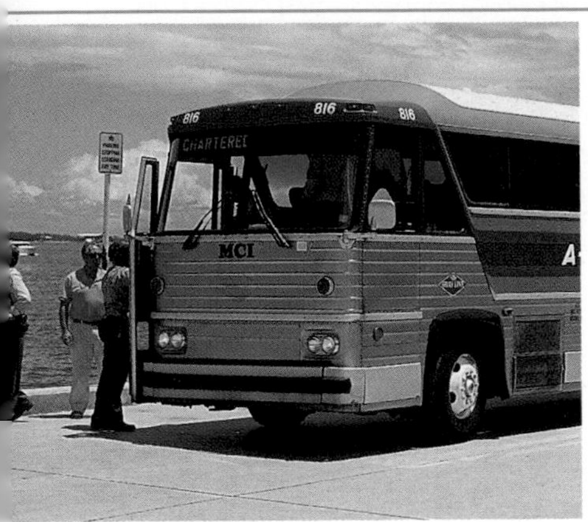

Interstate bus

doubt, the car (see **Driving**). For alternative, though less-convenient travel options, check out **Greyhound** which connects with more than 100 Florida destinations. **Amtrak** serves Miami, Jacksonville, Orlando, Tallahassee, Tampa, and 35 other stops.

Amtrak, 60 NE Massachusetts Avenue, Washington, DC 20002, tel: 202/906-3000 or 800/TELTRAK. Greyhound Lines Inc., PO Box 660606, Dallas, TX 75248, tel: 972/789-7000.

Taxi cabs can be picked up at airports, bus and train stations, or from major hotels. They tend not to cruise the streets looking for fares so you'll have to call for one.

Senior citizens
Many hotels, resorts, restaurants and attractions offer seniors discounts or special rates. Be sure to ask if no information is on display.

Sports and recreation
Regional visitor information bureaus can provide a wealth of information about sporting and recreational opportunities in their areas. For statewide information, contact the **Florida Sports Foundation**, 2964 Wellington Circle N., Tallahassee, FL 32308, tel: 850/488-8347; www.flasports.com. For information about state park facilities, contact the Department of Environmental Protection, Division of Recreation and Parks, Mail Station 535, 3900 Commonwealth Boulevard, Tallahassee, FL 32399-3000, tel: 850/488-9872; www.dep.state.fl.us/parks.

Student and youth travel
Florida has a limited number of youth hostels in prime locations, such as Miami Beach, Key West, Clearwater Beach and Orlando.

For information on affiliated properties, contact Hosteling International, 733 15th Street NW, Suite 840, Washington DC 20005, tel: 202/783-6161, or overseas branches of the Youth Hostel Association.

Telephones
Florida's telephone system is divided between half a dozen companies. Overseas visitors should note that some of these do not route overseas calls: AT&T and ITT do. The simplest solution is to call overseas collect via the operator (dial 0), who can also place telephone credit card calls (overseas credit cards are valid). To dial direct from a coin box (dial 011 + country code + area code + telephone number) bring at least $6-worth of quarters, dimes and nickels. This is an appalling juggling operation. Calling from a hotel room will cost more, but it can be worth the time and energy saved.

Codes At present Florida is divided into eight area codes. To call within the area code dial 1 + telephone number; to call outside the area code dial 1 + area code + number. All 800 and 888 (toll free) numbers must be prefixed with 1, ie 1 + 800 + telephone number. To call home from anywhere in Florida, you will need first to dial 011 to access an international line. Then dial the access code for the country: 44 for the UK, 353 for Eire, 61 for Australia, 64 for New Zealand.

Time
Florida has two time zones. Most of the state operates on Eastern Standard Time (GMT -5), while the Panhandle region west of the Apalachicola River keeps Central Standard Time (GMT-6). All clocks

go forward one hour for Daylight Saving between the first Sunday in April and the last in October.

Tipping
The standard tip for a restaurant bill or a taxi ride is 20 per cent; 15–20 per cent for full-service wait staff; and $1 per bag for bellboys, airport porters and doormen.

Tourist information
Most towns throughout Florida have a Chamber of Commerce. Major cities have Convention and Visitors Bureaus that will answer visitors' inquiries. For more information in advance of traveling, you should contact Visit Florida, the U.S.T.T.A. (U.S. Travel & Tourism Administration) or any of the main regional offices whose addresses and websites are listed as follows:

Visit Florida, 661 E Jefferson Street, Suite 300, Tallahassee, FL 32301, tel: 850/488-5607; www.flausa.com; (Canada) Taurus House, 512 Duplex Avenue, Toronto, Ontario M4R 2E3, tel: 416/485-2573; e-mail: jlutz@thermgroup.ca; (UK/Europe) Roebuck House, 1 Palace Street, London SW1E 5BA, tel: 020-7630 6602; e-mail: cbrodie@flausa.com

Daytona Beach Area Convention & Visitors Bureau, 126 E Orange Avenue, P.O. Box 910, Daytona Beach, FL 32114, tel: 904/255-0415 or 800/854-1234; www.daytonabeachcvb.org

Emerald Coast Convention & Visitors Bureau, PO Box 609, Fort Walton Beach, FL 32549-0609, tel: 850/651-7131 or 800/322-3319; www.destin-fwb.com

Florida Keys and Key West, 1201 White Street, #102, Key West, FL 33041-0866, tel: 305/296-1552 or 800/FLA KEYS; www.fla-keys.com

Florida's Space Coast Office of Tourism, 8810 Astronaut Boulevard, Cape Canaveral, FL 32920-4204, tel: 321/868-1126 or 800/USA 1969; www.space-coast.com

Greater Fort Lauderdale Convention & Visitors Bureau, 1850 Eller Drive, Suite 303, Fort Lauderdale, FL 33316, tel: 954/765-4466 or 800/356-1662; www.sunny.org

Greater Miami Convention & Visitors Bureau, 701 Brickell Avenue, Suite 2700, Miami, FL 33131, tel: 305/539-3000; www.miamiandbeaches.com

Jacksonville and The Beaches Convention & Visitors Bureau, 201 E Adams Street, Jacksonville, FL 32202, tel: 904/798-9111 or 800/733-2668; www.jaxcvb.com

Lee Island Coast Visitor & Convention Bureau, 2180 W First Street, Suite 100, Fort Myers, FL 33901, tel: 941/338-3500 or 800/237-6444; www.LeeIslandCoast.com

Naples/The Tourism Alliance of Collier County, 1400 Gulf Shore Boulevard N, Suite 123A, Naples, FL 34102, tel: 941/263-3666 or 800/605-7878; www.visit-naples.com

Orlando/Orange County Convention & Visitors Bureau, 6700 Forum Drive, Suite 100, Orlando, FL 32821-8087, tel: 407/363-5842 or 800/257-0060; www.go2orlando.com/cvb

Palm Beach County Convention & Visitors Bureau, 1555 Palm Beach Lakes Boulevard, Suite 204, West Palm Beach, FL 33401, tel: 561/471-3995 or 800/833-5733; www.palmbeachfla.com

Panama City Beach Convention & Visitors Bureau, PO Box 9473, Panama City Beach, FL 32417, tel: 850/233-5070 or 800/PCBEACH; www.panamacitybeachfl.com

Pensacola Convention & Visitors Information Center, 1401 E Gregory Street, Pensacola, FL 32501, tel: 850/434-1234 or 800/874-1234; www.visitpensacola.com

St. Johns County Visitors & Convention Bureau, 88 Riberia Street, St Augustine, FL 32084, tel: 904/829-1711; www.oldcity.com

St. Petersburg/Clearwater Area Convention & Visitors Bureau, 14450 46th Street N, #108, Clearwater, FL 33762, tel: 727/464-7200; www.floridasbeach.com

Sarasota Convention & Visitors Bureau, 655 N Tamiami Trail, Sarasota, FL 34236, tel: 941/955-0991 or 800/800 3906; www.sarasotafl.org

Tampa/Hillsborough Convention & Visitors Association, 400 N Tampa Street, Tampa, FL 33602, tel: 813/223-1111; www.gotampa.com

HOTELS

The choice of accommodation in Florida is enormous, varied and good value. You can save money by visiting Florida out of season (April to December) when prices plummet by as much as half. The exception is the Panhandle region and the northern East Coast, the only bit of Florida to feel the cold in winter, where prices are lower in October to May. Florida accommodation is generally spacious, with room for up to four people in some double rooms. There is often no charge for children under 18 sharing with their parents.

Rooms with self-catering facilities (called efficiencies) can be found in budget or moderately priced hotels and motels. Apartments are an excellent solution for families, though most require a minimum stay of three to seven days. Families should also look for hotel resorts. Many resorts now offer special children's programmes.

MIAMI

Expensive

Biltmore Hotel
1200 Anastasia Avenue, Coral Gables
tel: 305/445-1926 or 800/727-1926; www.biltmorehotel.com
279 spacious rooms in a luxurious Mediterranean Revival landmark. Elegant restaurants, tennis, golf, pool, fitness center.

Cavalier
1320 Ocean Drive, Miami Beach
tel: 305/604-5000 or 800/OUT–POST; www.islandlife.com
45 rooms/suites in Art Deco District gem remodelled in 1930s style.

Delano Hotel
1685 Collins Avenue, Miami Beach
tel: 305/672-2000 or 800/555-5001
208 rooms on the beach in one of Miami's coolest hotels; a popular haunt of visiting celebs. Restaurant, pool, fitness, women's rooftop bath-house.

Doral Golf Resort and Spa
4400 NW 87th Avenue tel: 305/592-2000 or 800/71-DORAL; www.doralgolf.com
Superb complex with 694 rooms and suites, five golf courses and Golf Learning Centre, tennis, swimming pool, restaurants, night-club child care.

Fontainebleau Hilton Resort and Towers
4441 Collins Avenue, Miami Beach
tel: 305/538-2000 or 800/548-8886; www.fontainebleauhilton.com
Monster jewel in Miami Beach's crown. 1,206 rooms and suites on 20 oceanfront acres. Tennis, watersports, seven restaurants, nightclubs.

Loews Miami Beach
1601 Collins Avenue, Miami Beach
tel: 305/604-1601; www.loewshotel.com
800 rooms in an elegant Mediterranean beachfront property with an art deco annex in the adjacent St Moritz Hotel and exemplary service.

Sonesta Beach Resort
350 Ocean Drive, Key Biscayne
tel: 305/361-2021 or 800/SONESTA; www.sonesta.com
304 rooms and suites in luxurious beachfront resort; tennis, water sports, free children's entertainment programme.

The Tides
1220 Ocean Drive, Miami Beach
tel: 305/604-5000 or 800/OUT–POST; www.islandoutpost.com
Ultra-chic showcase of the art deco boutique hotel group, Island Outpost. 45 rooms/suites with ocean views. Restaurants, pool and a fitness centre.

Moderate

Avalon/Majestic Hotel
700 Ocean Drive, Miami Beach
tel: 305/538-0133 or 800/933-3306
108 rooms in the heart of the Art Deco District in a deco building with modern amenities and restaurant facing the beach.

Bay Harbor Inn & Suites
9660 E Bay Harbor Drive, Bay Harbor Islands/Miami Beach tel: 305/868-4141; www.bayharborinn.com
46 attractive rooms and suites on Indian Creek waterfront; pool, good restaurants, complimentary breakfast served on a yacht.

Essex House Hotel
1001 Collins Avenue, Miami Beach
tel: 305/534-2700 or 800/553-7739; www.southbeachresorts.com
79 pastel-painted and refurbished rooms in a notable art deco hotel a block from the beach. Close to shopping and dining.

Governor Hotel
435 21st Street, Miami Beach
tel: 305/532-2100 or 800/542-0444; www.sunshinehotels.com
125 attractive, well-priced rooms one block from the ocean near the Convention Center. Pool; dining; walking distance to Lincoln Road shops.

Hotel Place St Michel
162 Alcazar Avenue, Coral Gables
tel: 305/444-1666 or 800/848-4683; www.hotelplacestmichel.com
Charming 27-room hotel on the expensive side of moderate. Ceiling fans, antiques, award-winning restaurant. Sundeck, pool, fitness.

Miami River Inn
118 SW South River Drive
tel: 305/325-0045 or 800/HOTEL-89; www.miamiriverinn.com
Historic B&B complex with 40 individual rooms furnished with antiques, close to downtown. Gardens and pool.

Budget

Banana Bungalow Beach – Hotel & Hostel
2360 Collins Avenue, Miami Beach
tel: 305/538-1951 or 800/746-7835; www.bananabungalow.com
85 budget dorms and rooms in tropical gardens across the street from the beach. Restaurants, bar and kitchen; pool, fitness.

Clay Hotel and International Hostel
1438 Washington Avenue, Miami Beach
tel: 305/534-2988 or 800/379-CLAY; www.clayhotel.com
Beach bargain, 80 rooms in the Art Deco District.

Hotels & Restaurants

Ocean Surf Hotel
7436 Ocean Terrace, Miami Beach
tel: 305/866-1648 or 800/555-0411; www.oceansurf.com
49 rooms in a charming family operated art deco hotel modelled on an ocean liner with porthole windows out to sea. Close to shopping and dining.
Park Washington Resort
1020–1050 Washington Avenue, Miami Beach
tel: 305/674-1930 or 888/424-1930; www.parkwashington.com
Four art deco hotels offering 150 rooms (some with kitchen) two blocks from the ocean. Gardens, pool, bike rentals; significant gay clientele.
Pelican Creek Hotel
6580 Indian Creek Drive, Miami Beach
tel: 305/868-2285 or 800/588-7918
45 spacious units (half with kitchens) which are a good option for families or groups. Two blocks from the beach; close to shopping and dining.

THE KEYS AND EVERGLADES

Expensive

Banana Bay Resort & Marina
2319 N Roosevelt Boulevard, Key West (MM2)
tel: 305/296-6925 or 800/226-2621; www.bananabay.com
50 spacious rooms/suites in small resort north of town. Excellent watersports facilities, dive shop, private beach, pool, fitness and spa.
Cheeca Lodge
MM 82.5, Islamorada tel: 305/664-4651 or 800/327-2888; www.cheeca.com
203 units in famous resort complex. Golf, tennis, fishing, watersports, fine dining, and kids' activities.
Marquesa Hotel
600 Fleming Street, Key West
tel: 305/292-1919 or 800/869-4631; www.marquesa.com
27 rooms in a collection of beautifully restored and furnished old Key West houses set in lovely gardens. Two pools; excellent casual restaurant.
The Moorings
123 Beach Road, Islamorada
tel: 305/664-4708
18 traditional Keys-style apartments (and a three-bedroom house) in charming, small, quiet grounds with gardens, beach, pool and tennis.
Westin Beach Resort
MM 97, Key Largo tel: 305/852-5553 or 800/539-5274; www.1800keylargo.com
Private beach, watersports, pools, tennis, four restaurants, children's activities; 200 rooms/suites.

Moderate

Faro Blanco Marine Resort
MM 48.2, Marathon tel: 305/743-9018 or 800/759-3276; http://florida–keys.fl.us/faroblan.htm
Ocean and bayfront hotel-marina complex with 60-plus units from houseboats and cottages to condos. Pool, dive shop, dining.
Flamingo Lodge Marina & Outpost Resort
Flamingo Lodge Highway, Flamingo
tel: 941/695-3101 or 800/600-3813; www.amfac.com
103 rooms and 24 cottages; pool, marina, restaurant.
Key Lime Inn
725 Truman Avenue, Key West
tel: 305/294-5229 or 800/549-4430; www.keylimeinn.com
Appealing Bahama-style cottage complex with 37 well-equipped rooms two blocks from Duval; pool.
Largo Lodge Motel
MM 101.5, Key Largo tel: 305/451-0424 or 800/IN THE SUN; www.largolodge.com
Seven efficiencies set in a tropical garden; air-conditioning, screened porches (minimum age 16).
Lime Tree Bay Resort
MM 68.5, Long Key tel: 305/664-4740 or 800/723-4519; www.limetreebayresort.com
30 units (some with kitchens) in attractive bayside gardens. Watersports, barbeque grills, hammocks.
Marina del Mar Resort and Marina
MM 100, Key Largo tel: 305/451-4107 or 800/451-3483; www.marinadelmar.com
76 rooms, suites, and villas in bayside resort and oceanside marina. Dive packages, watersports, tennis, dining and dancing.
Southernmost Motel
1319 Duval Street, Key West
tel: 305/296-6577 or 800/354-4455; www.oldtownresorts.com
127 rooms in tropical setting. Pool-side tiki bar; near restaurants and nightlife.

Budget

Accommodations Key West by Greg O'Berry
701 Caroline Street, Key West
tel: 305/294-6639 or 800/654-2781
Holiday rentals from Key West through Big Pine Key. Condos, cottages, and family houses.
The Grand
1116 Grinnell Street, Key West
tel: 305/294-0590 or 888/947-2630; www.keywestparadise.com
Ten rooms/suites (with kitchenettes) in spruce and friendly guesthouse. Terrific value.
Island Bay Resort
MM 92.5, Tavernier tel: 305/852-4087 or 800/654-5397; www.islandfun.com/islandbay
Ten small guesthouse/efficiencies in complex; dive boat and dock.
Parmer's Place Cottages
MM 29, Little Torch Key tel: 305/872-2157
44 spotless units (rooms, efficiencies, and apartments); family friendly atmosphere and staff; pool.
Ragged Edge Resort & Marina
MM 86.5, 243 Treasure Harbor Road, Islamorada tel: 305/852-5389 or 800/436-2023; www.ragged-edge.com
Ten oceanfront, wood-panelled units with decks or porches in two-storey buildings. Pool; kitchens.

CENTRAL FLORIDA

Expensive

Hyatt Regency Grand Cypress
1 Grand Cypress Boulevard, Orlando
tel: 407/239-1234 or 800/233-1234; www.hyatt.com
725 rooms, with tennis, golf, equestrian and fitness centres, nature reserve.

Portfino Bay
Universal Orlando, 5601 Universal Boulevard, Orlando tel: 407/224-7117 or 877/837-2273; www.uescape.com
795 luxurious rooms and suites in a pretty pastel Italian-themed resort. Pools, dining, health club.

WDW, **Grand Floridian Beach Resort**, **Polynesian Resort** (Magic Kingdom), **Dolphin, Swan, Yacht** and **Beach Club Resorts** (Epcot), **Wilderness Lodge**
Central Reservations, Box 10100, Lake Buena Vista, FL 32830 tel: 407/934-7639
Spacious family rooms, excellent facilities, dining, and transportation to parks.

Wyndham Palace Resort & Spa
1900 Buena Vista Drive, Lake Buena Vista tel: 407/827-2727; www.wyndham.com
1,014 deluxe rooms; pool, fitness, golf, tennis, restaurants, transport to WDW.

Moderate

Best Western Suite Resort – on Lake Cecile
4786 W Irlo Bronson Memorial Highway, Kissimmee tel: 407/396-2056 or 800/468-3027; www.bestwesternhotelfl.com
159 efficiency suites on lakeside close to WDW; pool, tennis, watersports, breakfast, grocery service.

Cabot Lodge Bed and Breakfast
3726 SW 40th Boulevard, Gainesville tel: 352/375-2400 or 800/843-8735
208 modern rooms off I–75; pool, fitness center, complimentary breakfast.

Chalet Suzanne
3800 Chalet Suzanne Drive (off CR 17A), 4½ miles north of Lake Wales tel: 941/676-6011 or 800/433-6011; www.chaletsuzanne.com
30 rooms in country inn on lake. Good restaurant.

Herlong Mansion
Cholokka Boulevard, Micanopy tel: 352/466-3322 or 800/437-5664
12 B&B rooms in antebellum mansion. Home-cooked breakfasts; charming historic village.

Radisson Resort Parkway
2900 Parkway Boulevard, Kissimmee tel: 407/396-7000 or 800/634-4774; www.radisson.com.kissimmeefl
712 large, bright rooms; pool, dining, free theme park transportation, kids-eat-free programme.

Seven Sisters
820 SE Fort King Street, Ocala tel: 352/867-1170 or 800/250-3496
Eight antiques-filled B&B rooms in a delightful Queen Anne-style house.

WDW Caribbean Beach Resort, Port Orleans, Dixie Landings
Central Reservations, Box 10100, Lake Buena Vista, FL 32830 tel: 407/934-7639; www.disneyworld.com
Caribbean/Deep South themed resort hotels; great Disney facilities at moderate prices.

Budget

CRS – Orlando Central Reservations Service
220 Lookout Place, Suite 200, Maitland, FL 32751 tel: 407/740-6442 or 800/548-3311; www.reservation-services.com

Econo Lodge Maingate Hawaiian Resort
7514 W Irlo Bronson Memorial Highway, Kissimmee tel: 407/396-2000 or 800/365-6935; www.enjoyfloridahotels.com
445 rooms with tropical theme; close to WDW; heated pool and whirlpool; dining, car rental.

Hojo Inn Maingate East
6051 W Irlo Bronson Memorial Highway, Kissimmee tel: 407/396-1748 or 800/288-4678; www.hojomge.com
367 rooms in sprawling chain hotel with swimming pools, free transport to WDW, close to shops and restaurants.

Unicorn Inn
8 S Orlando Avenue, Kissimmee tel: 407/846-1200 or 800/865-7212; www.touristguide.com/b&b/florida/unicorn
Ten rooms in friendly English B&B. Restored historic home downtown.

WDW All-Star Sports Movies and Music Resorts
Central Reservations, Box 10100, Lake Buena Vista, FL 32830 tel: 407/934-7639; www.disneyworld.com
5,760 rooms in Disney's three budget-priced resorts. Family friendly; good facilities.

WDW Fort Wilderness Resort and Campground
Central Reservations, Box 10100, Lake Buena Vista, FL 32830 tel: 407/934-7639; www.disneyworld.com
784 campsites and 408 one-bedroom cabins (sleep 4–6). Woodland setting; great facilities.

THE GOLD COAST

Expensive

Boca Raton Resort & Club
501 E Camino Real, Boca Raton tel: 561/447-3000 or 800/327-0101
963 deluxe rooms in superb Mizner/modern creation; golf, pools, tennis, health club, restaurants.

The Breakers
1 S County Road, Palm Beach tel: 561/655-6611 or 888/273-2537; www.thebreakers.com
572-room landmark on the ocean; golf, tennis, croquet, fine dining.

Colony Hotel
155 Hammon Avenue, Palm Beach tel: 561/655-5430 or 800/521-5525; www.thecolonypalmbeach.com
100 classy rooms between the beach and Worth Avenue; pool, fitness, restaurant.

Hyatt Regency Pier 66
2301 SE 17th Street, Fort Lauderdale tel: 954/525-6666 or 800/327-3796; www.hyatt.com
388 rooms and suites downtown. Pool, fitness room; California Café dining room.

The Pillars
111 N Birch Road, Fort Lauderdale tel: 954/467-9639 or 800/800-7666; www.pillarshotel.com
Elegantly appointed 23-room property a block from the ocean on New River Sound. Pool; charming service.

Moderate

A Little Inn by the Sea
4546 El Mar Drive, Lauderdale-by-the-Sea
tel: 954/772-2450 or 800/492-0311; www.alittleinn.com
Delightful 37-unit B&B on the ocean with views, pool, some efficiencies and cosmopolitan clientele.

Hollywood Beach Resort Hotel
101 N Ocean Drive, Hollywood
tel: 954/921-0990 or 800/331-6103
360 rooms and studios with art deco touches; pool, tennis, fitness, restaurants, shopping, child care.

Lago Mar Resort Hotel & Club
1700 S Ocean Lane, Fort Lauderdale
tel: 954/523-6511 or 800/524-6627
Attractive beachfront complex with 212 rooms and suites; pools, tennis, mini-golf, restaurant.

Manta Ray Inn
1715 S. Surf Road, Hollywood
tel: 954/921-9666 or 800/255-0595; www.mantarayinn.com
12 spacious, fully equipped apartments right on the beach and close to Hollywood's shops, restaurants and sports facilities.

Palm Beach Hawaiian Ocean Inn
3550 S Ocean Boulevard, South Palm Beach
tel: 561/582-5631 or 800/457-5631; www.palmbeachhawaiian.com
58 beachfront rooms and suites; attractive Hawaiian/Polynesian-style décor, pool, restaurant, patio bar with entertainment.

Palm Beach Historic Inn
365 S County Road, Palm Beach
tel: 561/832-4009
Nine rooms and four suites in B&B in walking distance from Worth Avenue and the beach.

Riverside Hotel
620 E Las Olas Boulevard, Fort Lauderdale tel: 954/467-0671 or 800/325-3280
109 spacious rooms in attractive, central, old hotel; pool, restaurant.

Sailfish Marina & Resort
98 Lake Drive, Palm Beach Shores
tel: 561/844-1724 or 800/446-4577; www.sailfishmarina.com
23 rooms two blocks from beach; pool, sportfishing charters, restaurant, bar and barbecue.

Budget

Beachcomber Apartment Motel
3024 S Ocean Boulevard, Palm Beach
tel: 561/585-4646 or 800/833-7122
Oceanfront location for 45 spacious units; some kitchens and balconies.

Riviera Palms Motel
3960 N Ocean Boulevard, Delray Beach
tel: 561/276-3032
Rooms and efficiencies near beach; pool.

Sea Chateau Resort
555 N Birch Road, Fort Lauderdale
tel: 954/566-8331 or 800/726-3732
17 pretty rooms and efficiencies 200 yards from beach; pool, coffee, pastries.

Tropic Cay Beach Resort Hotel
529 N Atlantic Boulevard, Fort Lauderdale
tel: 954/564-5900 or 800/463-2333
45 beachfront efficiencies and units. Close to watersports, tennis, shopping.

Villas-by-the-Sea Resort & Beach Club
4456 El Mar Drive, Lauderdale-by-the-Sea
tel: 954/772-3550 or 800/247-8963
141 smart rooms and efficiencies in landscaped grounds; pool, tennis, barbecue grills.

EAST COAST

Expensive

Adam's Mark Daytona Beach Resort
100 N Atlantic Avenue, Daytona Beach
tel: 904/254-8200 or 800/444-2326; www.adamsmark.com
437 rooms in a prime oceanfront location. Pools and fitness, dining, children's facilities.

Amelia Island Plantation
3000 First Coast Highway, Amelia Island
tel: 904/261-6161 or 800/874-6878; www.aipfl.com
Superb resort set in 1,000-acre nature reserve; beach, pools, tennis, golf, fishing, riding, fine dining.

Amelia Island Williams House
103 S 9th Street, Fernandina Beach
tel: 904/277-2328 or 800/414-9258; www.williamshouse.com
One of Fernandina's finest historic B&B homes. Oriental art and antiques. Four rooms.
Other historic B&B options include: Hoyt House (tel: 904/277-4300 or 800/432-2085), and The Bailey House (tel: 904/261-5390 or 800/251-5390).

Casa Monica Hotel
95 Cordova Street, St Augustine
tel: 904/827-1888 or 800/648-1888; www.casamonica.com
Superbly restored 137-room Flagler-era hotel. Handsome Spanish-Revival décor; pool.

Disney's Vero Beach Resort
9250 Island Grove Terrace, Vero Beach
tel: 561/234-2000 or 800/359-8000; www.dvcresorts.com
Rooms and one- and two-bedroom cottages in themed Old Florida beachfront timeshare complex, open to all. Pools, boating, tennis, fitness, fishing and golf.

Omni Hotel
245 Water Street, Jacksonville
tel: 904/355-6664 or 800/843-6664
354 classy rooms/suites around luxuriant atrium; pool, health club, excellent restaurant.

Ponte Vedra Inn & Club
200 Ponte Vedra Boulevard, Ponte Vedra Beach tel: 904/285-1111 or 800/234-7842; www.pvresorts.com
222 rooms and suites in luxurious old-style oceanfront country club resort. Golf, tennis, spa. Fine dining.

Moderate

Bahama House
2001 S Atlantic Avenue, Daytona Beach Shores tel: 904/248-2001 or 800/571-2001; www.daytonabahamahouse.com
87 tropically themed and well-equipped efficiencies. Right on the beach; pool, helpful staff.

Casablanca Inn
24 Avenida Menendez, St Augustine
tel: 904/829-0928 or 800/826-2626; www.casablancainn.com
20 rooms in gracious old town-centre B&B. River views, whirlpool, bicycles.

Driftwood Resort
3150 Ocean Drive, Vero Beach
tel: 561/231-0550
A 1930s inn decorated with driftwood and beach-combing finds, with 100 rooms and efficiencies.

Fawlty Towers Resort
100 E Cocoa Beach Causeway, Cocoa Beach
tel: 321/784-3870 or 800/887-3870
32 spacious and attractive rooms in shocking pink complex one block from the beach. Pool and pretty garden with bar.

House on Cherry Street
1844 Cherry Street, Jacksonville
tel: 904/384-1999
Four-room B&B in beautiful old house down leafy Riverside lane.

Hutchinson Inn Seaside Resort
9750 S Ocean Drive, Jensen Beach, Fort Pierce tel: 561/229-2000
21 units on ocean; pool, tennis, free barbecue on Saturday nights.

Sea Turtle Inn
1 Ocean Boulevard, Atlantic Beach
tel: 904/249-7402 or 800/874-6000
194 rooms by the ocean north of Jacksonville Beach. Pool; restaurant.

Sun Viking Lodge
2411 S Atlantic Avenue, Daytona Beach Shores tel: 904/252-6252 or 800/815-2578; www.sunviking.com
91 rooms and efficiencies in friendly family resort; activity programme, beachfront, pools, water slide, spa, café.

Budget

Bayfront Inn
138 Avenida Menendez, St Augustine
tel: 904/824-1681 or 800/558-3455
33 Spanish-style units around pool; convenient for historic quarter.

Beachside Motel
3172 S Fletcher Avenue, Fernandina Beach
tel: 904/261-4236
Beachfront bargain with 20 spotless and spacious rooms and efficiencies. Pool deck.

Best Western Aku Tiki
2225 S Atlantic Avenue, Daytona Beach Shores tel: 904/252-9631 or 800/258-8454
132 rooms and efficiencies on oceanfront; pool, restaurant.

Days Inn Oceanfront
1031 S First Street, Jacksonville Beach
tel: 904/249-7231 or 800/321-2037
155 rooms at some of the best rates on the beach. Pool; restaurant.

Dockside Harbor Light Inn
1160 Seaway Drive, Fort Pierce
tel: 561/468-3555 or 800/286-1745; www.docksideinn.com
65 units, some with kitchens and/or balconies on inlet; pool, barbecue, fishing.

Dream Inn
3217 S Atlantic Avenue, Daytona Beach Shores tel: 904/767-2821 or 800/767-9738; www.dreaminn.com
26 rooms in family-run oceanfront property. Balconies, pool, fishing pier, barbecue.

WEST COAST

Expensive

Don CeSar Beach Resort & Spa
3400 Gulf Boulevard, St Petersburg Beach tel: 727/360-1881 or 800/282-1116
Pink palace on beach with 226 rooms and 51 suites; pool, watersports, children's programs.

Edgewater Beach Hotel
1901 Gulf Shore Boulevard, Naples
tel: 941/403-2000 or 800/821-0196; www.edgewaternaples.com
124 attractive suites with kitchenette and balcony; friendly atmosphere; beach, pool, fitness, chic dining room.

Marriott's Marco Island Resort and Golf Club
400 S Collier Boulevard, Marco Island
tel: 941/394-2511 or 800/438-4373
One of America's best resorts: beachfront spread with great golf, watersports, gourmet dining, and children's entertainment.

Resort at Longboat Key Club
301 Gulf of Mexico Drive, Longboat Key, Sarasota
tel: 941/383-8821 or 800/237-8821; www.longboatkeyclub.com
232 fine suites, 45 holes of golf, 38 tennis courts, and a beachfront location, plus fine dining, fitness centre, and children's programmes.

Ritz-Carlton Naples
280 Vanderbilt Beach Road, Naples
tel: 941/598-3300
One of Florida's top resorts, with 463 rooms and grand public rooms, fine restaurants, golf, tennis, kids' programmes.

Saddlebrook Resort – Tampa
5700 Saddlebrook Way, Wesley Chapel
tel: 813/973-1111 or 800/729-8383
790 rooms and suites in countryside 15 miles north of Tampa; golf course, tennis, fitness, award-winning dining. Good value packages.

Moderate

Best Western Pink Shell Beach Resort
275 Estero Boulevard, Fort Myers Beach
tel: 941/463-6181 or 800/449-1830; www.southseas.com
180 family-style rooms/condos/cottages in landscaped surroundings; with pool, tennis, watersports, fishing, boat dock, dining.

Best Western Sea Stone Resort & Suites
445 Hamden Drive, Clearwater Beach
tel: 727/441-1722 or 800/444-1919
108 rooms and well-equipped one-bedroom suites with kitchenettes. Just across from beach; pool, spa, kids' programmes, marina.

Diplomat Resort
3155 Gulf of Mexico Drive, Longboat Key, Sarasota tel: 941/383-3791 or 800/344-5418; www.diplomatresort.net
50 spacious units in beachfront apartment complex (two-day minimum stay), with pool.

Duncan House Bed & Breakfast
1703 Gulf Drive, Bradenton
tel: 941/778-6858
Two one-bedroom apartments and two guest rooms in a Victorian house near the beach.

Half Moon Beach Club
2050 Ben Franklin Drive, Lido Key, Sarasota
tel: 941/388-3694 or 800/358-3245;
www.halfmoon-lidokey.com
85 rooms and efficiencies around pool and courtyard; beach frontage, restaurant and easy drive to sights.

The Inn by the Sea
287 S Eleventh Avenue, Naples
tel: 941/649-4124
Five pretty guest rooms in a 1927 B&B surrounded by tropical palms two blocks from the beach. Near shops and restaurants; bicycles to borrow.

Outrigger Beach Resort
6200 Estero Boulevard, Fort Myers Beach
tel: 941/463-3131 or 800/749-3131;
www.rooms@outriggerfmb.com
144 rooms and efficiences on Gulf; pool, tiki bar, dining, bicycle rental, children's programmes.

Song of the Sea
863 E Gulf Drive, Sanibel
tel: 941/472-2220 or 800/449-3923;
www.southseas.com
30 efficiencies in seaside B&B with pool. Alfresco breakfasts; close to tennis and golf.

Tradewinds Resort
5500 Gulf Boulevard, St Petersburg Beach tel: 727/562-1212 or 800/808-9821;
www.tradewindsresort.com
577 (moderate to expensive) rooms and efficiencies in excellent resort, with pools, tennis, sailing and children's activities.

Budget

Beach House
4960 Estero Boulevard, Fort Myers Beach
tel: 941/463-4004 or 800/226-4005;
www.travelbase.com/destinations/ft-myers/beach-house
14 rooms and apartments in delightful house amid condos.

Beach View Cottages
3325 W Gulf Drive, Sanibel Island
tel: 941/472-1202 or 800/860-0532;
www.beachviewcottages.com
Efficiencies in relaxed family style complex right on the beach.

Holiday Inn Busch Gardens
2701 E Fowler Avenue, Tampa
tel: 813/977-0155 or 800/206-2747
Sprawling family-friendly complex with 400-plus rooms/suites; pool, dining and shopping near by.

Island's End Resort
1 Pass-a-Grille Way, St Petersburg Beach
tel: 727/360-5023; www.islandsend.com
Six quiet and charming one- to three-bedroom B&B cottages on the Gulf. Fishing, barbecue grills.

Lido Beach Palms
148 Cleveland Drive, Lido Key, Sarasota
tel: 941/383-9505 or 800/237-9505;
www.longboatkey.com
One- and two-bedroom apartments. Pool, barbecue, near shops and restaurants.

Olde Naples Inn
801 S Third Street, Naples
tel: 941/262-5194 or 800/637-6036;
www.bestof.net/naples/hotels/oldenaplesinn
60 rooms and efficiencies in pleasant motel with pool, a short walk from the beach.

Palm Pavilion Inn
18 Bay Esplanade, Clearwater Beach
tel: 727/446-6777 or 800/433-PALM;
www.palmpavilioninn.com
Smartly restored deco hotel by the beach. 27 rooms/efficiencies; pool, rooftop sundeck.

THE PANHANDLE

Expensive

Edgewater Beach Resort
11212 Front Beach Road, Panama City Beach
tel: 850/235-4044 or 800/874-8686
464 deluxe units and villas by beach or golf course in good central location; pools, tennis, watersports.

Governor's Inn
209 S Adams Street, Tallahassee
tel: 850/681-6855 or 800/342-7717
40 luxurious rooms and suites; VIP treatment, elegant dining room, breakfast, airport shuttle.

Henderson Park Inn
2700 US 98 East, Destin
tel: 850/837-4853 or 800/336-4853
Romantic B&B escape, with antique furnishings, beach views, pool; 35 rooms with patio/balcony.

Marriott's Bay Point Resort
4200 Marriott Drive, Panama City Beach
tel: 850/234-3307 or 800/874-7105
355 elegant rooms, suites, and villas; beach, woods, golf, tennis, watersports, children's activities.

Seaside Cottage Rental Agency
PO Box 4730, Seaside, FL 32459
tel: 850/231-1320 or 800/231-2446
Holiday rentals in the Old Floridian-style beach resort of Seaside.

Moderate

Cedar Key Bed & Breakfast
3rd and F Streets, Cedar Key
tel: 352/543-9000 or 800/453-5051;
www.crestcomm.com/cedarkeyb-b
Pretty rooms in an 1880s gingerbread-trimmed residence.

Coombs House Inn
80 6th Street, Apalachicola tel: 850/653-9199
Grand Victorian B&B with ten rooms; plus eight more in a quiet cottage across the street.

Gibson Inn
Market Street, Apalachicola tel: 850/653-2191
30 rooms in fine restored building; dining.

Hampton Inn Pensacola Beach
2 Via De Luna Drive, Pensacola Beach
tel: 850/932-6800 or 800/320-8108;
www.hamptonbeachresort.com
181 large, well-equipped rooms on the beachfront. Pools, fitness; Continental breakfast included.

Inn at Killearn Country Club
100 Tyron Circle, Tallahassee
tel: 850/893-2186 or 800/476-4101
39 units in relaxing woodland setting; pool, city's finest golf course, tennis, fitness, fine dining.

New World Inn
600 S Palafox Street, Pensacola
tel: 850/432-4111;
www.newworldlanding.com
15 deluxe rooms and suites (each reflecting a famous US personality) with antique furnishings; excellent restaurant; airport shuttle.

Pelican Walk Condominiums
6905 Thomas Drive, Panama City Beach
tel: 850/233-0076 or 800/543-3307
Attractive beachside condo development with one-, two-, and three-bed apartments; good resort facilities.

Resort at Sandestin
9300 US 98 West, Destin
tel: 850/267-8160 or 800/277-0803
Huge sports-orientated complex offering rooms, condos and villas. Beachfront position, golf, pools, watersports, children's programmes.

Budget

Days Inn
710 N Palafox Street, Pensacola
tel: 850/438-4922
150 rooms and efficiencies near historic district; pool, coffee shop, Continental breakfast.

Flamingo Motel
15525 Front Beach Road (US. 98), Panama City Beach tel: 850/234-2232 or 800/828-0400
67 pleasant efficiencies around tropical garden on the beach, with pool.

Four Points Hotel by Sheraton
1325 Miracle Strip Parkway, Fort Walton Beach
tel: 850/243-8116 or 800/874-8104
229 oversize rooms, some efficiencies. Beachfront, pools, dining and fitness centre.

Georgian Terrace
14415 Front Beach Road (US 98), Panama City Beach
tel: 850/234-2144 or 888/882-2144
30 efficiencies on beach, with pool.

Leeside Inn & Marina
1350 US 98 E Fort Walton Beach
tel: 850/243-7359 or 800/824-2747
106 rooms and efficiencies adjoining National Seashore; pool, watersports, fishing, restaurant.

Mermaid's Landing
12685 SR 24, Cedar Key
tel: 352/543-5949 or 877/543-5949
Eight spotless wooden cottages (sleep 2–6) with kitchens in a small property on the back bayou.

RESTAURANTS

Florida's cuisine, like its culture, is diverse. The basic ingredients – seafood, fresh vegetables and exotic fruits, like the yellow Key lime used in Key lime pie – may be produced locally, but cooking styles can be worlds apart. Caribbean cooking has inspired the tasty new local 'Floribbean' style; Cuban cuisine, based in Miami and Tampa, has outposts throughout the state; and European cuisine from French to Greek all find a niche in Florida's numerous eateries. There is *nouvelle cuisine*, New American-style, spicy Cajun food and down-home country cooking with a distinctive Southern flavour. It will not cost a fortune to try out any of them.

Dining out in Florida is a casual affair. Families are welcome just about everywhere; special children's portions and money-saving 'early bird' specials (usually served between 5 and 7am) are standard.

MIAMI

Expensive

Astor Place Bar & Grill
Astor Hotel, 956 Washington Avenue, Miami Beach tel: 305/672-7217
Stunning atrium setting for sophisticated fusion fare.

Blue Door
Delano Hotel, 1685 Collins Avenue, Miami Beach tel: 305/674-6400
Fashionable dining room with a clientele and exotic French-Floribbean menu to match.

Chef Allen's
19088 NE 29th Avenue, Aventura
tel: 305/935-2900
New American contemporary cuisine at its best; elegant art deco interior.

Nemo
100 Collins Avenue, Miami Beach
tel: 305/532-4550
Gourmet magnet way down in SoBe. Amazing metalwork decor, garden courtyard and delicious Asian-influenced cuisine, plus Hedy Goldsmith's *pâtisseries.*

Norman's
21 Almeria Avenue, Coral Gables
tel: 305/446-6767
High profile chef Norman Van Aken's New World shrine has a casually elegant clientele to match his rum-and-pepper-painted grouper and other adventurous concoctions.

Pacific Time
915 Lincoln Road, Miami Beach
tel: 305/534-5979
Artfully casual and enormously popular eatery offering an enticing Pacific Rim menu with a Floridian twist, from the soft-shell crab tempura to baked Alaska Key West with tangy lime.

Restaurant St Michel
Hotel Place St Michel, 162 Alcazar Avenue, Coral Gables tel: 305/446-6572
Old World dining room; delicious French/American cuisine from Long Island duck to spring lamb.

Yuca
501 Lincoln Road, Miami Beach
tel: 305/532-9822
Airy, glass-wrapped pastel and blonde wood setting for young urban Cuban/Americans and other fans of imaginative Cuban food, with the occasional Asian influence. Guava-barbecued baby back ribs and three-bean terrine recommended.

Moderate

A Fish Called Avalon
Avalon Hotel, 700 Ocean Drive, Miami Beach
tel: 305/522-1727
New American cuisine and local seafood in a sleek Art Deco District setting.

Bangkok Bangkok
157 Giralda Avenue, Coral Gables
tel: 305/444-2397
Popular local Thai restaurant, with excellent curries.

Café Med
CocoWalk, 3015 Grand Avenue, Coconut Grove
tel: 305/443-1770
Mediterranean dishes and tasty thin-crust pizzas cooked in the wood-burning oven.

Café Prima Pasta
414 71st Street, North Miami Beach
tel: 305/867-0106
One of the best pasta cafés in town. Home-made pasta, fresh sauces. Always busy.

East Coast Fisheries
360 W Flagler Street, Downtown Miami
tel: 305/372-1300
Family operated fish market and restaurant in a fine spot overlooking the Miami River. Florida lobster and stone crab claws are specialities.

Joe's Stone Crab Restaurant
227 Biscayne Street, Miami Beach
tel: 305/673-0365
Closed: Jun–early Oct
Seafood institution; informal atmosphere, but expect queues.

Larios on the Beach
820 Ocean Drive, Miami Beach
tel: 305/532-9577
Cuban restaurant/sidewalk café brings Little Havana to the beach – has the best black beans in town.

Monty's Stone Crab Seafood House and Raw Bar
2550 S. Bayshore Drive, Coconut Grove
tel: 305/858-1431; and 300 Alton Road, Miami Beach tel: 305/673-3444
Seafood, steaks, snacks and entertainment.

NOA (Noodles of Asia)
801 Lincoln Road, Miami Beach
tel: 305/925-0050
Very stylish, very SoBe noodle shop where you can also tuck in to Thai beef salad, exotic cocktails and wild desserts.

Spiga
1225 Collins Avenue, Miami Beach
tel: 305/534-0079
Welcoming neighborhood Italian specialising in fresh homemade pastas, meat and salmon *carpaccios* and dessert flans.

Van Dyke Café
846 Lincoln Road, Miami Beach
tel: 305/534-3600
Trendy corner spot with pavement seating and an eclectic café menu throughout the day. Salads, omelettes, aubergine parmigiana and jazz.

Budget

Arnie and Richie's
525 41st Street, North Miami Beach
tel: 305/531-7691
A deli well worth seeking out. Mountainous pastrami-on-rye and other sandwiches, cheeses and kosher food.

Balans
1022 Lincoln Road, Miami Beach
tel: 305/534-9191
Astonishingly good value pavement bistro on fun Lincoln Road Mall. Mediterranean-Asian cooking plus sticky toffee pudding from English owners.

Café Tu Tu Tango
CocoWalk, 3015 Grand Avenue, Coconut Grove
tel: 305/529-2222
Funky-artsy tapas café serving up designer pizza, chicken wings, tortillas, kebabs and more.

La Carreta
3632 SW 8th Street, Little Havana
tel: 305/444-7501
Cuban specials served in casual, family atmosphere.

Daily Bread
2400 SW 27th Street, Coral Gables
tel: 305/856-0363
Budget sandwich shop with seating. Middle Eastern salads, and spinach pastries. Very generous portions.

Mrs. Mendoza's
1040 Alton Road, Miami Beach
tel: 305/535-0808
Cheap and cheerful Mexican joint. Home-cooked standards, such as pork *fajitas* and refried beans (*frijoles refritos*).

News Café
800 Ocean Drive, Miami Beach
tel: 305/538-6397
Hip café-society hangout with views to the ocean; great brunches; open 24 hours.

Orlando Seafood Restaurant & Fish Market
501 NW 37th Avenue tel: 305/642-6767
A stand-up affair: fresh swordfish, snapper, kingfish and delicious fish *croquetas* (deep-fried fish cakes).

San Loco
235 14th Street, Miami Beach
tel: 305/538-3009
Witheringly hot chili and hearty tacos, burritos and enchiladas. Open late.

Wolfie's Gourmet Deli
2038 Collins Avenue, Miami Beach
tel: 305/538-6626
Landmark deli-restaurant with mile-high bagel sandwiches.

KEYS AND EVERGLADES

Expensive

Café Marquesa
600 Fleming Street, Key West
tel: 305/292-1244
Creative New American fare made with fresh local ingredients and a dash of the Oriental. Pretty surroundings; excellent service.

Louie's Backyard
700 Waddell Avenue, Key West
tel: 305/294-1061
Innovative menu with local specialities featuring a Caribbean twist; has lovely waterfront views.

Marker 88
MM 88, Plantation Key tel: 305/852-9315
Spectacular sunset views accompany adventurous seafood and regional dishes (even alligator).

Morada Bay
MM 81, Islamorada tel: 305/664-0604
Delectable bayside dining room with an eclectic Caribbean-American menu; particularly strong on seafood.

Moderate

Bagatelle
115 Duval Street, Key West
tel: 305/296-6609
Historic 'conch' architecture and interesting Caribbean specials.

Fish House Restaurant & Seafood Market
MM 102.4, Key Largo tel: 305/451-4665
Homemade conch specialties and a singing waiter.

Frank Keys Café
MM 100, Key Largo tel: 305/453-0310
Cottage in the woods serving Floribbean-Mediterranean seafood, pasta and Key lime pie.

Green Turtle Restaurant
MM 81.5, Islamorada tel: 305/664-9031
Local favourite since 1947. Homemade Key lime pie and chowders.
Kelsey's
MM 48.5, Faro Blanco Bayside, Marathon tel: 305/743-9018
Dockside views of the Gulf; superb fresh seafood.
Pepe's
806 Caroline Street, Key West tel: 305/294-7192
Small diner with pine furnishings and garden seating. Big breakfasts, daily specials, barbecues.
Rick's Blue Heaven
729 Thomas Street, Key West tel: 305/296-8666
Funky old house with outdoor trestles and beer served from a bathtub. Great barbecue, vegetarian-Caribbean menu.
Rod & Gun Club
200 Riverside Drive, Everglades City tel: 941/695-2101
Old hunting and fishing lodge by the water. Dine on the veranda from small but well-prepared menu.

Budget
Anthony's
1111 Duval Street, Key West tel: 305/296-8899
Sunny yellow and blue decor, hearty Greek cooking, plus salads and good breakfasts.
El Siboney
900 Catherine Street (at Margaret), Key West tel: 305/296-4184
No frills Cuban neighbourhood spot. Generous piles of chicken and beans, paella and spicy picadillo.
Grassy Key Dairy Bar
MM 58.5, Grassy Key tel: 305/743-3816
Pint-sized and welcoming roadside dining room serving fine fresh seafood, steaks and regional favourites.
Half Shell Raw Bar
Land's End Village, Key West tel: 305/294-7496
Oysters, fish sandwiches and seasonal specials; overlooking the docks.
Herbie's
MM 50.5, Marathon tel: 305/743-6373
Informal and friendly; serves great spicy chowder.
Islamorada Fish Company
MM 81.5, Islamorada tel: 305/664-9271
A no-nonsense fresh fish shop and restaurant. Freshest fish available, shrimp, scallops and stone crab claws in season.
Mrs. Mac's Kitchen
MM 99.8, Key Largo tel: 305/451-3722
Home-cooked specials, like meatloaf and chilli.
Shuckers Raw Bar & Grill
MM 48.5, 1415 15th Street, Marathon tel: 305/743-8686
Nautical decor to match fishy menu; great value fish baskets.
Turtle Kraals
Land's End Village, Key West tel: 305/294-2640
Noisy, popular dockside bar-restaurant; turtles for viewing only.

CENTRAL FLORIDA

Expensive
Chalet Suzanne
3800 Chalet Suzanne Drive (off CR 17A), 4½ miles north of Lake Wales tel: 941/676-6011
Charming country inn with an award-winning small menu of American-Continental chef's specials.
Chefs de France
Epcot, Walt Disney World tel: 407/939-3463
French menu devised by three of France's top chefs: Verge, Bocuse and Lenôtre. Elegant surroundings in the French pavilion; a real treat.
Dux
Peabody Hotel, 9801 International Drive, Orlando tel: 407/352-4000
Sumptuous restaurant with innovative menu and fine cellar. Jackets requested.
Manuel's on the 28th
390 N Orange Avenue, Orlando tel: 407/246-6580
Sophisticated dining on the 28th floor of the downtown Bank of America building. Stylish Floribbean cuisine.

Park Plaza Gardens
319 Park Avenue South, Winter Park tel: 407/645-2475
Creative Florida cuisine in a pretty covered courtyard. Local favourite with a long wine list.

Moderate
Bongo's Cuban Café
Downtown Disney West Side tel: 407/828-0999
Fun atmosphere, live music and hearty Cuban cooking from chicken and rice to black beans.
Clewiston Inn
108 Royal Palm Avenue (at US 27), Clewiston tel: 941/983-8151
Fine old Southern-style dining room in historic inn.
Ming Court
9188 International Drive, Orlando tel: 407/351-9988
Serves Chinese food, regional favourites and seafood in attractive surroundings; dancing.
Pebbles
12551 SR 535, Lake Buena Vista tel: 407/827-1111
Also at 17 W Church Street, tel: 407/839-0892
New American menu, seafood and salads.
Portobello Yacht Club
Downtown Disney Pleasure Island tel: 407/934-8888
On the lagoon; serves great Northern Italian dishes, homemade pastas, pizzas, seafood.
Race Rock
8986 International Drive, Orlando tel: 407/248-9876
Restaurant with motor racing theme, packed with memorabilia. Serves American cooking, pizzas, pasta.
Rainforest Café
Downtown Disney Marketplace tel: 407/933-2800
Landmark mini-volcano decked out with trees and computer-animated wildlife. American menu with a Caribbean twist.

Steve's Café Americain
12 W University Avenue, Gainesville
tel: 352/377-9337
New American cooking in an open kitchen; smart and casual. Dinner only.
Teppankaki Dining Room
Epcot, Walt Disney World tel: 407/939-3463
Watch the preparations and sample traditional Japanese cuisine.
Wild Flowers Café
201 N US 441, Micanopy tel: 352/466-4330
Country dining room with a wide-ranging menu: Italian dishes, steaks, seafood and home-made desserts.

Budget

Café Tu Tu Tango
8625 International Drive, Orlando
tel: 407/248-2222
World cuisine (from Cajun to Greek) and cocktails served in a recreated artist's loft.
Hard Rock Café
Universal Orlando, CityWalk, Orlando
tel: 407/351-7625
Hamburgers, barbecue, salads and memorabilia in the world's biggest Hard Rock.

Jimmy Buffett's Margaritaville
Universal Orlando, CityWalk, Orlando
tel: 407/224-9255
Laid-back Florida Keys-themed joint specialising in cheeseburgers and margaritas.
Olive Garden
7653 International Drive, Orlando
tel: 407/351-1082
Good-value, friendly Italian restaurant chain.
Panache at the Wine & Cheese Gallery
113 N Main Street, Gainesville tel: 352/372-8446
Innovative bistro-cum-sandwich shop behind a deli/-wine merchant. Lunch only. Patio dining.
Wolfgang Puck Express
Downtown Disney Marketplace
tel: 407/939-3463
Exotic pizza toppings, focaccia sandwiches and salads. Also try the excellent **Wolfgang Puck Café** at Downtown Disney West Side.

THE GOLD COAST

Expensive

Armadillo Café
4630 SW 64th Avenue, Davie tel: 954/791-5104
Inspired Southwestern cooking. Blue crab nachos, great salsas, good crowd. Dinner only.
Burt & Jack's
Berth 23, Port Everglades, Fort Lauderdale
tel: 954/522-5225
Elegant Spanish villa on the waterfront with impressive American menu.
Darrel & Oliver's Café Max
2601 E Atlantic Boulevard, Pompano Beach
tel: 954/782-0606
Innovative New World-Floribbean cuisine; fresh seafood specialities and art deco styling.
Mark's Las Olas
1032 E Las Olas Boulevard, Fort Lauderdale
tel: 954/463-1000
Owner/chef Mark Militello's blend of creative contemporary cuisine made with fresh local ingredients is all the rage. Reservations a must.
La Vieille Maison
770 E Palmetto Park Road, Boca Raton
tel: 561/391-6701
Mizner-era setting for fine French cuisine.

Moderate

15th Street Fisheries
1900 SE 15th Street, Fort Lauderdale
tel: 954/763-2777
Award-winning seafood, waterfront views.
Blue Anchor
804 E Atlantic Avenue, Delray Beach
tel: 561/272-7272
Great British pub grub, from steak-and-kidney pie to Stilton cheese, plus beers and Sunday breakfast.
Café Protégé
2400 Metrocenter Boulevard, West Palm Beach tel: 561/687-2433
Restaurant showcase for master chefs and students from the Florida Culinary Institute.
Chuck & Harold's
207 Royal Poinciana Way, Palm Beach
tel: 561/659-1440
Tropical décor, tiles and beams; varied Californian menu. Live entertainment.
Las Olas Café
922 E Las Olas Boulevard, Fort Lauderdale
tel: 954/524-4300
Pretty courtyard and dining room off main drag. Tasty home-made soups, pastas and dairy specials.
Mark's at the Park
344 Plaza Real, Mizner Park, Boca Raton
tel: 561/395-0770
Lunch from the tempting Mediterranean-inspired menu is a reasonably priced experience; dinner is a little more expensive.
Martha's
6024 N Ocean Drive, Hollywood
tel: 954/923-5444
Nouvelle American with plenty of seafood. Waterside setting; live music at weekends.
No Anchovies
1901 Palm Beach Lakes Boulevard, West Palm Beach tel: 561/689-6100
Jolly, family friendly Italian with a long menu of pastas, pizzas, salads and meats from the oak-fired grill.
Sushi Blues Café
1836 Young Circle, Hollywood
tel: 954/929-9560
Sushi and live jazz (Thu–Sun) make a great pairing at this small but popular venue.

Budget

Banana Boat
739 E Ocean Avenue, Boynton Beach
tel: 561/732-9400
Casual waterfront spot; mostly seafood; dockside bar, entertainment.
Cheeburger, Cheeburger
708 E Las Olas Boulevard, Fort Lauderdale
tel: 954/524-8824
Mega cheeseburgers, onion loaf, milkshakes and low, low prices for this classy neighbourhood.
It's in the Bag
423 Clematis Street, West Palm Beach
tel: 561/655-4505
Generous pita sandwiches stuffed with classic and unusual fillings. Pavement tables.

John G's
10 S Ocean Boulevard, Lake Worth
tel: 561/585-9860
Busy, informal and on the beach; burgers, omelettes, pasta.

Lighthouse Restaurant
1510 U.S. 1, Jupiter tel: 561/7[illegible]6-4811
Good home cooking from beef stew to crab cakes and scrumptious desserts.

Tom's Place
7251 N Federal Highway, Boca Raton
tel: 561/997-0920
Barbecued ribs and chicken favoured by NFL players.

Toojays
313 Royal Poinciana Plaza, Palm Beach
tel: 561/659-7232
Local deli chain serving huge salads, sandwiches, desserts and kosher dishes.

EAST COAST

Expensive

Beech Street Grill
801 Beech Street, Fernandina Beach
tel: 904/277-3662
A series of small modish dining rooms in an 1889 historic district house. New American cuisine, local seafood and good wine list.

Black Pearl
4445 N US A1A, Vero Beach
tel: 561/234-4426
Fashionable fine dining spot with riverside views, a Martini bar and Continental menu with seafood a speciality.

Mango Tree
118 N Atlantic Avenue, Cocoa Beach
tel: 321/799-0513
Elegant tropical décor; delicious light, fresh American cuisine.

Matthew's at San Marco
2107 Hendricks Avenue, Jacksonville
tel: 904/396-9922
Smart San Marco district showcase for Matthew Madure's stunning cuisine fusing New American-Asian-Mediterranean influences.

95 Cordova
Casa Monica Hotel, 95 Cordova Street, St Augustine tel: 904/810-6810
Sumptuous decor, antique furnishings, and an eclectic–innovative Mediterranean–American southwestern menu.

Moderate

A1A Aleworks
1 King Street, St. Augustine
tel: 904/829-2977
Restaurant and micro-brewery with a New World menu (combining a spectacular array of ingredients and cooking methods) and outdoor seating.

Black Tulip
207 Brevard Avenue, Historic Cocoa Village
tel: 321/631-1133
Continental fare in the historic district.

Columbia
98 St. George Street, St Augustine
tel: 904/824-3341
Paella and other Spanish, Cuban and Continental dishes in the historic district.

Dolphin Depot
704 N First Street, Jacksonville Beach
tel: 904/270-1424
Popular seafood joint with excellent daily blackboard specials.

Down Under Restaurant
AIA at Intracoastal Waterway, Fernandina Beach tel: 904/261-1001
Feast off Alaskan king crab, baked grouper, oysters or ribeye steaks.

Live Oak Inn and Restaurant
448 S. Beach Street, Daytona
tel: 904/252-4667
Historic inn by the marina; fish, fillets, and more.

Mangrove Matties
1640 Seaway Drive, Fort Pierce
tel: 561/466-1044
Great waterfront views as well as sumptuous Sunday brunch.

Ocean Grill
1050 Sexton Plaza (Beachland Boulevard), Vero Beach tel: 561/231-5409
Local favourite; serves seafood, steaks, with ocean view.

Raintree
102 San Marco Avenue, St Augustine
tel: 904/829-5953
Beautifully restored old house; seasonal menu with plenty of seafood and marvellous desserts.

Riverside Café
1 Beachland Boulevard, Vero Beach
tel: 561/234-5550
Riverfront restaurant serving Continental fare. Outdoor seating, bar, entertainment.

Southend Brewery & Smokehouse
Jacksonville Landing, Jacksonville
tel: 904/665-0000
In-house micro-brewery and smokehouse-oriented menu, plus speciality pizzas, nachos and pasta.

Budget

Bubba's FishCamp
421 S Federal Highway, Stuart
tel: 561/220-3747
Rustic fish camp style and great Southern cooking: fried chicken, hush puppies.

Cruisin' Café
2 S Atlantic Avenue, Daytona Beach
tel: 904/253-5522
Motorsport-themed restaurant packed with memorabilia and racing videos. Refuel with burgers, steaks and seafood.

Florida Cracker Café
81 St George Street, St. Augustine
tel: 904/829-0397
Busy café serving up Florida coastal cuisine: shrimp, tuna, po'boy sandwiches and gator tail fritters.

Florida House Inn
22 S 3rd Street, Fernandina Beach
tel: 904/261-3300
All-you-can-eat homestyle Southern cooking, served boarding house fashion in Florida's oldest lodgings.

Homestead
1712 Beach Boulevard, Jacksonville Beach
tel: 904/249-5240
Country cooking and homey atmosphere.

Pearl's Bistro
56 Royal Palm Boulevard, Vero Beach
tel: 561/778-2950
Bistro sidekick of the Black Pearl featuring 'island cuisine': swordfish sandwiches, Rasta pasta and jerk chicken.
Rusty's Seafood & Oyster Bar
628 Glen Cheek Drive, Port Canaveral
tel: 321/783-2033
Also at 2 S Atlantic Avenue, Cocoa Beach
(tel: 321/783-2401)
Waterfront views and generous seafood specials.
Santa Maria
135 Avenida Menendez, St Augustine
tel: 904/829-6578
Seafood, steaks and chicken in family-run landmark by the marina.

WEST COAST

Expensive

Armani's
Hyatt Regency West Shore,
6200 Courtney Campbell Causeway, Tampa
tel: 813/281-9165
Stylish Northern Italian restaurant garlanded with awards. Amazing antipasta selection; grand rooftop views.

Bern's Steak House
1208 S Howard Avenue, Tampa
tel: 813/251-2421
Clubby decor, exemplary service, prime steaks accompanied by organic vegetables and huge wine list.
Café L'Europe
431 St Armands Circle, Sarasota
tel: 941/388-4415
Fashionably elegant, arty setting; delicate French *nouvelle cuisine* seafood, veal and beef dishes.
Marchand's Grill
Renaissance Vinoy Resort, 501 5th Avenue NE, St Petersburg tel: 727/822-2785
Wonderfully elegant dining room, bay views and a sophisticated New American-Floribbean menu. Long wine list.
Marek's Collier House
486 N Collier Boulevard, Marco Island
tel: 941/642-9948
American/international cuisine in gracious historic house. Smart-casual.
Terra
1300 Third Street, Naples tel: 941/262-5500
A culinary landmark in delightful surroundings; creative seasonal cuisine; also moderately priced café-bistro; truffles.

Moderate

Bob Heilman's Beachcomber
447 Mandalay Avenue, Clearwater Beach
tel: 727/442-4144
Popular casual restaurant with a broad American menu, welcoming atmosphere and local art on the walls.
Bubble Room
15001 Captiva Drive, Captiva
tel: 941/472-5558
Wacky 1940s kitsch decor; monster platters of home cooking and killer desserts.
Columbia
2117 7th Avenue, Ybor City, Tampa
tel: 813/248-4961
Landmark Spanish restaurant; rustic decor and traditional menu.
Dry Dock Waterfront Grill
412 Gulf of Mexico Drive, Longboat Key, Sarasota tel: 941/383-0102
Well-established seafood house that offers great chowder as well as grill specialities. Outdoor dining.
Louis Pappas' Riverside
10 W Dodecanese Boulevard, Tarpon Springs
tel: 727/937-5101
Busy tourist spot which serves great Greek food.
McT's Shrimp House & Tavern
1523 Periwinkle Way, Sanibel
tel: 941/472-3161
Mountains of seafood fresh off the dock, all-you-can-eat shrimp and crab platters, children's menus.
Mise en Place – An American Bistro
442 W. Kennedy Boulevard, Tampa
tel: 813/254-5373
Inventive New American cuisine with French-Italian-Japanese influences.
Prawnbroker
13451 McGregor Boulevard, Fort Myers
tel: 941/489-2226
Local favourite; mainly fish menu, steak and poultry.
Riverwalk Fish & Ale House
1200 S Fifth Avenue, Naples
tel: 941/263-2734
Dockside dining in the Old Marine Marketplace.
Veranda
2122 Second Street, Fort Myers
tel: 941/332-2065
Historical buildings with garden court; innovative regional Southern menu.
Wine Cellar
17307 N Gulf Boulevard, Redington Beach
tel: 727/393-3491
Warm atmosphere, plus award-winning American and Middle-European menu.

Budget

Cactus Club
1601 Snow Avenue, Tampa tel: 813/251-4089
Lively and fun; Southwestern cuisine, huge desserts.
California Pizza Kitchen
5555 US 41 N, Naples tel: 941/566-1900
Handy find in an upmarket mall. Designer pizzas and world cooking, salads, sandwiches and more.
Charlie's Fish House & Seafood Market
224 US 19 N, Crystal River
tel: 352/795-3949
Generous seafood dinners, oysters, grouper burgers and stone crab claws, with dockside views.
Lighthouse Café
362 Periwinkle Way, Sanibel
tel: 941/472-0303
Cosy café dishing up wonderful home-cooked meals. Breakfast, omelettes, steak sandwiches and seafood.
Roger's Real Pit Bar-B-Que
12150 Seminole Boulevard, Largo
tel: 727/586-2629
Baby-back ribs, franks and beans plus wonderful salad bar.

Seafood & Sunsets at Julie's
351 S Gulf Boulevard, Clearwater Beach tel: 727/441-2548
Beach shack with good seafood and sunset views.
Turtles
8875 Midnight Pass Road, Siesta Key, Sarasota tel: 941/346-2207
Central bayfront seafood joint with outdoor seating. Local favourite; child-friendly.

THE PANHANDLE

Expensive

Andrew's Second Act
228 S Adams Street, Tallahassee tel: 850/222-3444
Political district favourite serving small, elegant New American menu in a Frenchified setting.
Criolla's
Scenic 30A, Grayton Beach tel: 850/267-1267
Creative cuisine with a tropical New World flavour. Smart-casual dress; notable wine cellar.
Jamie's Wine Bar & Restaurant
424 E Zaragoza Street, Pensacola tel: 850/434-2911
Lovely historic district cottage setting for Floribbean-Mediterranean-Asian fusion cuisine, plus a huge and varied wine list.
Magnolia Grill
133 Avenue E Apalachicola tel: 850/653-8000
Sophisticated seafood from chef Eddie Cass, served up in a charming historic cottage.
Pandora's
1120 Santa Rosa Boulevard, Fort Walton Beach tel: 850/244-8669
Comfortably clubby surroundings for prime rib specialities and fresh seafood. Lounge entertainment area.

Moderate

Boar's Head
17290 Front Beach Road, Panama City Beach tel: 850/234-6628
Woodsy interior; generous prime rib and seafood platters.
Capt Anderson's
5551 N Lagoon Drive, Panama City Beach tel: 850/234-2225
Early diners can watch the fleet unload at this top seafood restaurant.
Chez Pierre
1215 Thomasville Road, Tallahassee tel: 850/222-0936
French café with large menu, light lunches, pastries.
Flamingo Café
414 E US 98, Destin tel: 850/837-0961
Chic decor, harbour views and a more casual patio area. Floribbean and fish specialities.
Flounders Chowder & Ale House
800 Quietwater Beach Road, Pensacola Beach tel: 850/932-2003
Lively pub-restaurant on Santa Rosa Sound serving a broad American menu with seafood specials. Entertainment and dance floor.
Gibson Inn
Market Street, Apalachicola tel: 850/653-2191
Historic inn serving varied menu of classic dishes and plenty of seafood. Semi-formal.
Island Hotel
2nd and B Streets, Cedar Key tel: 352/543-5111
Historic timber-built inn with a seafood restaurant specialising in local crabs, clams, and oysters.
Mesquite Charlie's
5901 N 'W' Street, Pensacola tel: 850/434-0498
Famous charcoal-grilled steaks and seafood. Western decor; 'Little Cowpokes' menu.
Nicholson Farm House
off SR 12 at Havana, 15 miles northwest of Tallahassee tel: 850/539-5931
Southern cooking in a fine 1820s plantation home. BYOB, and children's menu.
Oaks Restaurant
US 98, Panacea, 20 miles south of Tallahassee tel: 850/984-5370
Popular out-of-town dining spot serving seafood Southern style.
Staff's Seafood
24 SW Miracle Strip Parkway, Fort Walton tel: 850/243-3526
Cross to the mainland for heaped mixed seafood skillets, gumbo, Florida lobster or steaks.

Budget

Andrew's Capital Bar & Grill
228 S Adams Street, Tallahassee tel: 850/222-3444
New York-style deli and grill with outdoor seating in restored district.
Barnacle Bill's
1830 N Monroe Street, Tallahassee tel: 850/385-8734
Pasta and poultry, seafood; kids eat free on Sundays.
Billy's Oyster Bar I
3000 Thomas Drive, Panama City Beach tel: 850/235-2349
Oysters every which way; lobster, crawfish, crab and shrimp.
Blue Desert Café
SR 24, Cedar Key tel: 352/543-9111
Sandwiches, pastas, pizzas and home-made desserts dished up in a shotgun cottage.
Captain Dave's
3796 Old Highway 98, Destin tel: 850/837-2627
Family seafood spot overlooking the Gulf; dancing and entertainment.
Hopkin's Boarding House
900 N. Spring Street, Pensacola tel: 850/438-3979
A local institution since 1949. Southern specialities for breakfast, lunch and early dinner.
The Hut
US 98, Apalachicola tel: 850/653-9410
Rustic seafood and steak joint; a popular bar.
McGuire's Irish Pub
600 E Gregory Street, Pensacola tel: 850/433-6789
Ribs, burgers, sandwiches, seafood and good times to be had.
Magnolia Grill
Brooks Bridge 98 Center, 255 Miracle Strip Parkway, Fort Walton tel: 850/302-0266
Nostalgia-packed diner and good Cajun, Italian and seafood dining.

N

O

P

Q

R

Acknowledgements

The Automobile Association would like to thank the following photographers, libraries and associations for their assistance in the preparation of this book. **ALACHUA COUNTRY VISITORS & CONVENTION BUREAU** 26 Florida Fields Gainesville, 27 Gatornationaus; **ALLSPORT UK LTD** 173 Daytona race action (Jim Gund); **BABCOCK WILDERNESS ADVENTURES** 20, 32 Babcock; **BRUCE COLEMAN COLLECTION** 101 Key deer, 107 Florida Keys; **BUSCH GARDENS** 226 Adventure Island Tampa, 227 Bengal Tiger; **CORBIS IMAGES** Front cover b) Flamingo; **©DISNEY ENTERPRISES, INC.** 28 *Honey I Shrunk the Kids* set, 29 Main Street Magic Kingdom, 123 Kilimanjaro Safaris, 124 Festival of the Lion King, 127 Rock 'n' Rollercoaster, 128 Buzz Lightyear's Space Ranger Spin, 131 Main Street U.S.A., Cinderella Castle, 133 Blizzard Beach, Summit Plummet, 263 Hollywood Boulevard MGM; **HENRY FLAGLER MUSEUM** 160 Henry Flagler; **FLORIDA DEPT OF COMMERCE** 23 Rodeo, 41 Seminoles, 48 Miami Crandon Park, 64 Miami Seaquarium, Metro Tiger, 82 Horse-racing, 83 Skin diving, Orange Bowl, 164 Baseball, 175 Daytona Beach, 183 Jacksonville at night, 184 Fisherman, 188 Sunset, 190 St Augustine, 191 Sea Oats, 225 Ringling Museum, 244 Canoeing, 245 Sunset, 246 Panama City, 248 Shipwreck Isle, 251 Naval Air Museum, 255 Tallahassee; **GEIGER & ASSOCIATES** 15 Turkey Creek Sanctuary, 18/9 American Bald Eagle, 196 Port Canaveral, 197 F4-4 Fighter – Race Corsair, 214 Water fowl 253 Beach scene; **GRAND ROMANCE** 185 Rivership Grand Romance; **IMAGES COLOUR LIBRARY** Front cover a) Ocean Drive, South Beach; **KISSIMMEE ST CLOUD CONVENTION & VISITORS BUREAU** 184 Lake Tohopekaliga; **LEE COUNTY VISITORS & CONVENTION BUREAU** 200 Bonita Beach, Captiva Beach, 205 Fort Myers Beach Pier, 209 Tall Ship *Eagle;* **THE MANSELL COLLECTION** 36/7 Don Juan Ponce de León; **MARY EVANS PICTURE LIBRARY** 37 Philip II of Spain, 39 Pirates; **NATURE PHOTOGRAPHERS LTD** 95 Fire coral, 157 Osprey (P R Sterry), 159 Royal tern (W S Paton), 211 Queen conch (P R Sterry); **PICTURES COLOUR LIBRARY** 4 Captiva Island; **HENRY PLANT MUSEUM** 226 Henry Plant Museum; **POLK COUNTY TOURIST DEVELOPMENT COUNCIL** 135 Lake Wales; **POPPERFOTO** 42 Union guns at Fort Brady; **ROYAL GEOGRAPHIC SOCIETY** 32 Map; **ST AUGUSTINE/ST JOHNS COUNTY CHAMBER OF COMMERCE** 26 Tennis 43 St Augustine – The Castillo; **SARASOTA CONVENTION & VISITORS BUREAU** 222 Selby Gardens, Ringling Museum, 223 Sarasota Quay, 224 Circus galleries, Ringling Museum, Ca'd'Zan; **SEAWORLD** 118 Penguins; **SPECTRUM COLOUR LIBRARY** 170 Palm Beach shopping, 171 Worth Avenue, Palm Beach; **EMMA STANFORD** 34/113 Ocala Appleton Museum; **THE STOCK MARKET** 165 Sportfishing; **TAMPA/HILLSBOROUGH CONVENTION & VISITORS BUREAU** 228 Gasparilla Festival; **UNIVERSAL STUDIOS ORLANDO** Front cover c) Universal Studios entrance, 118 Le Jazz Hat, CityWalk, 119 Terminator 2:3-D, 120 Jurassic Park River Adventure, 121 Dueling Dragons; **ZEFA PICTURE LIBRARY (UK) LTD** 14 Middle Keys, 16 Flower, 17 Native palms, 19 Lake Okeechobee, 21 Blue Hole, 22 Fort Lauderdale, 33 Fairchild Gardens, Cranes Point, 38 Shipwreck Museum, Key Largo, Fisherman's Museum, Key West, 44 Gold Coast Museum, 45 Key West Steamer, 47 J Pennekamp State Park, 48 Miami Bayside, 50/1 Bayside at night, 52 Ocean Drive Miami, 53 Coconut Grove Miami, 54 Coral Gables Miami, 58 Bacardi Art Gallery, 61 Fairchild Gardens, 62 HMS *Bounty*, 65 Sailing Bay Miami, 70 Key West conch, 79 Opera, 80 M B Hotel, 81 Cardozo Hotel, 81 Colony Hotel, 87 Cypress airboat, 88 Everglades Big Cypress, 91 Mangrove, 92 Glades, 93 Everglades, 95 Ocean World, 98 Middle Keys, shrimp boats, 100 Audubon House, Key West, 138 Boca Raton Red Reef Park, 139 Boca Hotel, 140 Boca Children's Museum, 141 Market, Boca National Park, 142 Fort Lauderdale, 148/9 Fort Lauderdale, 150 H Taylor Birch Park, 152/3 Fort Lauderdale Ocean World, 156 Stranahan House, 160 Flagler Railroad, 161 Palm Beach, 162 Flagler House, 166 West Palm Beach, 167 Dreher Zoo, 168 Norton Gallery, 169 Polo, 170 Worth Avenue Palm Beach, 171 Fort Lauderdale Las Olas, 194 Keys, 213 Naples City Dock, 218 St Petersburg Pier, 244 Fort Zachary Taylor State Park, 245 J Pennekamp State Park, 250 Westwear Grove, 261 Old Flagler Bridge; **ZIMMERMAN AGENCY** 257 Tallahassee Old Town Trolley, 259 Tallahassee Junior Museum.

The remaining photos are from the Association's own library (**AA PHOTO LIBRARY**) and were taken by Pete Bennett, with the exception of the following: **KIRK LEE AEDER** 195; **P BENNETT** Back cover, North Miami Beach; **JON DAVISON** 4, 10, 25, 51, 72, 74, 78, 99, 102/3, 163, 241, 242; **DAVID LYONS** 154, 155; **KEN PATERSON** 102; **TONY SOUTER** Spine, Fort Liberty, Kissimmee, 116, 134; **JAMES A TIMMS** 2, 3, 5a, 5b, 6, 6/7, 7, 8, 9a, 9b, 49, 63, 71, 87, 94, 97, 104, 105, 106, 109, 137, 144, 145, 149, 173, 199, 210, 211, 220, 235 and 237.

Contributors

Original copy editor: Audrey Horne Revision verifier: Emma Stanford

Revision copy editors: Becky Norris, Maria Morgan